Bristol

PEVSNER ARCHITECTURAL GUIDES

Founding Editor: Nikolaus Pevsner

PEVSNER ARCHITECTURAL GUIDES

The Buildings of England series was created and largely written
by Sir Nikolaus Pevsner (1901–83). First editions of the county
volumes were published by Penguin Books between 1951 and 1974.
The continuing programme of revisions and new volumes has
been supported by research financed through the Buildings Books
Trust since 1994.

The Buildings Books Trust gratefully acknowledges
Grants towards the cost of research, writing and illustrations
for this volume from:

THE HERITAGE LOTTERY FUND

THE C J ROBERTSON CHARITABLE TRUST

THE OPEN CHURCHES TRUST

STACKS

Assistance with photographs from:

ENGLISH HERITAGE
(photographer: James O. Davies)

Assistance with maps from:

BRISTOL COUNTY COUNCIL

Bristol

ANDREW FOYLE

with contributions by

BRIDGET CHERRY

PEVSNER ARCHITECTURAL GUIDES

YALE UNIVERSITY PRESS

NEW HAVEN & LONDON

For my parents, with love

YALE UNIVERSITY PRESS
NEW HAVEN AND LONDON
302 Temple Street, New Haven CT06511
47 Bedford Square, London WC1B 3DP

www.pevsner.co.uk
www.lookingatbuildings.org
www.yalebooks.co.uk
www.yalebooks.com

Published 2004
Reprinted with corrections 2009
10 9 8 7 6 5 4 3 2

Copyright © Andrew Foyle

Set in Adobe Minion by SNP Best-set Typesetter Ltd., Hong Kong
Printed in China through World Print

Library of Congress Cataloging-in-Publication Data

Foyle, Andrew.
Bristol / Andrew Foyle ; with contributions by Bridget Cherry.
    p. cm. – (Pevsner architectural guides)
    Based on: North Somerset and Bristol / Nikolaus Pevsner. 1958.
    Includes bibliographical references and indexes.

    ISBN 978-0-300-10442-4 (pbk. : alk. paper)
    1. Architecture – England – Bristol – Guidebooks. 2. Bristol
(England) – Buildings, structures, etc. – Guidebooks. I. Cherry,
Bridget. II. Pevsner, Nikolaus, Sir, 1902 – North Somerset and
Bristol. III. Title. IV. Series.
    NA971.B8F69 2004
    720′.9423′93–dc22
                                    2004002260

Contents

Acknowledgements viii
How to use this book xii

Introduction 1

Major Buildings 49
Bristol Cathedral 50
Clifton Cathedral (R.C.) 63
St Mary Redcliffe 66
Council House 73
Central Library 75
Exchange 78
Wills Memorial Building 82
Clifton Suspension Bridge 85
Temple Meads Railway Station 88

City Churches 91
All Saints 92
Christ Church 94
St George 95
St James 97
St John the Baptist 98
St Mark (or the Lord Mayor's Chapel) 100
St Mary le Port 102
St Mary on the Quay (R.C.) 103
St Michael on the Mount Without 104
St Nicholas 104
St Peter 106
SS Philip and Jacob 107
St Stephen 108
St Thomas the Martyr 110
Temple (or Holy Cross) Church 111

City Centre 113

The Inner City 153
Walk 1. Around Queen Square 154
Walk 2. Castle Park and Broadmead 169
Walk 3. Temple and Redcliffe 178
Walk 4. Park Street and Brandon Hill 189
Walk 5. Canon's Marsh 199

Outer Areas 207

    Walk 6. Hotwells and the Clifton Slopes 208

    Walk 7. Central Clifton 221

    Walk 8. North Clifton 232

    Walk 9. The University and St Michael's Hill 239

    Walk 10. Kingsdown to Stokes Croft 253

    Walk 11. The Eastern Fringe 260

    Walk 12. Spike Island 269

    Walk 13. Bedminster 275

Excursions 281

    Arno's Vale 282

    Ashton Court 285

    Blaise Castle House and Blaise Hamlet 288

    Kingsweston House 291

    Tyntesfield 293

    Further Reading 296

    Glossary 299

    Index of Artists, Architects and Other Persons Mentioned 305

    Index of Localities, Streets and Buildings 313

    Illustration Acknowledgements 324

1. Bristol Cathedral, detail of Chapter House, mid-c12

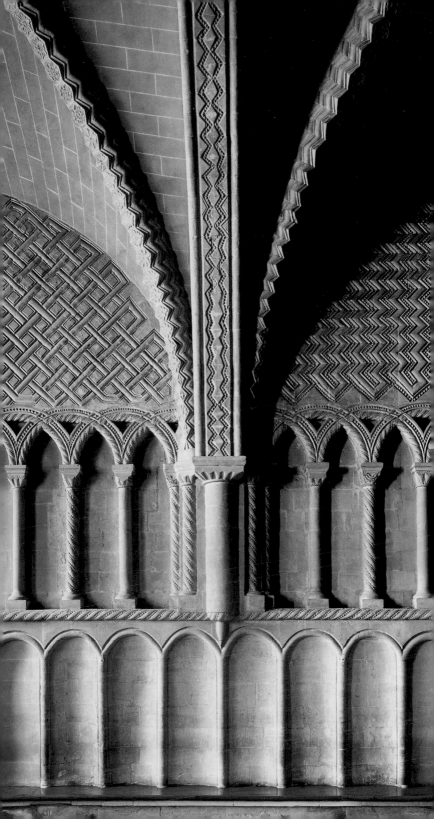

Acknowledgements

Sir Nikolaus Pevsner set exacting standards both in terms of scholarship and writing style. My indebtedness to him is measured in the number of places where his judgement has stood the test of time, and where his words in *North Somerset and Bristol* (*The Buildings of England*), 1958, remain the best expression of Bristol's architectural wealth. Bridget Cherry wrote the entries for Bristol Cathedral and St Mary Redcliffe church, and offered her immense knowledge and personal support throughout. James O. Davies of English Heritage took all the new photographs (assisted in part by Henry Williamson): his eye for the quality of place is remarkable. Karen Evans researched in national resources with great efficiency, while Sue Thurlow read the text and suggested common-sense clarifications. This book was published with the aid of a generous grant from the Heritage Lottery Fund.

Bristol City Council supported the project unstintingly. Thanks to Bristol City Museums Service, especially its Director, Stephen Price, and to Roger Clark, David Eveleigh, Alison Farrar, Sue Giles, Andy King, Sheena Stoddard and Karin Walton. I am also indebted to Bruce Williams, John Bryant, and the late Rod Burchill (Bristol and Region Archaeological Service); Alastair Brook, Chris Heath, Tina Speake, Jon Brett (Conservation Officer) and Bob Jones (City Archaeologist) in the Planning Department; and Dave Holdaway and Barbara Robertson of the Visual Technologies group, who produced the maps. Anthony Beeson, Dawn Dyer and Jane Bradley at the Central Reference Library were endlessly helpful, and staff at Bristol Record Office under John Williams patiently produced thousands of building plans.

Numerous architectural histories on Bristol have inevitably coloured this book (*see* Further Reading). Thanks to their authors, both living and dead. In particular, Mike Jenner generously contributed his formidable expertise. I am grateful to the Special Collections, Public Relations and History of Art Departments at the University of Bristol, and to Mark Janaway, Ann Longney and Annie Burnside for additional information. Access to the archives of the Society of Merchant Venturers was by kind permission of the Master. I am grateful also to Bristol and Gloucestershire Archaeological Society; Bristol Record Society; the Architecture Centre under Mark Pearson; Bristol Industrial Archaeology Society; Avon Gardens Trust; the Friends of Arno's Vale Cemetery; and Brislington Conservation and History Society. I am indebted to Phil Draper and his authoritative Churchcrawler website for such unstinting help.

English Heritage has given unfailing support, through Elain Harwood, Francis Kelly, Nick Molyneux, and the National Monuments Record. John McVerry and Fiona Jenkins graciously organised access to Tyntesfield, and Francis and Mary Greenacre contributed their expertise. Thanks also to the Churches Conservation Trust, the British Museum, the RIBA library, and the Royal Academy of Arts, and to specialists including Professor Colin Barnes of Leeds University, Dr Joseph Bettey, Oliver Bradbury, Julia Elton, Peter Hardie, Dr Hughes-Games, Susan Kellerman, Frank Kelsall, Dr Roger Leech, Douglas Merritt of the Public Monuments and Sculpture Association, Michael Ponsford, Alan Rome, Jonathon Rowe, James Russell, Anita Sims, Rosemary Thomas and John Winstone. Sir George and Lady White enlightened me on James Bridges, and Alan Brooks shared his vast knowledge of stained glass. Mike Bone, Steven Brindle, Angus Buchanan, Richard Davis and Gavin Watson unravelled the complexities of Temple Meads Station; and Sarah Whittingham contributed generously from her doctoral research on Sir George Oatley.

Many architectural and building firms assisted, among them Acanthus Ferguson Mann, Alec French Partnership, Atkins Walters Webster, Barton Willmore, Colin Beales, Ray Bowden, Building Design Partnership, Geoff Haslam, Inscape Architects, Roger Mortimer, Richard Pedlar, Stride Treglown and Whicheloe Macfarlane. Numerous custodians and administrators gave access, notably at Bristol's Cathedrals and churches, Bristol Cathedral School, the Theatre Royal, and Ashton Court. Martin Laker, Alan Canterbury, Jeffrey Spittall and Mark Topping provided valuable information. Private owners with huge enthusiasm for the buildings in their care include John Hardy at Kingsweston House, John Avery, the Bourgnana family, Rupert Curtis, John and Maggie Garland, Garrad Hassan Ltd, Rowland Morgan and David Stevenson.

Special thanks go to the editorial team at Yale University Press. Simon Bradley's and Bridget Cherry's painstaking editing enriched and deepened the text hugely. The Commissioning Editor, Sally Salvesen oversaw the design and production, assisted by Emily Winter. Emily Lees coordinated the illustrations, Alan Fagan produced the text figures, Stephany Ungless was the copy editor and Judith Wardman compiled the index. The other City Guides authors patiently answered my obscure enquiries. Lastly, readers' responses dating back to 1958 were considered for this revision, including lengthy contributions from Lady Georgina Crauford, Phil Draper, Glyn Duggan, John Fisher, the late Bryan Little, David W. Lloyd, and D. Palliser. I hope this will encourage a new generation of readers to respond to the traditional appeal for corrections and significant omissions.

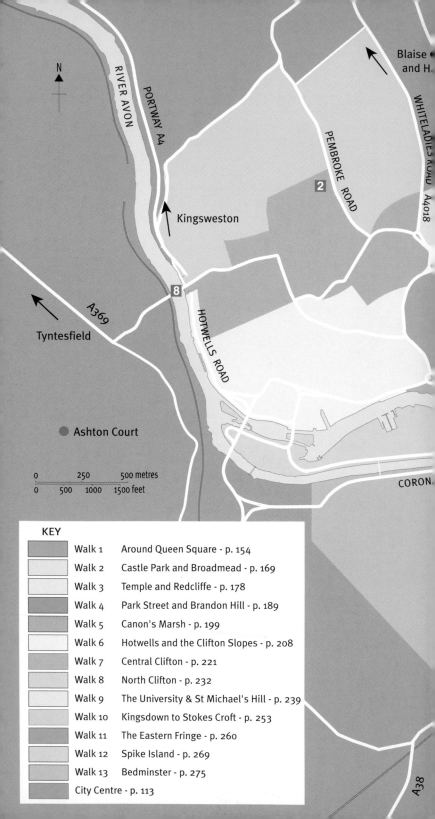

N

Blaise
and H.

RIVER AVON

PORTWAY A4

WHITELADIES ROAD A4018

PEMBROKE ROAD

2

Kingsweston

8

HOTWELLS ROAD

A369

Tyntesfield

Ashton Court

CORON.

0	250	500 metres
0	500	1000	1500 feet

KEY

Walk 1	Around Queen Square - p. 154
Walk 2	Castle Park and Broadmead - p. 169
Walk 3	Temple and Redcliffe - p. 178
Walk 4	Park Street and Brandon Hill - p. 189
Walk 5	Canon's Marsh - p. 199
Walk 6	Hotwells and the Clifton Slopes - p. 208
Walk 7	Central Clifton - p. 221
Walk 8	North Clifton - p. 232
Walk 9	The University & St Michael's Hill - p. 239
Walk 10	Kingsdown to Stokes Croft - p. 253
Walk 11	The Eastern Fringe - p. 260
Walk 12	Spike Island - p. 269
Walk 13	Bedminster - p. 275
City Centre - p. 113	

A38

House

STOKE CROFT A38

NEWFOUNDLAND STREET

M32

BOND STREET

OLD MARKET STREET

7

6

TEMPLE WAY

4
5 1

3

9

ROAD

Arno's Vale

EAST STREET

BATH ROAD

WELLS ROAD

WEST STREET

KEY - Major Buildings

1 Bristol Cathedral
2 Clifton Cathedral (R.C.)
3 St Mary Redcliffe
4 Council House
5 Central Library
6 Exchange
7 Wills Memorial Building
8 Clifton Suspension Bridge
9 Temple Meads Station

How to use this book

This book is designed as a practical guide for exploring the buildings of central Bristol and its inner suburbs. The divisions between the sections are shown on the map on pp. x–xi. After a historical Introduction, the gazetteer begins on p. 49 with entries on nine Major Buildings. A separate section follows devoted to the fifteen city churches. The chief streets of the inner city are then treated alphabetically, and five Walks cover the rest of the central area. Eight further Walks cover the outer areas (i.e. the inner ring of suburbs). Each Walk is provided with its own street map, and the texts of Walks 3, 6, 7 and 11 are subdivided for ease of navigation. The final section suggests five excursions to places of outstanding interest nearby, in outer Bristol or the historic county of Somerset. These areas will be fully surveyed in the forthcoming *Buildings of England* hardback volume *Somerset 1: Bristol, Bath and the Mendips*.

In addition, certain topics are singled out for special attention and presented in separate boxes:

Topographical Records: The Braikenridge Collection p. 19

Planning and Development: Georgian Speculative Development p. 25, Geography of the 1240 Frome Diversion p. 124, Lewins Mead Development p. 140, The Economic Collapse of 1793 p. 217

History and Trade: Bristol's Population Growth in the C19 p. 24, The Bristol Riots p. 161, Bristol Blitzed p. 170, Bristol and Slavery p. 202

Bristol Architects: Architectural Dynasties in Bristol p. 30

Private Architectural Patronage: Private Money, Public Works p. 38, The Canynges Family in Redcliffe p. 186, Raja Rammohun Roy p. 283

The Medieval Churches: How Important is Bristol Cathedral? p. 56, Bristol Cathedral Monuments p. 60, The Earlier Church [St Mary Redcliffe] p. 70, William Worcestre and an Early Architectural Drawing [St Stephen] p. 110

Civic Buildings and Defences: Bristol Corporation's Premises p. 134, Civil War Defences p. 246

2. *Overleaf* Bristol, showing areas covered by walks

Introduction

Medieval Bristol 6

Bristol from *c.* 1530 to *c.* 1700 12

Bristol from *c.* 1700 to *c.* 1850 16

    Early Eighteenth-Century Bristol 17

    Mid-Georgian Bristol, *c.* 1740 to *c.* 1800 20

    Bristol *c.* 1800–50 23

Victorian and Edwardian Bristol, *c.* 1840–1914 27

The Twentieth Century and Beyond 37

Introduction

The late Sir John Summerson wrote 'If I had to show a foreigner one English city and one only, to give him a balanced idea of English architecture, I should take him . . . to Bristol, which has developed in all directions, and where nearly everything has happened.' Bristol has been a major centre of population, manufacture, commerce and transportation for almost one thousand years. It was made a county by royal charter in 1373, and at several periods it was the second city after London. In ecclesiastical terms, however, it remained a distant outlier of the Diocese of Worcester until the See of Bristol was created in 1542. After *c*. 1800 it was no longer a contender for second city, although still the chief regional centre of sw England. Perhaps because of this relative decline, the modern city has grown up piecemeal, allowing survival of pre-C19 buildings alongside the new. Bristol's uniqueness lies in the range and extraordinary juxtapositions of its buildings, constantly surprising with their richness of texture.

From the C12 on, every century is represented by outstanding buildings. Although Bristol's foundation was not primarily religious, the earliest survivals are churches. Fifteen churches and religious foundations of medieval origin still exist in the city centre. There are Jacobean and Carolean timber-framed houses, early Nonconformist chapels, Georgian terraces in brick and stone, *Wood*'s Palladian Exchange, riotously carved Venetian-Victorian banks, Byzantine warehouses, and some fine Art Nouveau façades. Of Bristol's last golden age in the C18 there are some especially fine merchants' villas. This mercantile middle class has left the city ringed by Georgian and Victorian suburbs unparalleled in England, notably Hotwells, Kingsdown and, the best known, Clifton.

However, the nature of Bristol's development and the traumatic after-effects of Second World War bombing have led to a mystifying disjointedness, a constant staccato in the city's rhythms often remarked upon by visitors. Bristol is quirky, revealing its charms only slowly. One plunges from sheltered medieval alleys into alienating traffic routes amidst high-rise offices and back again with alarming suddenness. Certain areas have an unplanned and aimless air. As well as dealing with individual buildings, this volume will attempt to unravel

3. City centre, Bristol Cathedral and Wills Memorial Tower, from the harbour

and explain that disjointedness, and to make sense of the complexities of the city of today.

It is essential first to grasp the **geography** of the surrounding region, the single factor responsible for Bristol's existence. It sits in a favoured position in the valley of the River Avon, which runs w to the Bristol Channel flanked by two limestone outcrops: the Mendip Hills to the s and the Cotswolds to the N. The Bristol Channel, or Severn Estuary, is a giant funnel with the toe of the Cornish peninsula and sw Wales as its outermost limits. Its tidal range of up to *c.* 50 ft (*c.* 15 metres) is the second highest in the world. Bristol sits some five miles inside the mouth of the Avon, but the force of the Severn waters makes the river tidal well to the E of Bristol. Its narrow, winding channel was Bristol's blessing and its curse, providing a defensible location and protection from weather, but proving a handicap in the race to expand the Atlantic trade in the C18. Ships waited up to a month in the channel for a favourable wind and tide to make the perilous dash into port. To fail to make it on one tide was to risk running aground and breaking the ship's back as the waters receded. Nevertheless Bristol's position provided all the prerequisites for great wealth: a port and bridgehead, well situated to trade with the w coast of England and with Wales, Ireland, the Atlantic coasts of Europe, and later the New World; river access to inland England; a focal point for trade in West Country produce, primarily wool, but also wheat, leather and many foods; access to alluvial clays, sands and gravels, excellent building stones and abundant timber; nearby coal seams and water from the hills; and trade routes providing copper, lead, zinc, iron, etc. – the raw materials for manufacturing.

The local **geology** is complex. The low-lying areas around the rivers Avon and Frome are alluvial deposits. Outcrops of red Triassic sandstone form low hills at Redcliffe, College Green and beneath the Saxon town (Corn Street, etc.). Higher slopes to the N (Brandon Hill and St Michael's Hill) are formed of Brandon Hill Grit, a hard red Carboniferous sandstone. To the w Clifton sits on Hotwells limestone, a grey stone containing crinoids and corals. Quarries E of Bristol (e.g. at Hanham) provided **Pennant sandstone**, once widely used for rubble walling and flagstones. It is soft and flaky, ill-suited to smooth finishing or precise cutting. One of the subtle underpinnings of Bristol's character is its grey colour – sometimes a dour battleship grey, but often cast with slate blue, moss green or ochre. More rarely, Pennant ranges from soft chocolate brown to plum. Any of these colours may have splashes of rich orange iron-staining. For fine work, medieval masons favoured **Dundry stone** from the Mendip escarpment a few miles s. It takes fine carving and is not hard to work. At a distance it is virtually indistinguishable from Bath stone, but close inspection reveals ribbon-like layers of sedimentary deposits. Both are oolitic limestones, creamy-white when newly cut, weathering to a honey colour. **Bath stone** has a more regular granular structure like coarse sand. It was infrequently used in Bristol until Ralph Allen began to quarry Bath stone and market it

4. Building materials (left to right): top – terracotta, Bath stone, c19 brick; middle – shuttered concrete, copper slag blocks, Dundry stone; bottom cobbles, Pennant sandstone, Brandon Hill Grit

aggressively, taking advantage of the newly navigable course of the River Avon from Bristol to Bath, opened in 1727. Dundry stone required road transport and was consequently more expensive. Its use declined and Bath stone became the ubiquitous Georgian material. Even during the Regency, stucco found little favour, being reserved for disguising the rubble walls of lesser buildings.

Of other **building materials**, oak was used for timber-framed buildings, a natural adjunct to shipbuilding. Most medieval structures must have been timber-framed, and the tradition continued until the end of the C17. It is unclear when brick was first made in Bristol. There may have been one or two kilns by the C16, for building contracts of that date specified brick for chimneys, etc. Local manufacture seems to have begun in earnest in the late C17 and building contracts regularly specified brick frontages from *c*. 1700.

Roman settlement can be described very briefly. There was no town corresponding to Bristol, merely a small port at *Abonae* on the River Avon, now the suburb of Sea Mills. A road along the Avon valley connected *Abonae* with *Aquae Sulis* (Bath), with scattered villas along the route. One has been excavated at Lawrence Weston. Others were at Brislington, Newton St Loe and two at Keynsham, one of them very large. A small Romano-British settlement was excavated near present-day Upper Maudlin Street, the first Roman site found within the modern city.

Medieval Bristol

Modern Bristol is of **Anglo-Saxon** foundation. Coins were minted by *c*. 1009–16, suggesting that a settlement existed by the late 900s if not before. In 1051 the town is mentioned in the Anglo-Saxon Chronicle, and in 1063 was the base from which the future King Harold launched his campaign against Wales. It was probably defended from the first, the walls being strengthened after the Conquest. The Saxon defences are traceable in the street plan of St Nicholas Street, Leonard Lane, Bell Lane and Tower Lane, with settlement inside this near-circular boundary and E of High Street up to and including the castle. The castle sat above a curve of the River Avon, blocking the E end of the shallow bluff on which the town was built. This traditional view of the topography was challenged in the 1970s, principally by Michael Ponsford, who posited that the Saxon centre lay entirely E of High Street; however Saxon finds around Small Street, etc., now favour the earlier view. Nothing certain is known of Bristol Bridge before its 1240s rebuilding but the name *Brycgstow* (place of the bridge) implies its existence. It was presumably of timber construction. The Saxon settlement was large enough to have several **churches**, including St Mary le Port, St Peter [49] and possibly St Werburgh (formerly in Corn Street, rebuilt in the suburb of St Werburgh's in the 1870s). Only the early C11 Harrowing of Hell relief at Bristol Cathedral tells of the power of pre-Conquest art.

Bristol came under **Norman** control in 1068. A motte-and-bailey castle (probably wholly or partly of wood) was established by the 1080s under Bishop Geoffrey of Coutances. Bristol was handed by William the Conqueror to his wife Matilda. It was clearly a prized possession already, but the c12 seems to have been a high point in its further expansion and its political and economic importance. Henry II issued the first royal charter in 1155. The castle was strengthened c. 1120, with a stone keep comparable in scale to that at Rochester, Kent. Commerce flourished, notably in the new districts of Temple and Redcliffe s of the River Avon, which became centres of the wool and leather industries, with busy wharves.

There was also notable growth in the number of **religious foundations**. Many of the eighteen **parish churches** that existed at the Reformation had c12 origins: All Saints, c. 1140; Temple, before 1150; St Nicholas, before 1154; St Mary Redcliffe, before 1160; St John, before 1174, SS Philip and Jacob, before 1174, and St Thomas, late c12. Sizeable and wealthy **monastic foundations** ringed the town outside the walls. There were Benedictine monks at St James's Priory, c. 1134, Augustinian canons at St Augustine's Abbey (later Bristol Cathedral), 1140, and Whitefriars or Carmelites on the present site of Colston Hall. St Mark's Hospital was founded in 1220, and St Bartholomew's c. 1230. The Greyfriars or Franciscans were at Lewins Mead by c. 1250. Parts of the Dominican (or Blackfriars) Priory remain at Quakers' Friars. The Norman works of c. 1160 in the monastic parts of Bristol Cathedral – the chapter house and the two gateways near College Square [108] – are of the best quality, and the w front of St James is of some distinction too. Of **domestic building**, there are fragmentary remains of an arcade possibly from an aisled hall house, later reused at the chapel of St Bartholomew. Masonry from another late Norman aisled hall house in Small Street – a precious survival – was wantonly destroyed as recently as 1961. The s wall and cellars of the Deanery (now part of Bristol Cathedral School), which have yet to be documented fully, may prove to be a significant survival of Norman domestic work.

Early English Gothic work of high quality is rare in Bristol. The outstanding examples are Bristol Cathedral's Elder Lady Chapel and the inner n porch of St Mary Redcliffe, both of c. 1220. Also of the 1220s is St Mark, College Green; although the surviving E.E. elements are not especially striking now, the original design was probably quite impressive. At SS Philip and Jacob the E.E. tower and transeptal arches are of some refinement. The Wells Cathedral masons were influential. A mason was loaned from there to work on the Elder Lady Chapel, and sculptures at St James and St Bartholomew derive from the Wells workshop.

In 1240–7 Bristol Bridge was rebuilt as a four-arched stone structure; by c. 1300 it was lined with tall houses [6]. The **harbour** was enlarged substantially by the digging of a new channel, St Augustine's Reach, to divert the River Frome (*see* topic box, p. 124), also 1240–7. A secondary effect was the dumping of a layer of clay spoil 40 ins (1 metre) deep on the marshy N margin of the Frome, creating a raft-like foundation for buildings: a long street called Lewins Mead was laid out here *c.* 1250. Also in the mid C13 new **town walls** were built outside the Saxon defensive line, coinciding with similar projects in other prosperous centres, e.g. Oxford, 1224–40, York, *c.* 1250, and Newcastle, *c.* 1265. Their function was as much to regulate trade as it was defensive. Two new walls protected the S expansions. One ran across Town Marsh from St Augustine's Reach to Welsh Back, on the line of the later King Street. The second ran S of Temple and Redcliffe along the line of Portwall Lane, meeting the Avon N of the site of Temple Meads station. Gates survived at Redcliff and Temple streets until the C18. A new N wall followed the Frome along today's Nelson Street, joining the NE corner of the castle. One sees something of the older inner wall only at the gateway beneath St John's church, and of the C13 wall at the surviving bastion N of King Street. The new walls, bridge, harbour and monastic foundations must have given mid-C13 Bristol a dramatic air of forwardness and change.

Already by the C14 Bristol maintained valuable overseas trade links, notably with Gascony, Anjou and Poitou, where wool (in high demand in Flanders and Italy) and other commodities were traded for wine. Trade was also carried on with Norway, Iceland, Ireland, Spain, Portugal and the Mediterranean. Bristol was by *c.* 1330 the wealthiest town after London, and among the most populous at perhaps *c.* 10,000 people. By the mid C14 cloth displaced unwoven wool as the chief export, although the cloth trade gradually declined after that time. But we should not try to link the ups and downs of trade too closely to the development of architecture, for Bristol's buildings continued to display abundant evidence of wealth and prestige throughout the late Middle Ages.

Pevsner and others have held Bristol's moment of greatness, architecturally speaking, to be that point just after 1300 when the **Decorated**

5. Bristol Cathedral, detail of Elder Lady Chapel, early C13

6 Old Bristol Bridge, from a mid-c18 drawing

style of Gothic was at its most capricious and inventive. Above all else it is the E arm of the abbey church (now Bristol Cathedral), and especially the vaulting there, that establishes that claim. The view that, for a moment, Bristol nurtured the most advanced and original architecture in Europe is not now accepted without argument, though neither has it been demolished (*see* topic box, p. 56). The recent redating implies that the work was less crucial than Pevsner believed for the transmission of ideas from France, however it takes up and reworks French *Rayonnant* themes with a curious, almost perverse inventiveness. In addition, contemporary metalwork and manuscript illustrations were delightfully translated into ornamental stone details. The distinctive brilliance in the handling of space in the choir vaulting is indisputable. The tiny skeletal vault outside the Berkeley Chapel is further proof [27]. Such a conceit, a rib-vault that reveals rather than hides the prosaic flat ceiling above, 'may sound merely playful, [but] is in fact aesthetically of the greatest charm' (Pevsner). At St Mary Redcliffe, one of the grandest parish churches in England, the ambitious tower [31] was begun in the late c13, and the glorious outer N porch *c.* 1320, part of a virtual rebuilding of the church that was not completed until the Perp style was well established. The inventive Dec work shows the abbey's influence, although the differences suggest that other masons were responsible: principally the dense knobbly foliate decoration around the N porch door and the use of nodding ogee arches.

Many parish churches were rebuilt or extended in **Perpendicular** style from the later c14. Among these are St Stephen, St Werburgh, All Saints, St John, St Peter [49], St Mary le Port, Temple and St Michael (some of which were later demolished or rebuilt). Distinctive characteristics are the high naves (unclerestoried at all except the first), the long high ranks of aisle windows (e.g. Temple Church [52]) and the towers. The showy projecting crown at St Stephen (1470s) [50] derives from Gloucester Cathedral. Many c15 towers exhibit a distinctive Bristol spirelet over the stair-turret.

7. St Mary Redcliffe, the nave looking E

The best place to see the significance and wealth of early Perp work is in the later parts of the C14 rebuilding at St Mary Redcliffe, i.e. the upper parts of the choir, transepts and nave, perhaps completed *c.* 1390. Of the other parish churches, St Stephen's interior is still

8. Spicer's door, Bristol Museum, *c.* 1330–50

impressive despite heavy C19 restorations. St John has two great rarities: a one-bay clerestory w of the chancel arch to light the rood,* and a full crypt, built in two sections [46]. The vault pattern of the w part here matches that at Bristol's other crypt, St Nicholas. This is probably of *c.* 1350–80, and very fine. The best late Perp work is the Poyntz chapel at St Mark, decorated in honour of the patron's friendship with Henry VIII and Catherine of Aragon, and bearing their arms in the vault.

Medieval **church furnishings** include fragments of C14–C16 glass at Bristol Cathedral and at St Mary Redcliffe [33]; a fine C15 brass lectern now at St Stephen, and a rare candelabrum in the Berkeley Chapel of the cathedral. The cathedral misericords are of *c.* 1520. Bishop Miles Salley embellished the chancel at St Mark *c.* 1500–20 with a fine reredos and his own tomb in a matching style. The neighbouring Berkeley tomb and the similar late C15 Mede tombs at St Mary Redcliffe have richly ornamented canopies with lacy stonework. **Sculpture** includes the fine alabaster effigies of William Canynges the Younger, d.1474, at St Mary Redcliffe, and of Walter Frampton d.1388, at St John. The Poyntz Chapel at St Mark was floored with richly decorated C16 Spanish tiles, evidence of the strong trading links with the Iberian peninsula.

Secular buildings are less well represented. No public buildings of the period remain. Illustrations of the elaborately decorated C15 Guildhall show it to have had a carefree asymmetry that inhibited any sense of civic grandeur. At the historic centre of the city, that is, the crossroads formed by High Street, s, Wine Street, E, Broad Street, N, and Corn Street, w, stood the C14 **High Cross**. An outstanding C14 fragment is **Spicer's Door** [8], a panelled and traceried oak door of *c.* 1330–50, with the stubs of a rib-vaulted porch, originally from Welsh Back and now displayed at the Museum and Art Gallery. The tracery clearly derives

---

*Another, at St Thomas, was destroyed in C18 rebuilding.

from religious architecture. The most extravagant house was undoubtedly that of the Canynges family at Redcliff Backs (*see* p. 186). It had by the late C15 a high tower overlooking the harbour. Canynges's House, like others of the richest C15 merchants, had a great hall open to the roof. We know from C15 Bristol inventories and wills that such halls were often not used for everyday living, but were decorated with symbols of the owner's civic status and militia associations – a phenomenon that continued in Bristol as late as the end of the C17. The less wealthy might live in 'shophouses', that is they traded from the ground floor and lived above, with a great chamber on the first floor. Following the demolition of the fine rooms at the so-called Colston's House,* the best secular stonework is Guardhouse Arch, of *c.* 1520, now also at Bristol Museum.

Bristol from *c.* 1530 to *c.* 1700

Bristol's population in the mid C16 was *c.* 9,500–10,000, virtually the same as it had been before the Black Death in 1348. It began to increase in the late C16, to *c.* 12,000 by *c.* 1605, and *c.* 16,000 by the 1670s. Between *c.* 1630 and *c.* 1700, the pattern of Bristol's trade was also transformed. At the start of that period just a few ships made the annual voyage to the newly opening Americas; by its end, voyages to Virginia, the Caribbean and Newfoundland accounted for about half the ships leaving the port.

The effects of the **Reformation** are familiar. The monastic foundations were stripped, demolished or robbed for materials, their property divided and sold. Abbot Newland's untimely half-built nave at St Augustine's Abbey was demolished and houses built against the abbey crossing. The abbey at least became a cathedral in 1542, giving Bristol city status. The buildings of other monastic foundations were used as guild halls, schools (e.g. St Mark and St Bartholomew) or private houses.

We should note briefly the **expansion** beyond the medieval walls. NE of the medieval city, the Broadmead and Old Market districts were already established by 1480, but they became more densely populated and suburban in character during the C17. To the N, St Michael's Hill developed from the C15, with scattered houses and garden lodges in parkland, and humbler houses clustered around the road up the hill. King Street was laid out in the 1650s along the outer side of the s wall on Town Marsh, and housing straggled w towards Hotwells and s towards Bedminster too. The city was 'in every respect another London that one can hardly know it to stand in the country' (Samuel Pepys, 1668).

By the C16 Bristol's **military** importance was much reduced; Bristol Castle had long since ceased to be maintained as an occasional royal residence – a common phenomenon nationally – and its fabric was ruinous. For its role in the Civil War, subsequent demolition, and other Civil War defences, *see* topic box, p. 246. No new churches were built in

---

*These rooms were an addition, probably of the 1540s, to the C12 hall house at Small Street, mentioned above. Both were incorporated in the C19 Assize Court, and demolished when it was remodelled in 1961.

Bristol from 1530 until the C18. There is however a rich legacy of **church furnishings** including pews, communion table, rails and font at St John, and pulpit and font cover at SS Philip and Jacob. Monuments are well represented, e.g. at St Mark, St Stephen and St James. Ionic columns support the canopy of Bishop Bush's monument of *c.* 1558 at Bristol Cathedral [9], the earliest surviving use of classical motifs in Bristol.

The Bush monument raises the wider issue of the infiltration of **classicism** into Bristol. The spread of the style was assisted by the availability of prints and books from Northern Europe, and was at first mainly used for monuments, chimneypieces and ornamental details. But all this is well-established fact and applies to England as a whole. What is Bristol's story? Classical columns, though probably crudely formed, were considered appropriate for public buildings by the mid C16

9. Bristol Cathedral, monument to Bishop Bush, d.1558

(*see* below). The Orders are rendered with approximate accuracy in late C16 monuments. The s front at Ashton Court was refaced *c.* 1634 (*see* Excursions, p. 285). For all its irregularity of rhythm and spacing, the organizing principle here is truly classical. Although only two miles from the city, it was however a country house and its frame of reference was the style fashionable with the court and aristocracy, exemplified by the designs of Inigo Jones. It was another half-century before the gap between the taste of the London court and nobility and that of the Bristol merchants began to close. Until that time mercantile middle-class buildings remained essentially Jacobean. Merchants (at least some of them) had regular contact with London. They must have been aware of changing fashions there and had the money to follow suit. That they did not was probably for two reasons: first, the local craftsmen and builders had neither the skills nor the understanding necessary; more fundamentally, the patrons probably saw London's classicism as irrelevant to Bristol's traditions.

Public buildings of *c.* 1530–*c.* 1700 are known only through a few illustrations, principally those on the excellent illustrative maps of 1671–1710 by Jacob Millerd and his son, and from the Braikenridge Collection of drawings (*see* topic box, p. 19). The Tolzey, a covered structure for trade and official business, rebuilt in 1551, appears to have had Corinthian columns, as did an open sided Corn Market in Wine Street, with crested coats of arms above the eaves. All such early examples were destroyed by C18 and C19 improvements.

There is better evidence for **domestic buildings**, due partly to the absence of a Bristol equivalent of the Great Fire of London. The best, and effectively the only, Elizabethan survival is the Red Lodge, Park Row, of *c.* 1577–85, on the N outskirts below St Michael's Hill. It originally had an Italian-influenced arched loggia. The interiors – especially the Great Oak Room [133]– rival the best of their size and date anywhere in England. St Peter's Hospital (bombed in 1940) was rebuilt in 1612 around a C14 core as the mansion of Alderman Robert Aldworth, wealthy merchant and sometime mayor. Its highly decorated timber-framing, rich interiors, and zoomorphic figures supporting the jetties and bays made it the most conspicuous C17 production of Bristol's mercantile élite. The Dutch House, High Street, 1676 (also bombed, 1940), was timber-framed and unusually high at five storeys. Its main corner-post was transformed into a howling grotesque figure, carved as if anchored with iron bands onto the woodwork – an arresting device. Both in terms of height and ostentation, a parallel can be drawn with the mid-C17 timber-framed houses of Newcastle. By contrast, stone-built gabled houses had begun to supplant timber-framing in Bath by the 1620s.

Surprisingly large numbers of C17 houses survive, e.g. at St Michael's Hill, King Street, Old Market, Temple Street and St Thomas Street. The layman might mistake them for Tudor work, but there are subtle differences as carpenters absorbed the new ideas. The ground-floor jetty becomes shallower; upper parts are given either a small pent roof or a moulded wooden beam at each floor, and the wall surface becomes flatter, with little or no actual projection between the storeys. Securely dated evidence is scarce, but this flattening seems to have started later than *c.* 1615, and is obvious by the late 1630s at Nos. 23–29 St Michael's Hill. The houses in King Street of the 1660s [75] have a new expansive air about them, with groups of up to five houses treated as unified symmetrical compositions. 'Ipswich' bay windows with arched centres are favoured, perhaps referring to the Venetian motif. Quasi-Ionic pilasters are incised into structural timbers, e.g. at the Llandoger Trow, King Street (*c.* 1664). Urban buildings in the Vale of Gloucestershire exhibit similar continuity with late medieval tradition until the late C17. In Bristol, timber-framing died out with remarkable suddenness in the 1690s. The earliest known examples of classical principles used to organize urban façades are the White Lion Hotel, Broad Street (demolished 1864); Colston's Almshouses, St Michael's Hill [131]; and the Manor House nearby [132]. All three were begun in 1691. Flat brick or stone façades and horizontal eaves cornices soon became the norm, being enforced for the first time in the building contracts for Queen Square (from 1699). By *c.* 1705 the transformation in Bristol's expectations was complete, although their fulfilment lagged slightly behind.

Interiors of the C16 and C17 rarely survive complete, but much can be gleaned from the Braikenridge Collection and other sources. The Red Lodge interiors have been remarked already. Several panelled rooms are known, of which the 1620s State Room from Langton's Mansion, Welsh Back, was reconstructed *c.* 1906 at New Place, Shedfield, Hampshire. Panelling from a good but humbler room at No. 28 Redcliff Street, perhaps of *c.* 1650, is in Bristol Museum's collection. Its frieze is highly decorated with masks, foliage, shields and hounds' heads, similar to the plaster frieze at No. 33 King Street.

Stone chimneypieces of *c.* 1580–*c.* 1680 form a special group with a distinctive Bristol style. The fire opening (often Tudor-arched) was framed with pilasters, paired half-columns or terms. Simple patterns of rosettes, dots or pairs of incised lines decorated the inner border. Above was a broad horizontal frieze, richly carved with interlace, scrolled foliage, or occasionally with iconographic figures and emblems (e.g. the chimneypiece formerly at No. 28 Redcliff Street). Elaborate overmantels, sometimes ceiling-high, frequently combined strapwork with figures and emblems from Continental engravings. Only the chimney-pieces at the Red Lodge [133] and some minor ones at Ashton Court remain *in situ*. Many have been resited.* They would amply reward further study.

Plaster ceilings are represented by the Red Lodge, and the similar though later example now at Shedfield, Hampshire (*see* above). At the Museum is a panel with the arms of Charles I from a building in Bristol

*Guildhall, Broad Street; Bristol Water Works offices, Telephone Avenue; Museum Café; Red Lodge Wigwam; etc.

10 No. 33 King Street, great chamber, ceiling detail, 1650s

Castle – possibly the Constable's house – which survived the 1650s demolition. Humbler ceilings of *c*. 1650–65 in King Street [10] have a flat ground with isolated patterns outlined by lozenges or quatrefoils, and with moulded rose, vine or pomegranate motifs, both attractive and economical. It is clear that C17 Bristol's enjoyment of pattern, decoration and colour flourished under skilled local craftsmen combining and reinventing familiar themes.

Bristol from *c*. 1700 to *c*. 1850

Bristol began to outstrip York and Norwich as second city after London from *c*. 1700. The years 1700–50 are regarded in particular as the city's golden age. At the start of the C18, the population was about 25,000. By 1735 that may have increased to *c*. 35,000, by 1750 to nearly 50,000, and to *c*. 67,000 by the 1801 census. The growth was fed by commercial markets including the slave trade, and new **industrial developments**. The earliest pottery operated at the outlying village of Brislington from *c*. 1650, joined by others, mainly at Temple and Redcliffe, from the 1680s. By 1745 experiments were being made with soft-paste porcelain at Redcliffe. Nine glass kilns existed by 1696 – the largest concentration outside London – stimulated by the availability of sand, limestone, red lead and coal for the furnaces. Pottery and glass cones dominated the c18 townscape. Brass was being produced in Bristol by *c.* 1696, and Abraham Darby's brassworks was established by *c.* 1702. Brass was an important export commodity for slave traders (*see* topic box, p. 202). The refining of Caribbean sugar was another major c18 industry, although few buildings survived the many fires occasioned by sugar-boiling; there are fragmentary remains of a factory at Lewins Mead. The diversity and inventiveness of c18 manufacturing industry made Bristol a seedbed of the Industrial Revolution. In general, much industrial activity was carried on in small or mid-sized workshops, in the dense heart of the city, a situation that pertained at least in residual fashion until the Second World War.

This digression gives some context to the architectural riches of the years *c.* 1700–1850 to which we now turn. This long time-span is subdivided into early, *c.* 1700–*c.* 1740, middle, *c.* 1740–*c.* 1800, and late, *c.* 1800–*c.* 1850. The late end-date encompasses Bristol's Greek Revival which continued, particularly in Clifton, until 1850 and even slightly beyond, overlapping the start of Victorian developments.

Early Eighteenth-Century Bristol

During this period Bristol saw significant changes in **building materials**, principally because of the industrial and technological improvements outlined above. Brick was little used until *c.* 1700, after which date it quickly became the standard material for terraced housing. The introduction of Bath stone from 1727 has been referred to as well as the speed with which it supplanted all rivals in the best public buildings and large houses. After the mid c18 it was increasingly used for the most fashionable terraces. Slag from brass furnaces was compressed whilst still hot into building blocks of an iridescent purplish-black colour. This was exploited most notably at the Black Castle, Arno's Vale [11], and was used, e.g. for wall copings, until *c.* 1900. **Joinery** was revitalized with the import of mahogany from the Americas: the panelled parlour at Goldney House, Clifton [114], of *c.* 1723, is perhaps the best example. At least two houses in Queen Square had **murals** painted in oil on plaster. No. 15 (*c.* 1711, demolished *c.* 1912), had an ambitious scheme of five mythological panels covering the hallway, possibly by *Pierre Berchet*, a follower of Verrio. Of decorative **plasterwork**, a ceiling at No. 12 Guinea Street, of *c.* 1718, has a richly moulded frame surrounding a charming bas-relief of hunting scenes. These examples, and the panelled hall at No. 28 Orchard Street [68], show the great elaboration that could be displayed in relatively ordinary domestic settings; a trend continued in the mid-c18 Rococo plasterwork discussed below (p. 22).

Little need be said of **church architecture** until later in the century. A fine rebuilding of the tower at All Saints took place in 1712–17. There are also some excellent funerary monuments and architectural details e.g. Colston's monument, All Saints [42], and Baroque doorcases at Temple

11. The Black Castle, Brislington, w front, c. 1764

Church and St Stephen. Redland Chapel, by *John Strahan* and *William Halfpenny*, c. 1739–43, was a private chapel for John Cossins, in a late Baroque style with excellent woodwork by *Thomas Paty* and sculpture by *Rysbrack*. Although it is outside our boundary, in the suburb of Redland, it deserves mention because its spatial and decorative refinement raised the stakes in the rest of the city. Superb examples of **ironwork** are provided by the church screens and gates of *William* and *Simon Edney*, e.g. at St Mary Redcliffe, St Mark and St Stephen. The best bear comparison with the work of the court favourite Jean Tijou. Sword rests were also a speciality. The early C18 examples at St Stephen and St Mark equal the gates and screens in delicacy and richness. Eight churches could boast fine wooden reredoses, but the only survivor is at St Thomas the Martyr.

Bristol's new status resulted in **public buildings** of some flamboyance but less refinement. The demolished Merchants' Hall, home of the

Society of Merchant Venturers, was rebuilt in 1719 with an entrance façade remarkably like *George Townesend*'s unexecuted design for a dairy at Kingsweston House. Townesend, a member of the Oxford family of masons, settled in Bristol in the 1690s and is the first identifiable local architect in the line that covers the C17–C21. Bristol is also rich in **almshouses** of this period; the best are Colston's on St Michael's Hill, 1691–6 [131], and the Merchant Tailors' in Merchant Street, 1701. Ridley's Almshouses, Milk Street, 1738 (demolished in the 1950s) were humbler, and despite their late date still had mullioned and transomed windows. Fortunately, two **guild halls** – or at least, their façades – survive: Merchant Tailors' Hall off Broad Street, and Coopers' Hall, King Street [76], both of the early 1740s and both attributed to *William Halfpenny*. They demonstrate that point of contradiction between the exaggerated proportions of late Baroque motifs and the more rule-bound approach of Palladianism. The best early C18 **sculpture** is *Rysbrack*'s great brass equestrian statue of William III in Queen Square [78]. At Goldney House, Clifton is a lead statue of Hercules, *c.* 1715, tentatively assigned to *John Nost the Elder*. *Randall*'s Neptune (Broad Quay), of 1722 and also of lead, is a good and lively example of local statuary.

House building was transformed by the rise of **terraces** and planned **squares**. Queen Square (1699–*c.* 1727) is the first of the Bristol squares, and the grandest for its size and breadth rather than for its individual houses. These were constructed piecemeal, the only coherence being dictated by building leases that stipulated regular brick fronts, cornices and sash windows, etc., in emulation of the City of London's post-Fire regulations. Queen Square is Bristol's first attempt at urban planning and belatedly set the seal on the brick façade as the fashionable model. Early C18 houses were generally of three, five or, very unusually, seven bays, invariably double-pile in plan, and the staircase generally aligned with the front door. Variations were a lateral staircase between front and rear rooms, e.g. No. 68 Prince Street [83], or a three- or four-bay house

The Braikenridge Collection

George Weare Braikenridge (1775–1856) was a successful Bristol merchant and antiquarian collector. His collection included antiquities of many types, notably architectural fragments salvaged from medieval Bristol houses and churches. When it was dispersed in 1908, his collection of *c.* 1,400 topographical views of Bristol commissioned from some thirty artists was fortunately bequeathed to Bristol City Museums and Art Gallery. They are among the finest and most complete pre-photographic records of any British city. Most were made *c.* 1820–30, i.e. just before the changes wrought by Victorian improvers and church restorers. Braikenridge was particularly interested in the churches and in the picturesque C13–C17 houses then still abundant throughout the city. Panoramas and views, e.g. of Georgian Kingsdown, were also included.

with a wide staircase hall at the front, as at No. 28 Orchard Street [68]. In larger houses, services might be in a rear yard, sometimes with separate kitchen block, as seems to have been the case in Queen Square.

Other squares quickly followed, such as St James's Square, 1707–16, and Dowry Square, Hotwells, 1721 onward. From the early c18, divisions between adjoining houses are generally marked with **lesenes**, projecting vertical strips, either plain, quoined or in the form of a pilaster. Although not uncommon elsewhere, they were almost universally adopted here, and remained common in terraces (and later, semi-detached houses) until the early c20. Special **decorative devices** before *c.* 1740 include cherub rainwater heads, shell-hooded doors and foliate window keystones modelled as grotesque masks: *see* No. 28 Orchard Street (p. 145); No. 29 Queen Square (p. 164); Nos. 10–12 Guinea Street (p. 182); Chapel Row, Hotwells (p. 211); and No. 5 Broad Plain (p. 266).

Nos. 66–70 Prince Street, *c.* 1725–8, are the best surviving early Georgian merchants' houses of their type [83]. They have unusually vigorous façades, although the repeated pediments and projecting centres are slightly awkward. The architect was probably *John Strahan*, who seems to have worked for John Hobbs, one of the owners of the Prince Street houses, at Kingsmead, Bath. The lively Baroque façade at No. 59 Queen Charlotte Street [80], of the 1730s, is now attributed to *Nathaniel Ireson*, from Wincanton, Somerset. A minor characteristic of Bristol's late Baroque was a brief fashion *c.* 1720–50 for curved and shaped parapets or gables.* The most notable work in the hinterland was Vanbrugh's Kingsweston House [157], of *c.* 1710–19, covered here as an excursion. Bishopsworth manor house (outside the boundary of this book) has Kingsweston's arcaded chimneys in miniature, the only evidence of its direct influence in Bristol.

Mid-Georgian Bristol, *c.* 1740 to *c.* 1800

Contemporary observers seem to agree that, while it was prosperous, Bristol exhibited little taste or sophistication. Horace Walpole called it 'the dirtiest great shop I ever saw'. Its people were constantly 'in a hurry, running up and down with cloudy looks and busy faces' (Thomas Cox, *Magna Britannia*, 1727). For its much-needed new Exchange, the Corporation consciously chose, in *John Wood the Elder* of Bath, an architect compatible with its sense of self-importance. Vanbrugh excepted, this is the first known example of Bristol using an architect of national standing. Wood's Exchange, Corn Street, 1741–3 [36], is undoubtedly Bristol's most significant c18 building for its sophistication of design and richness of detail, and its reliance on Palladian models interpreted with academic rigour. The 1740s saw something of a building boom: two guild halls and several Nonconformist chapels were built, as well as Redland Chapel (*see* above, p. 18) and some big mercantile villas, of which Clifton

---

*E.g. warehouses at Narrow Quay, *c.* 1730, demolished; Lunsford House, Park Row, 1738; No. 10 Guinea Street; a gateway beside the Old Library, King Street, 1740; a demolished house next to Cooper's Hall, King Street, *c.* 1740; No. 28 Clifton Wood Road, 1738.

Court and Clifton Hill House [112] are the best. Housing schemes include the completion of Dowry Square and much in Prince Street, and the layout of King Square, Unity Street and Park Street. Wesley's New Room, Broadmead [87], is the first purpose-built Methodist chapel, a space of great simplicity and homeliness. The Friends' Meeting House of 1747 in nearby Quakers' Friars is by *George Tully* and is perhaps the most architecturally ambitious of its type and date in England. Anglican **church architecture** is well represented. St Nicholas and St Michael were both rebuilt, in the 1760s and 1770s respectively. *James Bridges*'s remarkably early and accurate Neo-Perpendicular design at St Nicholas [48] outshines *Thomas Paty*'s weak Georgian Gothic at St Michael. Another burst of church building in the 1780s produced Christ Church, Broad Street [43]; St Paul, Portland Square [141]; the Unitarian Meeting House, Lewins Mead [67]; and St Thomas the Martyr, St Thomas Street. At St Paul, the mason-architect *Daniel Hague* attempted to synthesize Gothick and classical motifs, naïvely and with limited success if judged by the purist, but with great spirit. The only national figure involved was *William Blackburn,* for the Unitarians at Lewins Mead.

James Bridges had considerable talent, and was responsible for two other projects of great interest. He designed the new Bristol Bridge in 1757–60 and was probably the main architect at Royal Fort House [130], a dazzling Rococo villa of 1758–61. The son of a Hertfordshire clockmaker, Bridges arrived in Bristol in 1756 having recently taken his late father's great clock, the Microcosm, on a tour of the American colonies – hence the inaccurate supposition that he was American. Regrettably his career after leaving Bristol in 1763 is unknown.*

Bristol's productive essays in Rococo and Gothick are worth considering in tandem. Firm evidence of names and dates for the local work is frustratingly scanty. The national fashion for **Gothick** as an alternative to the Palladian mainstream was spread via the pattern books of Batty Langley, etc. It was taken up in Bristol in the 1750s with great enthusiasm by wealthy merchants including the Quakers William Reeve and Thomas Goldney III. Reeve's house (later Arno's Court) was Gothicized and the nationally significant castellated stable block [11] added c. 1764. His Gothick bath house was demolished but its façade survives at Portmeirion, North Wales. No designer is known, but *Thomas Paty* (and perhaps his brother *James*) are associated with a number of houses where Gothick work crops up, and may have been its main exponents in Bristol. Thomas Paty may have designed the rotunda at Goldney House, Clifton, which has the characteristic ogee-curved battlements also seen at Arno's Court gateway. Paty must have designed St Michael's rectory too, which has ogee-arched windows, etc., similar to a house at Brandon Steep. Several other houses of the 1760s in the locality have or had Gothick work.† The circular folly tower at Blaise

*Information from Sir George White.
†Cote House (1759, demolished), Stoke Park at Stoke Gifford, Ashton Court (NW wing), Corsham Court, and Clevedon Court (W wing, demolished).

12. Royal Fort House, Rococo doorcase in the dining room, early 1760s

Castle (*Robert Mylne*, 1766) is a good example of romantic landscape building. Locally the craze seems to have faded by *c*. 1780.

The French-inspired **Rococo** style was current nationally from *c*. 1730–70. Its chief architectural manifestation was in interiors, characterized by serpentine lines, scrolls, shells and organic forms rendered in plasterwork, etc. In Bristol it enjoyed a brief but intense fashion from *c*. 1750–70, concurrent with the Gothick and taken up by some of the same patrons. The Rococo elements in *Joseph Thomas*'s plasterwork at Clifton Hill House are rigidly contained within compartments, probably at the architect Ware's insistence. This compartmentalizing also dominated *Thomas Stocking*'s handsome ceiling at St Nicholas (destroyed 1940). By contrast his spectacular free-flowing work at Royal Fort House [12] make it among the most exciting interiors of its date in England. Stocking probably also did the bath-house and reception-room ceilings at Arno's Court. Other examples include the hall at No. 15 Orchard Street, and the style even filtered down to a quite humble parlour ceiling at Northview Cottage, Bedminster. There is no parallel for these urban Rococo interiors at Bath.* Timothy Mowl makes the plausible argument that the work of Dublin *stuccatori* may have influenced the style in Bristol. The grounds are stylistic and circumstantial, and further research is needed to establish the nature of the links.

The more prosaic mainstream of mid-Georgian **domestic** work consisted of speculative developments put up for the middle class (*see* topic box, p. 25). Rows of individual houses were gradually supplanted by terraces planned as unified compositions, as at Albemarle Row, Hotwells, of 1762–3 [111]. The *Paty* family was responsible for many terraces of this type, which tend to be overladen with blocked Gibbs surrounds and repetitive stepped keystones to the windows. The later work of *Thomas Paty* is difficult to distinguish from that of his son. However, it was probably *William Paty* who introduced the sparer designs seen from the 1780s, of Bath stone with unadorned openings, e.g. Charlotte Street [100] and Berkeley Square. It is generally referred to as the 'late Paty style'. There are many good terraces of middling status around Hotwells, Kingsdown and St Paul's, but the most fashionable late C18 developments were, of course, in Clifton, e.g. Prince's Buildings and Royal York Crescent. They are only rivalled at Portland Square, St Paul's, designed *c.* 1787–8 by *Daniel Hague*, where the planning approaches the scale and consistency of C18 London squares.

In the later C18, a new wave of **industrial development** began to encroach on a still basically medieval city centre. Champion's (later Merchants') Dock, Hotwells, was dug in 1765; lime and glass-kilns were built. Potteries and iron works sprang up e.g. in St Philip's and at Guinea Street, Redcliffe. A shot tower on Redcliff Hill and early C18 warehouses at Narrow Quay were among the saddest losses to 1960s redevelopment plans. Virtually the only survivors are the truncated glass cone at Redcliffe, of *c.* 1780, and a gunpowder storage house on the banks of the River Avon at Shirehampton, although this is now a dwelling house and well outside the city centre.

Bristol *c.* 1800–50

During the early C19, Bristol's population growth was much less spectacular than that of Liverpool, Manchester or Birmingham. The industrial capacity of the Northern towns fast overtook Bristol's, inviting the suggestion that late C18 Bristol had failed to develop the infrastructure, particularly port facilities, that might have allowed it to keep pace. Moreover Bristol's role in the slave trade had declined in

*The Rococo plasterwork at Midford Castle near Bath is attributed to *Thomas Stocking*.

	1801	1821	1841	1861	1881	1901
Bristol	68,000	98,000	143,000	179,000	266,000	337,000
Liverpool	78,000	119,000	286,000	444,000	553,000	685,000
Manchester	75,000	126,000	235,000	339,000	341,000	347,000
Birmingham	71,000	107,000	183,000	296,000	401,000	522,000

Note: Some figures may vary because of boundary changes.

favour of Liverpool, and Bristol had become an early centre of the abolition movement. These trends undoubtedly affected Bristol's prosperity in the early C19.

The most important of all C19 developments was the creation of the **Floating Harbour** by the engineer *William Jessop* in 1804–9 [104]. After decades of debate and various proposals, the tidal River Avon was enclosed with lock gates to the W and E of the city. This removed the limitation on loading and unloading caused when the tide went out and ships in harbour were lowered to the mud. The Floating Harbour required two new channels: the Feeder Canal crossed St Philip's Marsh to the E, giving small boats an exit towards Bath and feeding water into the harbour via sluice gates; the New Cut from Temple Meads to Hotwells acted as a tidal bypass, taking the downstream flow of the River Avon and diverting incoming tides that could no longer flow into the harbour. Inside the lock gates at Hotwells, the Cumberland Basin was dug, where shipping awaited exit at high tide. But the Floating Harbour did not solve the problem of the winding and tidal five-mile channel from the sea (*see* p. 4). Moreover it came too late – the deep-water port of Liverpool had already overtaken Bristol in the Atlantic trade – and cost some £600,000; the harbour dues needed to pay for it made trading through Bristol uncompetitive for many decades after.

Nationally, expanding populations needed new **churches**, and their provision was met by the Church Building Act of 1818 (sometimes called the 'Million Pound Act') and the allocation of a further half million pounds in 1824. The programme was controlled by a Government-appointed Commission – hence the term Commissioners' Churches. In Bristol three were built in the 1820s. The first and most prominent, St George, Brandon Hill [44], by *Robert Smirke*, is also Bristol's first Greek Revival church. The Commissioners eventually agreed to meet the full cost of £10,042, although it served much the wealthiest congregation. The other two examples were both in the thin Gothic Revival style synonymous with Commissioners'. *Charles Dyer*'s church of St Paul, Bedminster, of 1829–31, received £7,796 of £9,796, and *Thomas Rickman & Hutchinson*'s Holy Trinity in St Philip's of 1829–30, received £6,031 of £8,231. The Renaissance-inspired arch and heavy handling at *Charles Cockerell*'s Holy Trinity, Hotwells, of 1829–30, foreshadow early Victorian

The model for C18 speculative development was common across England. In theory it was simple: a landholder leased land for development to one or more builders in return for a ground rent. The builder contracted to finish the houses within a fixed term (usually one to three years) to the landholder's specification, and leased them on. When the lease expired, the buildings and land reverted to the owner. In the early C18, land tenure was often for a term of ninety-nine years or three lives. From *c.* 1750 it became increasingly common to grant fixed-term building leases usually for forty years, a feature also common in Ireland at this time. They were frequently converted later to perpetual leases in return for an annual ground rent.

The system became complicated for larger developments, where the head lease was taken up by a middleman or a consortium of investors, often in professions related to the housing market, to spread the financial risks of large schemes. The developers laid out the plots, provided water, drainage and street surfacing and usually engaged an architect, as at Kingsdown Parade. Single plots or small groups were then subcontracted to builders. Such terraces were rarely built entirely by one builder. In addition the fittings within the shell were often specified by the buyer. The buyer might be the occupier or, as was common in Clifton, a landlord who then rented out rooms or floors by the season. The system was complicated further by multiple layers of leases and financing. Often the leaseholders or landowners lent money to those below them in the chain, in the interest of seeing the work completed while earning money in interest. 'Tontine subscriptions' were another popular arrangement: subscribers each paid a set sum to fund the building, and any profits were divided annually between them. As subscribers died off, the profits were divided between the survivors in ever-larger shares. The system was later made illegal because of a tendency for subscribers to die mysteriously.

In the late 1780s the building boom accelerated to the point of mania, and many developers were hopelessly over-committed. The financial collapse of 1793 (*see* topic box, p. 217) thus had devastating consequences for Bristol business.

work. *Henry Goodridge* designed the Roman Catholic Pro-Cathedral, Clifton, in *c.* 1834. Its completion to a reduced design and present dereliction cannot hide the megalomaniac conception, which again prefigures Victorian trends. *R.S. Pope*'s St Mary on the Quay, 1839, is controlled and austere, with an academic rendering of a Greek Corinthian temple front. As for **Nonconformist chapels** of 1800–30 only the plain Grecian Zion Congregational chapel, Bedminster, survives in the city and inner suburbs [150]. At least seven others have been demolished.

13. Old Council House, by Sir Robert Smirke, 1823–7. Early C19 engraving

Public buildings of the early C19 are more numerous, and the tendency to seek designs from outside architects becomes very noticeable, perhaps due to the bankruptcy of many local firms in the economic crash of 1793 and the end of the Paty domination. Among the few local architects to bridge the gap is *James Foster* (*c.* 1748–1823), founder of a very significant C19 firm, but of limited abilities himself. Little building of note was done until the Assembly Rooms in The Mall, Clifton, of 1806; its architect *Francis Greenway* was the son of a humble Gloucestershire mason. Tellingly, the committee in charge of building the Commercial Rooms (1809–11), Corn Street [65], a new merchants' club, looked to Thomas Harrison's works in Liverpool and Manchester for inspiration. The resulting design, by *Charles Busby* of London, is really good, despite his youth and inexperience. So what else was done by national names in Bristol? *Cockerell* designed the Philosophical and Literary Institution, Park Street, of 1821–3, while *Smirke*'s Old Council House, Corn Street (1823–7) [13], has much pleasing Greek Revival detail, yet is far from purely Grecian. The scale is surprisingly small, but the interiors are of great interest. The private Arno's Vale Cemetery (*see* p. 282) is by *Charles Underwood*, 1837–9, with paired Greek Doric gate lodges of immaculate purity, and two mortuary chapels, one Italianate and one Ionic. In 1838 *Charles Dyer*, that most competent of local classicists, designed the admirable Victoria Rooms in Clifton [120]. Its giant portico and broad pilastered wings with bulky attics introduce a new Roman Corinthian grandeur which is distinctly Victorian in outlook. Nearby on Queen's Road, *Dyer* used a collegiate Tudor Gothic style for the Bishop's College (1835–9), while next door, the Asylum and School of Industry for the Blind (*Thomas Rickman & R.C. Hussey*, 1835–7) was in a pinched lancet style. Both were demolished long ago.

The fundamentals of late Georgian **housing** did not change significantly from the designs of before 1800. Terraces continued to spread across Clifton, Cotham and Kingsdown. New and more distant suburbs flourished too (e.g. Montpelier) and scattered villas appeared on the slopes as far out as Ashley Down. The trend to individuality which led eventually to the Victorian villa appears first at Ashley Place, Montpelier, c. 1788, where tall single houses are made into a terrace only by single-storey links. The design was developed further at Prince's Buildings, Clifton, of 1789, and Kingsdown Parade, 1791. At both, pairs of houses are linked by lower wings: one step towards semi-detached houses. Prince's Buildings and Ashley Place are definitely by *William Paty*, and Kingsdown Parade is attributed to him. As for details, the pedimented doorcases at Nos. 48–86 Kingsdown Parade are supported on short brackets that die back into the wall with a neat concave curve (here they are fluted too). This type only seems to occur in houses finished after the 1793 crash; it quickly became widespread in the humbler terraces, a useful marker when there is so little architectural detail on which to base dating.

Housing in **Clifton** after 1800 can be viewed as a special case, both for the size and cost of the developments, and for its Greek Revival which continues as late as c. 1850. The Clifton Walks follow this in detail, principally at Litfield Place [123], Queen's Road, Clifton Park, Vyvyan Terrace and Worcester Terrace [119]. Research over the last twenty years, and new work done for this volume, has led to significant adjustments of dating.* This makes clear both how concentrated was the development of Clifton in the years c. 1833–48, and how the slide towards the rich Italianate of Victoria Square was delayed until as late as the 1860s. *Charles Dyer*, *Charles Underwood* and *R.S. Pope* were the most prominent architects at Clifton, combining Grecian and other motifs with almost Mannerist freedom. The interaction and borrowing of stylistic details between them is hard to unravel, and sparse evidence means some reliance on attribution.

Victorian and Edwardian Bristol, c. 1840–1914

The **economic characteristics** of Bristol during this period are complex, and what follows must be taken only as a generalization. No single industry predominated. Bristol's industrial adaptability lay in a diversified economy of up to a dozen key industries at any one time. Some traditional trades continued to flourish, e.g. sugar, brass, shipping, iron-founding, leather, soap-making and potteries. They operated from small and medium-sized factories and workshops dispersed throughout the city and suburbs. From 1800–40 there was economic growth, albeit sluggish and uneven, followed up to the 1860s by a period of stagnation as Bristol's position faltered under the force of industrialization elsewhere. From the 1860s–80s there was economic revival and substantial growth, based on changes in the organization and finances of the port, and on

*Design dates are given first, followed by the 'old' dates in brackets. West Mall/Caledonia Place, 1832–3 (1840); Vyvyan Terrace, 1833–4 (c. 1845); Dorset House, Litfield Place, 1833–4 (c. 1825–8); Clifton Vale, c. 1836 (1840); Lansdown Place, Victoria Square, 1842 (1835/8); Royal Promenade, Victoria Square, 1847 (1837); Buckingham Vale, c. 1847 (c. 1840); Worcester Terrace, c. 1848 (1851–3); Victoria Square sw side, 1863 (1855).

14. **Nos. 12–13 Buckingham Vale, possibly by R.S. Pope, 1847–50**

newer industries, e.g. tobacco, chocolate, printing, paper and board. After *c.* 1880 growth slackened off. Bristol's population growth rate exceeded the national average at the beginning and end of the century, but fell below it in the middle decades. Dr Bernard Alford judges Bristol's C19 performance as 'generally mediocre' with 'few monuments to civic pride and local enthusiasm' common to other large industrial cities, a view which the following account certainly supports.

Bristol architects followed the national tendency to professionalization and specialization, and formed the Bristol Society of Architects in 1850. It favoured no one style, instead establishing a code of practice. For the first time Bristol architects as a group had a consciously local identity. The scene had for the previous century or more been dominated by a number of family firms, usually descended from quite humble builders and masons, generally favoured locally for run-of-the-mill work. Brief summaries are given in the topic box on p. 30 of three of the most active during the C18 and C19, with names, dates and some key buildings.*

The years 1840–70 saw a spate of enthusiasm for new **public buildings**. *Charles Cockerell*'s Bank of England branch office at Broad Street (designed 1846) [55] shows a sure and skilful handling of Greek and Roman motifs synthesized in a distinctively personal way. Next door and equally instructive is *R.S. Pope*'s Guildhall of 1843–6 [56]. Its Perpendicular Gothic evokes its predecessor on the site. Although not yet fully convincing, it is a significant step towards the local manifesta-

---

*Still the most comprehensive survey of Bristol architects appears as an appendix to A. Gomme, M. Jenner and B. Little, *Bristol: An Architectural History* (1979).

tion of the Gothic Revival in its archaeological phase. The Assize Courts, Small Street, 1867–70 by *Popes & Bindon*, is a disappointing and ill-judged work, its sting all the sharper for the memory of *E.W. Godwin*'s excellent design that won the competition but was then rejected. *Foster & Wood* produced two fine almshouses, Trinity Hospital South, Old Market (from 1857) and Foster's, Colston Street (1861 and later) [63], both decked in a rich Burgundian Gothic. They also designed Colston Hall (1864–73), Bristol's first major concert and meeting hall, in a North Italian round-arched style. Lastly, the former Museum and Library, Queen's Road, by *Foster* and *Ponton*, 1867, introduces the Venetian Gothic of Ruskin's *Stones of Venice*. But a comparison with the town halls, courts, museums and libraries of, say, Manchester, Birmingham or Liverpool confirms the bald truth regarding Bristol's status and civic ambition in the mid-Victorian years.

The economic upswing of the 1860s resulted in a **building boom**. *George Godwin*, editor of *The Builder*, noted in 1867 that 'The growth of Bristol in the last eight or ten years is something to wonder at and the change now being made in the city itself is equally marvellous. Hundreds of houses faced with stone, many of them costly and of considerable size, have been built . . . The Corporation are to spend nearly £200,000 in forming new roads.' Among the works he mentioned are some of the public buildings above, Elmdale (now the Mansion House), Clifton (shameless self-propaganda as *Godwin* designed it), Clifton College chapel [124], the Royal Hotel on College Green, the restoration of St Mary Redcliffe [31], a new Post Office (*see* Small Street), and Prince's Theatre.

We have not yet touched on changes in **transportation**. Early C19 improvements to the roads were administered by the Bristol Turnpike Trust, supervised from the 1820s by its surveyor John MacAdam. One tollhouse survives at Ashton Gate, and a fine cast-iron Doric signpost of 1833 at Three Lamps junction, Totterdown (outside our area). Road developments were overshadowed by the advent of **railways**, synonymous here, of course, with the Great Western Railway from London to Bristol, opened in 1841. Its engineer, *Isambard Kingdom Brunel*, supervised every detail of the line, the stations and the Temple Meads terminus building (q.v. Major Buildings), especially the technically ambitious wooden roof to the train shed [40]. The Royal Western Hotel (Brunel House) in St George's Road [102] is the remnant of Brunel's unrealized scheme for an integrated rail and sea route from London to New York, although *R.S. Pope* seems to have played a large part in the hotel's design. But undoubtedly his single overriding achievement here is Clifton Suspension Bridge (1829–64), its design initially regarded by many as an impossibility. It is perhaps the most recognizable symbol of Bristol to outsiders [39].

The **port** underwent significant administrative changes in the mid-Victorian years. In 1848 the private docks company was taken over by the City Corporation, and in 1861 the Society of Merchant Venturers

Three families dominated c18 and c19 architecture. The **Paty** family (variants Patty or Patey) were masons, carvers, gilders and architects. There were at least seven Patys active in the c18. *James Paty the Elder* (died 1748) probably designed the Old Library, King Street. *Thomas* (1712/13–89), perhaps a nephew of James, was masonry carver at the Exchange, Corn Street, and Clifton Hill House. He built St Nicholas church and the Theatre Royal, King Street, and designed much speculative housing. Thomas's son *William* (1758–1800) designed, e.g., Christ Church [43], Blaise Castle House.

James Foster (1748–1823) was a pupil of William Paty and set up his own business in 1806. His sons *James* (d.1836) and *Thomas* (1793–1849) were joined by *William Okely* between 1827 and 1840. *John Foster* (*c.* 1820–*c.* 1902), probably Thomas's son, did much excellent work with *Joseph Wood* from 1849. The firm continued well into the c20. Foster works include Caledonia Place, West Mall and Clifton Vale in the 1830s, Queen Elizabeth's Hospital School of 1844–7 [101], Foster's Almshouses [63], the Grand Hotel and Colston Hall in the 1860s.

Thomas **Pope** was a late c18 builder and district surveyor. His son *Richard Shackleton Pope* (1791–1884) favoured a classical style and at his best produced designs of considerable quality. There were various partnerships, notably with *John Bindon* (1849–69), and from *c.* 1864 with his less talented son *Thomas Shackleton Pope*. Key works include Bush House on Narrow Quay [82], Vyvyan Terrace, Clifton, the Royal Western Hotel (Brunel House) [102], St Mary on the Quay (all 1830s) [47], Guildhall, Broad Street, 1843–6 [56], and the Assize Courts, Small Street, 1867–70.

surrendered to the Port Authority all the wharfage dues on ships that docked in harbour, which it had been paid since the early c17. Avonmouth Docks, a private operation opened in 1877, and Portishead Docks (1879) were in 1884 also taken over by the Port Authority.

Mid-Victorian **commercial buildings** exhibit a startling rush of self-confidence, even brashness, which yet invites a sort of grudging admiration. The foremost among these is Lloyds TSB bank on Corn Street, by *Gingell & Lysaght*, 1854–7 [64]. It outdoes its Venetian model (St Mark's Library by Sansovino) for density of decoration. Everything is emblematic of the bank's activities, amounting to a manifesto for its business. This is also true of the former Liverpool, London and Globe Insurance offices, by *Gingell*, 1864–7, in the same street. The mercantile city states of North Italy were the favoured models for banks and offices for their allusions to commercial power. Shops are represented by a row in St Nicholas Street, by *Archibald Ponton*, *c.* 1866, and his excellent design for Pointing's Chemist, High Street of about the same date (bombed 1940), in a more strongly Gothic idiom. No. 51 Broad Street

15. Former Grand Hotel, Broad Street, by Foster & Wood, 1864–9

(*Ponton & Gough*, 1868) is related to both. Italianate was preferred for the Royal Hotel, College Green, and the Grand Hotel, Broad Street [15], both of *c.* 1865. The latter, by *Foster & Wood*, is very accomplished. Bristol has no C19 **pubs** to rival London's grandiloquent gin palaces. The ostentatious Palace Hotel in Old Market, is the only surviving purpose-built pub of the C19 that attempts any architectural show. The King's Head, Victoria Street has a good interior of *c.* 1865 in a C17 frame.

Commentary on **industrial buildings** has been dominated since the mid C20 by the notion of the Bristol Byzantine style. But its boundaries are ill-defined, and no clear evidence has come to light that this was a self-conscious stylistic development or 'school'. The term 'Byzantine' is also vexing, for there are various models for the buildings, none of them especially Byzantine. The forefather of them all seems to have been *R.S. Pope*'s warehouse for Acramans' Ironworks at Narrow Quay, 1830 (now Bush House), which exploited coursed Pennant rubble walling, big round arches and a four-square silhouette [82]. *W.B. Gingell* developed the theme, e.g., in his basement warehousing at Bristol General Hospital (1852–7) and at Rogers' Brewery, Jacob Street *c.* 1865. His rock-faced walling and arch surrounds are magnified to giant proportions. The model was perhaps C15 Florentine palazzi. *E.W. Godwin*'s Carriage Works in Stokes Croft (1862) [139], now in scandalous disrepair, deploys two round-arched arcades above double-width segmental arches on the ground floor. *Ponton & Gough*'s The Granary, Welsh Back (1869) [74] is the apogee of the Bristol style, in red, black and yellow

16. Bathurst Basin, Venetian Gothic warehouse and offices for Robinson's Oil Seed Manufactory, by W.B. Gingell, 1874

brick, a layer-cake of arcaded openings each treated differently. Sienese, Gothic and Venetian motifs are detectable, all coloured by the influence of Ruskin. Bristol Byzantine was not restricted solely to industrial buildings – it can be seen, for example, at Colston Hall too. A parallel strand was the use of simple Gothic, e.g. at *Godwin*'s warehouse in Merchant Street, Broadmead (1858, destroyed).

A survey of C19 **churches** must begin with *G.E. Street*'s completion of Bristol Cathedral nave, 1867–88. Pevsner judged it 'rather dull, though admittedly very earnest'. More recent assessments have been kinder; Andor Gomme explains how Street's nave, in more conventional C14 forms than the choir, was designed to prepare one for the magnificence of the E end. Street's other Bristol work, All Saints Clifton, of 1863, was a design of great power and originality, but it was bombed and later demolished almost entirely for the 1960s rebuilding. St Raphael, Spike Island, by *H. Woodyer*, 1859, was also bombed but not rebuilt – accounting for the two best Victorian churches. For the rest, the first hints of archaeological Gothic are *Charles Dyer*'s Christ Church, Clifton, 1841 [118], and *Butterfield*'s Highbury Chapel (now Cotham Parish Church), 1842–3. Most unusual is the archaeologically minded Gothic exterior of Buckingham Baptist Chapel, Clifton, 1842–7. The later 1840s saw good local examples of Ecclesiological influence (at least in the archaeological use of medieval precedent), such as *Samuel Gabriel*'s St Jude, Braggs Lane (Old Market), 1848–9. But Bristol was a bastion of Evangelicalism, and the association of Ecclesiology with the High Church was an inhibiting factor. Perhaps the best locally bred practitioner in the mid-Victorian period was *John Norton*. He designed several good local churches (e.g. St John, Bedminster, 1855), most of which have been bombed or demolished.

Housing constitutes, of course, the vast majority of Bristol's Victorian buildings but it can be dealt with in relatively few words. The years after 1850 saw the terrace in decline as a fashionable place to live, being replaced by the single or semi-detached villa. The biggest of these are at The Promenade, Clifton Down, dating from *c.* 1840–70. Much else in N Bristol was done from *c.* 1860 by local architects such as *W.H. Hawtin, George Gay* and *J.A Clark*. The names are barely relevant, for one would be hard-pressed to distinguish the works of one from another. The characteristic style is debased Italianate with paired round-arched windows, big curving bays and indiscriminate carved ornament. Tudor, Jacobean or Gothic might be substituted for variety. Workmanship could be shoddy, and a villa pair in Redland notoriously collapsed in 1868. Suburban expansion and the absorption of surrounding villages continued apace. The only other form requiring mention is 'Industrial Dwellings', although in Bristol these were rare. Those by *Elijah Hoole* in Jacob's Wells Road, of 1875, were in an unusually full-blooded Gothic for this type of building. They were demolished in the 1950s. A less striking example of 1856 survives, externally at least, at St Bartholomew's, Lewins Mead.

This expansion of the city was necessarily accompanied by far-reaching changes in **sanitation**. The C19 growth in population and industry took place within an essentially medieval fabric, with the harbour and rivers serving as open sewers and drains for industrial effluent. But with the creation of the Floating Harbour by 1809, the tidal flow effectively ceased and the harbour stagnated. A Parliamentary Report in 1845 found Bristol among the dirtiest cities in Britain, with a mortality rate (thirty-one per thousand) exceeded in only two towns. Bristol was hit particularly hard by cholera outbreaks. A new Local Board of Health spent £155,000 laying sewers from 1855 to 1873. By 1847 new water supplies were tapped in the Mendip Hills, but consistent and universal supply was established only in the 1870s. By 1883 the mortality rate had dropped to eighteen deaths per thousand. Nationally, the introduction of plumbed bathrooms constitutes perhaps the major change to house design in the C19. Among the earliest local examples in a private house was at Elmdale (now the Mansion House), Clifton (1867). From *c.* 1870, the introduction of bathrooms spread down the social scales, not reaching the poorest new houses until *c.* 1920.

The mushrooming population coincided with changing ideas on leisure, health and education. A few examples of buildings for **entertainment** survive. Right at the end of this period is *Frank Matcham's* Hippodrome, St Augustine's Parade (1911–12) [69]. This is intact (internally at least), but of the People's Palace, Baldwin Street, a music hall of 1892, only the façade is relatively unchanged. The Prince's Theatre, Park

Row (by *C.J. Phipps*, 1867) was bombed in 1940. The former Hotwells baths, Jacob's Wells Road, by *Josiah Thomas*, 1881, reflect the growing understanding of the importance of exercise in healthy development. There were formerly many C19 city-centre **schools**: privately funded, 'industrial schools', National Schools and other church schools: almost all are now gone. Three good examples of fee-paying schools remain. Queen Elizabeth's Hospital School, Brandon Hill (*Foster & Son*, 1844–7) [101] is in a sparse Tudor style. Clifton College (1862 and later by *Charles Hansom*) is in a richer collegiate Tudor [124], as is Bristol Grammar School, University Road (*Foster & Wood*, 1875). The 1870 Education Act necessitated an energetic programme to construct **Board Schools**. The Bristol School Board appointed *W.L. Bernard* as their architect in 1888, though not to the exclusion of others, such as *W.V. Gough*, *F.B. Bond* and *H.D. Bryan*. While the London Board adopted the Queen Anne style from the 1870s, Bristol clung to a rather dour Gothic or Tudor until the 1890s, when it half-heartedly followed London. Unlike London, these schools frequently had just a high central hall with spreading single-storey blocks around. Bedminster has the best remaining late C19 schools, a group of five. The **University of Bristol** was founded as a college in 1876, and has a small group of C19 buildings from 1879, although most of its premises are C20. They are covered in detail in the Gazetteer (*see* Walk 9).

The postscript to Victorian Bristol covers the years *c*. 1885–1914. In the 1880s mild forms of Queen Anne and Renaissance Revival crept in, e.g. at *Foster & Wood*'s Bristol Municipal Charities Offices, Colston Avenue, and *W.V. Gough*'s Port Authority Offices, Queen Square. *Alfred Waterhouse*'s Prudential Building, Clare Street (1899) [60] is in a Loire Renaissance mode. *Frank Wills* developed his own distinctive free Gothic of red brick with giant pointed arches. His Wills tobacco factories at East Street, Bedminster, of the 1880s–1910 develop from Gothic to a simplified classicism [151]. For the Art Gallery, Queen's Road (1900–5) [127], Wills resorted inevitably to a weighty Edwardian civic Baroque. Some good **industrial buildings** can be singled out. The offices of Lysaght's St Vincent's Works in St Philip's, by *R.M. Drake*, 1891, are Neo-Norman outside and have fantastical tiled interiors by *Doulton & Co.* [143]. The monumental former Tramways Generating Station, Counterslip, of 1899 is by the young *W. Curtis Green* [91]. *Edward Gabriel* designed a transit shed for the Port Authority (1894–6), now the Watershed Media Centre.

More fundamental than these superficial stylistic variations was the introduction of **reinforced concrete** structures. It was employed fairly early in Bristol, for instance at the GWR goods shed, Canon's Marsh (1904), which used the *Hennebique* system. The local builders *Cowlin & Son* (responsible for many of Bristol's bigger C20 buildings) became licensees for the *Coignet* patent system, in which the tension and compression bars within the concrete are linked by diagonally braced steel

17. St Mary Redcliffe, detail of s aisle w window, by Heaton, Butler & Bayne, 1867

wires to resist horizontal shearing when the beam is under load. Cowlins built three bonded tobacco warehouses at Cumberland Basin (1903–19) [147], two using the *Coignet* system. *W.H. Brown*'s WCA warehouse, Redcliff Backs, of 1909 [93], has a reinforced concrete frame with brick infill. In about 1905 Jamaica Street Carriage Works belatedly introduced exposed cast-iron framing.

The **Arts and Crafts** movement enjoyed some popularity in Bristol, notably in the work of *Edward Gabriel*, *F.B. Bond* and *H.D. Bryan*. Gabriel excelled at pubs with English vernacular embellishments, although the plasticity and liveliness of Edinburgh Chambers, Baldwin Street (1896–8) suggests potential that was unrealized in his later career. Some of Bond's best work is at Shirehampton (especially the public hall of 1904) and Bryan designed some fine houses in Leigh Woods, Sneyd Park, etc. His best work in the city is perhaps the Jacobean revival Western Congregational College (1905–6), Cotham [136]. *James Hart*, a minor player in the Arts and Crafts style, designed the excellent trio of houses and shop of 1902 on Park Row. Does more work by him await discovery? Bristol's outstanding Art Nouveau building is at Everard's Printing Works, Broad Street (1900), which has a scintillating tiled façade by *W.J. Neatby* of *Doulton & Co.* [57].

Bristol boasts two pre-First World War buildings that are notably advanced, to the extent that Pevsner saw them almost exclusively as preludes to Modernism. *Charles Holden*'s Central Library, 1902–6 [35], and his Bristol Royal Infirmary King Edward VII wing, 1909–12 [70], were both competition wins, and thus surprising in a city that so often steered a middle course and ignored the most up-to-date architecture. Their reliance on complex intersecting masses and subtle modulations of surface show Holden's awareness of the work of architects such as Mackintosh in Glasgow. At the library, progressive features exist in tandem with an Arts and Crafts concern with context and materials, whereas at the hospital the Arts and Crafts influence is much less. After the library Holden 'did not produce anything so uncompromising again until he started on the chain of small Underground stations in London in 1932' (Pevsner).

George Oatley was a giant in both character and output, whose work here began *c.* 1881 and continued until his death in 1950. He did some fine suburban churches, notably All Hallows, Easton, from 1899. His many banks and offices are usually mildly Arts and Crafts or free classical. From *c.* 1910 he was the favoured architect of the Wills family, and was thus central to the development of the University buildings and many of their other projects (*see* topic box, p. 38). He settled on a Tudor, Cotswold-manor-house or Jacobean style e.g. at the Bristol Baptist College, Woodland Road (1913) [128], reserving Perp Gothic for public buildings. Of these none is more prominent than the University's Wills Memorial Building (1912–25) [37]. Although its date, and the reinforced concrete that makes it stand up, are firmly of the C20, in intention it is one of the last great instances of Gothic Revival architecture. It is a good point at which to end this chapter.

The **economic** and demographic framework for C20 developments is complex. In 1901 Bristol's population was *c*. 337,000. By the mid century, after boundary extensions to take in former Somerset villages, etc., it was 442,000; but by 2001 it had decreased to *c*. 380,000. (Large new estates on the N outskirts are in Gloucestershire and not included in the official figure for Bristol.) It is now the seventh largest city in Britain. Established trades and industries such as printing, paper and packaging, tobacco, wine and sherry importing, and chocolate-making flourished until after the Second World War. Of new ventures, the Filton aircraft works was both prominent and profitable. But one change is inescapable: the city ceased to be a commercial port after almost a thousand years. Expansion at Avonmouth Docks in 1908 and later accommodated ever-larger ships, and shipping entering the city docks slowly declined. The wartime damage to traditional industrial areas and, on a larger scale, the move to a post-industrial economy in the later C20 led inexorably to the closure of the city docks in 1973. Perhaps because the city had been adjusting to this fate for almost one hundred years, this had less impact than it might have had on a smaller port. Within a few years motorways opened linking Bristol with London and the Midlands. Financial and service industries were already taking over, and from the 1970s information was the new cargo. Media and technology have dominated late C20 developments.

Bristol architecture in the C20 is a mixed bag. Holden's work at the Library and Bristol Royal Infirmary had few followers in Bristol. Much **church** building was going on in Bristol up to 1939, but none of it in the city centre. *Rodway & Dening* and *Oatley & Lawrence* used a simplified late Gothic influenced perhaps by E.S. Prior, while the churches of *P. Hartland Thomas* are even leaner. But these are all suburban. An industrialized centre with shrinking population meant no new churches there until after the wartime depredations. Of **public buildings** in this era, if one excepts Oatley's essentially Edwardian Wills Memorial Building, only one stands out: *E. Vincent Harris*'s Council House, College Green [34]. Its bland Neo-Georgian is hardly a triumph, but the interior details lift the whole, and its size, location and status ensure its place in our attentions. *Oatley & Lawrence* continued to design solid and competent buildings for the University of Bristol, generally in pared down Tudor Gothic or other revival styles. In 1934, J.B. Priestley's *English Journey* captured interwar Bristol's sense of its own comfortableness: it 'arrives at a new prosperity, by selling us Gold Flake and Fry's chocolate and soap and clothes and a hundred other things. And the smoke from a million gold flakes solidifies into a new Gothic Tower for the university; and the chocolate melts away only to leave behind it all the fine big shops down Park Street, the pleasant villas out at Clifton, and an occasional glass of Harvey's Bristol Milk for nearly everybody.'

Some good **commercial** interwar buildings are scattered through the city centre. *Sir Giles Gilbert Scott* contributed the former Friends

The contribution of private donors to Bristol's fabric and cultural life is immeasurable. From *c.* 1890 to 1930, a few wealthy families and individuals raised public philanthropy to a high art. The Wills family were Congregationalists whose money came from tobacco. The Fry family were Quakers who made fortunes from chocolate. Sir George White's wealth derived from transport and technology. The Willses favoured the University; by the 1920s it is believed they had given over £1,250,000. The following list is partial and excludes religious buildings. Some figures are unknown.

Wills Family: St George's Free Library, 1897: £3,000; Convalescent Home, 1897: £40,000; Art Gallery, 1900–5: *c.* £40,000; Shaftesbury Institute, St Philip's, 1900: £2,000; Colston Hall Organ, 1900: £5,000; Establishment of Bristol University, 1908–9: *c.* £160,000; University Athletic Ground, 1911: unknown; Extension, Royal West of England Academy, 1912: unknown; Wills Memorial Building, 1912–25: *c.* £501,000; Gift of Royal Fort House to University, 1917; Homoeopathic Hospital, 1920–5: £123,000; Gift of Victoria Rooms to University, 1920; H.H. Wills Physics Laboratory, 1921–7: £200,000; Wills Hall of Residence, 1922–9: £145,000+; Art Gallery extension, 1925–30: £98,000; St Monica Home of Rest, 1929: *c.* £490,000

Vincent Stuckey Lean: Central Library, 1899: £50,000; University College, 1899: £5,000

Fry Family: Convalescent Home, 1897: £12,000; Albert Fry Memorial Tower, 1904: *c.* £4,000; Establishment of Bristol University, 1908–9: £17,500

Sir George White: Stock Exchange building, 1903; Edward VII Memorial Building, Bristol Royal Infirmary, 1912: *c.* £16,500; Red Cross, Bristol branch: unknown

Provident office, Corn Street (1931–3) [18], distinguished by its precise severity, sculpture, and excellent cast-metal detailing, and Electricity House, Colston Avenue (1935–48). *Ellis & Clarke*'s Northcliffe House, Colston Avenue, 1929, follows the Art Deco London newspaper offices of its day. *Alec French* started work in Bristol by 1920 and his work developed along 'Moderne' lines in the 1930s; the former Halifax offices, Nos. 1–2 St Augustine's Parade (1937) and St Stephen's House (1938) are typical. His practice designed much in post-war Bristol. *C.F.W. Dening*'s modest Central Health Clinic (1935) is a good example of the Moderne style. Lastly *Cecil Howitt*'s Odeon, Broadmead, is the only city cinema of its date to preserve even a modicum of the original appearance. *W.H. Watkins*'s opulent Regent Cinema, Castle Street (1928) was bombed. The flashiest work of this genre, the News Theatre, Little Peter Street – faced with apple green and black glass – was demolished in 1959.

18. No. 37–39 Corn Street, elevation by Sir Giles Gilbert Scott, 1931–3

During the 1930s slum clearances e.g. in Bedminster, St Philip's, etc., contributed further to depopulation around the centre. However, suburban **housing estates** were built by the Council, e.g. at Shirehampton, Sea Mills, Knowle West and Fishponds, inspired by Garden City ideals.

The physical and psychological impact of **Second World War** bomb damage (*see* topic box, p. 170) cannot be over-emphasized. About a quarter of the medieval city was destroyed, and remained as car parks until Castle Park was created in 1978. There was also heavy damage in Temple and Redcliffe, Park Street, the Triangle, Broadmead and Bedminster. After the war, the city was surrounded by a 'ring of blight', e.g. St Paul's and St Jude's – a pattern common across the USA and Great Britain. These factors perhaps prepared the way in people's minds for a different approach to planning in the post-war era.

J.N. Meredith, the City Architect, produced a very early **reconstruction** plan in 1941, which picked up some threads of pre-war slum clearance and road building (*see* below). By 1943 the City Council determined on a new retail district at Broadmead and a new cultural and civic centre on the old shopping area around Castle Street. The Broadmead shops were the only element of the early schemes to be executed comprehensively, despite their unpopularity with traders and the public. The Western Chapter of Architects' proposal (1944) would have swept away everything between Bristol Bridge and Bristol Cathedral, except All Saints' and St Stephen's churches. Not even Wood's Exchange was to be spared. This and other plans tended to ignore existing land use and street layouts in favour of grand planning, zoning and uniform building designs, ideas expanded to megalomaniac proportions in the Reconstruction Plan of 1946. It covered 771 acres (312 hectares; most of the area of this volume except Hotwells and Clifton) but by 1948 the Ministry of Town and Country Planning had reduced this to a permitted compulsory purchase of just 4.5 acres (1.8 hectares) in Broadmead, insufficient for the ambitions of the city planners. Bristol was three years ahead of the nation in producing a list of historic buildings – the foundation of the present listing system – in 1941. However, this offered little protection for historic buildings in the redevelopments of *c.* 1950–75, when demolition losses probably equalled those from bombing.

Traffic planning was central to these post-war schemes. Ring roads had been proposed in *Sir Patrick Abercrombie*'s Bristol and Bath Regional Planning Scheme as early as 1928, the inner circuit road being partly implemented at Temple Way and Redcliffe Way from 1936. A twenty-five-year Development Plan of 1952 provided for an outer circuit road through the southern suburbs, across the harbour w of Canon's Marsh and up Brandon Hill into Clifton, thence through Cotham and St Paul's. Only Easton Way in the e was completed, but some five hundred houses were demolished at Totterdown in the 1970s for a road junction that was never built. By 1969 plans had apparently been made to ease the route by filling in a large section of the harbour, a proposal that provoked massive protest. *Casson, Conder & Partners'* City Docks Report (1972) for the Council abandoned this idea but still had to accommodate the City Council's desire for road bridges across the harbour, which would have been almost as destructive. The City Centre Policy Report of 1966 featured 'vertical segregation' of traffic and people by means of pedestrian decks above the roads, especially in The Centre and Lewins Mead. The scheme was watered down then abandoned *c.* 1973, although some inadequate footbridges were nevertheless completed, at Lewins Mead. In summary, the conflicting interests of all the grand plans proved too much, and Bristol's traffic system today is a series of compromises and part-built schemes with the joins smoothed over.

Church building between 1945 and *c.* 1970 often meant no more than bomb-damage repairs, and, given the depopulation of the inner city, many losses were not replaced. St Peter, St Mary le Port and Temple were stabilized and left as ruins, while St Augustine the Less, a mainly c15 church with relatively minor damage, was demolished in 1962. The interior of Holy Trinity, Hotwells, was rebuilt by *T.H.B. Burrough*, very simply and with no attempt at restoration. There are two exceptionally good post-war churches. All Saints, Clifton, incorporates small survivals

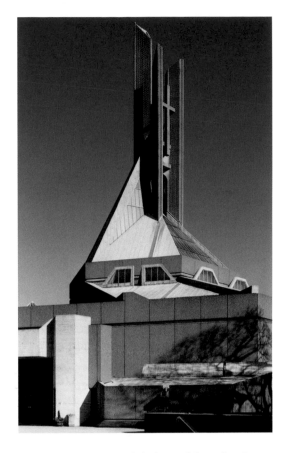

19. Clifton Cathedral (R.C.), Pembroke Road, by Percy Thomas Partnership, 1965–73

from *G.E. Street*'s bombed predecessor, while the work by *Robert Potter*, of 1962–7 [125], is angular and thrilling, the internal impact heightened by *John Piper*'s richly muted fibreglass windows. Undoubtedly the best late C20 church is the Clifton Cathedral (R.C.), by *Percy Thomas Partnership*, 1965–73 [19]. It resulted not from bombing but from the lack of a Roman Catholic cathedral since the Diocese of Clifton was created in 1850. It cost *c.* £600,000 – a remarkably small sum even then – and achieves an impressive austerity. Anyone who has confessed a dislike of post-war concrete buildings should come here before repeating that prejudice. Would that Bristol could muster **public buildings** to match it. But 1945–70 produced little to speak of, either good or bad. The University buildings of the period are generally dull. As for the planned Civic Centre in Castle Park, the reduced scheme for a new Museum and Art Gallery was abandoned *c.* 1966. The Central Library extension of 1966–8 is at least straightforward and avoids any pastiche of Holden's fine work.

Housing from the 1940s was concentrated in new suburbs. A few inner areas were redeveloped, notably Barton Hill, 1956–65, where poor

C19 terraces were replaced with fifteen-storey blocks, then the highest in the West of England. The area s of St Mary Redcliffe, intended as a housing zone for key workers in the 1944 Reconstruction Plan, was one of the few elements to come to fruition. The design was by the *City Architect's Department*, the river front of Waring House (1958–60) being especially lively [92]. By contrast, the excellent low-rise, high-density housing at High Kingsdown, 1971–5 [137], is a rare example of a private scheme re-engineered from the wreck of a dismal high-rise proposal by the City Council.

Of post-war industrial buildings the Shot Tower in St Philip's [20] is the most arresting. **Commercial buildings** of 1945–70 are numerous. Most such buildings of the 1950s were in the range of 1,500–5,000 sq. ft (140–465 sq. metres) of floor space. From 1960 to 1975 the largest were around 16,000–18,000 (1,480–1,670 sq. metres). The 1980s saw reductions to 5,000 or less, although some were bigger. *Alec French & Partners* did The Gaunt's House (1953), very tall for its time at ten storeys. The construction of Broadmead shopping precinct from 1950 to 1960 required the demolition of many C17–C19 vernacular and industrial buildings that had survived the patchy bomb damage in this area. The planning was unimaginative, with two axial streets crossing at a central hub. The shop façades are generally dull, and the plan to have attached weather-protection canopies throughout the precinct was abandoned after Woolworths refused to conform. This encapsulates the City Architect's problem at Broadmead. Unable to impose the strict uniformity of design he desired in the face of powerful developers, he had to accept a series of half-hearted compromises. Only Lewis's store is of any distinction. In 1960 *Group Architects DRG* designed the fifteen-storey Robinson Building, Victoria Street [95], admirably pure in line and colour. The arched window heads are the earliest conscious borrowing in Bristol from Victorian commercial architecture. Although in the wrong place, its starkness is better by far than the *retardataire* classicism that the client apparently wanted. *Raymond Moxley*'s Clifton Heights at the Triangle, Clifton, came within a year. It included offices, shops and flats. *Moxley Jenner & Partners* Colston Centre [62], completed in 1973, is tall but infinitely better than most of its size. There was no tall buildings policy beyond a gentlemen's agreement of the early 1960s restricting heights to *c*. 120 ft (36.6 metres), a limit broken in several cases before it was made. The Civic Society meanwhile developed a sophisticated building-height policy, eventually adopted by the Council in 1972, which protected the historic centre and five 'viewing corridors'. This did not prevent damaging speculative office developments at Lewins Mead and Nelson Street, St James Barton, Bond Street, The Pithay and All Saints Street. The blocks in Lewins Mead are hardest to accept not only because of their height but their crushing bulk and inhumanity. The district is carved through by wide racetrack roads, intended to be hidden below high-level decks and walkways (*see* topic box, p. 140). In contrast, the bespoke design of the Bristol United Press building,

20. Lead shot tower, St Philip's, by E.N. Underwood & Partners, 1968–9

Temple Way, by *Group Architects DRG*, 1970–4, retains humanity in its scale, colour and form. A national property crash in 1973 left Bristol vastly over-supplied with office space. 1973–6 were years of standstill, and later developments tended to be smaller and more circumspect (*see* below).

The impact of these redevelopments was enormous and generally negative, prompting intense debate about the future of Bristol's **historic environment**. Before 1970 instances of sensitivity are rare: Park Street's bomb gaps were filled from 1953 with replica Georgian façades at the City Architect's insistence, and Lower Arcade, Broadmead [88], was saved and restored in 1948. The 1960s were characterized by growing dissent and protest at controversial schemes. It was feared Bristol might come to resemble 'one of those Middle Western towns with streets you can drive for ever without finding the centre of town' (Gordon Russell). Meanwhile the Planning Department negotiated privately with developers, resenting the interference of the public and amenity groups. Embryonic amenity groups were formed in response, beginning in 1968 with the Clifton and Hotwells Improvement Society.

The **conservation movement** came of age *c.* 1970–5, the turning point in Bristol's post-war development. It was a manifestation of both national and local trends. In the space of a few years, the closure of the docks left 175 acres (71 hectares) of unused water, while hospital and university building plans put increasing pressure on the historic districts of St Michael's Hill and Kingsdown. Other plans included an intrusive 300 ft (91.4 metre) high tower N of King Street, and a crass eight-storey hotel in the Avon Gorge just 550 ft (167.6 metres) from Clifton Suspension Bridge. Last-minute campaigns, local and national press reporting and interventions by national bodies led to both schemes being dropped. Other campaigns halted the clearance programmes at St Michael's Hill, Kingsdown and Old Market, although not before significant losses of historic buildings in each of these cases. Six Conservation Areas were designated in 1970–2, and six more in 1974–5. The Planning Department's role changed radically to a cooperative one in which reuse or smaller new buildings were favoured over clearance. The department also became more active in controlling design quality, including the encouragement of a 'dockside warehouse' aesthetic, which generally resulted in improved new schemes after 1975. There was a national trend to schemes of conservation, repair and reuse, encouraged by government grants; local examples include the Arnolfini (Bush House) and the Watershed, which together set the pace for the regeneration of the harbour (*see* below). Nationally, the practice of façading – where an old façade is retained with entirely new buildings behind – was seen at first as an acceptable and imaginative compromise, although its over-use and abuse has caused its fall from favour. It was much used in Bristol, e.g. at Brunswick Square and St Augustine's Parade; both are schemes which paid lip-service to conservation.

As for **public buildings** after 1975, the University of Bristol fared better than it had before, notably in the fortress-like Arts and Social Sciences Library, by *Twist & Whitley*, 1975. Minor notes include an excellent refurbishment at Goldney Hall, and the Arts Faculty lecture theatres, tactfully grafted onto Victorian villas in Woodland Road. *Moxley Jenner*'s small theatre at Queen Elizabeth's Hospital School, Brandon Hill, is quietly stylish in banded coloured bricks. In the city the Crown Courts, Small Street, by *Stride Treglown*, 1994, are remarkably unobtrusive given their bulk. **Public spaces** have received increased attention in the last twenty-five years. Castle Park (1978 and 1993) put back some much-needed green space. At Queen Square, a dual carriageway was removed in 2000 and the C18 layout reinstated, creating a popular retreat for office workers and residents. The remodelled Centre has many faults, but in the face of general disdain it must be said that the concept is right: Bristol needs at this crucial hub a real public space, not a hole in the ground with water at the bottom of it. Millennium Square, Canon's Marsh, is paved rather than planted, yet is animated by water and light sculptures. *Walter Ritchie*'s reliefs in brick at Bristol Eye Hospital [72] are among the best of much recent **public art** mentioned in the gazetteer.

We look now at **commercial** work after 1975. At the Scottish Life building, Welsh Back (*Burnet Tait Powell & Partners*, 1975) the reemerged dockside aesthetic is evident in the crisply detailed brickwork and arched window heads. The Bristol & West extension, Broad Quay, and Broad Quay House, both of 1981, represent the numerous later commercial examples of the style. Distinctive bespoke offices include Wessex Water's building in Passage Street, 1978, and London Life, Temple Street, 1982. Both are of brick, handled differently, and neither attempts any dockside trickery. *Alec French Partnership*'s One Bridewell Street, 1987, introduces a full-height glass-fronted atrium to the street, and injects colour in its rain-cladding and red trim [54]. In the face of 1980s appliqué Postmodernism, No. 31 Great George Street [21], also by *Alec French Partnership*, makes the style seem the most natural thing imaginable in this sensitive setting – a really likeable design. Lloyds Bank, Canon's Marsh (*Arup Associates*, 1988–90) [107] manages its paired columns and other classical allusions with less aplomb. River Station, a restaurant by *Inscape Architects*, 1998, sits easily on the harbour wall, balancing sophistication and intimacy perfectly.

The **harbour** has been regenerated since *c.* 1980, with new leisure activities on the water and the dockside. The return of the S.S. *Great Britain* in 1970 was critical for the harbour's future, obstructing damaging road-building plans. But redevelopment has eroded the texture of the working docks, which is now best appreciated at The Grove and Princes Wharf [145]. For the first time since the early C19 there is large-scale **housing** development in the city centre. New harbourside housing began with Rownham Mead, Hotwells, *c.* 1975–80, and Merchants Landing, Spike Island, of 1980–4. From the mid 1980s bigger and more mediocre developments were built around the w arm of the harbour. The last phase of regeneration – the w end of Canon's Marsh – has yet to be completed (*see* p. 47).

Apartment blocks have become ubiquitous, the most fashionable and expensive with views over water (e.g. Capricorn Quay, Canon's

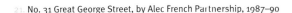
21. No. 31 Great George Street, by Alec French Partnership, 1987–90

Marsh) or those created from reused industrial buildings (e.g. The Granary, Welsh Back, 2002). The former Courage Brewery site off Victoria Street is a mixed-use conversion for flats and offices. Rehabilitation of the inner suburbs has happened partly through planned schemes, but also through individual owners. At Hotwells, Windmill Hill, Totterdown and Brandon Hill, this is marked by the habit of painting houses in bright and contrasting colours, particularly terraces on the crests of hills [22].

Urban Development Corporations (UDCs) were established by central government in 1987 for Bristol, Leeds and Manchester. Bristol's UDC aimed to regenerate the under-used land a mile or so E of Temple Meads. It was deeply controversial for its perceived imposition, and for its lack of accountability. Its main achievement was the link road N from Brislington to the M32 motorway of c. 1994, and associated leisure, industry and housing developments in St Philip's Marsh and St Anne's. Plans for Temple Quay were implemented in changed form in the late 1990s, after the UDC was dismantled. Here and at Temple Quay North, the poor architectural quality of much of the building, and the absence of the promised mixed use and leisure facilities, cast doubt on its effectiveness.

Several late C20 trends are worth noting. **Infill** development has become more common with rising land values; yet original designs are rarer than one would like. Nos. 2 and 4 Alfred Place, Redcliffe, are uncompromising in the face of their Georgian neighbours. The ecology movement is represented by the Ecohome at Smeaton Road, Cumberland Basin, 1996 by *Bruges Tozer Partnership; a* lozenge plan with monopitched roof, of renewable materials, it makes efficient use of heat and water to reduce its environmental impact. Changes to building procurement include **design and build**, by which a single organization is responsible for the entire design, engineering and construction of a building, with the aim of reducing costs. The Bristol company *JT Group Ltd*, formed in 1961, was responsible for the conversions of both the Arnolfini (1975) and Watershed (1980), unusually early for such prestigious projects. Nationally, public consultation in building projects came to the fore during the 1970s, leading in the 1980s to community architecture, with varying degrees of success. **Community-led development** took a leap forward at Prior's Close, Kingsdown, of 2000–4. Local people formed a company, raised capital by subscription, ran an architectural competition, selected a design by *Inscape Architects*, and took it from planning to completion, funded by pre-sales of flats on the site. Profits will be returned to the shareholders, and local people maintained real control of development on a sensitive site.

The **Millennium project** known as At-Bristol was notably successful architecturally, commercially and socially, amidst many that fell short of expectations. It occupies two related buildings on the N edge of Canon's Marsh: Wildwalk, by *Michael Hopkins & Partners*, and Explore, by *Wilkinson Eyre* [23]. They are set in admirable public spaces by

Ambrose Road, Hotwells, brightly painted terrace

Concept Planning Group. The complex sits N of *Arup*'s Lloyds TSB building (*see* p. 204), but presently the two bear little relationship. The **Canon's Marsh redevelopment** scheme to the w has a long and acrimonious history. Dereliction set in after the closure of the docks in the early 1970s. Three proposals in 1981 got nowhere, and the scheme coming to fruition now was outlined in 1992. A plan for mixed office, residential and leisure facilities by *Arup Associates* for developer Crest Nicholson was rejected in 1999, as was a modified version in 2000. A particular sensitivity was the disruption to views of Bristol Cathedral to the N. A new masterplan by *Edward Cullinan Architects* gained consent in 2001 after much public consultation. It includes 425 dwellings, 371,000 sq. ft or 34,500 sq. metres of office space and a multiplex cinema; the scheme is lower than its predecessors, with buildings stepped down towards a new harbour inlet. The controversial block-like massing is broken up, and vistas are planned between the Cathedral and the harbour. Building began in 2004.

Bristol Cultural Development Partnership launched the **Legible City** initiative in 2001. This ambitious project aims to improve Bristol's identity and legibility through signage and maps, information systems and public art. It has won national recognition and put the city at the forefront of thinking in the planning field – a situation of which Bristol has had too little experience. It is anticipated that the new approach will be incorporated into planned **future changes**. Of these, the most crucial are the Canon's Marsh scheme, discussed above, and the extension of Broadmead into an awkward cul-de-sac of dereliction E of the inner circuit road. The latter includes the remodelling of the SE quadrant of Broadmead around Quakers' Friars. A third area of need is the bewildering traffic

23. Explore At-Bristol, N facade, by Wilkinson Eyre, 2000

mayhem between Temple Meads Station and the city centre, which is many visitors' first experience of Bristol. Here, there have been several proposals, but no prospect yet of a solution being implemented. Likewise, the promise of harbourside regeneration could easily descend into a twee monoculture of steel-and-glass café bars. To avoid the mediocrity of a city where bland commercial development swamps a few historic façades stripped of meaning or context, Bristol must tread a highwire, applying planning controls and conservation principles sensitively, without stifling the energy and innovation of good new architecture that the city deserves.

Major Buildings

Bristol Cathedral 50

Clifton Cathedral (R.C.) 63

St Mary Redcliffe 66

Council House 73

Central Library 75

Exchange 78

Wills Memorial Building 83

Clifton Suspension Bridge 85

Temple Meads Railway Station 88

Bristol Cathedral

College Green

Bristol Cathedral originated as an Augustinian abbey founded in 1140 by Robert Fitzharding, who became the first Lord Berkeley and died a canon of his foundation. His family continued as the major patrons. From the C12 there remains the notable Chapter House and from the early C13 a Lady Chapel to the E of the N transept. But Bristol's unique importance lies in the innovative and original work begun in 1298 by Abbot Knowle (treasurer from 1298, abbot from 1306): a new aisled choir

24. Bristol Cathedral from the NW, W towers completed by J.L. Pearson, 1887–8

and eastern Lady Chapel; and s of the choir aisle the Berkeley Chapel, and its antechapel. Knowle (d.1332) and his successor Abbot Snow (d.1341) were buried before the rood altar in the nave. In 1339 the church was 'in ruins' according to a Bishop's Visitation, but by 1353 Abbot Asshe could be buried in the new choir. The s transept was rebuilt from the C14; N transept and crossing tower from the later C15, under abbots Hunt (1473–81) and Newland (1481–1515). By the Reformation, a new nave had been completed only up to the sills of the windows. After Henry VIII decreed in 1542 that Bristol should become one of the six new dioceses, the eastern end was reordered for cathedral use. The incomplete nave was demolished and houses built on its site. In 1859, a campaign to enlarge the inadequate accommodation was begun by Dean Gilbert Elliott; destructive internal changes made in 1860–1 under *T.S. Pope* on the advice of *G.G. Scott* were much criticized. In 1866 Canon J.P. Norris launched a campaign to raise funds for a more ambitious new nave, prompted by the supposed rediscovery in 1865 of the C15 nave foundations; *G.E. Street* was engaged, work began in 1867 and the nave was complete in 1877 [24]. The w towers were completed only in 1887–8, after Street's death, by *J.L. Pearson*, also responsible for major restoration work in 1890–1900. The building is largely faced with smooth ashlar of creamy yellow limestone, from Dundry near Bristol, used from the C14. Earlier walls are of red Brandon Hill Grit.

Exterior

The building lies alongside College Green. Transepts and central tower separate the evenly balanced E end and nave. The Perp crossing tower rises vigorously to two storeys, each face crowded with five transomed two-light windows. Strong set-back buttresses rise to broad diagonal ones; parapet with blank arcading and pinnacles. *Street*'s two w towers with sturdy corner pinnacles provide a dominant accent from the w. Street's N porch is adorned with much sculpture. The prominent figures of Evangelists in the buttress niches date from 1878, replacing Church Fathers by *James Redfern*, ruthlessly torn down in 1876 by Dean Elliott following popular protest at their allegedly popish character. Funding diminished after this row, and Street's grand w end in the French manner remained without its intended sculpture.

Street introduced minor differences to distinguish his nave from the medieval parts. He followed the choir in making the aisles as high as the nave and giving the windows transoms, but details of nave and N transept are in the more calmly ordered manner of the later C13. Pevsner called it 'the respectable performance of a sensible architect'; Priscilla Metcalf, more sympathetic to Street's dilemma, saw it as 'a vestibule to a work of genius which he did not see it as his business to upstage.'

E of the N transept is the so-called Elder Lady Chapel, its early C13 date recognisable by the use of red sandstone and stepped lancets divided by buttresses. The more elaborate E window is later C13; parapet and pinnacles are Perp. Beyond, the C14 chancel aisles are the first introduction to the insistent ingenuity of Bristol work of this period. The heads of its tall windows alternate between a group of four quatrefoils, and an elongated quatrefoil between two trefoils. There is tracery also below the transoms: it can be read either as pairs of two-light arches with Y-tracery, or as intersecting ogee arches. The three-light aisle E windows show further variety in their tracery. The Lady Chapel's broad E window has nine lights, the centre three under a clumsily spreading trefoil, flanked by steeply arched lights with reticulated tracery. The s side is only accessible from the cloister and a brief description of the exterior there is given below, *see* p. 62. For the monastic survivals beyond the cloister, *see* Walk 5, Canon's Marsh.

Interior

This account describes the medieval, eastern parts first. From the Norman church little evidence remains apart from the masonry of the transepts. A small C12 window is visible high up in the E wall of the s transept, and there is a C12 block capital in the sw corner. The C13 **Elder Lady Chapel** was added E of the N transept by Abbot David (1216–34), following the new fashion for elaborately decorated chapels dedicated to the Virgin (cf. the earlier ones at Glastonbury and Tewkesbury). Stylistically, the closest link is with Wells. Indeed two letters survive of *c.* 1220–30, from the abbot to the Dean of Wells, asking for the loan of a mason called 'L' to 'hew out the seven pillars of Wisdom' for the Lady Chapel, and for contributions to the building costs. The chapel is in the mature Early English style, four bays long, vaulted and slender in its proportions, and following the E.E. liking for materials of contrasting colour. Shafts of Blue Lias (rather than the more usual Purbeck marble) are used around the windows, between the bays and in the dado of blank arcading. Much lively stiff-leaf carving, also genre scenes in the spandrels [5]; the **piscina** and **sedilia** are treated similarly. All this relates closely to the w parts of Wells nave. The roll-moulded stringcourse below the windows even terminates in small heads swallowing the roll, as in Wells's N porch. Triplets of lancet windows on the N side. The more advanced E window with different mouldings may be of *c.* 1270–80 (cf. Wells chapter-house staircase). The vault with its naturalistic foliage bosses is perhaps of the same date, quadripartite with ridge rib and transverse arches of equal width. In the s wall, two inserted Perp arches open into the N choir aisle, one housing a tomb. They have boldly quatrefoiled tunnel vaults on ribbed coving, with disconcertingly large bosses, and belong with the C14 work to which we must now turn.

The **choir** is the great surprise. Bristol is a hall church, i.e. the aisles are the same height as the central vessel. Whatever the source of inspiration – suggestions include English retrochoirs, earlier hall churches in France or, perhaps most convincingly, secular timber-framed buildings – the idea is adapted here with unprecedented originality. The central vessel is broad rather than high (only 50ft, 15.2 metres, to the apex of the vault) and has broad arches with two wave mouldings carried down the piers,

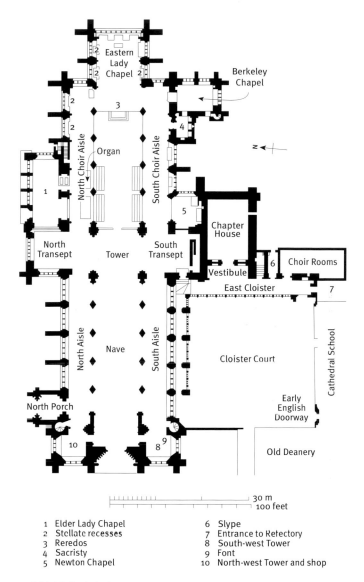

Bristol Cathedral, plan

Scale: 30 m / 100 feet

1 Elder Lady Chapel
2 Stellate recesses
3 Reredos
4 Sacristy
5 Newton Chapel
6 Slype
7 Entrance to Refectory
8 South-west Tower
9 Font
10 North-west Tower and shop

Labels within plan: Eastern Lady Chapel, Berkeley Chapel, North Choir Aisle, Organ, South Choir Aisle, Chapter House, Choir Rooms, North Transept, Tower, South Transept, Vestibule, East Cloister, North Aisle, Nave, South Aisle, Cloister Court, Cathedral School, North Porch, Early English Doorway, Old Deanery

interrupted only by capitals to thin triple shafts facing the nave. Continuous mouldings, a challenge to the consistent distinction of parts usual in E.E. work, became a characteristic of the Dec style, though precedents can be found in minor West Country detail such as the Wells nave triforium. *Thomas Witney*, who worked at Wells, has been suggested as the designer; perhaps in the second decade of the C14.

The **lierne vault** of the choir, that is a vault with additional ribs linking the ribs springing from the wall-shafts, is, with that of Wells Lady

Chapel, among the first in the West Country [26]. Richard Morris attributes it to *William Joy*, who also worked at Wells. The principle appears earlier (lower chapel of St Stephen, Palace of Westminster, completed by 1297), but here, with the exception of the eastern bays, there is the novelty of cusping the parts emphasized by the liernes, as if it were window tracery; a trick taken up also at Wells choir, Tewkesbury choir and St Mary Redcliffe. The cusping, emphasized by standing proud of the vault cells, defines a chain of kite-like lozenge shapes along the centre of the vault, in place of a ridge rib.

The most striking feature of the **aisles** is the unforgettable device by which the weight of the main vault is conveyed to the outer aisle walls. The buttresses thrown across the aisles at the level of the springing of the main vault are given the form of bridges from arcade pier to outer wall, comparable to timber tie-beams on arch braces. The aisles are vaulted transversely, each with two bays of rib-vaulting with ridge ribs. In each little vault the cell resting on the bridge is omitted, so that one can see through from vault to vault. Pevsner rightly called this a 'flash of genius' which made 'the transverse arch and ribs on the middle of the bridge stand as it were on tip-toes, a tight-rope feat right up there', extending the diagonal vistas into the vaulting zone. There is much delightful minor sculpture, e.g. the heads above the arches to the wall passages in the outer walls. The w bay of the s choir aisle has a vault of a different design, a more solid transverse tunnel vault with eight ribs; possibly this and the simpler and adjacent Newton Chapel E of the s transept were the first parts to be built.

Lady Chapel, at the E end. Two bays, the same height and width as the choir. As a result of C19 restorations, and those of the early C20, when the original fittings were brightly painted by *E.W. Tristram* following existing fragments of colour, the painted stonework and complete set of glazed windows (albeit only partially C14) give some impression of the colourful character of a medieval interior. Elaborately decorated C14 **reredos**, with three cusped ogee arches and narrow steeply gabled niches between. The centre, defaced at the Reformation, was restored after 1839, following the removal of a C17 classical altarpiece. The crested parapet to the wall-passage above has the initials WB (for Abbot Burton, 1526–39). **Sedilia**, much restored; four pointed arches, and above them, inverted arches like those beneath the crossing at Wells, with big finials. In the N and s walls three elegantly eccentric **tomb recesses** [28], of the stellate design used also in the aisle walls and the Berkeley Chapel. They now have effigies of later abbots (*see* Monuments, p. 59). They are Pevsner's '*nec plus ultra* of the . . . cavalier treatment of Gothic precedent . . . [a] sharply spiced meeting of straight and curved'. The inner frame is a half-octagon of straight lines, the outer one is made up of four semicircles on two quarter-circles, arranged concavely. Their large scale creates a powerfully exotic impression, but the details relate to native C14 art. There are familiar crockets and finials, and splendid heads and busts as stops, reminiscent

26. Bristol Cathedral, choir with early c14 lierne vault, attributed to William Joy

of the miniature ornament found on c14 metalwork and manuscripts such as the Luttrell Psalter.

The **Berkeley Chapel** and the adjoining **antechapel** or **sacristy** lie s of the s choir aisle. The date is unclear. The tomb between chapel and s choir aisle is that of Lady Joan Berkeley (d.1309), but the chapel may be a c14 reworking of something older (see the different ground level). The

Pevsner, following the German art-historical interest in the handling of space, was the first to alert English readers to the originality of Bristol's C14 work: he found the hall church with its diagonal vistas 'from the point of view of spatial imagination – which is after all the architectural point of view *par excellence* – . . . superior to anything else built in England and indeed in Europe at the same time. It proves incontrovertibly that English design surpassed that of all other countries during the first third of the C14' (*Buildings of England, North Somerset and Bristol*, 1958). Pevsner saw this work as the creation of a man 'of supreme inventiveness . . . who experimented with certain subtly applied discordances, with sudden straight lines and right angles in the middle of Gothic curves . . .' and who achieved 'a superb synthesis of structural ingeniousness with spatial thrills'. Debate continues over whether Bristol choir is a 'European prodigy or regional eccentric' the title of an essay by Richard Morris. He argues that building continued over a longer time span, into the mid C14, and that the range of mouldings suggests several designers, rather than a building accomplished by one master in a single burst of creative energy. However, as to its wayward originality there is no dispute. Bristol is also one of the supreme examples of how intricate and inventive carved work, found both in the cathedral and in St Mary Redcliffe (q.v.), contributes to the Decorated style of the C14.

antechapel, built up against the chapel, is full of puzzling curiosities. Below a flat stone ceiling is a miniature skeletal rib-vault system, without cells to the vault [27]. Corbels with naturalistic foliage, but large, more stylized bosses. In the s wall are three deep recesses within ogee arches carved with huge knobbly leaves, the overscaled detail similar to that in the arches off the Elder Lady Chapel. One recess has a flue leading to an outlet in a pinnacle; it is suggested as a place for baking communion wafers. In the NE corner an odd diagonal niche below an open-mouthed head. The doorway into the chapel has an eccentric order of ammonites or snails, and an inner order of diminishing ballflower. Was this a mason's experiment, or is there some hidden meaning, related to the preparation of the Eucharist? The Berkeley Chapel is visually quieter, of two bays with a simple cross-ribbed vault with ridge ribs. In the s wall three trefoil-headed niches with the perverse feature of straight gables over little carved heads. In the N wall, the tomb-chest of Lady Joan Berkeley (mentioned above) is framed by another spiky stellate recess, as in the Lady Chapel. The chest itself has the capricious motif of three-quarter-circles left open at the bottom and connected by diagonal bars.

Transepts and **crossing**, although with Norman fabric, appear principally late C15–early C16. Perp s window, high up, because the monastic buildings adjoined here; a worn stair with vault over led to the

27. Bristol Cathedral, sacristy or antechapel with C14 skeletal rib-vault

former dormitory. The s transept vault may date from the time of Abbot Hunt (1473–81). It carries on the idea of the lierne vault of the choir; the N transept and crossing vaults confuse the design with additional ribs. The N transept N window is by *Street*.

The interior details of *Street*'s **nave** are illuminatingly different from the choir, although he follows its proportions and main features. The eccentricities are toned down. There is a normal tierceron vault; no cusped liernes. The piers have big naturalistic capitals to nave and arch, with Purbeck shafts. The aisles have bridges, but the vaults above are different, so that the gaps are vertical planes, not vault cells. The aisles have standard arched tomb recesses with big cusps.

Furnishings

The dominant features now are *Pearson*'s, installed after completion of the nave: large high altar **reredos** of 1899, with Cosmati-type inlaid pavement in front; **pulpit**, 1903, incorporating Flamboyant panels said to come from the pulpit given by Abbot Elyot in 1525. **Screen** with ogee arches, by *F.L. Pearson*, 1904–5. – The **choir stalls** survive from a rich refurnishing by Abbot Elyot (1515–25). Back panels and ends are carved with Flamboyant tracery. – The fine set of twenty-eight **misericords** combines traditional subjects with narrative inspired by new Continental sources: scenes from the *Romance of Reynard the Fox*, others based on popular prints, with frequent use of nude figures and bawdy detail. – The stalls survived the Reformation reordering, when medieval pulpitum and rood screen were swept away. Until the new nave was built, the crossing and two bays of the choir became the space for the lay congregation. The stalls were moved E and divided off by an elaborate stone rood screen acquired from the Whitefriars, given to the cathedral in 1542 by Thomas White. This was removed in 1860, but parts are incorporated in the stone **screens** N and S of the choir, including, S side, fragments of the carved frieze, a shield with White's initials and arms of Edward, Prince of Wales.

From the C17 there remains a pair of **organ cases**, 1682–5, with very rich carving. – **Sculpture**. In the S transept, large slab with relief carving of the Harrowing of Hell, a remarkable piece; the disorderly and excited drapery suggests a late Saxon rather than early Norman date. It stands on a pair of colonnettes with decorated scalloped capitals, probably from the Norman cloister. It was perhaps used as a tomb lid although that may not have been its original purpose. – **Metalwork**. In the Berkeley Chapel a rarity, a late C15 **candelabrum** from Temple Church. Square leaves decorate the arms. In the middle, St George, with the Virgin above.

Stained Glass

The coherence of the **Lady Chapel windows** is largely the result of *Joseph Bell*'s sympathetic restoration and repair of the C14 glass in the mid C19. E window with Tree of Jesse across nine lights incorporating C14 pieces, notably the figure of the Virgin. Crucifixion in the upper central three lights, emphasized by the tracery pattern. N and S windows have standing figures against red or green backgrounds; the most complete of the old glass was placed in the SW window, which includes the Martyrdom of St Edmund. There are **medieval fragments** in the N transept E window, mostly early C16; in the Berkeley Chapel vestibule, reset; and (easily visible) in the cloister, arranged as part of a post-war scheme by *Arnold Robinson* of *Joseph Bell & Son*.

From the C17, an unusual date, N choir aisle E, two windows of brightly coloured enamelled glass given *c.* 1665, with lively Old and New Testament scenes. Of a matching window, fragments are now in S choir aisle. From the later C19 the most interesting work is by *Hardman*, employed by Street for the windows in the new W end: excellent rose window of 1877, N tower 1877 and 1887, S tower S 1883, all with standing figures below elaborate white canopies. The nave windows were to have two bands of small scenes, as in S aisle first from W, designed by *Street* himself, but not completed as planned. Also by *Hardman*, the Elder Lady Chapel E, a dense Magnificat of 1894. In the C20 lighter tones were introduced, first seen in the delicately drawn and coloured Childhood of Christ series in the Berkeley Chapel, by *Ernest Board,* painter, with *Arnold Robinson,* 1925. The present nave glazing followed wartime damage; providing more light was a priority, but the results do not complement the architecture. The N side has Robinson's meticulously detailed figures of the local wartime Civilian Services, 1947, awkwardly set against clear glass. 1920s s nave windows, with dull figures of Bristol notables by *G.J. Hunt*, also reset in clear glass. In total contrast is *Keith New*'s dynamic Holy Spirit window (s choir aisle E, replacing the damaged C17 window), a vividly coloured abstract design of 1965.

For a full account *see* M.Q. Smith, *The Stained Glass of Bristol Cathedral*, 1983.

Monuments

The earliest tombs are simple coffin lids of the C13, but the C14 rebuilding provided ostentatious spaces for a sequence of monuments in the s choir aisle and off the N side for the Berkeleys, chief patrons of the church. Three C15–early C16 abbots in traditional recumbent position

28. Bristol Cathedral Lady Chapel, N side, stellate tomb recess, C14

Lady Chapel

[N] Abbot Newbery (d.1473). Recumbent effigy, in C14 recess. – Abbot Hunt (d.1481). Recumbent effigy, in C14 recess.

[S] Abbot Newland (d.1515). Recumbent effigy, four angels, in C14 recess.

N choir aisle

[E] Bishop Bush (d.1558). Cadaver on straw mat under low classical canopy. – John Campbell (d.1817). By *Tyley*. Urn with seated woman. – Robert Codrington (d.1618). Two kneeling figures below canopy.

[N] Robert Southey (d.1843). Bust by *Baily*. – 'Villam le Someter'. C13. Coffin-lid, foliated cross and inscription in French. – William Powell (d.1769). Signed *J. Paine*, 1771. Obelisk; genius and portrait medallion. – Philip Freke (d.1729). Small curly cartouche, cherub heads and skull. – Mary Mason (d.1767), wife of W. Mason, poet. J.F. Moore, designed by *James Stuart*. Sarcophagus with portrait medallion.

S choir aisle

[E] Mary Spencer Crosett (d.1820). Big Gothic tomb-chest, unusually of cast-iron, with marble Bible on marble slab.

[N] Harriet Middleton (d.1826). Large kneeling female figure, by *Baily*.

[S] Georgiana Worrall (d.1832). By *Tyley*. Relief of a child in bed. – Lady Joan Berkeley (d.1309). Tomb-chest without effigy, in arch between choir aisle and Berkeley chapel. – Maurice III, 7th Lord Berkeley *(?)* (d.1326). In wall recess. Military effigy. – Thomas, Lord Berkeley *(?)* (d.1243). In wall recess. Military effigy with crossed legs. – Mary Brame Elwyn (d.1818). By *Chantrey*, 1822. Woman seated on Grecian chair in front of altar. – William Brame Elwyn (d.1841). By *Baily*. Deathbed relief with mourning relatives.

Newton Chapel

[E] Early C16. Purbeck marble short tomb-chest with lozenges. Perp canopy; panelled sides and fluted columns.

[S] Sir Henry Newton (d.1599). Big tomb-chest with recumbent effigies. Small kneeling children. – Sir John Newton (d.1661). Recumbent effigy, Baroque frame with two twisted columns.

[W] Elizabeth Stanhope (d.1816). By *Westmacott*, woman and angel. – Bishop Trelawny. *c.* 1900. By *Alfred Drury*. Bronze Art Nouveau plaque with angels.

S transept

[S] Emma Crawfurd. 1823. By *Chantrey*. Grecian altar with double portrait.

[W] Bishop Gray (d.1834). By *Baily*. Urn with portrait on pedestal; two standing angels.

Elder Lady Chapel

[S] Maurice 9th Lord Berkeley (d.1368) and mother. Recumbent effigies, slender figures, originally finely carved, on tomb-chest with ogee niches.

N transept

[N] Abbot David (d.1253). Coffin-lid, head in relief, very worn. – Joseph Butler (d.1752). Inscription in elaborate Gothic frame, by *S.C. Fripp*, 1833. – Major W. Gore (d.1814). By *Tyley*. Portrait medallion on base of an urn; two theatrical standing figures of soldiers left and right. – Mary Carpenter (d.1877). By *J. Havard Thomas*, 1878. Portrait medallion.

Crossing

[NW] Canon J.P. Norris (d.1891). By *Frampton*. Bronze relief portrait.

N nave aisle

[N] Dean Elliott (d.1891). By *Forsyth*, 1895. Marble recumbent effigy in wall recess.

Nave

[w end]   Joan Young (d.1603) and Sir John Young. By *Samuel Baldwin* of
     Stroud. Recumbent effigy; tomb-chest with kneeling children; two small
     winged genii. Other figures missing. – Sir Charles Vaughan (d.1630).
     Reclining effigy; allegorical figures (columns and pediment).

s nave aisle

[s]   Dean Pigou (d.1916). By *N.A. Trent*. Recumbent effigy in wall recess.

Crossing

[sw]   Jordan Palmer-Palmer (d.1885). By *Singer* of Frome. Large brass with figure.

Cloister

     Eleanor Daniel (d.1774). Coloured marble, big putto. – Elizabeth Draper.
     1778. By *John Bacon Sen.* Figures of Genius and Benevolence. – Elizabeth
     Cookson (d.1852). By *Tyley*. With surround like a Rococo fireplace. – A.A.
     Henderson (d.1807). Figure of a kneeling young Roman.

now occupy the Lady Chapel niches. The new taste of the Renaissance
appears with the tomb of Bishop Bush d.1558, the first to occupy the see,
with its cadaver below a flat canopy on Ionic columns [9]. But Bristol
was a poor see; most bishops moved on and were buried elsewhere. The
chief C16–C17 memorials are secular; the Newton Chapel has an evocative family group, two others are in the nave (not in their original position), to Joan Young d.1603, by *Samuel Baldwin* of Stroud, and Sir
Charles Vaughan d.1630. They are of the type with recumbent or reclining effigies below a canopy, sometimes embellished with allegorical figures, or with children along the tomb-chest. The more compact hanging
wall monument with kneeling figures below curtained canopy is represented in the choir, by Robert Codrington d.1618. There is little to bridge
the gap between these painted memorials and the metropolitan designs
in the sparer Neoclassical taste of the second half of the C18, which com-
bine a portrait medallion with an urn or obelisk. They start with Mary
Mason, designed by *James Stuart*, and William Powell, designed by *James
Paine*, and enjoyed continued popularity in the C19 (monuments by
Chantrey and *Baily*). Among alternative themes are *John Bacon Sen.*'s
fine monument to Elizabeth Draper (Sterne's Eliza) with two unusually
lively allegorical figures, *Westmacott*'s to Elizabeth Stanhope with more
romantic woman and angel, and *Baily*'s to William Brame Elwyn, a
touching deathbed scene. The local firm of *Tyley & Sons* produced
numerous minor memorials in the earlier C19, the most ambitious being
that to Major Gore, with portrait and two stiffly theatrical soldiers. Later
C19 memorials to senior clerics revert to formal recumbent figures or
portrait reliefs. Exceptions to the standard types are the curious Gothic
iron tomb-chest to Mary Crosett, 1820, and the attractive Art Nouveau
bronze plaque designed by *Alfred Drury* to commemorate the C17
Bishop Trelawney.

The Precinct

The remains of the Augustinian abbey lie s of the church, interlarded with C19 work, and partly incorporated within the Cathedral school (*see* p. 205). The **cloister**, with Perp traceried windows, is reduced to the E walk and a narrow N corridor, all C19 rebuilding. At the s end an early C14 door with depressed ogee gable. Crockets up both jambs and gable, partly cut into by a wall with late C15 openings. E of the cloister is the **chapter house**, a remarkably complete work of *c.* 1150–70. Entrance is through the **vestibule** of the same date, consisting of three arched openings on columns with many-scalloped capitals. The vault ribs have beaded fillets and big roll mouldings. The chapter-house doorway, flanked by twin-arched windows, leads into a rectangular vaulted space two bays deep. It rises through the dormitory level above to allow for an impressive vault. The side walls are lined with seats, above which are shallow niches with continuous mouldings. Above this is a tier of enriched and intersecting arches, and higher again the entire wall is covered with a variety of interwoven lattice and zigzag. The w wall has intersecting arches up to the apex. In the E wall, much rebuilt after 1831, are three plain large windows. The vault ribs are high and broad, thick with zigzag, while the broad, square-sectioned transverse arch has two rows of zigzag arranged to form a frieze of lozenges. The whole ensemble is a striking example of what animated effects the late Norman style could achieve with nothing but abstract motifs. The **slype** passage leads to the secluded **churchyard** to the E, from where one can study the irregular exteriors of C14 choir and C12 s transept with their projecting chapels. By the eastern Lady Chapel, three coped **tombstones**, the earliest to Canon Norris d. 1891, instigator of the new nave.

The mid-C12 **Abbey Gatehouse**, once the main entrance to the abbey precinct, lies w of the C19 nave, with a postern gate and carriage arch. The larger arch has two orders of mouldings on the N, four on the s, densely decorated with nailhead, zigzags with angle rolls, and beaded interlace work. Some column shafts have zigzag or spiral enrichment. Inside the main arch, arcaded side walls and a vault, with decoration as in the chapter house. The upper parts were rebuilt *c.* 1500 (arms of Abbot Newland), modernized with sashes, etc., in the C18, and restored in 1888 by *J.L. Pearson*. The style is late Perp, with double-height oriel, statuary niches, and panelled parapets. Pearson retained what stonework he could and replicated the old oriels and parapets quite closely. Four figures of abbots on the s side by *Charles Pibworth*, 1914. Plans by *Allies & Morrison* were approved in 2004 for a **visitor centre** s of the courtyard between the gatehouse and cathedral. Starkly new, with much glass, sandstone walls and mono-pitched roof.

Bridget Cherry

Clifton Cathedral (R.C.)
of St Peter and St Paul

Pembroke Road, Clifton

Bristol (named Clifton to differentiate it from the Anglican see) was one of thirteen Roman Catholic sees established in England in 1850. The present structure is the newest c20 English cathedral, replacing the Pro-Cathedral in Park Place (*see* Walk 7, p. 230). It was beset with constraints: a small four-acre site; an unpromising suburban context; and a small budget (*c.* £600,000 – the result was called the 'ecclesiastical bargain of the 1970s'). Despite or because of these, and in less than eight years from commissioning to consecration, the architects and craftsmen produced a church of superlative quality. Three-dimensionally complex, yet the simple spatial arrangement is immediately clear. It attains a mystic simplicity through careful use of humble materials and masterly manipulation of light. Mary Haddock described it as 'a heart-lifting Christian temple, inspiring reverence but not awe. A sermon in concrete.'

Set amidst Victorian villas w of Pembroke Road, the cathedral has a surprising piquancy, yet it does no violence to its neighbours. Commissioned in 1965 from *R. Weeks*, *F.S. Jennett* and *A. Poremba* of the *Percy Thomas Partnership*, it was the world's first cathedral designed in

29. Clifton Cathedral (R.C.), nave, by Percy Thomas Patnership, 1965–73

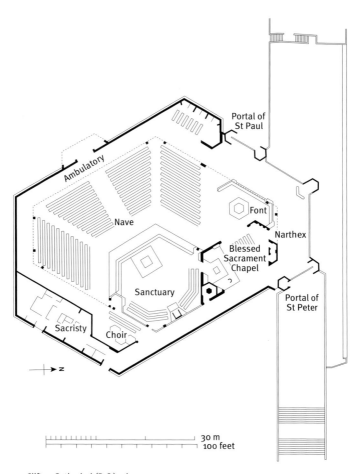

Portal of
St Paul

Ambulatory

Font

Nave

Narthex

Blessed
Sacrament
Chapel

Sanctuary

Portal of
St Peter

Sacristy

Choir

z

30 m
100 feet

30. Clifton Cathedral (R.C.), plan

response to the Second Vatican Council's emphasis on liturgical essentials. The primary requirement was for a congregation of nine hundred grouped as closely as possible around the altar during mass. The major elements were established in three months and were executed essentially unchanged, in 1970–3.

The two main entrances are the portal of St Paul from Clifton Park and the portal of St Peter from Pembroke Road, both reached via stepped bridges, with an additional processional entrance at the liturgical w. Exterior cladding is pre-cast concrete panels of pink Aberdeen granite aggregate, with contrasting white concrete piers. Concentric stages of walling rise to a steep double-pyramid roof [19]. A crowning cross sits within the slim tripartite spire of bevelled fins, rising to 167 ft (51 metres). In the spire hang two bells, the only fittings taken from the former Pro-Cathedral. Car parking beneath the building, and a presbytery to the N.

In plan the church is an irregular hexagon subdivided into varied polygons. The controlling module for all dimensions is an 18 in. (46 cm.) equilateral triangle, contributing to the building's apparent unity. Exposed concrete walls inside, cast *in situ* with Russian redwood formwork, the crisp textures dramatised by concealed natural lighting. The portal of St Peter leads to a **narthex**, then to the **Blessed Sacrament Chapel**, and a **baptistery** enclosed by a low wall beneath deep galleries. **Lady Chapel** at the NW angle. There is a palpable sense of emergence as one enters the nave [29] – a broad and simple space beneath complex roof, with timber acoustic cones. Seats in fan form, so that no-one is over 50 ft (15 metres) from the sanctuary steps: a more succinct plan than at Liverpool, where seating 'in the round' places some of the congregation behind the celebrant. The structure is based on three concentric hexagons tied together with radiating beams: the outer walls; then the nave walls, supported on piers that define a low **ambulatory**; and an inner ring suspended over the sanctuary. This supports a funnel-like lantern which floods the sanctuary with concealed light and gives an impression of ever-increasing height.

Fittings: The original **doors** of fibreglass and metallic filler by *William Mitchell* were replaced in glass, 1995. – Narthex **windows** by *Henry Haig*, the larger representing Pentecost and the smaller Jubilation. Stained glass set in epoxy resin. – **Stations of the Cross** around the ambulatory, in low-relief cast concrete by *William Mitchell*, each worked in an hour and a half. Their raw brutality jars with the setting. Lectern by *Ronald Weeks,* who also designed the Portland stone altar. – **Font** by *Simon Verity:* a Portland stone base with sculpted doves and fish, and a big Purbeck stone bowl. It is toplit and stands in a shallow pool lined with black stone, typical of the intensely spiritual symbolism achieved here. – **Screen** to the Blessed Sacrament Chapel and votive **candlestand** by *Brother Patrick* of Prinknash Abbey. – Bronze **Madonna** in the Lady Chapel by *Terry Jones*. – **Organ** with ash case and tin pipes, by *Rieger* of Austria.

St Mary Redcliffe

Redcliffe Way

St Mary lies in the suburb of Redcliffe, on a sandstone bluff, outside the medieval town walls. It is first mentioned *c.* 1160. Although eulogized as 'the fairest, goodliest, most famous parish church in England', its building history is remarkably obscure, and confused by C19 restorers who laid undue emphasis on the role of the wealthy Canynges family in the C14 and C15. Recent studies show that it was conceived as a coherent whole in the C14, but the order of work remains unclear. The unusually substantial and ambitious C13 predecessor must have conditioned and complicated the rebuilding, which probably began with the s transept, *c.* 1320–30. Burials and bequests of the 1380s–90s suggest the new E end was complete by then, and possibly the nave as well. St Mary [31] has aisled transepts, an ambulatory and projecting Lady Chapel, a stone vault throughout and a clerestory so tall that it requires flying buttresses, and elaborate s and N porches. The church is 240 ft (73 metres) long inside and the spire rises to 292 ft (89 metres). Many English parish churches were totally rebuilt and given a dominant tower in the later Middle Ages but, as Pevsner remarked, aesthetically there is no other example 'so frankly endeavouring to be a cathedral'. It shares with Bristol Cathedral a taste for the eccentric, but the later details changed from fanciful Dec to more rigorous Perp.

Exterior

The proud NW tower is C13, an addition to the previous building. Battered plinth with filleted roll, broad angle buttresses with trefoiled niches and crocketed gables, and typical late C13 tracery: N and w windows with foiled circles; Y-tracery in the w window. Above are trefoil-headed niches, with C19 figures (two of them copies of C13 originals). Bell-stage with ogee gables and much crocketing; the main buttresses end here with ogee gables and pinnacles. Parapet with openwork frieze, polygonal corner pinnacles. C14 ballflower motifs appear on the parapet and spire. The early C14 spire of Salisbury is likely to have been the inspiration. The bands of decoration and the lucarnes are C19. The spire suffered from lightning in 1446 and remained truncated until rebuilt in 1870–2 by *George Godwin*, the culmination of an appeal launched in 1842 by the antiquary John Britton and the engineer William Hosking. As for the rest of the building, much of the exterior stonework which one sees now is refacing. Repairs were carried out by *A. W. Blomfield* (1890s) and

31. St Mary Redcliffe from the NW, with C13 tower; C14 spire rebuilt 1870–2

George Oatley, 1930–3. Godwin used grey Caen stone, Oatley used Clipsham stone to replace the original Dundry limestone.

The w wall of nave and s aisle is C13, continuing the plinth of the tower. Renewed early C14 cusped and subcusped doorway. Above, inserted later, is a tall Perp five-light transomed window below a low-pitched gable. On the s side the **transept** has an immensely tall four-light s window with two transoms and pretty flowing tracery. Broad flanking buttresses with thickly crocketed gables. Remarkable upper w and E windows, framed by glazed quatrefoils so that the centres appear to float (cf. Wells, doorways from transepts to choir aisles). Pevsner called this 'the questionable charm of the Bristol style of the early C14'. The Dec rebuilding probably began here. The other windows of the nave, choir and s transept have Perp tracery. The clerestory is very tall, the windows of six lights filling the whole space between the flying buttresses, with blind tracery in the spandrels above. The parapet, continued round the transept, has pierced cusped triangles, as on the tower, and delicate pinnacles. Aisle and Lady Chapel have pierced quatrefoil parapets and simpler Perp windows; in the choir aisles the arches are more angular. The lower masonry of the nave s aisle wall may be earlier than the Perp windows above. But apart from the s transept, the general effect is of Perp uniformity despite the minor variations. The only exception is the seven-light E window over the opening to the Lady Chapel, which has reticulated tracery. The Lady Chapel was at first of one bay ending in two polygonal turrets, the eastern bay is an addition, the passage beneath possibly C15.

Back now to the C14 s **porch**, richly decorated with pinnacles, pierced quatrefoil parapet and crocketed gables to the buttresses. Outer and inner entrances are cusped and subcusped with niches left and right. Above is a tall niche flanked by two very odd windows, lancet-shaped, shouldered, and topped with very sharp, steep straight-sided triangles – a sign of the capriciousness more strongly expressed in the N porch. Side walls inside have five-light blind windows under four-centred arches, with central canopied niches. These are truncated by an inserted lierne vault with cusped panels, the square centre subdivided into four – a bold design similar to the retrochoir vault at Wells.

In general, the N **side** resembles the s side. N of the choir, a two-storey **vestry** and **library** above an undercroft. A second undercroft outside the N porch was added by *Sir George Oatley* in 1939–41, during clearances for the construction of Redcliffe Way. The exceptional N **porch** is the church's greatest curiosity. This was added *c.* 1320 in front of an older N porch. It is hexagonal, like the Eleanor Cross at Waltham of 1291, deliberately contradicting the clarity of the C13, avoiding 'the repose of rectangularity' (Pevsner). The outer doorway is framed by three bands of the most intricate foliage of that bossy, knobbly, flickering kind which replaced naturalistic foliage *c.* 1300. Tiny figures are almost hidden in the jungle of leaves. The doorway is ogee-cusped and subcusped. But the outer framing consists of concave arches, on the pattern of the tomb recesses in the cathedral, swinging up to points, the opposite of the pointed arch. The sources of the design have been much debated; the details can be paralleled in small-scale C14 English ornament but, as at the cathedral, the total effect is strangely exotic; Islamic or Indian influences have been suggested. The sides of the porch are covered in niches and crocketed gables, almost obscuring the upper windows. The newly fashionable nodding or three-dimensional arch (not found in the cathedral) is the prevalent arch form. The niches have lost their

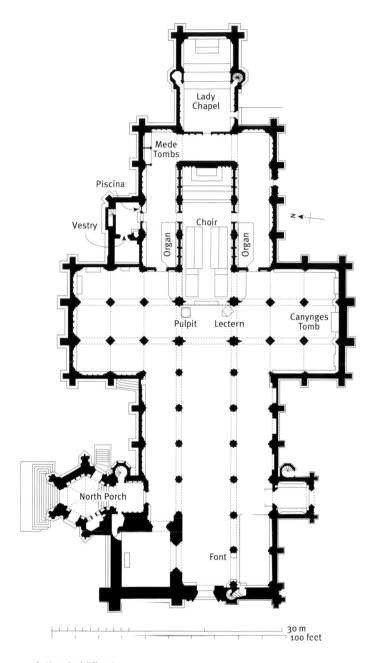

32. St Mary Redcliffe, plan

original figures, but their plinths are carried by many small figures, crouching men and the like. Virtually all the exterior was recarved in the C19; some of the original plinth figures are displayed in the N aisle.

The **porch interior** is equally ingenious. Six piers against the six angles, between niches with seats, and hardly an indication of the ogee, apart from the doorway, which surfs up above the line of the wall-passage that runs around the walls and through the piers. On the w side a tiny room recessed in the thickness of the wall, a later alteration possibly for the display of relics. Does the use of the porch as a cult centre explain its lavish treatment? Upper windows of three lights, a foiled shape in the middle. Vault with a hexagon of liernes in the centre, twisted so that its points face the outer walls rather than their corners. Big knobbly vault bosses and more figure sculpture hidden in the foliage throughout the porch interior. The **inner N porch** is excellent work of c. 1215–20. Blue Lias shafts, tall blank arcading left and right, stiff-leaf capitals, elaborate arch mouldings. Quadripartite rib vault. The arched top of the inner doorway is C19.

Interior

'The interior is of a splendour of which the Perp style does not often seem capable' (Pevsner) [7]. The whole church is vaulted, and the vaults richly decorated with bosses, so that the first impression is one of unity. Closer examination reveals a variety of detail, perhaps explained by a long building period, though the exact sequence is uncertain. A tour can start with the lower parts. The tower was given a C14 lierne vault, cusped, like the choir vault of the cathedral. The C13 w wall of the nave also has C14 enrichment, with the inserted w window framed by panels with three-dimensional ogee heads. The s aisle wall has (much restored) C14 tomb recesses similar to those in the cathedral, an ogee arch within an outer frame of concave curves. The s aisle also has a lierne vault with cusps, but with the centre panel of each bay given concave sides. Curved ribs of this kind are very unusual in England; the closest comparison is with Ottery St Mary, Devon. The vault must have been built with the s arcade of the nave (evidence in the roof space shows it is later than the s aisle wall). It is similar to the probably earlier one in the w aisle of the s transept.

The Earlier Church

From the C12 church pieces of stone with chevron decoration have been recorded. In addition to the inner N porch, survivals from the early C13 church include a substantial amount of masonry of the w wall of nave and s aisle, with a staircase between them with round-headed doorway. Warwick Rodwell has observed that this led to w galleries at two levels, comparable to arrangements at the cathedrals of Wells and Salisbury for elaborate liturgical ceremonies. On the s wall of the tower, a stiff-leaf corbel remains from two bays of stone vaulting over the nave (a rarity in a C13 parish church). C13 masonry has also been identified E of the crossing in the roof space above the clerestory, implying that the earlier choir was aisled. Whether there was a C13 crossing and transepts remains unclear.

The treatment of the upper parts shows the transition from Dec to Perp. The s transept has large pointed trefoils in the arcade spandrels and, above, a blind arcade with mullions descending from the curious clerestory windows noted outside. The high vault has square centres as in the s porch. The n transept is similar, but in nave and choir the wall treatment is more emphatically vertical: no horizontal breaks, and vaulting shafts thinner and more numerous. Other vaults offer further variety; the choir vault is the grandest: three parallel ridge ribs (cf. Gloucester, pre-1360). The Lady Chapel has a star vault with four lozenges in the first bay. The nave vault is less disciplined, with many triangles of tiercerons and no ridge ribs. The date of the upper parts of the nave is unclear, but the nave piers with numerous shafts for the vault responds suggest a complex vault was intended from the beginning. Finally, in the n aisle of the nave the vaults have straight ribs, and the window mullions continue down as wall panelling.

Below the Lady Chapel is a crypt and a passage, the latter with single-chamfered ribs and foliage bosses. Below the n transept a larger crypt, three by two bays, with chamfered ribs. (It houses a fine C15 **vestment armoire**.)

The **furnishings** have been repeatedly reordered. Little remains from the medieval fittings or of the numerous side altars (there were twenty-four chantry priests by 1380). **Lectern**: brass eagle, given 1638. C18 embellishments were lavish. From 1710 to 1756 the choir was divided off by a magnificent wrought-iron **screen** by *William Edney*, now in the tower. The e end had a three-part altarpiece by *Hogarth* of 1755, removed in the C19.* Also in the tower a baluster **font** by *Thomas Paty*, 1755, and a surprising painted **statue** of Queen Elizabeth from the grammar school, wood, large, with lively drapery, probably made after her visit to Bristol in 1574. In the nave and aisles is more C18 **ironwork** including a screen and gates possibly by *Edney* from Temple Church, 1726. **Royal arms**, 1670; **sword rest**, C18. In the Lady Chapel: elegant C17 brass **candelabrum**. The **pulpit**, Dec style, 1856 by *William Bennett*, remains from a C19 refitting intended to be in keeping with the architecture. A reredos of 1871 was removed in 1958, thus creating an awkward vista into the Lady Chapel which would not originally have existed.

Stained glass.† A rich assortment from medieval to C20. Reglazing began in the 1860s at e and w ends. The medieval glass was reset in the tower, by the local firm of *Joseph Bell* in 1872. The tower n has a delightful collection of roundels [33], the tower w has large, pale Somerset-style C15 figures. *Clayton & Bell* did much, starting in the 1860s with the good choir aisles e and the lively s nave aisle first from w, ending in the 1880s–90 with the choir clerestory and e window. Bell's 1880s work is worthwhile too: n nave aisle first from e (Noah); n transept w, first from n; s transept w first from n. The main w window is by *Hardman*,

*Now at St Nicholas, *see* p. 104.
†Details kindly supplied by Alan Brooks.

33. St Mary Redcliffe, medieval glass roundels in tower N window

1868, with much blue, but the most spectacular, with its arresting greens and purples, is the rich nave s aisle w, by *Heaton, Butler & Bayne*, 1867 (Life of Moses) [17]. s transept s is by *Comper*, 1914, pale figures in clear glass. The Lady Chapel has a complete set of windows by *Harry J. Stammers*, 1965, a boldly drawn and coloured Life of Christ.

Monuments

The C15 monuments testify to the importance of the citizens of Redcliffe. s aisle, in the wall recesses: John Lavington d.1411, worn stone effigy; foliated cross. – s transept. Civilian, a lively figure with purse and dog with a bone, late C15. – William Canynge the younger, MP and five times mayor, and wife. Two stiff effigies beneath a routine late C15 canopy. – The same William Canynge, d.1474, shown as Dean of Westbury, to where he had retired after the death of his wife. Fine alabaster effigy with sensitive face, a bedesman at his feet. Brought from Westbury. – N choir aisle: pair of canopied tomb-chests for the Mede family; straight canopies with pinnacles springing from angel corbels, ogee arches in between, chest and back panels with Perp panelling. On the w tomb effigies of Thomas Mede, three times mayor, d.1475 and wife; the E one, for his brother Philip Mede, has a rectangular brass at the back, with kneeling figures, scrolls with prayers, and demi-figure of Christ, a type sometimes associated with Easter Sepulchres. – N transept. Assigned to Robert, 3rd Lord Berkeley (but later than him). Large, slender military effigy with crossed legs, late C13. – Nave N, high up: Admiral William Penn d.1670. Architectural, with cannons above curved inscription. His armour above. – In the tower several early tombstones with floriated crosses, and some good C17–C18 memorials, among them Richard Sandford d.1721, by *James Paty*.

Brasses. Lady Chapel (under carpet): John Juyn d.1439 – Choir (under carpet): John Jay d.1480 and wife, 3 ft (91 cm.) figures under canopies, kneeling children – John Brooke d.1522 and wife, also with 3 ft figures – N choir aisle: two brasses from Temple Church: merchant, 1396, half-figure; priest *c.* 1460.

Bridget Cherry

Council House

College Green

Increased civic administration made a new municipal headquarters for Bristol on a larger site imperative by the early C20, despite enlarging the Old Council House in Corn Street in 1899. This site was proposed in 1913, and land purchased *c.* 1919–24. A design competition was abandoned in 1930, and *E. Vincent Harris* produced a plan in 1931 after another assessor, G.C. Lawrence, declined. The RIBA censured Harris for professional misconduct but he was appointed architect in 1933. Harris specialized in civic buildings in a Neo-Georgian manner (e.g. Sheffield, Leeds). No record has been located of the design development up to 1938, when construction began by *Cowlin & Son*. War and austerity delayed completion until 1952. The official opening in 1956 ended an extraordinary forty-three-year gestation for a building of questionable merits.

The crescent plan closes the w end of College Green effectively.* Over a Portland stone basement a high structure of concrete faced with muted brown Blockley Gloucester bricks, which Harris had also used at Exeter University, chosen here to avoid competing with Bristol Cathedral. Now it seems unsympathetic rather than respectful. The rigidly symmetrical four-storey façade [34] has thirty-six repetitive bays of sashes emphasized further by a steep leaded roof; intermittent ground-floor window architraves provide inadequate variation. The composition is relieved only by full-height arched end pavilions leading via ramps to a lower domed porte cochère. The latter is spiced with Lutyens's influence   New Delhi in the dome and the Thiepval Memorial in the stepped profile and monumental arches. On the pavilion roofs are two sculptures of majestic gilded unicorns (supporters of Bristol arms) by *David McFall*. The Council wanted a statue of an Elizabethan sailor (but not John Cabot) to stand beneath the porte-cochère. In the end *Charles Wheeler* gave them Cabot, complete with fur-trimmed tunic and charter, but without conviction. Tall sculptures planned to stand before the pavilions were not executed. The curved plan, the unicorns and the central domed porch save the day – but only just. Harris's aloof and chilly achievement is difficult to admire.

The setting is not an easy one, with the cathedral, Norman gateway and Central Library all close by. College Green was a fine tree-lined

*Harris used a crescent plan at the smaller Somerset County Hall, Taunton (1932).

34. Council House, College Green, E front, by E. Vincent Harris, 1938–52

space, raised and railed with paths around *John Norton*'s C19 replica High Cross. Harris swept all this away in 1950 for the billiard-table expanse that he hoped would 'make his building'. It might flatter a fine composition, but only exposes a flawed one. There is a shallow pool in front of the façade – better that than municipal paving. At least Harris turned to advantage a steep decline at the back, with a vast Rates Hall in the basement. Above, on the rear roofs, two children riding river horses, also by *McFall*.

The major **interiors** are sited centrally. The porte-cochère leads to a curved **entrance hall** with Doulting stone walls, and geometric floors of Belgian black marble and Bianco del Mara. A fine blue and gilt clock, with zodiacal signs and wind dial, is set over studded leather doors to the **Conference Hall**, a vast stony space with full-height w windows. The N and S walls list the names of Bristol's mayors, 1216–1956, incised and gilded by *Angello del Cauchferta* and *Beryl Hardman*. Ceiling painted *in situ* by *W.T. Monnington*, in a semi-abstract design of atomic structures orbiting the earth, in pale blue, pink and grey tempera.

The **Council Chamber** adjoins the Conference Hall to the N. Black oak and crimson pigskin fittings with facing benches, Parliament-style. Ceiling painted on canvas by *John Armstrong*; a remarkable fantasy on Bristol, with Bristol buildings along the sides, allegorical figures of Wisdom, Enterprise, Navigation and Industry in the corners, and a blue sea with innumerable close-packed sails occupying the whole centre. The two curving wings have office ranges served by spine corridors. In the S corridor, the Neo-Georgian **Lord Mayor's Reception Suite** evokes Bristol's C18 golden age, with panelling and pilasters in rich English walnut, and gilded details. Committee rooms in similar style. Harris procured the joinery before the war, otherwise post-war austerity would doubtless have prevented its execution.

Central Library

Deanery Road

In 1613 Robert Redwood gave the Corporation his lodge in Town Marsh (now King Street) for use as a library; and Dr Tobias Matthew, Bristol-born Archbishop of York, donated the core of a book collection. It was the second-earliest public municipal library in England. The lodge was rebuilt *c.* 1740, but by 1900 was wholly inadequate. In 1899 Vincent Stuckey Lean bequeathed £50,000 for a new building. The architectural competition in 1902 was won by the firm of *H. Percy Adams*, with designs by his assistant *Charles Holden* (1875–1960). As completed in 1906, it differs relatively little from the 1902 competition designs. It shows Holden's precocious maturity at just 27; and he gained a partnership in the firm at about the time of its completion. Holden's education in the c19 tradition of historicism is evident (Neo-Tudor without, classical within). Why, then, is the library regarded as so significant in the development of the Modern Movement in Britain? Firstly, as Pevsner says, the styles are used with a 'freedom instigated by Mackintosh's Glasgow Art School' – juxtaposed, stripped down and stylized. Secondly, for the innovative exterior composition and handling of volume and mass, especially the s and e fronts.

The plan form is simple: the entrance and main staircase are at the e end, with (originally) three floors of public space to the n; offices and storage to the s are on five floors, taking advantage of the sloping site. Here there is a light well, and glass-block panels in the floors, to illuminate the lower levels. The building budget of £30,000 was not extravagant for a structure of this size and complexity. Holden overcame this by using brick on steel framing, with facings of Bath stone. Internal ornament is kept to a minimum, and much is executed in plaster; but quality is never skimped. All the joinery and furniture was designed by Holden and executed in durable teak, and *William Aumonier* of London did most of the stone carving.

The most influential element was the composition of the s and e façades [35]. Although the s approach was relatively unimportant, Holden held to the Arts and Crafts principle of equal attention to back and front. Bold chimneystacks and framing towers establish the dominant verticals, and the central arched and buttressed bays echo the n front. There is a complex play of projection and recession both here and on the high blank e walls, reminiscent of the library wing of Mackintosh's

35. Central Library from the SE, with stair turret, by Charles Holden, 1902–6

Glasgow School of Art (1906–9) and Hill House, Helensburgh (also designed in 1902). The stair-turret at the latter is sited in the re-entrant angle as at Bristol, but one hesitates to claim precedence for Bristol, since Mackintosh had rehearsed the major compositional elements at Windyhill, Kilmalcolm, by 1901. Rather, Holden draws on the same set of ideas – mathematical logic, spatial manipulation and Arts and Crafts respect for locale – while synthesizing a new and infinitely pleasing design.

The design of the N front had to respect the adjoining Norman Abbey Gatehouse. Holden kept his parapet slightly lower, and the upper parts recessed. The gatehouse is echoed in the tower-like ends and round-arched entrance below a Neo-Tudor oriel window. Symmetrical centre of three segmental bays with pointedly small oriels against chequer panels of Westmorland stone. Between these are broad flat buttresses, and under the arches figure groups by *Charles Pibworth*, representing English literature from St Augustine and Bede to Chaucer. Beautifully detailed rainwater heads and downpipes subtly underscore the angles. Westward extension of 1966–8 by the City Architect *A.H. Clarke*, with associate architects *Burrough & Hannam*. Its N façade has square oriels and chequerwork echoing Holden's work. Wide stone wall panels rise above roof level, the incomplete stubs of a planned third floor. Glass-canopied access ramp and entrance lobby added at the W end (2000, by *Architecton*). It all works surprisingly well with Holden's building.

Interiors

The **vestibule** has a broad central space and narrow flanking aisles, with a low vault of pendentive domes tiled in turquoise vitreous mosaic. Otherwise, the room is entirely faced in marbles: Piastraccia for the floor, walls of dramatically figured green Cipollino with Irish marble capping rails and Grand Antique for the skirtings. This Byzantine setting would do justice to the painted fantasies of Alma-Tadema. Beyond glazed screens, the secondary ground-floor rooms (originally the Newspaper, Magazine and Lending libraries) are of lesser significance architecturally. At the end of this dark vestibule, a stone screen offers a glimpse of the high, light space of the main **staircase**, which rises in a single semicircular flight. A low vaulted corridor provides a dramatic spatial contrast to the **Reading Room**, a cool, noble space similar in its general form to C.R. Cockerell's Old University Library, Cambridge. Tunnel vaulted with glass-block panels for top lighting and transeptal ends lit by floor-length mullioned windows. Two tiers of galleries, providing extra book stacks, accessed by spiral staircases. Three small oriels in the N wall light the area beneath the lower gallery, which continues around the room by means of narrow bridges across the transepts. The upper gallery has mildly Art Nouveau railings and, on the N side, a mullioned clerestory. The details are unexpectedly classical, given the faintly Tudor windows, etc. Giant Ionic main piers, and a subsidiary Tuscan order supporting the galleries. Scrolled oculi, fruity festoons and segmental arches reminiscent of Wren, and groined vaults and transepts suggesting Roman *thermae*. Fixed reading desks and revolving map tables in the bays designed by Holden.

The **Bristol Room** was designed for the fittings from the reference room of the former library in King Street (*see* p. 160). Panelling, bookcases and some furniture of *c.* 1/40. At the S end a spectacular *Grinling Gibbons* overmantel, purchased in 1721 from Gibbons's studio sale by a Bristolian and donated to the old library. Beneath an open segmental pediment, drops of fruit, game birds and miraculously delicate sprays of corn, etc., carved with Gibbons's usual artistry. The chimneypiece beneath is provincial early C18.

Exchange

Corn Street

The Exchange by *John Wood the Elder* of Bath, 1741–3, with the attached
C18 and C19 market buildings, occupies an approximately rectangular
plot between Corn Street and St Nicholas Street. The Exchange is Wood's
outstanding public building and is in the highest canon of C18 civic structures. It balances refined Palladian proportion and detail with more
solidly prosaic qualities likely to appeal to Bristol's mercantile oligarchy.
Previously merchants had transacted business in the open arcaded Tolzey
outside All Saints nearby. In 1717 the Corporation started planning a
replacement, and an Act of Parliament was obtained in 1722. Apart from
William Halfpenny's wayward design published in 1731, the project
remained dormant until 1738–41, when Halfpenny, *John Jacob de Wilstar*
and *George Tully* all submitted plans without success. In 1740, *George
Dance the Elder* (the recent architect of London's Mansion House) was
asked to submit designs. Almost immediately *John Wood* was also invited
to participate. His local connections clearly prevailed with the
Corporation, and building took place to his design, 1741–3. Among the
craftsmen were *Thomas Paty*, 'ornament carver', *John Griffin*, 'ornament
plaisterer', *Benjamin and Daniel Greenway*, 'marble and freestone
masons, carvers and vase-makers', *Robert Parsons*, 'freestone mason and
house carver', and *William Biggs*, 'freestone mason'. In 1745 Wood published a self-aggrandizing account of the design and construction.

In **plan**, the main entrance is from the N, in Corn Street. The flanks of
the N range were originally occupied by a tavern and a coffee house,
with a square vestibule in the centre leading to an open courtyard
where the merchants transacted their business. In the E and W ranges
were insurance offices, etc. The S range and the area beyond house St
Nicholas Market. The eleven-bay N **façade** [36] is a more tautly expressed
development of Wood's N range of Queen Square, Bath. Rusticated
ground floor with V-joints, and plain arched entrance with iron-
studded and bossed oak doors bearing massive lion masks. One-and-a-
half-storey piano nobile with giant pilasters to the flanks, and deeply
projecting attached columns in the three-bay pedimented centre. A
Venetian window occupies the wider centre bay. The first-floor windows have alternating pediments on Corinthian pilasters. Beneath the
entablature is a richly embellished frieze of garlands, after Inigo Jones's
Banqueting House at Whitehall, with attributes symbolizing Bristol's

36. Exchange, Corn Street, by John Wood the Elder, 1741 3

worldwide trade. All the mouldings and breaks are richly embellished with egg-and-dart, waterleaf, etc. Below the pediment, the clock of 1822 has two minute hands, showing the difference between London and Bristol time before national standardization. Fine C18 spear-headed iron railings front the area, with early C20 lamp standards beside the door. On the pavement in front are four brass **nails**, flat-topped balusters on which merchants transacted business – hence 'to pay on the nail'. From the E, two are late C16, the first with embossed foliage and scroll pattern; the third given by Nicolas Crisp, 1625, and the fourth by George White, 1631.

The **vestibule** emulates Palladio's tetrastyle hall, with four Corinthian columns defining an inner square. Steps lead up to side doors surmounted by Gods: Bacchus for the former tavern; and for the coffee house, where newspapers were sold, Mercury, messenger of the Gods. In the s arch leading to the Exchange court, C20 glazed doors have replaced Wood's rich wrought-iron gates, which are stored at Bristol Museum.

And so to the **Exchange** proper, now home to a teeming and atmospheric market. Wood argued strongly for an Egyptian Hall after Vitruvius; that is, a carefully proportioned rectangular colonnaded room, the centre covered in with a tall lantern-like second storey. It had recently been the model for Lord Burlington's York Assembly Rooms. The Corporation preferred an open square court with arcaded walks, the traditional model for exchanges since Antwerp and London in the mid C16. But the executed design retains elements of Palladio's published version of an Egyptian Hall, with its flat entablature over colonnades rather than arcades. The s and N colonnades are deeper than the sides, to make the most of the shade in summer and the sun in winter when the courtyard was open. Outer walls punctuated by niches below a fine frieze of shells, fruit and flowers, with a female head central to each bay. Over the E, s and w doorways is playful Rococo plasterwork, with personifications of Asia, Africa and America; stuccoists *Boni* of London. Garish paint colours reduce the plasterwork to exceptional vulgarity. The architecture has been scandalously abused, parts of the stone capitals having even been sawn off to accommodate cables. Everything needs expert repair and conservation. In 1870–2 *E.M. Barry* added ranges of arched lights and terms above the colonnade to carry a high iron and glass roof. This was replaced by the present disfiguring roof in 1949, although the supporting stonework for Barry's roof survives above.

Markets and Environs

On Corn Street, two small flanking buildings are set forward from the line of the Exchange front, almost certainly designed by Wood to imply a shallow courtyard setting for his building. To the right is No. 48 Corn Street by *Samuel Glascodine*, 1746, originally housing the Old Post Office, see inscription on the platband. The matching left flank (then and now a coffee house) was built by *Thomas Paty*, 1782. Both have one-bay pediments and ground floors with heavily detailed arcades. In All Saints Lane, left, the plain but carefully composed side elevation is visible, including a splendid door framed with an oak-leaf band. At the s end of All Saints Lane, E side, the decaying **Market Tavern**, by *John Wood the Elder*, 1744–5, a rebuilding of the medieval Rummer Inn.* A simple well-proportioned entrance front, to a 1:3:1 bay design, the flanks slightly set back. Internally the Market Tavern connects with a C16–C17 building eastward (upper room reported to have linenfold panelling and a plain C17 stone chimneypiece).

s of the Market Tavern is **St Nicholas Market**; a planned subsidiary to Wood's Exchange, executed 1744–5 by *Samuel Glascodine*, a local

*Confusingly the C20 Rummer is directly E on High Street.

carpenter-builder. There were three covered halls: the East Arcade hall, and the Gloucestershire and Somersetshire market halls, around an open square, originally with butchers' shambles (roofed timber stalls). The s range of Wood's Exchange building, now a café, was originally the Gloucestershire Market Hall, and had no direct access from the Exchange proper. Its open arcaded s front was blocked and glazed *c.* 1813 when it became a Corn Exchange. Its s door leads to the **Glass Arcade**, an avenue running E–W, and now lined with C19 wooden stalls. Glazed roof on wrought-iron framing, by *R.S. Pope*, 1854–5, repaired 2002–3. At its E end, *Samuel Glascodine*'s simple and pleasing **Market Gate** leads to the High Street via a vaulted arch, with narrow pedestrian entrances, now blocked. On the High Street front is a small pediment above a Serlian window. Given the success of this design, the untutored Glascodine may have been guided by Wood or another experienced architect. Inside the gate and s of the Glass Arcade, is Glascodine's East Arcade Market Hall, now the ground floor of a pub. The arcaded first floor was added by *Pope* to carry the new roof in 1854. The richer niched screen wall N of East Arcade may be by Wood, though it is somewhat at variance with a plan of 1793; if so it may be Pope's attempt to emulate Wood. He was a learned classicist and could have done so.

Directly s of the Exchange building, on the site of the C18 shambles, is the arcaded **Market Hall** by *R.S. Pope*, 1848–9, the lower s part having a very plain façade to St Nicholas Street. Again Pope heightened the N front with a pierced screen wall to carry the roof of the Glass Arcade. At the sw extremity of the complex is **Market Chambers**, by *R.S. Pope*, 1848–9, replacing Glascodine's Somersetshire Market Hall. Its entrance is on St Nicholas Street. Tucked into a corner at its N end, a good lead rainwater head *c.* 1740, with acanthus-leaf throat, surviving from the Barber-Surgeons' Hall which was demolished after war damage.

Wills Memorial Building

Queen's Road

The University of Bristol's main building by *George Oatley*, 1915–25, houses an entrance hall, great hall, libraries, council chamber, and a majestic tower – a major Bristol landmark. All is on a monumental scale, and an exceptionally late example of Perpendicular Gothic Revival style, wholly backward looking to the C19 and beyond to the C15. It is nevertheless 'a *tour de force* . . . so convinced, so vast, and so competent that one cannot help feeling respect for it' (Pevsner). University College was founded in 1876 largely by the Rev. John Percival and Benjamin Jowett, Master of Balliol College, Oxford, with donations from wealthy local Liberals and Nonconformists. University College offered non-degree courses in sciences, languages, engineering, history and literature. It gained university status in 1909 following a gift of £100,000 from Henry Overton Wills (1828–1911), which was quickly increased to £203,000 with donations from others. He was made the first Chancellor and is regarded as the University's founder. Following their father's death, Sir George Arthur Wills and Henry Herbert Wills commissioned the building as his memorial. Contrary to the local myth that the patrons rejected concrete in favour of the proven and lasting qualities of stone, the structure throughout is of ferro-concrete, faced with Bath stone and carvings in Clipsham stone. Designed 1912–14; building began 1915–16, and was completed 1919–25 at a cost of *c.* £501,000.

The 215-ft (65.5-metre) tower is dramatically sited, angled and set forward on its plot at the top of Park Street [97]. From the SE, the whole height is framed by the stepped buildings of Park Street. Oatley composed this consciously, pencilling his design onto a photograph. The main door nestling in the plinth is the university's ceremonial entrance, announced by the two-stage tower above, which has one vast window on each face at each stage. The upper windows have three lights beneath a blind tracery head. Chunky buttresses clasp the angles, and thin pinnacles mask the transition to octagonal turrets with beautifully judged concave caps. The octagonal lantern with delicate traceried panelling houses Great George, a bell of over nine tons. The fine carving was designed in collaboration with *Jean Hahn* of King's Heath Guild,

37. Wills Memorial Building, entrance hall, by George Oatley, built 1915–25

Birmingham, whose big, lively gargoyle-like masks portray identifiable members of the University staff. Everything is subordinated to the bold composition necessary at this scale. What can be said against it? Compared with medieval towers, the proportions are too broad in relation to the height, but this gives majestic solidity to the distant silhouette and can hardly be described as a fault. The traceried panels to the buttresses appear pasteboard-thin. The octagon's blind tracery, although correctly Perpendicular, is wiry and repetitive, and perhaps less inventive than the detailing of Giles Gilbert Scott's Liverpool Cathedral. The design is often compared with the c15 Boston Stump, Lincolnshire, but Oatley always denied any influence.

The **entrance hall** [37] occupies the floor area of the tower and extends into the wing behind it. It is vastly impressive, with panelled stone walls and fan-vaulting, higher at 75 ft (23 metres) than Wells Cathedral nave. Over the door, the prodigiously big Founders' Window (the glass replaced to a new design after war damage). Opposite the main door, twin staircases run straight up 'as spectacular as their opposite number at Beckford's [c18] Fonthill and three times as solid' (Pevsner). They lead to a lateral fan-vaulted corridor; at its NW end the oak-panelled **reception room** has a Neo-Jacobean plaster ceiling. The **Great Hall** is oak-panelled below large windows, with an apse behind the dais, and an oak hammerbeam roof with pierced traceried panels. The hall was destroyed by bombing and reconstructed 1959–63 by *Ralph Brentnall*, Oatley's surviving partner, to the same design but with some carving omitted to reduce costs. The **Council Chamber** to the SE is to a truncated polygonal plan, with stone-panelled walls above oak linenfold panelling. Central light fitting set flush with the vault, rendered as a rose window. The SW wing houses a galleried **library** complete with fittings and furniture to *Oatley*'s design. Plaster barrel vault of Jacobean panels and pendants. A narrow bridge carries the gallery in front of the end bay, reminiscent of Holden's at the Central Library Reading Room (q.v.). In the SE wing, *Brentnall*'s library extension (1962) continues the theme in a simplified fashion.

For adjacent University buildings to the SE and N, *see* Walk 9, The University and St Michael's Hill.

Clifton Suspension Bridge

Suspension Bridge Road

The major Bristol work of *Isambard Kingdom Brunel*, designed in 1829 when he was just twenty-three, and built 1836–64. This iconic symbol is for many synonymous with Bristol. Its visual impact is due to the great height of the gorge (245 ft, 74.7 metres, from high-water mark to the bridge deck) and the drama of the 702-ft (214-metre) span. It is perhaps 'the most beautiful of early English suspension bridges . . . largely due to the felicitous design of the stone pylons' (Pevsner). The vertical suspension rods appear wonderfully light, supporting the bridge deck with daring and grace. Understandably, Brunel referred to it in his journal of 1835 as 'my first child, my darling'.

William Vick, a merchant, bequeathed £1,000 in 1753 for a bridge across the Avon Gorge. There was no pressing need to link Clifton with the open country on the Somerset side (the suburb of Leigh Woods

38 River Avon and Clifton Suspension Bridge

39. Clifton Suspension Bridge from Sion Hill, by I.K. Brunel, 1836–64

largely post-dates the bridge). The challenge of the gorge itself was suf-
ficient reason. In 1829 Vick's money had grown to £8,000 and designs
were invited. *Brunel* submitted four designs in various styles, based on
the suspension principle, perhaps inspired by the competition judge
Thomas Telford's recently completed Menai Straits Bridge. After a second competition a modified version of one of Brunel's designs was
placed second. Brunel then persuaded the bridge committee in 1831 to

adopt his design anyway. Although it exceeded the 600 ft (183 metres) that Telford believed was the maximum possible, Brunel calculated that suspension bridges could achieve much wider spans.

Brunel wrote that 'A work of art thus thrown across such grand and imposing scenery should be as simple and unobtrusive as possible, that it should fix the observer rather by the grandeur of the ideas that it gave rise to than attract his attention by anything inconsistent with the surrounding objects'. Despite this, the accepted 'unobtrusive' Egyptian design included sphinxes topping the pylons, and cast-iron decoration of scarabs, etc. Work commenced in 1831 but was soon suspended because of the Bristol Riots (*see* topic box, p. 161). The massive Somerset-side abutment was built 1836–40, and the pylons raised by 1843. But the £45,000 raised (including Vick's legacy) was spent, and work ceased, with a half-hearted intention to continue when funds allowed. In 1853 the time allowed for construction by an 1830 Act of Parliament expired. The project was abandoned and the ironwork sold for reuse at Brunel's Royal Albert Bridge, Saltash.

The barren pylons were an embarrassing reminder of failure and there were moves to demolish them. Brunel died in 1859, and in 1861 members of the Institute of Civil Engineers resurrected the scheme in Brunel's memory, reusing the chains from Brunel's Hungerford Bridge, London, then being demolished. Work resumed under *Hawkshaw & Barlow* in 1862, using three chains on each side instead of two and a wrought-iron deck frame instead of Brunel's timber and iron one. It was completed in 1864 [39].

The piers on which the pylons stand are honeycombed with recently rediscovered vaults, to reduce the weight of masonry and increase their structural strength. Brunel changed the original rectilinear design of the pylons before construction, for reasons unknown. Their apparently curving sides are in reality battered at two sensitively judged angles, the change of angle occurring at the level where the tall parabolic opening is bridged by a segmental arch over the carriageway; again a happy motif. They are of Pennant rubble below, with pale ashlar caps and cornices of harmonious proportions. The chains are fastened to iron saddles on top of the pylons and where they meet the ground, allowing the chains to move and flex. The outer ends are anchored 70 ft (21 metres) into the rock with tapering brick plugs. The planned cast-iron cladding of the pylons was happily omitted for lack of money, revealing the magical fusion of Victorian engineering and architecture.

Temple Meads Railway Station

Temple Gate

Temple Meads is actually parts of three stations, although the travelling public generally does not realise it. Of these three, *Isambard Kingdom Brunel's* Great Western Railway (GWR) station, 1839–41, is probably the world's first example of the mature form of railway terminus with integrated train shed, passenger and office facilities.

The GWR was a Bristol initiative to provide a railway link to London. *Brunel* (1806–59) was appointed its Chief Engineer in 1833, aged twenty-seven. He had won the design competition for Clifton Suspension Bridge and other Bristol projects followed, including the S.S. *Great Western*, 1837, the Royal Western Hotel (Brunel House, q.v. Walk 4), and S.S. *Great Britain*, 1843. The Bristol–Bath section of the line was opened in 1840 and the whole Bristol–Paddington line in 1841, controversially using 7 ft ¼ in. (2.1 metre) broad gauge tracks.

First some orientation: in Temple Gate are *Brunel's* offices, Tudor Revival, with the train shed (now the Empire and Commonwealth Museum) N of the approach ramp. To its s is the Bristol & Exeter (B&E) Railway office, 1852–4, in Jacobean style with ogee-capped towers. Facing down the approach, a big Gothic tower marks *M.D. Wyatt's* Joint Station of 1871–8, with 1930s extension behind.

The **GWR offices**, 1839–41, have a symmetrical Tudor façade, apparently of Dundry limestone. *R.S. Pope* has been proposed as joint architect, but the archive material suggests that Brunel was probably solely responsible. A tall oriel in a five-bay centre, and one-bay flanks outside octagonal angle turrets. Across the centre is a black-letter inscription on a long scroll: 'Great Western Railway Company Incorporated by Act of Parliament MDCCCXXXV'. The left entrance arch was once matched by an exit arch at the right. The medieval revivalist Pugin favoured Gothic for railway stations, but argued for 'a massive architecture . . . in the simplest and most substantial manner'. He thundered against the 'architectural display', the 'mock castellated work and . . . all sorts of unaccountable breaks' of the GWR stations; but Brunel saw nothing incongruous in using C15 collegiate Tudor to dress up a C19 building type. Having bridged the harbour to the E, the tracks came in 15 ft (4.5 metres) above ground level on brick vaults, through which a road for passengers' carriages passes beneath the train shed. Brunel's platforms were dedicated to departure (N side) and arrival (s); carriages

40. Temple Meads Station, Brunel's train shed. Lithograph by J.C. Bourne, *c.* 1846

had to be lifted and rolled across the tracks between on hydraulic 'traversers' before departing from the other platform. N of the train shed was a large goods depot (demolished), with dock and wharfs to take harbour traffic.

This new building type created complex problems that challenged even the most resourceful of Victorian engineers. The **train shed**'s impressive mock hammerbeam roof [40] of yellow pine spans 72 ft (22 metres), with 20 ft (6 metres) aisles behind Tudor arcades. But the hammerbeams and arches are set-dressing to add architectural presence; the thin side walls over high vaults would not bear the outward thrust of true arched construction. Instead, in Brunel's first design, each bay was treated as two independent crane-like structures, not quite meeting at the ridge. Most of the roof's weight was transferred to the slim iron columns of the aisle arcades, which were bolted to the substructure on cast-iron rockers to allow fine adjustment during construction. Each column thus acted as the fulcrum for a cantilevered rafter, the downward thrust at the centre being resisted by a vertical iron tie-rod anchoring the triangulated frame over the aisle to the platform. This design probably proved unstable during testing, for it was executed in amended form [41], with a crown piece plugging the central gap and wrought-iron straps binding the two crane-like structures into a rigid portal frame. These compromises reintroduced some characteristics of arch construction and the consequent outward thrust caused significant bowing in the columns and side walls. Brunel was still attempting to stabilize the roof in 1849.

The **Bristol & Exeter** line was constructed 1841–4, and joined the GWR lines from the first. There was originally a timber train shed across the present approach ramp at right angles to the GWR shed. s of the ramp, opposite the train shed, are the symmetrical Jacobean **offices**, 1852–4, with shaped gables, towered roofline and a pleasing Doric

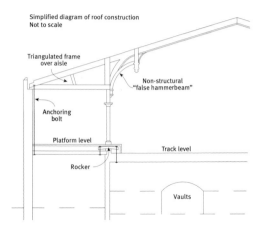

Simplified diagram of roof construction
Not to scale

Triangulated frame
over aisle

Non-structural
"false hammerbeam"

Anchoring
bolt

Platform level

Track level

Rocker

Vaults

41. **Temple Meads Station**, diagram of train shed roof construction

columned doorway. The architect was *S.C. Fripp*, who had been Brunel's 'assistant' (probably meaning clerk of works) at the GWR station.

Matthew Digby Wyatt designed a **Joint Station** serving the GWR, Bristol & Exeter and the Midland Railways, 1871–8, on a curving **Y**-plan. The Midland shed extended Brunel's train shed E, in similar if plainer style, with much brick inside, but abandoning the mock hammerbeam roof. The external walls are of chunky pink conglomerate from Draycott near Cheddar, with Bath stone dressings. The coarsely detailed tower had a French pavilion roof, destroyed by bombing. Austere red brick Gothic interiors. **Train shed** roofed in an elegant 125-ft (38-metre) arch formed of two segments, designed by *Francis Fox*, using the Cheltenham iron founders *Vernon & Evans*. M.D. Wyatt had collaborated with Brunel at Paddington in 1851–5 and Sir Charles Fox, Francis's father, engineered the Paddington roof after Brunel's sketches. It may have something to do with Wyatt's progressive views that the Bristol roof's construction has interesting reminiscences of Viollet-le-Duc's *Entretiens* (particularly Vol. II, 1872).* A further **extension** by *P.E. Culverhouse*, 1930–5, added five platforms on the E side. Platform buildings in GWR chocolate-and-cream faience, in an anachronistic pared-down Tudor style.

*The *Entretiens* was a programme for an iron-based architecture free from dependence on historical styles.

City Churches

All Saints 92

Christ Church 94

St George 95

St James 97

St John the Baptist 98

St Mark (or the Lord Mayor's Chapel) 100

St Mary le Port 102

St Mary on the Quay (R.C.) 103

St Michael on the Mount Without 104

St Nicholas 104

St Peter 106

SS Philip and Jacob 107

St Stephen 108

St Thomas the Martyr 110

Temple (or Holy Cross) Church 111

The city churches are treated here as a group to make comparisons and contrasts between them easier. The group includes all the surviving churches of medieval foundation except Bristol Cathedral and St Mary Redcliffe, which are described under Major Buildings. Two later churches in or near the city centre are listed, but Nonconformist chapels and churches of the inner suburbs are excluded. At the Reformation Bristol had nineteen parish churches, of which five are still churches, six are lost, three ruinous, one semi-derelict and four in alternative use. Two churches of monastic foundation still function as places of worship. Of two C19 churches, one is still in use.

Many of the medieval churches underwent ambitious Perp re-buildings: Norman, E.E. and Decorated work is less common. Four churches were rebuilt in the C18. There are some outstanding furnishings: the Jacobean woodwork at St John: C18 woodwork at St Thomas; tombs and Continental glass at St Mark; and in several churches, very fine Baroque ironwork by the *Edney* brothers. Bristol also has perhaps the best group of C17 and C18 sword rests outside London.

All Saints

Corn Street

Currently a Diocesan Education Centre; not generally accessible to the public.

A medieval parish church possibly of late Saxon foundation, near the site of the High Cross on the High Street–Corn Street junction, so cramped by surrounding buildings that little is visible externally apart from the C18 tower. Part of a Romanesque nave arcade is incorporated in a largely Perp rebuilding. In 1443 a room over the N aisle was rebuilt for the Guild of Kalendars, a charitable religious foundation that also provided a library and kept legal records.

The medieval tower was rebuilt 1712–17. Begun by *Thomas Sumsion*, a Colerne mason, but completed 1716–17 by *George Townesend* with *William Paul*. It has three stages, the lower two having oddly assorted arches and windows. Belfry stage of simple recessed panels with an oculus on each face, and an open-arcaded domed octagonal cupola, for which Wren's St Magnus the Martyr, London, may be the source. Townesend's bell-shaped dome was replaced in 1807 by *Luke Henwood*, District Surveyor, with one of more conventional profile, restored 1930 by *Sir George Oatley* without altering the form. *Thomas Paty* rebuilt the three-bay N aisle wall 1782 in a reasonable imitation of Perp, at the same time as he reconstructed the NW corner as a coffee house to *John Wood*'s design (*see* Major Buildings; Exchange, p. 78). The w wall, six-light w window and entrance are largely C19. Adjoining at the sw, a rubble-walled glebe house (or parsonage) built in 1422, substantially rebuilt *c.* 1585 and heavily restored 1905–6 by *Oatley*.

Inside, a high five-bay nave (without a clerestory), aisles and long

42. All Saints, detail
of monument to
Edward Colston, by
J.M. Rysbrack,
c. 1729

chancel. Two w bays of the nave survive with round piers, multi-scalloped capitals and square-sectioned arches of *c.* 1140. They supported structures built over both aisles, and thus could not be removed in the rebuilding of *c.* 1430–50. Awkwardly stilted piers at the junction of the Norman and Perp work. Slim, elegant later piers, with four attached shafts, intervening continuous wave mouldings, and foliated capitals. In the s aisle, an oversailing bulkhead of the glebe house with two tiny windows from which priests could see the altars, and fragments of painted c16 text with foliate border. The chancel was largely rebuilt in 1850 and shortened by 6 ft 6 ins (2 metres). In the s wall, a three-seat **sedilia** and **piscina** beneath ogee arches, with coarsely scraped stonework.

Reredos, Dec Gothic, of three bays, apparently from Bristol Cathedral. – **Stained glass**. E window by *Arnold Robinson*, 1949; Colston window 1907–8 by *H. Holiday*. – **Monuments**. Many good c18 tablets with urns, etc., by local masons, principally the *Patys* and *Tyleys*. – Chancel s wall. Small tablet to Troth Blisset d.1805, by *Flaxman*, with reclining Grecian-looking figure under a segmental arch with Gothic hoodmould. – s aisle, E end. Edward Colston d.1721, wealthy merchant and Bristol philanthropist. Colston's executors were governors of St Bartholomew's Hospital, London, as was *James Gibbs*, whom they commissioned to design the architectural frame in 1728–9. Gibbs recommended *J.M. Rysbrack* for the effigy. The Bristol mason *Michael Sidnell* carved Gibbs's design splendidly in black and white marbles, with Ionic columns, pulvinated frieze and putti flanking Colston's escutcheon of arms. Rysbrack's outstanding reclining figure [42] is urbane and dignified. The head was made from a painting by *Jonathan Richardson*; the terracotta model is at Bristol Museum and Art Gallery. – N aisle, w end. Tablet to Colston's mother Sarah, d.1701, with Corinthian frame on scrolled brackets, swan-neck pediment, and putti opening a draped canopy to reveal the inscription.

Christ Church
Broad Street

One of the medieval churches at the junction of the four streets where the High Cross once stood; rebuilt 1786–90 to the design of *William Paty*. The entrance front consists only of the base of the tower. Bombing exposed the featureless s side in 1940. All is focused on the tower, according to Pevsner 'not a specially refined member of the large

43. Christ Church, nave looking E, by William Paty, 1786–90

progeny of St Martin-in-the-Fields' (Westminster). The upper stage sits awkwardly over the pediment of the stage below, while subtly diminishing upper stages and the elegantly proportioned octagonal spire increase its apparent height. On the clock, two quarterjacks by *James Paty*, 1728. The main doorway is a fussy Neo-Renaissance alteration by *Henry Williams*, the only external sign of his unfortunate reordering (1883) which so disrupts *Paty*'s interior.

The **interior** [43] is the most accomplished of Bristol's surviving C18 churches. A rectangular aisled space, the high windows on three sides now with round-arched tracery and poor coloured glass of the 1883 reordering. Six tall Corinthian columns form the nave arcades, originally painted to resemble Siena marble. From their entablature blocks springs a 'vaulted' ceiling – actually a series of pendentive domes held taut on elliptical vault ribs enriched with guilloche. Several models have been suggested: St Martin-in-the-Fields; Badminton church, Gloucestershire (1783–5); Sir Robert Taylor's Transfer and Stock Offices at the Bank of England (1765–8); and George Dance the Younger's Guildhall Common Council Chamber, London, 1777–8. Only the last had the essential element of Christ Church: the pendentive dome. *Paty*'s daring innovation was to employ twelve such domes together. Ceiling decoration of gilded Adamish grotesques and big rosettes. At the NW corner a tiny circular **baptistery** (1898), domed, toplit and with Baroque plasterwork. Vestries by *Drake & Pizey*, 1908.

Fittings. Clumsy stone **reredos** of 1883 replacing *Paty*'s original, with its fluted columns twined with rose garlands. This was reinstated in the 1920s as the **rood screen** with a big Crucifix above. – Delicate demi-lune **communion table** by *Charles & William Court*, 1791–2, to *Paty*'s design, in the Hepplewhite style, framed by a semicircular wrought-iron and mahogany **rail**. – C18 wrought-iron **sword rest**. – Brass eagle **lectern**. – **Pulpit**, plain oak with big gilded cherubs on the panels. Octagonal **tester** of 1816. – **Organ** from the old church by *Renatus Harris*, *c.* 1708, on the W **gallery**. This has a heavy carved front (1883) with an C18 cherub frieze below. – C17 octagonal stone **font**, reputedly from the long-demolished St Ewen's church. *Paty*'s mahogany baluster font is in the vestry anteroom. – Numerous **memorial tablets** of the late C18 and early C19, Neoclassical or Gothic, many by the firms of *Paty*, *Wood* and *Tyley*.

St George

Great George Street, Brandon Hill

By *Sir Robert Smirke*, 1821–3. A Commissioners' church, the first of eight in Bristol, built as a chapel of ease to Bristol Cathedral serving the new residential development on Brandon Hill. *Smirke* was one of three official architects to the Board of Works, who had produced model church designs for the Commissioners in 1818. This design, costing over £10,000, was used again at St James, Hackney. Of the 1,416 sittings, 496 were rented and 920 free. Austere Doric E portico set imposingly above

44　St George Brandon Hill, by Sir Robert Smirke, 1821–3

a full-width flight of forty-eight steps [44]. The order is from the 'Theseum' (Temple of Hephaestus, Athens); chosen no doubt because its proportions were calculated for the optical distortion of being viewed from the bottom of a steep slope. Above the pediment a narrow and somehow bloodless domed lantern. The functionless portico is at the ritual E (actually SE) end, behind the altar (cf. Hawksmoor's St Alphege, Greenwich). Congregational entrance reached from Charlotte Street. Seven-bay sides with tall round-headed windows.

Plain 'preaching box' **interior**, with flat ceiling and galleries on three sides. Canon John Pilkington Norris (prime mover in Street's completion of the cathedral) became vicar in 1870 and had the chancel reordered for High Church worship, 1871–6. Made redundant in 1984, St George was saved from a planned office conversion when the BBC remarked its near-perfect acoustic and commissioned a concert-hall conversion, admirably achieved by *Ferguson Mann* in 1985. Italianate marble sanctuary fittings by *G.E. Street* and *Foster & Wood*, of the 1870s reordering, were put in storage and replaced with a stage. *Sir Arthur Blomfield*'s painted **reredos** of 1876 remains. Brick-vaulted **crypt**, now performers' facilities, foyer, bar and restaurant.

Whitson Street

Now R.C. church of the Little Brothers of Nazareth.

St James's Priory was founded before 1134 by Robert Earl of Gloucester as a cell of the Benedictine Abbey of Tewkesbury. The nave became a parish church in 1374; the monastic E end was converted to a large house at the Reformation. The body of the present church consists of five C12 bays from the nave of the Benedictine church.

The lower part of the W **front** [45] is of red rubble stone, with ashlar limestone above. Across the centre is a clever device: an interlaced arcade with every third column omitted, and three round-arched windows in the wider intersections thus formed. The ends are resolved with lancet arches. Above, an unusual and early wheel window, perhaps *c.* 1160, now badly weathered. Eight circular openings frame a central octagon, with rope interlacing and a chevron band. The gable lancet is C19. The S aisle and tower may be late C14 or C15, with later alterations. A print of 1630 at the British Museum shows both substantially in their present forms. The building of a new tower was a condition of the grant of parochial use in 1374. It has two ashlar faces and two (N and E) of rubble, and a Bristol Perp spirelet. S porch and upper vestry room by *James Foster*, 1802–3, in a well-observed Perp Gothic for its date, though, of course, not archaeological.

Inside, a wide nave with five-bay Norman arcades of sturdy circular piers with four attached shafts at the cardinal points, and multi-scalloped capitals. Round arches of stepped square profile, with a roll

45. St James, W front, largely of the C12

in one angle, and outer mouldings of lozenges and billets. Simple clerestory openings. The E wall, with high triple window and Romanesque blind arcades (the two tiers handled quite differently and very awkward-looking), dates entirely from *S.C. Fripp*'s restoration, 1846. N aisle added 1864 by *Popes & Bindon*, to support the leaning nave arcade. It is now divided into a narrow aisle and a church room. Aberdeen granite piers with shaft-rings and broad foliate capitals. The nave and s aisle have open timber roofs, both with corbel heads perhaps of the late C15. In the s aisle, a bizarre corbel – half woman, half pig.

Fittings. Simple **altar** of three Portland stone slabs, 1990s. – Neo-Norman **font** probably by *Popes & Bindon*, 1864. – Stuart **royal arms** over the w door. – For the **glass**, the E windows have very bright geometric patterning, 1846. Two s aisle windows by *Joseph Bell & Son*, 1900 and 1909.

Monuments. From the s aisle working E to w: good pictorial brass to Henry Gibbes (d.1636), his wife and eight children, in stone frame with strapwork. – Bust of Thomas Biddulph by *E.H. Baily*, 1842. In the s wall a stone effigy reputedly of Robert Earl of Gloucester (d.1142), but with elegant linear drapery derived from the w front sculpture at Wells Cathedral, thus probably early C13. – Thomas Edwards, d.1727, by *Michael Sidnell*, a Corinthian design closely related to Rysbrack's Innys monument at St John, *see* below. – Mary Edwards d.1736, possibly also by *Sidnell*, and influenced by James Gibbs – w wall, Sir James Russell d.1674, first governor of Nevis, with martial motifs. – Henry Dighton, d.1673, probably by the same mason.

St John the Baptist
Broad Street

The last survivor of four churches that sat astride the city gates. A church existed here in 1174; the present Perp building dates from *c.* 1350–1500, with full crypt and superb Jacobean fittings. It picturesquely frames the view up Broad Street.

Embattled late C14 tower and elegant spire with roll-moulded angles, over the arched **city gate**, with portcullis slot and unusually elaborate vaulting. Side-arches for pedestrians added in 1828. On the s face are **statues**, possibly C17, representing Brennus and Bellinus, legendary founders of Bristol. Between them, the arms of the City and Merchant Venturers, and the Stuart royal arms above. Embattled nave and chancel atop the line of the town wall, cramped by surrounding buildings. On the N side is the outlet of St John's Conduit (1866), which has flowed since 1376 via a C13 conduit from Brandon Hill. The outlet was moved here in 1827 from the s side, its former site now occupied by the entrance to the church.

Interior. Late C14 six-bay nave, aisleless and unclerestoried, with simple timber roof. Tall Perp recessed windows with continuous arch mouldings, divided by wall-shafts; seen in perspective they ripple and dissolve, giving the nave an expansive air. Unusually, the E nave bay has

46. St John the Baptist, C14 crypt looking E

its own transept-like clerestory that lit the rood screen; another was formerly at St Thomas the Martyr (q.v.) before its C18 rebuilding. Graceful moulded chancel arch and two-bay chancel; vestry beyond lit by a N oriel.

Furnishings. Complete set of **pews**, *c.* 1621, altered in the C19. Not yet of box type. – **Communion table** (1635), with stretchers, gadrooned top rail, five tapered columnar legs and the sixth, the central front leg, a caryatid with a chalice. – C17 **communion rails**, square uprights with drops of foliage and fruit, and spiral turned columns between. – **Reading desks** made or perhaps remade in the C19, incorporating C17 double-arched panels that were part of a screen in the crypt until at least the 1820s. – Over the chancel arch, the **royal arms** of George I. – Late C17 brass **lectern** on baluster stem with acanthus decoration. – Early C18 wrought-iron **sword rest**. – C19 **pulpit** on the S side. – Unusual cruciform **font**, 1624, on scrolled legs with claw feet, cherubs' heads and rosettes on the square body, and an open **cover** of curved stays with a dove. – Late C17 W **gallery** with seven arched panels containing C18 paintings of saints in Dutch style. Below, fine late C16 carved **doors**, incorporated into a later screen. **Stained glass**. N chancel window by *Joseph Bell*, 1957. Christ with St John the Baptist and St

Lawrence. Some medieval fragments high in the nave. **Monuments**. Tomb-chest to the church's patron Walter Frampton d.1388, a very fine alabaster civilian effigy with angels, and a dog at his feet. – Brass to Thomas Rowley and his wife, *c.* 1478. – Wall tablet to Andrew Innys d.1723, by *Rysbrack*.

Crypt. A rare rib-vaulted crypt [46], entered independently from the N side. Built in two parts, the older at the E, but both C14. The chapel of the medieval Guild of the Holy Cross, it was perhaps partly independent of the church above. E part three bays long. Wall-shafts with moulded capitals supporting tierceron star vaults; each bay of vaulting is domed, giving an undulating movement to the whole. Wider two-bay W part, perhaps *c.* 1380, with vaults of more fanciful plan, the same as the crypt at St Nicholas (*see* p. 105). Defaced **piscina** on s wall. – **Monuments**. Late medieval alabaster tomb-chest to unknown merchant and ten children (represented in the panels). – Thomas and Chrystina White, d.1542, a flat slab with incised cross, under a Dec ogee canopy with crockets and pinnacle.

St Mark (or the Lord Mayor's Chapel)
College Green

A monastic foundation instituted by Maurice de Gaunt in 1220 (the church completed *c.* 1230) and transformed by his nephew Robert de Gournay into **The Gaunt's Hospital**. In 1541 it was granted to the Corporation for £1,000. Used as a Huguenot chapel from 1687 until 1722, when it became the official Corporation church. Still the only church in England owned and used for worship by a local authority.

The original chapel was unaisled, cruciform and oriented NE–SW. The nave was later extended to the ritual s. Alterations of *c.* 1830 were largely undone in 1889 by *J.L. Pearson*, who rebuilt the N transept and made a new W entrance with flanking blind arcades in the E.E. style. Of the exterior only the W front, parts of the s side and tower are visible. In the gabled W end a big eight-light window, grouped 3:2:3, with a twelve-petalled rose window above. It is seemingly a C15 modernization of a C13 idea. The fabric is however a replica of *c.* 1830. Lower s aisle gable with an early C14 three-light W window overladen with ballflower ornament. At the SE, a tower of coral-pink sandstone with pale limestone dressings, diagonal buttresses and Bristol spirelet. We know from a mason's inscription that 'In the yer off our Lorde god MCCCC LXXX VII [1487] the III Day of Novemb the masonry off thys Tower was fynyshyd.'

Interior. A narrow nave of *c.* 1230, with original three-stepped lancet windows (two being replicas by *Pearson*). Slightly cambered timber roof, *c.* 1500, panelled, with deep moulded beams and stylized and gilded foliate bosses. Impressive Perp chancel rebuilt *c.* 1500 by Bishop Miles Salley, all the lacy detail subordinated to a strictly rectilinear composition. Unusually three-dimensional four-seat **sedilia** and **piscina**, *c.* 1500. At the SW, two arches with double wave mouldings dying against an octagonal central pier. They open into the s **aisle** added in *c.* 1280, with three blocked Geometric Dec windows on its s wall. At the E, a panelled Perp arch leads to a lower s **aisle chapel**, of *c.* 1510. Panelled roof with Tudor rose and portcullis bosses, and four-light Tudor-arched s windows separated by elaborate canopied niches. E again, but only accessible from the chancel, the base of the tower forms the entrance to the **Poyntz Chapel**, added in 1523 for a chantry to Sir Robert Poyntz, d.1520. Fan-vaulted in two bays with the arms of the Poyntz family and Henry VIII and Catherine of Aragon in the bosses. Eight elaborate canopied niches around the walls, and a pair of deep recesses in the N wall, possibly confessionals.

Furnishings. **Reredos**, *c.* 1500. Delicate pinnacled frieze, three big niches beneath pierced octagonal domes. Statues *c.* 1917. – **Altar triptych** of the Baptism, Transfiguration and Resurrection, painted by *Malcolm Ferguson*, 1990–1. – **Tiles**, Poyntz Chapel. Highly coloured C16 Spanish floor tiles, probably imported by Poyntz's son, interspersed with some medieval English armorial tiles. – Fine large **sword rest**, made by *William Edney*, 1702, from Temple Church. – **Royal arms** of Charles II on the nave s wall. – In the nave, seven C18 and C19 **hatchments**. – **Wall paintings**. s aisle, three fragmentary early C16 wall paintings on stone, representing the Nativity, Resurrection and Appearance of Christ to Mary Magdalene. – Wrought-iron **gates** to the s aisle chapel, by *Edney*, 1726, also from Temple Church.

Stained glass. The Continental glass, of remarkable quantity and quality, was mostly purchased at the sales of Sir Paul Baghott (Stroud, 1820) and William Beckford (Fonthill, 1823), installed without order and later disordered further. E window, with main lights including SS Catherine and Barbara, French C16. – **Poyntz Chapel**, E window: three C15 bird roundels, and C16 saints from Steinfeld Abbey in the Rhineland, dated 1527. – **Nave** N side, second from the E, much orange-red heraldic glass, 1829; third, C16 French Mannerist glass from Ecouen, with much grisaille. – s side, C16 French Biblical scenes. – s **aisle**, E, St Thomas à Becket, designed by *Benjamin West* for Fonthill, dated 1799. – s **aisle chapel**, twenty-four Flemish C16–C17 roundels, and a squint with C14 roundel of a knight's head.

Monuments. Chancel, N wall: Bishop Miles Salley d.1516. Tomb-chest with thin blank arcading. Tudor arch with openwork spandrels. Frieze of the same design as the reredos. – Sir Maurice d.1464 and Lady Ellen Berkeley. Big tomb-chest with eight blank arches with ogee gables. Big ogee or 'Berkeley arched' canopy with cusps and subcusps; extremely high finial rising above the superstructure.

Nave, N wall: Thomas Harris d.1797. By *William Paty*. Flowery garlands and angel bearing portrait medallion. – Small brass plate of 1666, to William and Anne Searchfield. – NW corner, William Birde d.1590. Unashamedly brash tomb-chest with superstructure on fluted Ionic columns, and frieze of biblical scenes. Caryatids and a shell pediment above, but no effigy. – sw corner, Sir Richard Berkeley d.1604. Recumbent alabaster effigy in court armour.

s **aisle**. NW corner, Thomas James d.1619, Corinthian frame with broken segmental pediment. – W wall, Henry Bengough, by *Sir F. Chantrey*, 1823, a dignified if rather aloof seated profile figure. – s wall, William Hilliard d.1735. By *Thomas Paty*. Big standing wall monument on rusticated base with arched recess. Black sarcophagus flanked by putti, with a good portrait bust. Open pediment and crowning obelisk. – Rare civilian effigy *c.* 1360, placed on a C15 tomb-chest with quatrefoils and shields, under an ogee-arched recess. – John Cookin d.1627. Poignant alabaster of a kneeling schoolboy with his books and pens, in Corinthian frame. – NE corner, Henry Walter d.1737. Architectural tablet with cherubs' heads in the predella. Swan-neck pediment on fluted pilasters. – Late Perp tomb-chest with pointed quatrefoils and shields.

s **aisle chapel**, centre: two effigies of knights, slim and with crossed legs, traditionally (but doubtfully) the founders Maurice de Gaunt d.1230 and Robert de Gournay d.1269. – E wall, Dame Mary Baynton d.1667. Triptych composition with steeply pedimented flanks and domed baldacchino with four obelisks above. Two kneeling sons hold back the draperies of the baldacchino to reveal their mother kneeling awkwardly in a niche. A late, provincial version of a London type developed by Maximilian Colt from *c.* 1615. Strong Mannerist details, e.g. the projecting scrolls beneath the sons. – N wall, John Aldworth d.1615 and his son Francis d.1623, their alabaster effigies kneeling beneath a remarkably late Perp canopy. – Lady Margaret and Sir Baynham Throkmorton, d.1635 and 1664 respectively. Her reclining effigy, cradling an infant, clearly rearranged to make room for his and to effect the addition of their clasped hands. Coloured marble canopy with mutilated angels holding an inscription. – George Upton d.1608. Stiff reclining figure. Arched canopy with excellent strapwork.

St Mary le Port
Castle Park

Hidden behind post-war buildings just E of High Street. One of two Castle Park churches blitzed in 1940. The visible remains are Perp, but excavation (1962–3) revealed late Saxon or early Norman origins. The C15 name Mary le Port indicates proximity to the market.

Intact late C15 three-stage Pennant tower with limestone dressings. Simple Perp windows, arcaded battlements with central niche in each face, taller panelled stair-turret with crocketed spirelet. On the E face are two roof lines; post-war concrete reinforcing to the arch below. Everything else is merely low rubble walls describing a five-bay nave and a N aisle with E chapel. On the N wall, the foundations of a porch. It led to Mary-le-Port Street through C17 houses built over the former churchyard. The stump of a rood-stair-turret survives in the s nave wall. To its E a narrow two-bay chancel with a low door in its s wall. Outside the NE corner is a C16 or later domestic cellar beneath a metal grille.

St Mary on the Quay (R.C.)
Colston Avenue

Designed by *R.S. Pope* in 1839 for the Irvingites, but purchased in 1843 by the Roman Catholics, who added the legend 'VIVAT CHRISTVS REX' in the entablature. An aloof Greek temple on a high base with a richly carved portico of six deeply fluted Corinthian columns [47]. The order is from the Lysicratic monument at Athens, which Pope had also used at Brunel House (*see* Walk 4, p. 198). Pilasters within the portico employ only the upper half of the full capital. Screen walls with channelled rustication. Returns push forward to the pavement, framing symmetrical entrance staircases rising through the plinth. Above the steps, tall blind windows in pilastered frames. The flanks look slightly unconvincing, like theatrical flats drawn round to mask the shabby sides of the building.

The interior is slightly disappointing; a plain box lit by very tall side windows. The only enrichment is the toplit chancel: a narrower recessed bay marked by two columns *in antis*, and backed by pairs of fluted and gilded columns of the same order as those outside. Galleried N transept now arranged as a side chapel and another gallery on cast-iron Doric columns at the ritual w end. Two fittings of unexpected genesis: **altar** with domed tabernacle, *c.* 1900 by *J.F. Bentley*, and **font** by *G.E. Street*, 1860, formerly at St George, Brandon Hill (*see* p. 95).

47. St Mary on the Quay, by R.S. Pope, designed 1839

St Michael on the Mount Without
St Michael's Hill

Now closed. A C15 church built on the steep slopes N of the city and well outside the walls, to serve a growing suburb of merchants' houses on the hill. The raised site has a paved forecourt to the S, screened by trees. Against a Georgian Gothic nave is a late Perp w tower of four stages, with diagonal buttresses and SE stair-turret carrying a spirelet. It was described by William Worcestre in *c.* 1480 as new built. By 1774 the body was crumbling and was rebuilt in 1775–7 by *Thomas Paty*. Five-bay nave of Pennant rubble with thin window-mouldings, etc., quite poverty-stricken. N and S aisles with two-light Y-traceried windows, and short projecting chancel.

Oddly, the interiors are not Gothic. Prominent nave arcades with vaguely Doric columns with fluted necks, supporting flat beams from which springs a plaster tunnel vault over the nave (a post-war replacement after bomb damage). The aisles are flat-ceilinged with beams dividing the bays. – Late Victorian **font**, **reredos** and **pulpit**. – **Monuments**: Joseph Percivall d.1764, three graceful Neoclassical female figures against an obelisk, the central figure holding an oval portrait medallion. Signed *J. Walsh*, London. – Mary Stretton d.1794, by *William Paty*; the usual female figure leaning on an urn. – James Drew d.1835, a Gothic tablet. – **Sword rest**. The date is not known. It probably dates partly from 1683.

St Nicholas
St Nicholas Street

Now City Council premises; not generally open to the public.

Prominently sited N of Bristol Bridge. A church was recorded here by 1154. Its chancel was built out over the S gate to the city. In 1760 plans for a new Bristol Bridge entailed demolishing gate, nave and chancel. *James Bridges*'s new design [48] was begun 1762 on top of the old crypt, the S wall of which incorporates part of the medieval town wall. Following his departure in 1763, it was completed by *Thomas Paty*, 1763–9. Horace Walpole called it 'neat and truly Gothic'. Bridges intended to retain the decayed steeple but Paty replaced it with his own design. The lavish Rococo interior was destroyed by bombing in 1940 and a new interior created by the *City Architect's Department*, 1974–5, for a Church Museum (now closed).

Box-like nave with arcaded parapet and seven bays of five-light windows, probably, as Michael Jenner suggests, the result of observing local Perp examples, and remarkably accurate for their date. The ogee intersecting tracery betrays its C18 origins. Windowless E wall with five spindly buttresses. Paty's w tower and slim elegant spire are every inch C18 Gothic. Clasping pilaster buttresses with Gothic panels, parapet with pinnacles at the angles, and spire rising from within the parapet.

48. St Nicholas, by James Bridges and Thomas Paty, 1760s. Photograph, 1920s

Paired ogee belfry lights with cusped Y-tracery. Octofoil window over an ogee doorway on the N tower flank. Inside, a long, high nave with no remaining C18 features. Deep w balcony, 1974–5.

Some **fittings** remain from its time as a museum.* – **Altar triptych** by *William Hogarth*, 1755–6, on the E dais, painted for St Mary Redcliffe. Depicting the Resurrection and Ascension, in total *c.* 53 ft (16 metres) wide by 28 ft (8.5 metres) high. Large religious work was an unfamiliar genre for Hogarth, who seems to have looked back to Continental models, and particularly the style of Sebastiano Ricci. Frames carved by *Thomas Paty*. – **Sculpture**. Four C14 statues of debated identity, perhaps Edward I and Edward III (from Lawford's Gate), and Bishop Geoffrey of Coutances and Robert Fitzroy (from Newgate). – Very fine oak **pulpit** *c.* 1758, from Cowl Street Unitarian Chapel, Shepton Mallet, Somerset. Hexagonal, on wineglass stem with large tester and flaming urn-finials.

Pevsner called the **crypt** one of Bristol's most precious survivals of medieval church architecture. It housed a chapel of the Holy Cross. Perhaps dating from *c.* 1350–80, it is four bays long and divided by broad piers into a nave and a narrower s aisle. Generously carved vault bosses, mostly foliate but some with heads and C14 costume details. The present NE bay has a central boss depicting Christ crucified, and in the next bay w the Virgin and Child flanked by two praying donors. The whole vault is consistent, each bay a four-pointed star diagonally set around a lozenge. The design is identical with the w bays of St John's

*St Nicholas's lectern, sword rest and gates are at St Stephen's church (q.v.).

crypt (q.v.). The ribs have long concave sides to a narrow ridge, like the secondary ribs at St John. Half hidden at the nave E wall, one arch rib, *c.* 1250, to a wider vault. A further bay existed to the E, presumably the chapel sanctuary. – **Font**. Early C18 baluster shape with octagonal gadrooned bowl. – **Monuments**. John Whitson, d.1629. Shallow standing monument with arched canopy on pilasters topped by pinnacles. Stiff reclining effigy. – Nearby on a C20 plinth, a second effigy of Whitson, by *Clarke*, 1822–3, a close paraphrase.

St Peter

Castle Park

A pre-Conquest foundation, sited s of a Saxon sunken way running w to St Mary le Port. The Norman castle's w wall was *c.* 100 ft (30 metres) E of St Peter. By the C19 the surrounding streets had become the heart of Bristol's old shopping centre. Both district and church were heavily bombed in 1940 and the shopping centre relocated at Broadmead after the war. Castle Park was laid out from the 1970s around St Peter, which is now a memorial to Bristol's civilian war dead [49].

The Pennant rubble walls are particularly varied in colour. Unbuttressed NW tower, with two-light Perp windows in the upper stages; at its base, possibly C11 stonework around the w door. Generous Perp nave and s aisle both *c.* 1400, the aisle with five-light Perp windows between narrow buttresses. High N arcade with slender Perp piers of quatrefoil plan. Narrow N aisle on Norman plan, with a large bullseye window. The E window was blocked, probably for the Baroque reredos (1697) lost in the blitz. The tower and N arcade were consolidated with concrete 1975.

49. St Peter, Castle Park, from the sw

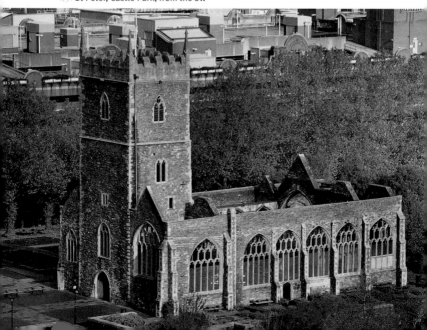

Narrow Plain

SS Philip and Jacob was established before 1174 as the church for a large parish on the E outskirts of Bristol. Of Pennant rubble and sitting low in its churchyard, it retains something of the feel of a country church. Three-gabled nave and aisles. The ramped w gable, pinnacles and battlements are probably of 1764. The two N porches, tall square-headed aisle windows, and big projections N and S for gallery stairs all date from a partial rebuilding by *William Armstrong*, 1837–41. Four-stage s tower with broad clasping buttresses and unshafted E.E. lancets low down, paired shafted lancets above, and Perp top stage with Bristol spirelet. Perp E window.

Interior. An aisled nave, long chancel and N chapel. Perp wagon roof to the nave, with good C15 corbel heads and bosses. Broad arcades, remodelled 1764, when every second pier was removed and segmental arches added. The original cruciform plan is discernible in some fine work of *c*. 1200 around the former transepts. The once-vaulted **tower room** in the s transept has springers on short Purbeck shafts with excellent stiff-leaf capitals. From this transept to the chancel is an arch, now blocked, with moulded capitals and deep keeled roll mouldings. Of the corresponding N transept arch, part of the left jamb remains. The **aisles** were probably added shortly after the transepts were built. The outer face of a good lancet window to the former N transept remains high on the E wall of the N aisle. Offset to the right, an arch with moulded capitals was inserted below to connect with the N aisle. Between the tower room and s aisle a fine, smaller E.E. arch: shafted inner order with capitals of shallow upright foliage, and continuous outer mouldings with deep hollows. This composite design probably derives from Wells school work of *c*. 1200. Its E face respects the tower-room vault springers, so must post-date the vault.

The E end is spatially confused by recent unsympathetic partitions. Long **chancel**, probably essentially C13 but with Perp alterations including the simple wagon roof, and (to the N) blocked four-centred arches to the C15 **Kemys Chapel**, which took in the former N transept and extended E.

Furnishings. Much-restored Norman **font**, square with scalloped underside. Oak **font cover**, 1636 (the later inscription plate is inaccurate): a box-like cage of open arches, then eight big S-scrolls carrying a finial. – **Pulpit**. Oak, *c*. 1630. Octagonal, each face having an arched panel below another with scrolled cartouche. Broad cornice on figure brackets, and later tester. – **Sword rest**. (Now in storage.) Of 1610, the earliest in Bristol. A simple iron rod with flat metal ornaments at three points. – **Stained glass**. E window (Day Memorial), restored by *Godwin & Crisp*, 1865. Glass by *Heaton, Butler & Bayne*, perhaps to designs by *E.W. Godwin*. Remarkably clear figures in purples, pinks and blue. – N chapel, three N windows 1869–*c*. 1875, by *Heaton, Butler & Bayne*. –

N chapel E, one big figure, by *Joseph Bell & Son*, 1937. – S aisle, Dunkirk Veterans window, 1995 by *Sampson & Son* of Bristol. **Monuments**. Many good tablets of *c.* 1750–1850. All below are in the N chapel. SW corner, head of a knight, early C14. – N wall, Henry Merrett d.1692. Big architectural frame of barley-sugar columns, segmental pediment inside swan neck, and half-figure in an oval wreath surrounded by cherubs and skulls. – SE corner, John Foy d.1771, by *James Paty Jun*. Obelisk with a portrait medallion. In the predella, good relief of a woman with children.

St Stephen

St Stephen's Avenue

A fine late Perp church of *c.* 1470 now set among commercial buildings, between The Centre and Corn Street. On the site of a C13 Benedictine cell of Glastonbury Abbey. Here Bristol's C15 mercantile wealth is evident.

The late C15 rebuilding was entirely in ashlar except for the S aisle. At the SW and at a slight angle to the nave, a majestic Somerset-type tower, paid for by the merchant John Shipward. Of four stages increasing in elaboration. Showy openwork crown with angled corner panels, comparable with Dundry and Gloucester Cathedral. Tower and crown have been repaired and refaced several times, most recently the angled panels to the crown in reinforced fibreglass in the 1970s. Good Baroque W door with blocked pilasters and segmental pediment. S porch completed by 1480, with two rows of leaf carvings over deep concave mouldings around the entrance arch, and C20 parapet. Fan-vaulted interior with unusual flat panelled centre.

Interior. A high nave with full-length aisles and no structurally separate chancel, a typical Perp plan form. Elegant piers of diaper plan with concave sides and a thin shaft set in each curve, and angel capitals. Blocked clerestory rood door one bay W of the current chancel. W window possibly *c.* 1540. The arcade mouldings collide with the W wall; was it realigned in the C16? Baptistery beneath the tower; corner springers indicate lost fan-vaulting. Restorations of 1875–98 replaced the roofs, floor, reredos, pulpit, font and all the tracery and glazing except in the W window, without destroying the church's spatial unity. Reredos and E window by *Charles Hansom* (1875); the later restorers not known.

Fittings. Simple stone **altars** in chancel and N aisle by *J. Ralph Edwards*, 1964. – Magnificent wrought-iron **sword rest** by *William Edney*, *c.* 1710, from the blitzed St Nicholas. – N aisle **chapel** of St Nicholas and St Leonard defined by a low screen wall, by *J. Ralph Edwards*, 1958. **Gates**, *c.* 1710, by *Edney*, from St Nicholas. Behind the altar, **statues** of St Nicholas by *Gerald Scott* and St Leonard by *Ernest Pascoe*. – **Pulpit** of 1890, designed by *Pope & Paul*, made by *Harry Hems*. – Splendid late C15 brass eagle **lectern**, from St Nicholas church, on tall

stem with disc-like turnings. – **Organ** by *Nicholson of Malvern*, 1964. – **Stained glass**. E window by *Hardman & Co.*, 1882. *Clayton & Bell* glazed the N aisle (1898), two tower windows (1901), and probably the clerestory (1902–4).

Monuments. s aisle, tomb of Sir George Snygge d.1617, in judge's robes, amid Corinthian columns and much strapwork. – N aisle, three C14 ogee tomb recesses, one with much-restored cusped mouldings. The lower part of this wall must predate the rebuilding. Two contain effigies not designed for them: that at the w reputedly of Edmund Blanket (d.1371) and his wife, on a panelled chest; E, Sir Walter Tyddesley d.1385, resited from the s aisle in the C19. – N of the pulpit, an oval plaque to Martin Pring d.1626, the naïve figured surround embellished 1733 by *William Pugh*. – Robert Kitchin d.1594, a brass plate with kneeling figures, in stone frame.

William Worcestre and an Early Architectural Drawing

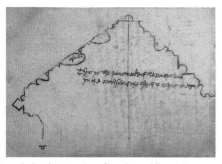

The Bristolian William Worcestre (1415–85) was secretary to Sir John Fastolf of Caister, Norfolk. He returned in 1478 and 1480, compiling a uniquely detailed survey of Bristol's buildings with historical comments, distinct from his better-known *Itineraries*. Worcestre was impressed with St Stephen's porch, noting the 'ingenious . . .

51 St Stephen, section of porch moulding. Late c15 drawing

handiwork of Benet the Freemason' (elsewhere named *Benet Crosse*), and included a precise sectional drawing, probably by Crosse, of the right-hand arch jamb. Worcestre also noted that the tower's foundations are 31 ft (9.4 metres) deep; assuming Crosse told Worcestre this, it may indicate that Crosse masterminded the whole rebuilding. A unified late medieval church, contemporary documentation for its master mason, and an architectural drawing in his hand are a rare combination of survivals.

Further reading: F. Neale (ed.) 'William Worcestre: The Topography of Medieval Bristol', Bristol Record Society vol. 51 (2000).

St Thomas the Martyr
St Thomas Street

Founded before 1200 but extended and rebuilt until, by the c15, it was a Perp church of some magnificence. This was replaced except the tower in 1789–93 by *James Allen*, a local statuary mason little-known as an architect. Its quiet classicism is evidence of Allen's unfulfilled potential. Substantially reordered 1878–80, by *W.V. Gough*; now redundant.

Plain exterior with handsome E end. Neoclassical garlands beneath a shallow pediment, the wall below articulated by a large Venetian motif. A lunette in the arch was replaced with a crass rose window by *Gough*. Ramped parapets link the aisles and nave. c15 three-stage W tower with an unusual combination of clasping and setback buttresses. 'Bristol' spirelet, and diminutive corner pinnacles set inside a pierced parapet, all added 1896–7 by *Gough*. W entrance S of the tower; in the inner doorway two small defaced c15 **statues** from the demolished Burton's Almshouses nearby. Five-bay nave arcade on substantial square piers with tunnel vault penetrated by segmental clerestory windows. Transverse ribs spring from projections to the cornice, supported by Baroque cherubs' heads, the latter perhaps after Redland Chapel. Lower flat-ceilinged aisles, with poor late C19 **stained glass** in arched windows. The nave E bay was reordered as a chancel in 1878, with contemporary **choir stalls** and **altar**. Coffered sanctuary flanked by paired Ionic pilasters with one-winged cherubs squashed into the corners – a most unhappy design that shows Allen's inexperience.

Other fittings. The **woodwork** is the glory of St Thomas, largely C18 and from the previous church. Fine **reredos** of Flemish oak, 1716 by *William Killigrew*, worthy of a Wren church in the City of London.* The two-tier arrangement seems to have been a Bristol speciality. It has garish paintings by *F. von Kamptz*, 1907. The panels, with late C19 Aesthetic Movement painted decoration in leafy C18 frames, are now in the s aisle. – Balustraded **altar rail**. – Dignified Roman Doric **w gallery**, 1728–32, with inlaid clock. – Plain **pulpit** (1740) with gadrooned base; cut down in 1878 from a three-decker. – Wooden **lectern** converted from a font. – Elegant 1790s lunette-plan mahogany **font rail** (s aisle), with tapered supports and lozenge inlays. – **Royal arms**, 1637, an unusually early survival, in a square frame still with strapwork and terms. – **Organ case**, 1728 by *John Harris*, with foliage panels and cherubs' heads. – Stone **font**, s aisle, late C19 Neo-Renaissance style. – Early C17 **sword rest**; square rod with central cage of four flat scrolls.

Temple (or Holy Cross) Church
Temple Street

Gutted 1940. The Knights Templar built an oval church here *c*. 1150 (revealed by excavation), a variation on the circular model in London and elsewhere. Either just before or just after the suppression of the Templars in 1312, the church was rebuilt on a rectangular plan: the lost nave arcade and parts of the E end were probably from this building campaign.

Dramatically leaning tower (now *c*. 5 ft, 1.5 metres, out of true), begun *c*. 1390 [52]. Despite the subsidence, a third stage was added *c*. 1460; the corrected angle is obvious from the s. Frieze of cusped triangles below two fretted 'Somerset' belfry lights, separated by a shaft rising from the belfry-stage stringcourse. Offset buttresses die into insignificant pinnacles below the parapet, giving a monumental flat-topped tower. The parapet and pinnacles that were presumably intended were never added; the masons must have lost their nerve. At the tower base three delicate Perp statue niches. Baroque NW door with big segmental pediment. Embattled N and s aisles with large early Perp windows. Rood-stair turret on the s, and further E a finely framed late C17 memorial, now much weathered; another is hidden high within the tower. Dec traceried E windows.

---

*The only survivor, and the best, of eight C18 reredoses in Bristol. Others were at Bristol Cathedral, St Mary le Port, St James, St Peter, St Stephen, Temple and St Nicholas.

52. Temple Church, tower, begun c. 1390, upper stage c. 1460

Five-bay nave with quatrefoil piers (the arcades now dismantled).
Very long chancel with shorter flanking chapels, that on the N for the
Weavers' Guild. Early C14 Dec windows in the E end, including, in the N
chapel, square-headed windows of four cusped lights beneath convex-
sided triangles. In the S chapel and throughout the nave, good Perp
windows.*

*Some furnishings survive elsewhere. St Mark – gates (from the parclose screens at Temple
Church), and sword rest, both by *William Edney*, early C18; Berkeley Chapel, Bristol
Cathedral – C15 candelabrum; Holy Cross church, Inns Court (not included in this volume)
– C18 font.

City Centre

(Area bounded by St James Barton roundabout (N); Bristol Bridge (E); the Council House (SW); and Bristol Royal Infirmary (NW))

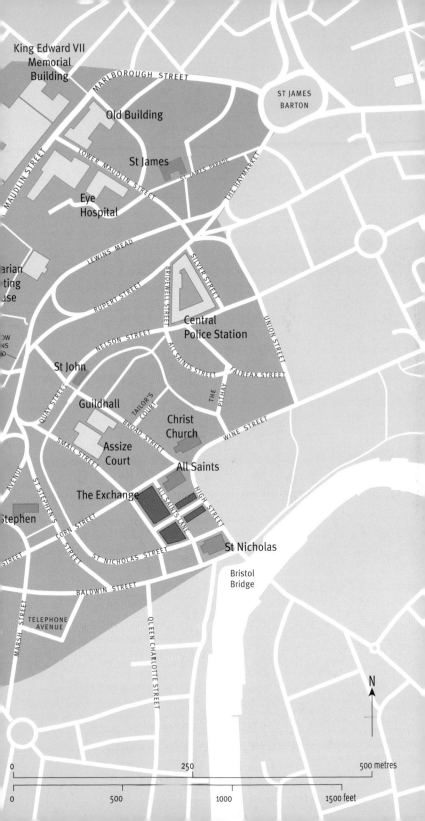

A dense and disparate assemblage: intact areas of historic buildings survive around College Green and Corn Street, and a few in the hospital quarter, N. In between, poor post-war offices around Lewins Mead, which runs s to The Centre, once an arm of the harbour. No walk route is offered: streets are dealt with alphabetically.

All Saints Lane

A narrow alley running SE off Corn Street on the E side of the Exchange. s of All Saints' church is **All Saints' Court**, with modest early C18 town houses of brick. Then *Oatley & Lawrence*'s **All Saints' House** of 1903, mildly Arts and Crafts and pleasingly done. Red granite plinth contrasting with ochre-coloured Ham stone which has weathered to reveal sedimentary layering. Beyond is the Market Tavern (*see* Major Buildings: Exchange, p. 80).

All Saints Street, Including The Pithay and Fairfax Street

To the w of Union Street is a small area on steep slopes, historically just outside the E line of the town walls. The whole area was redeveloped with office blocks in the 1960s. **The Pithay**, a steep lane of medieval origin, was formerly the site of Fry's chocolate factories, and before that, C17 and earlier timber-framed merchants' houses. The River Frome is carried in a C19 culvert running roughly beneath **Fairfax Street**, the E end of which disappears beneath the Galleries shopping centre. Excavation in 2000 for shops w of Union Street revealed early medieval riverside houses here. Opposite, Tower House (*Wakeford*, *Jerram & Harris*, 1966) dominates. **All Saints Street** is defined by a monolithic curve of concrete at Pithay House by *R.S. Redwood & Associates*, 1966. Both demonstrate the architectural manner that mesmerized Bristol's post-war planners and builders.

Baldwin Street

Baldwin Street is a busy route running w from Bristol Bridge to The Centre; the E end is early medieval, and originally curved N along present-day St Stephen's Street, outside the town wall. The w extension towards The Centre was opened in 1881, with major redevelopment along the whole street *c.* 1880–1900. The central section around the junction with Queen Charlotte Street suffered Second World War bomb damage, and was redeveloped again *c.* 1950–70.

Starting from The Centre. On the N side, No. 2 Clare Street and Nos. 1–5 Baldwin Street are described under Clare Street (p. 127). At Nos. 2–12, opposite, the whole block is taken up by the former Dunlop & Mackie's shop, 1879, by *John Bevan*. In brown brick with repetitive pedimented dormers; the monotony underscored by the loss of its

53. *Overleaf* City Centre

original riot of chimneys, turrets and cupolas. Continuing the s side, E of Marsh Street, Nos. 14–16, *Edward Gabriel*'s **Edinburgh Chambers** of 1896–8. A façade of Baroque projections and recessions, with surprisingly tough blocked and rusticated ground floor and a curved corner topped by a copper dome. It has none of Gabriel's customary vernacular detail. Then Nos. 18–24, originally for **Refuge Assurance** (now O'Neill's Bar), 1926 by *Stanley Birkett* of Manchester, their house architect. The last gasp of classicism, with Portland stone marking the infiltration of metropolitan standards. Recessed centre above the ground floor, with pairs of stocky Doric columns, flanking shallower recesses with quarter-pilasters, and chunky blocked attics. Next, No. 26, built *c.* 1896 for the Inland Revenue (hence the royal monogram in the entrance pediment).*

On the N side between Marsh Street and St Stephen's Street is the **People's Palace**, a variety theatre of 1892 by *James Hutton* for the Livermore Brothers, theatrical impresarios (hence LB in the fanciful central aedicule). It was successively music hall, cinema, dance hall and now nightclub. Unfortunately, the façade has been whitewashed. The blank upper storeys, now rendered and incised like stone, carried the words 'People's Palace' emblazoned in light on dark brick. Giant Ionic pilasters, added in the mid C20 to disguise blocked side windows, stop mid-wall, supporting nothing. Next door, standard Late Victorian offices at Nos. 23–25, **Carlton Chambers** by *Thomas Lysaght* (1884), of red brick with stone dressings.

In the central section of Baldwin Street, the spirits are dampened by a series of mediocre post-war offices, such as New Minster House (Nos. 27–29) at the junction with St Stephen's Street, by *Alec French & Partners*, 1965. On the s side, the Queen Charlotte Street junction is dominated by the sweeping curve of **Bridge House**, 1961, also by *Alec French & Partners*, every window and bay treated with scrupulous equality, avoiding anything that might give focus to the design. Part of this site was occupied by the medieval Back Hall. The N side E of St Stephen's Street is typical late Victorian commercial. The first and largest is the façade to the **Fish Market**, an addition of 1897 to the earlier market building on St Nicholas Street. Usually given to *W.B. Gingell* on uncertain grounds, but looking more like W.V. Gough's Loire Renaissance style with much elaborate carving. Then Nos. 59–63, by *Gingell*, 1894, formerly Bigwood's fish merchants, now a pub. The red and yellow brick typifies Gingell's later work. The street widens at the approach to Bristol Bridge, where until 1844 a fish market obstructed the roadway. St Nicholas dominates here (*see* City Churches, p. 104).

---

*In **Telephone Avenue** is Armada House, by *Henry Williams*, 1902, formerly the Bristol Water Works offices, and rarely accessible. It contains two much older chimneypieces. That in the hall has Ionic herms and strapwork in the overmantel, perhaps late C16. On the first floor is another of *c.* 1620, with rich strapwork and Ionic and Corinthian columns. The overmantel bears a later cartouche, A.M.E 1700, denoting Abraham and Mary Elton. Both chimneypieces came here in 1902 from the Eltons' house, No. 7 Small Street (demolished).

54. One Bridewell Street, by Alec French Partnership, 1987

Bridewell Street

Named from the old Bridewell prison, demolished *c.* 1878 for the disused **Police Courts** by *Josiah Thomas*, 1879, E of the street. Large porch of flattened Renaissance design. Iron railings and gates influenced by the Aesthetic Movement. The building is now surrounded on three sides by the Police and Fire Station (*see* Nelson Street). At the junction with Rupert Street is **One Bridewell Street**, *Alec French Partnership*, 1987, built for Ernst & Young [54]. L-shaped six-storey block with an angled glass foyer set in the return. White rain-screen panels with scarlet details, relieving the grey monotony around.

Bristol Bridge

The reason for the modern settlement of Bristol, and once the only crossing over the River Avon from Bristol to Redcliffe and the road to Bath. *James Bridges* designed the present structure in 1757–60, but the Corporation's indecision, and bitter disputes over alternative designs advanced by others, caused Bridges's departure in 1763. The bridge was built by *Thomas Paty*, 1764–7, on the pier foundations of the previous C13 bridge. An elliptical central arch is flanked by two semicircular ones. The long-and-short voussoirs and domed tollhouses were based on Westminster Bridge of 1750. The tollhouses were demolished for a widened deck standing on paired Doric columns, by *T.S. Pope*, 1861 and later, obscuring the arches beneath. A 1960s steel parapet completes the desecration.

The SE side of The Centre, and something of a hotchpotch. At the N end, Nos. 1–6 of 1830, possibly a refronting of C18 buildings, with later shopfronts. s towards the harbour, the **Bristol & West Building**, by *Alec French & Partners* (1967–8). Seventeen storeys of henge-like granite-chipped concrete with an open, loggia-like top floor. Its first-floor banking hall, originally with access from outside, is a remnant of 1960s plans for pedestrian decks over The Centre. The grid-like elevations seem clumsy by comparison with the Colston Centre visible to the N (*see* Colston Avenue). To the s, the lower Bristol & West **Extension Building** by the same architects, instructive of the shift in national and local planning policy in the 1970s towards a more contextual approach. With guidance from planners, a grey concrete rotunda proposed in 1973 evolved into the present dark brick polygon approved in 1980. Contextual references include windows in recessed panels, a leaded mansard roof with cupola and gilded weathervane, and decorative concrete panels with the City arms. On its Prince Street side is a bronze **statue** of I.K. Brunel, by *John Doubleday*, 1981–2.

Broad Street slopes picturesquely NW from Christ Church to the medieval city gate at St John (*see* City Churches, pp. 94, 98). It is one of the main streets of the late Saxon town. Broad Street gives a good sense of the narrow, enclosed character of the old city. The crashing post-war intrusions of Lewins Mead and the University buildings rear up behind St John.

We begin at the s end, w side. Nos. 5–8 is of uncertain origin. The details match *Sir Robert Smirke*'s adjoining Old Council House (*see* Corn Street), and Smirke designed a shop on this site, but that was only two windows wide. The present building may be late C19, perhaps an extended rebuilding of Smirke's structure. Then **Holbeck House**, originally for North British & Mercantile Insurance. By *Sir Frank Wills*, 1911, proving that he had in full measure the Edwardian aptitude for putting on a good show, here a blend of Baroque and Neoclassical motifs. A broad first-floor bow with a Diocletian window above. Wrought-iron clock bracket. Then a narrow building of 1843, which provided a Broad Street entrance to Albion Chambers, built by 1833 and previously entered only from Small Street. The doorway and a narrow window occupy the full width of the building, which nevertheless manages framing Corinthian columns. Above, two storeys of tripartite windows topped by a pediment. Decorative refinement carries the day.

At Nos. 13–14, the former **Branch Bank of England** [55] by *Charles Cockerell*, a design of exceptional panache and subtlety, whilst maintaining the *gravitas* necessary to a national institution. Bristol in the C18 and C19 rarely looked to outside architects, but here it had no say. In 1844 the Bank commissioned branches for Manchester, Bristol and Liverpool from its official architect. They conform to the same general

mould: two storeys with superimposed Doric columns, then an attic storey between entablature and pediment. Contract drawings for Bristol were completed early in 1846; uniquely of the three it had to be slotted into a continuous building line. It is set back a few feet to give some visual separation. Channelled return walls create a sense of enclosure, reinforced by projecting porches. Scholarly and correct Doric columns frame windows divided by firm grids of stone and a band of Greek key ornament. By the 1840s Cockerell had moved away from his pure Grecian training to a Graeco-Roman idiom, evident in the break-back of the pediment cornice and the arcaded attic recessed behind railings over the entablature. Little remains of Cockerell's interiors and the building is now empty.

On the other (NE) side of the street, the **Grand Hotel** [15] (now Thistle Hotel) commands the block. By *Foster & Wood*, 1864–9, and one of Bristol's most persuasive Victorian buildings. Pevsner called it 'a cool but competent essay in the Venetian Quattrocento'. Originally designed as a five-storey block with lower flanks, but only one flank was built, and the centre was given a loggia with free-standing columns below a massive bracketed cornice. The ground floor is fronted by what were originally shops – allowing the building to stand back from the street line and carry off its bulk. The lower pilastered block effects the transition to Christ Church next door (p. 94).

At No. 51, NE side, the **Avon Insurance** building by *Ponton & Gough*, 1868, although Ponton was probably the chief designer. An exercise in

polychromatic Gothic by an underrated architect, and a precursor to his Welsh Back Granary begun the following year. Middle Pointed arches on the first floor, embellished with much carving, paired shouldered arches on the second floor, and a miniature arcade to the attic. Full-width sashes set behind stone arcading. The ribbed tooling of the attic stonework gives a Ruskinian emphasis to the wall surfaces. No. 50, Hort's pub, is C18 with sturdy segmental arches on the ground floor, of *c.* 1870. Pevsner questioned whether it is Free Gothic or Free Renaissance. Perhaps it is better left as simply High Victorian.

Returning to the sw side, the **Guildhall** by *R.S. Pope*, 1843–6, is the earliest Perpendicular Gothic Revival town hall built in England [56]. A long three-storey façade with higher central tower and oriel, three symmetrically placed entrances under four-centred arches. Perpendicular Gothic was perhaps chosen to echo the previous C15 Guildhall, and with Barry's Houses of Parliament and New College, Oxford (1842), in mind. However, the oriel projects on very un-Perp curved brackets instead of the robustly moulded published design: and the odd extension of the hoodmoulds to the side gates, the round-arched parapet openings, and the wilful lines of the stringcourse around the tower all suggest a classicist's attempt at Perp. The window tracery at least seems convincing. Good sculptures of Bristol figures by *John Thomas* on the façade. Its predecessor was by 1843 no longer the seat of local government, housing only the mayor's parlour, quarter sessions, assizes and occasional Corporation business such as elections. But Pope's building was harshly criticized at the time for being too small, badly planned, ill-lit and poorly ventilated. Most of the interiors except the main staircase have been modernized. (One of the courts reportedly has a fine Jacobean chimneypiece dated 1626, from Welsh Back.)

The lower end of the w side has mainly c18 façades, with plentiful five-stepped voussoirs, and at No. 26 a rich shopfront, late c19. No. 27 was seemingly built as a music hall, looking quite Edwardian despite its indisputable appearance in a photograph c. 1865–70. A narrow façade, big arched entrance and loosely classical. Opposite is a good mix of c18 and c19 building, now mainly offices. At No. 43, a rare survival of a c15 dwelling, refronted in the late c18. Walk through the alley at the left into **Tailor's Court**. The rear elevation here has two jetties and probably original fenestration patterns; truncated timbers suggest there may once have been an oriel window. On the ground floor is a narrow doorway with two-centred arch and moulded surround, and two small mutilated c15 stone figures set in the wall. Also in Tailor's Court on the left side is the former **Merchant Tailors' Hall**, 1740–1, now apartments. A single-depth plan with large guild hall expressed in a simple front of five big sash windows with alternating pediments, and a door at the E end. Attributed to *William Halfpenny*, whose Coopers' Hall, King Street, and No. 40 Prince Street (demolished) employed similar proportions. Ison's proposal that the fine shell-hood with the Tailors' arms and head of St John the Baptist is reset earlier work (perhaps from the Tailors' previous hall) is plausible. Bristol was not so backward as to make new work of this character in 1740.

Further up, SE side, is **Court House** of 1692, built for James Freeman whose initials are on the shell-hood. A provincial design for this date, but Bristol's later c17 artisan classicism was still backward-looking. Three storeys of cross-windows with c20 leaded casement lights, and inside, a staircase with twisted balusters and two principal rooms with early c18 panelling. Its Norman rear wall survives from an adjoining c12 hall to the SE (demolished 1859). At the end of Tailor's Court, **St John's Churchyard**, consecrated 1409. Tomb to Hugh Browne, died 1653, with crude effigies beneath a Late Georgian arch-fronted shelter, perhaps formerly at St John.

Returning to Broad Street, at the bottom of the NE side, the extraordinary **Everard's Printing Works**, 1900–1 [57]. Onto an architectural shell by *Henry Williams* is grafted a polychrome vision in Carrara-ware faience by *Doulton & Co.*'s chief designer *W.J. Neatby*. In the first storey are depicted Gutenberg (spelt 'Gutenburg' in the tiling) and William Morris, who revived craft printing in the 1890s, each with his typeface, presided over by the Spirit of Literature. Above them a figure bearing a lamp and mirror represents Light and Truth. Edward Everard's name appears in the typeface he designed, with 'EE' in repoussé copper surmounting the wrought-iron gates (one a recent copy after a theft). Of

57. Former Everard's Printing Works, by H. Williams and W.J. Neatby, 1900–1

the architecture, radial voussoirs and octagonal turrets with dumpy columns and helmet-like caps perhaps derive from C. Harrison Townsend's early plans for Whitechapel Art Gallery (1896), as may the deeply coved entrance arch. Unfortunately the interiors were demolished for **National Westminster Court** by *Alec French Partnership*, 1972, which weaves through the site behind Broad Street. It owes its present form to negotiation with the client and architect by the Council's Development Control officer, changing the proposed design to preserve the medieval street pattern NE of Broad Street. The drab concrete is a poor foil to Neatby's tilework. Finally No. 35, a handsome three-storey house, dated 1711 on the rainwater head. The jettied ground floor suggests this is a remodelling of a timber-framed house perhaps of the C17. Good early C19 shopfront with Greek key ornament.

Geography of the 1240 Frome Diversion

58. The Quay, detail from Jacob Millerd's map, 1673

By 1240 Bristol's harbour capacity was inadequate, so a new channel, St Augustine's Reach, was dug to divert the River Frome southward. The huge undertaking took seven years to complete. The new quay took large vessels that traded with France and the Mediterranean. The old port s of Bristol Bridge became known as The Back (later Welsh Back), and dealt mainly in inland and coastal trade with the West Country, Wales and Ireland. The increased port capacity was probably partly responsible for Bristol's economic boom in the following century.

The Quay enabled ships to moor right in the heart of the town. In 1739, Alexander Pope described the scene: 'in the middle of the street, as far as you can see, hundreds of ships, their Masts as thick as they can stand by one another, which is the oddest sight imaginable. This street is fuller of them, than the Thames from London Bridge to Deptford'. By the C19 the bridge at the quay head was a bottleneck and, inevitably, the process was reversed by culverting the N end (which became Colston Avenue) in 1892. The space thus created became Bristol's transport hub (as it still is) and was called the Tramways Centre – soon shortened to The Centre. A further section s from Baldwin Street was culverted in 1937–9.

The Centre

On conventional street maps this does not exist, being composed of St Augustine's Parade, Colston Avenue and Broad Quay. Ask any Bristolian for directions to one of these and they will probably look blank; but everyone will be able to direct you to 'The Centre'. The buildings are described under their respective street names, while the statues, public spaces, etc., down the middle are described below.

The question 'Where is the centre of Bristol?' is still much debated. It is not a question of points on a map, but of an emotional heart perceived by Bristolians. Until the Second World War, it was undoubtedly the shopping centre around Wine Street and Castle Street (now Castle Park). With the removal of the shopping precinct to Broadmead, that focus was lost. The Centre sits between the commercial core, the harbour and College Green, yet is part of none of them and has no major public buildings. It is however the focus of Bristol's nightlife and entertainment. Like the Tin Man, Bristol may find one day that The Centre is the heart it had all along.

The N end of The Centre is laid out with low walls and trees around the **Cenotaph** (unveiled remarkably late, 1932), a competition win by the obscure local firm of *Heathman & Blacker*. Predictably it follows Lutyens's Whitehall model. Decorated with the city arms, regimental medallions and a wreath over a sword. At the s end of Colston Avenue is a **drinking fountain** of 1893, moved here 1901. Of grey and red granite with brass mountings, commemorating an Industrial and Fine Arts Exhibition held 1892–3. Further s is the **statue** of Edward Colston by *John Cassidy*, 1895. Bronze plaques on the plinth, an early manifestation of Art Nouveau in Bristol. Colston (1636–1721), the city's most famous benefactor, invested in the Royal African Company and profited significantly from slavery. Suggestions that the statue be removed as an acknowledgement of Bristol's shameful role in the slave trade have not been followed, but the city has made other gestures, e.g. Pero's Bridge (*see* Walk 5, p. 201). s again, the bronze **statue** of Edmund Burke by *J.H. Thomas*, 1894.[*]

The deeply controversial **Centre remodelling**, debated since the early 1990s, was completed in 2000, replacing municipal flowerbeds to a design by the *Concept Planning Group*. Against a strong local desire to reinstate the open waters of the River Frome (*see* topic box, facing), this or any other scheme was bound to face difficulties. There are too many changes of texture and surface, and it was let down in execution by problems of access and safety. The supposedly synchronized fountains and beacons often do not work. If The Centre's revival has not yet captured Bristol's heart, people have nevertheless voted with their feet: it is a much-used public space, where open water would have created another barrier to movement.

[*]Douglas Merritt of the Public Monuments and Sculpture Association points out the common C20 fallacy that it is a replica of William Theed's at the Palace of Westminster. That was the original intent but Thomas's design won the day.

From N to S, opposite Baldwin Street is *Ferguson Mann*'s octagonal mast-and-sail structure (*c.* 1997). Then a vigorous lead **statue** of Neptune, cast by *John Randall* in 1722. The date and spelling on the plaque are wrong. In the C18 he was painted in naturalistic colours; his later bronze coating was replaced by battleship-grey paint at his fifth and latest resiting in 2000. The landscaping mixes cobbled, paved and decked surfaces. Three shallow pools with angled water jets, and to their w ten illuminated metal **Millennium Beacons** by *Martin Richman* striding in line to the harbour, where the pools finish in a stepped cascade.

Christmas Steps

An alley running uphill from Lewins Mead to Colston Street [59]. Much photographed and painted for its picturesque streetscape, largely of C17–C19 vernacular buildings, some of them doubtless timber-framed behind later façades. It narrows considerably from top to bottom, exaggerating its plunging perspective when viewed from above. At the top an arrangement of seats in niches, six each side, rebuilt 1881. Above the s side, we are told that Christmas Steps was 'steppered, done & finished September 1669' at the expense of Jonathan Blackwell, sometime Sheriff of Bristol and alderman of London.

On the s side, the basement of Foster's Almshouses (*see* Colston Street) has a range of shops of 1883 by *Foster & Wood*, with massively hewn round arches on stumpy chamfered sandstone columns. No. 5, s side, has two small C17 figure sculptures mounted on the first floor, removed from the Merchant Venturers' Hall. At the bottom, the Three Sugar Loaves pub, built as a bakery *c.* 1747–8, in an old-fashioned manner with hipped tiled roofs, deep wooden cornice and flush-framed sashes. Heavily restored *c.* 1980 after reaching total dereliction.

Clare Street

Created 1771–5 by *Thomas Paty* to link Corn Street with Broad Quay, requiring the demolition of St Leonard's church astride its medieval city gate. A few of Paty's original houses (e.g. No. 10) survive with alterations. On the corner of St Stephen's Street, the former **Scottish Provident Institution** is a beautiful small office building of 1903 given grandeur by its dome and subtly overscaled Baroque twin façades with giant Ionic columns. Immaculately detailed, as one would expect from *Oatley & Lawrence*. At the corner with St Stephen's Street, s side, No. 28 Clare Street by *Henry Crisp*, 1883, was the company offices of George White, a Bristol entrepreneur in railways and trams. Prodigiously wealthy already at twenty-nine, White wanted everyone to know it with this flashy design overburdened with Renaissance trim and ranks of dormers. Two doors down, No. 24 shows *W.B. Gingell* still reworking Ruskinian Gothic themes as late as 1890, suggesting his, or his client's, inertia.

Further down, the orange terracotta of **Prudential Building** (1899), one of twenty-four commissions by their house architect *Alfred Waterhouse* [60]. In the Loire-chateau style, with turreted corners.

59. Christmas Steps, c17 and later

Massive central chimneystacks and steep pyramid roof emphasize its height and compactness. Rough-hewn green slate contrasts with the terracotta. Opposite to the w is No. 15 Clare Street, the **County Fire Office**, 1889 (now a fast-food restaurant). *E. Henry Edwards* drew freely on Norman Shaw and much else, with an unusual arcaded gallery in the attic. *The Builder* called it 'picturesque and satisfactory'.

Beyond St Stephen's Avenue, s side, the former Capital & Counties Bank (now a bar). Little survives of the narrow building of 1883 by *Frederick Mew* of London; the current appearance was determined by *R.M. Drake*, 1895, with a widened Neoclassical revival façade, extended E in 1924 by *Benjamin Wakefield*. At No. 2 Clare Street, *Charles Hansom*

ably furnished the tight corner to Baldwin Street with a shop and offices in 1881, richly carved in a hybrid Loire-Renaissance style with pilasters and portrait roundels. Opposite, the uninteresting back of **Sun Alliance House** (*Wakeford, Jerram & Harris*, 1972) mars the approach to Broad Quay.

College Green

College Green is framed to the w by the Council House and to the s by Bristol Cathedral. (For the cathedral, Central Library and Council House, *see* Major Buildings, pp. 50, 75, 73). The Green's roughly triangular shape describes the precinct of St Augustine's Abbey before the Reformation. Before College Green was levelled for the Council House in 1950, it was somewhat higher, being the top of a low hill with slopes down toward The Centre and a steep gully dividing it from Brandon Hill.

Climbing the curved approach from The Centre, the cathedral and Council House are revealed as one approaches the Green. The marble **statue** of Queen Victoria, 1888, by *Sir Joseph Boehm*, then the Queen's favourite sculptor, commemorated her Golden Jubilee the previous year.

To the left is the **Royal Hotel**, 1864–8, by *W.H. Hawtin*. Unexceptional architecture, but, now a horrendous 1960s canopy has been removed, the rich detailing adds to the streetscape. After years of dereliction it was reopened *c.* 1990, with a weighty E extension by *Denny & Bryan*. A domed turret echoes the neighbouring Watershed (*see* Walk 5, p. 199), and the fenestration and heavy cornice emulate the parent building. But the detailing and finish are less than a match for the C19 parts. The site was occupied by the church of **St Augustine the Less** (rebuilt *c.* 1480 and much altered in the C19), bomb damaged 1940–1, and demolished 1962.

w of the hotel are four terraced brick houses (now façades only). That at the left, perhaps *c.* 1750, has continuous moulded architraves and segment-headed windows in the manner of *George Tully* at Nos. 10–11 Dowry Square. The three at the right are slightly later. On Deanery Road, between the Abbey Gatehouse and the Council House, stands a bronze **statue** of the Calcutta reformer Raja Rammohun Roy (*see* topic box, p. 283) by *Niranjan Pradhan* of Calcutta, 1997.

The NE side of College Green begins s of Mark Lane facing The Centre, and continues up the slope on to the green proper. First Nos. 44–47, a stepped terrace probably of *c.* 1850 with C20 shopfronts. Then Nos. 39–43, by *Alec French & Partners* (1962), filling a bomb gap. Well-proportioned, with a taller recessed stair-tower and square windows suggesting an attic above the grid-like upper floors. The same firm designed Nos. 32–36 (also 1962) a few doors up, less interesting and more prominent.

At No. 38, the **Cabot Café** by *Latrobe & Weston*, 1904, for an estate agent, Walter Hughes. Now offices. Edwardian Baroque façade with excellent Art Nouveau details. Repoussé copper hoods to the side windows. Between the upper windows, pomegranate mosaic with enamel insets [61] by the client's daughter, *Catherine Hughes*, taken from Charles Ricketts's bookbinding for Oscar Wilde's *A House of Pomegranates*, 1891. The unmoulded and crisply chamfered red granite frame of the shopfront (altered) is often mistaken for a post-war addition. The engaged column and gablet at the right introduce the requisite asymmetry. Inside, an Arts and Crafts staircase, and remnants of two panelled tearooms (oak in the Cabot Room, walnut in the Camelot

Room), with some Art Nouveau marquetry. All was calculated to offer 'a high tone of ornamentation and comfort', after the Glasgow fashion for artistic tearooms.

The NE side of the Green had, before the Second World War some fine C18 houses. One of few to survive the bombing is No. 30, mid-C18, of five bays, the centre three broken forward and pilastered. Ionic capitals and broad splayed voussoirs were lost to bomb blast and a poverty-stricken 1980s refacing. A fine arcaded shopfront was added by *Foster & Wood*, 1865–6, of contrasting granite, pink sandstone and Bath stone, with inlaid black mastic decoration. Directly NW is the Lord Mayor's Chapel (*see* City Churches: St Mark, p. 100).

Colston Avenue

The N end of The Centre, now an elongated traffic roundabout. A broad central space created by culverting the River Frome 1892 (*see* topic box p. 124); for sculpture here, *see* The Centre.

Clockwise from Colston Street, first the **Colston Centre** by *Moxley Jenner & Partners*, 1961–73 [62], a fourteen-storey rectangular tower raised over a long podium curving round the tight Colston Street junction. A development of *Raymond Moxley*'s Clifton Heights (*see* Walk 4, p. 195). A pedestrian walkway was to have launched from its prow across The Centre. Glazed walls behind a skein of balconies and vertical struts

62. Colston Centre from Colston Street, by Moxley Jenner & Partners, 1961–73

lend the tower surprising lightness, anchored visually by a stilted plinth over the podium and a solid-looking white capping band. Perhaps it is too tall for the site, but it escapes the contempt heaped upon (for instance) Lewins Mead, and has an elegance of its own. Next St Mary on the Quay (*see* City Churches, p. 103), and beyond it **Northcliffe House**, completed 1929 by *Ellis & Clarke*, also responsible for Lord Northcliffe's London offices. This was the newspaper baron's attempt to establish the *Evening World* in Bristol in competition with the *Bristol Evening Post*. A stepped Art Deco clock tower with sculptural decoration, set slightly off-centre in an otherwise reserved façade. Redeveloped as apartments 2002.

At the head of The Centre, between Lewins Mead and Rupert Street, is the white Portland stone **Electricity House**, designed 1935–7 by *Giles Gilbert Scott*, the showrooms and offices of the Electricity Company. The shell was requisitioned for wartime aircraft construction, delaying completion until 1948. Prow-like composition taking full advantage of the site at the former quay head. The top two storeys step back, with a loggia emphasizing the curve. On the E side of Colston Avenue, **Quay Head House**, 1884 by *Foster & Wood* for Bristol Municipal Charities, in the Queen Anne style, never as widely used here as it was elsewhere. Crisply carved and panelled brick with big curvaceous gable and ogee-capped dormers, pilasters, festoons, urns, etc. It is carefully detailed and handsome but the composition just misses the relaxed feel of the work of Shaw or J.J. Stevenson. s of the junction with St Stephen's Street, a Portland stone office block by *C.F.W. Dening*, 1935, with sculpture framing a second-floor balcony on the side elevation; surely derived from Nos. 37–39 Corn Street (*see* p. 137). Next door, St Stephen's House in similar vein, by *Alec French* for Bristol & West Building Society, 1938, articulated by sharply projecting full-height fins at each bay, and the windows more regularly and severely disposed than Dening had dared.

Colston Street

Colston Street runs N from The Centre uphill to Perry Road; the route N of Colston Hall was cut through *c.* 1870 to St Michael's Hill and Park Row, previously reached via steep medieval lanes. Facing The Centre at the bottom of Colston Street is **Colston House**, formerly Bristol Gas Company showrooms by *Whinney, Son & Austen Hall*, 1935, a refronting in the 'Moderne' idiom with horizontal window bands following the bellied curves of the projecting centre, and columned recesses in the attics. The side of the building facing Pipe Lane, left, reveals the flank of *W.V. Gough's* predecessor building of 1904; a new front has been pasted on to bring it up to date.

Immediately N, **Colston Hall**, by *Foster & Wood*, Bristol's major concert hall, is an underrated Bristol Byzantine design. Two-phase construction: the hall with its basement of bonded warehousing first (1864–7), then the entrance front and lesser hall (1869–73). The seven-bay façade derives from Renaissance palazzo models, with an open arcade on the ground floor and another with paired columns above, originally glazed. The first-floor arcade openings are now filled by discordant concrete render with three relief sculptures of *c.* 1960, depicting music, wrestling and dance. Below, the outer arches were bricked up and windows inserted, probably *c.* 1900. These changes mute the massive scale and insistent rhythm of the arcades, qualities necessary to counterpoint the staccato details of polychrome brick voussoirs and richly ornamented cornices. Major fires in 1898 and 1945 destroyed the imperial staircase and the Great Hall modelled very closely on that of St George's Hall, Liverpool. The replacement is in a drab sub-Festival of Britain style by the City Architect *J.N. Meredith*, 1951. Large organ behind the stage facing a steeply raked balcony brought forward with staggered and angled boxes.

Immediately N, **Friary House** by *J. Ralph Edwards*, 1938, is one of the earliest buildings in Bristol to express Modernist motifs with any clarity; the nine-bay centre is emphasized by deeply recessed flanking bays, and by windows in four horizontal strips with slim vertical divisions and continuous sill mouldings. Beyond, the former **YMCA** building by *Oatley & Lawrence*, 1930, in dark brick with stone dressings, unusually dour and weighty. Higher up on the E side the fanciful Burgundian Gothic **Foster's Almshouses** [63], founded by John Foster in 1483, was rebuilt by *Foster & Wood* modelled loosely on the Hôtel Dieu at Beaune. The L-shaped S wing was begun 1861, extended 1873, and the E and N wings completed in 1883. Much diaper-work in the brick walls and tiled roofs, on a courtyard plan with towers at the internal corners and timber porches linked by a timber-railed balcony. On the N range this terminates in an open stair-tower with conical roof. The delight here is in the details: dragon hoppers to the downpipes; rich foliate eaves cornice; cast-lead roof finials; an ogee-capped oriel launching off one corner; and excellent ironwork to the boundary wall. Terminating the N range, the almshouse **Chapel of the Three Kings of Cologne** was founded by John Foster in 1484. Comprehensively refaced to a new design of 1872 by *Foster & Wood*, but executed in simplified form, 1883 in Pennant and White Lias stones. The sculpture niches appear to have been renewed in 1960 when *Ernest Pascoe*'s statues of the Three Kings were installed. Inside, a simple rectangular plan with a collegiate arrangement of facing stalls. The woodwork is mostly C19. E window by *Patrick Pollen, c.* 1960.

Continuing uphill, beyond Christmas Steps is a good row of older houses. At Nos. 54–56 an attached pair of early C19 date; Nos. 58–60 perhaps *c.* 1710, with differing fenestration but a common cornice and roofs; No. 60 has an early C19 bowed shopfront. No. 64 appears early C18, rebuilt in replica *c.* 1990. No. 66 has a brick façade of *c.* 1780, possibly on an older core. At the top, Nos. 68 and 70 are of *c.* 1650–70, with one jetty, first-floor canted bays, and gables. The whole row was refurbished *c.* 1990 under the architects *Peter Ware* and *Richard Pedlar*.

63. Foster's Almshouses, Colston Street, by Foster & Wood, 1861 and later

The Corporation's home until 1827 was the Guildhall, Broad Street, a c15 Perp building which also housed the courts. The medieval Tolzey, at the junction of Broad Street and Corn Street, was an open loggia where the Corporation dispensed justice. After the first Council House was built on the Tolzey site in 1704, the Guildhall was used mainly on election days, etc. *R.S. Pope* rebuilt the Guildhall in 1843–6 to house various courts, and new Assize Courts (*see* Small Street) were added by *Popes & Bindon* in 1867–70. There have been three Council Houses. The first (1704) was replaced in 1824–7 with *Sir Robert Smirke's* design, hereafter called the Old Council House. The Council Chamber soon became inadequate, and a new chamber was added in 1899. Finally the present Council House on College Green was completed in 1952 (*see* Major Buildings, p. 73).

Corn Street

The commercial heart of Bristol, once the route from the High Cross towards The Quay, now substantially composed of c18 and c19 banks and offices. In the 1990s many of these became bars and restaurants, and Corn Street is now busiest at night.

At the E end, s side, is All Saints (*see* City Churches, p. 92). Then *John Wood the Elder's* Exchange, 1741–3 (*see* Major Buildings, p. 78), now home to St Nicholas Market. Opposite, first the surprisingly small **Old Council House** by *Sir Robert Smirke*, 1823–7 [13]. Smirke designed a larger scheme including a Guildhall in 1823, abandoned because the street here needed widening and the site was insufficient. Bath stone exterior articulated by antae and central recessed entrance between Ionic columns *in antis*. The frontage is a near-copy of Smirke's design for the Royal College of Physicians, London. Despite its Grecian elements, the parapets include Italianate balustrades. Central figure of Justice by *E.H. Baily*. The three-bay W extension by *R.S. Pope* and *George Dymond*, 1827–9, housed the Magistrates' Court, replacing one by Smirke that proved to be inadequately lit. An accomplished design of deceptive simplicity. Inside, the hall has a coffered segment-vault. Staircase with brass Doric balusters and brass treads inlaid with red composition. The Council Chamber has a beamed and panelled ceiling with a lantern, and a remarkable decorative scheme (perhaps Late Victorian) of Grecian motifs with much gilding. A larger council chamber in thin Jacobethan style was added in 1899.

Directly w of the Old Council House, is the astonishingly sumptuous **Lloyds Bank** (originally the West of England and South Wales District Bank) 1854–7, by *W.B. Gingell & T.R. Lysaght* [64]. How they must have enjoyed knocking out their Grecian neighbour! The model was Sansovino's St Mark's Library, Venice, with Roman Doric ground floor

64. Lloyds TSB, Corn Street, by W.B. Gingell and T.R. Lysaght, 1854–7

and Ionic above, and a subsidiary order forming the Venetian motifs. Of Bath stone, with contrasting Portland stone for the sculptural elements. Originally five bays with a central door, the current entrance bay was added at the left probably *c*. 1900–10, all in Portland stone, reputedly because the contrasting stones of the rest were invisible under grime. Now cleaned, it upsets the balance of the façade considerably. Sculpture by *John Thomas* representing (on the ground floor, right to left) Newport, Bath, Bristol, Exeter and Cardiff – the main towns where the bank operated – with their rivers, coats of arms and wealth-generating products. On the first floor are paired female figures representing 'the elements and sources of wealth', such as Peace and

Plenty, Justice and Integrity. The weighty entablature is swamped with coats of arms of the bank's minor towns, and *putti* improbably engaged in the pursuits of banking. Inside, paired Composite columns define the wall bays, and deep panelled coving surrounds an Edwardian glazed skylight replacing the original ceiling. The construction was fireproof. Next door, **HSBC Bank** on the corner of Small Street, by *T.B. Whinney* (of *Whinney, Son & Austen Hall*) 1921–3, in Portland stone bankers' classicism, with a domed corner lantern.

Opposite is a row of commercial buildings that gives the street much character and unity. First, No. 48 Corn Street (*see* Major Buildings: Exchange, p. 80). Its arcaded ground floor establishes a pattern followed by its neighbours to the w. Next door is **London & Lancashire Assurance** by *Edward Gabriel*, 1904, now a restaurant. An eclectic riot of rustication, giant columns, bow windows and segmental pediment, with sculpture by *Gilbert Seale*. The high domed lantern echoes both All Saints up the street and the Scottish Provident Institution down it (*see* Clare Street). No. 40, of *c.* 1810–20, was in the c19 Miles and Harford's bank. *John Nash* is known to have designed for the firm in Corn Street, but almost certainly not their later premises at No. 35 (*see* below, now known to be *c.* 1790). Could No. 40 therefore be by Nash? Originally a four-bay façade, two e bays added *c.* 1925 by *W.H. Watkins*, the masonry joins still visible.

Further w, the Neo-Baroque **NatWest Bank**, originally for the Liverpool, London and Globe Insurance, by *Gingell*, 1864–7. A high ground floor with narrow outer entrance bays, the next two storeys unified by a giant order, all rippling movement. The paired columns are stacked two high and four wide. An attic storey with caryatids and doubled pediment completes the visual indigestion. The joy is in *Thomas Colley*'s sculpted details. Keystones illustrate the need for insurance: firemen with axes and helmets; and in the centre, Time with an hourglass. Oval plaques proclaiming Old Bank, from No. 35 opposite. Interiors entirely rebuilt behind the façade *c.* 1977. In the banking hall, a 16.5 ft by 13 ft (5 by 4 metre) intaglio **relief panel** in Napoleon marble by *Walter Ritchie*, *c.* 1977, commemorates events from Bristol's history. Finally Nos. 32–34, now part of NatWest's premises, formerly Stuckey's Bank, by *R.S. Pope*, 1852–4, holds the corner to St Nicholas Street. Conservatively classical, with bold vermiculated rustication and heavily bracketed cornice. Fine Doric apsidal banking hall, a remodelling by *Oatley & Lawrence*, 1914.

On the n side, w of Small Street first No. 47, formerly London and South Western Bank, a leaden four-storey composition by *James Weir*, 1878–80, with none of Gingell's swagger. Then the single-storey **Commercial Rooms** of 1809–11 by *Charles Busby* [65], small but engaging, among the first youthful essays of an architect later instrumental in creating Regency Brighton. It was a merchants' club and is now a bar. The secretary and chairman of the Commercial Rooms inspected Thomas Harrison's Liverpool Lyceum and his Portico Library in

65. Commercial Rooms, Corn Street, by C.A. Busby, 1809–11

Manchester, from which Busby adapted many features at Bristol. Ionic portico flanked by narrow wings with pedimented sashes, and a high blocking course behind the pediment. Figure sculptures (Commerce, Bristol and Navigation) and the frieze inside the portico all by *John G. Bubb*. Sober Great Room (presently blighted by orange and purple paint), with black marble chimneypieces of Egyptian form, and pendentive dome with lantern supported on graceful caryatids probably derived from Soane's Consols Transfer Office (1798–9) at the Bank of England. Heavily scrolled iron ventilation grilles in the ceiling. At the rear a mahogany buffet with more caryatids, and above, a wind dial to advise merchants on the arrival of their shipping. Behind is a toplit reading room.

At Nos. 37–39, the former **Friends Provident Building** [18], 1931-3 by *A.W. Roques* (elevation by *Sir Giles Gilbert Scott*). A stylish metropolitan-looking production of Portland stone on a steel frame. Its lean Art Deco interpretation of Neoclassicism is enlivened with white 'anodium metal' windows, grilles and a frieze of jaunty dancers above the door. First-floor relief figures by *Hermon Cawthra*.

No. 35 (now **Pizza Express**) is of *c.* 1790, the façade remodelled probably by *Gingell*, 1879. Previously ascribed to John Nash *c.* 1811 (*see* No. 40, above) but signed and dated plasterwork in the lantern proves that the interior existed in its present form in 1791, making Nash and 1811 improbable. The premises were later used by Miles and Harford's Bank. Beneath is a C14 or C15 cellar with some rib vaulting. Behind a courtyard (now glazed in) is the banker's house, with a Neoclassical plaster ceiling in the principal first-floor room. *William Paty* is the likely author. Nos. 31–33, now a bar, originally a bank by *W.B. Gingell* 1862–4, refaced

66 Nos. 31–33 Corn Street, banking hall ceiling, by W.B. Gingell, 1862–4

in 1930 by *F.C. Palmer*, house architect for National Provincial Bank. Reserved Neo-Palladian front of brown brick, with four-column portico over a high ground floor of Portland stone, and with all the polish but none of the charm of the C18. Gingell's lusciously ornamented toplit banking hall has a coved ceiling and central dome defined by beams [66].

Here, the junction with St Nicholas Street marks the end of medieval Corn Street, and the site of St Leonard's church and gate. Everything to the w is in Clare Street (q.v.). To the NW Leonard Lane follows the curve of the original inner town wall to Small Street.

Denmark Street

A narrow street between The Centre and Frogmore Street. Working NW from The Centre, Nos. 1–11, s side, late C18–early C19 terraced artisan houses. The rear of The Hippodrome (*see* St Augustine's Parade) dominates the N side. Opposite, **The Gaunt's House**, 1953 by *Alec French & Partners*, with ten relief sculpture panels set on the upper storeys. Beneath the street here are partly medieval **cellars** once associated with The Gaunt's Hospital. Beyond, four-square C19 **warehouses** of plain Pennant rubble with deeply recessed window openings, converted to apartments *c*. 1998.

See All Saints Street.

Running along the valley between College Green and the slopes towards St Michael's Hill, Frogmore Street roughly marked the northern limits of the medieval city. It now runs under the road viaduct carrying Park Street, of 1870. The only building left of obvious antiquity is **The Hatchet**, now a pub marooned on a curve of the road. A timber-framed house of 1606, substantially rebuilt in 1967. Two-storey oriels and on the second floor even a little West Country timber ornament, an oval and a lozenge keyed in bars. Opposite, the **New Bristol Centre** *c.* 1963–6, by *Gillinson, Barnett & Partners*, combined cinema, dance hall, ice-rink, nightclub and bingo hall. It brutalizes everything around by its scale and texture. Much charming early C18 housing around Culver Street was demolished for it. The architecture was deliberately anonymous, as a backdrop to intended night-time illuminations, never fully executed and long since removed. The sw end was replaced in 2000 by student accommodation by *Unite.* sw towards Park Street viaduct is a Greek Revival façade, probably *c.* 1830, with Doric attached columns, now much altered and neglected. The architect and original use are unknown.

Pre-war photographs reveal a narrow bustling street of tall C19 and earlier buildings. It was devastated by bombing in 1940–1, particularly on the e side, which has a lax, dissipated air, its former tension bled away on expanses of shabby paving. Vaulted C15 **cellars** under the pavement on the e side. The w **side** is an incoherent C18–C20 mixture. Typical of the rebuilding is **St Nicholas House** (*Alec French & Partners*, 1959) on the corner of St Nicholas Street. Further up is the arched Market Gate by *Samuel Glascodine*, 1744 (*see* Major Buildings: Exchange, p. 81). To the n, the **Rummer** pub, refaced by *Alec French c.* 1936. At No. 41, a two-bay façade with mildly Greek Revival battered window frames (reported to have a partly surviving timber roof, perhaps C15). Nos. 44–45 have a veneer of half-timbering apparently of 1908, over a C17 core at No. 45.

On the e side, nearest Bristol Bridge, the former **Norwich Union Building** by *Wakeford, Jerram & Harris*, 1962, deflates one of the city's prime sites with its receding angled entrance between wide, blank walls. The glass-walled foyer reveals the blitzed tower of St Mary le Port behind. Then the **Bank of England**, 1964 by *Easton, Robertson & Partners*, merely occupying the land, with bleak fenestration and a puny corner entrance. On this wide corner stood the timber-framed Dutch House, of 1676, bombed in 1940. At the top, the junction of High, Wine, Corn and Broad streets was the centre of the medieval city: here stood the C14 **High Cross**, removed in 1733 and re-erected at Stourhead, Wiltshire, in 1764, where it still makes a picturesque eye-catcher in the gardens.

The NE continuation of Colston Avenue. Originally a C13 street sand-wiched between the NW bank of the River Frome and the steep escarp-ment below St Michael's Hill. Lewins Mead was laid out *c.* 1250 (*see* Introduction, p. 8), and several religious houses were founded here. High-status merchants' houses of the C16 and C17 were demolished for C19 industry and post-Second World War redevelopment.

From the bottom of Christmas Steps, **Narrow Lewins Mead** is a short alley leading NE to Lewins Mead. The **Centre Gate** office devel-opment by *Moxley Jenner & Partners*, 1984, re-creates the enclosure of the old street pattern. A partially colonnaded walkway runs through it. Opposite, a timber-framed house (a long-established fish and chip shop), the upper storeys mid-C17 with Ipswich windows in canted bays, but the depth of the ground-floor jetty suggesting a core possibly of the C15 or earlier. On its right is **St Bartholomew's Hospital**, founded *c.* 1230–40, converted *c.* 1538 for use by Bristol Grammar School and later Queen Elizabeth's Hospital School. After 1847 it was adapted as housing and a printer's premises. Entry is by a deeply moulded E.E. arch, broken and reset lower in the C17. Within the gate, a trefoiled arcade of *c.* 1250, and a precious but much defaced **statue** of the seated Virgin, probably C13 and by a carver associated with the Wells school. The medieval and later buildings were refurbished as offices at the same time as Centre Gate (above), by *Moxley Jenner & Partners,* 1984. New

Lewins Mead Development

By 1960 Lewins Mead, Rupert Street and Nelson Street consisted of run-down Victorian industrial sites, C17 and C18 buildings and bomb gaps. The area was sandwiched between Broadmead to the E and the Centre to the W, on the line of the planned inner circuit road. Redevelopment was proposed in 1963–4 and partially implemented by the mid 1970s. The circuit road split along Lewins Mead (eastbound traffic) and Rupert Street (westbound). Speculative developers cherry-picked the sites, the planned diversity of use was never achieved, and hulking towers turned the streets into windswept canyons.

Key to the plan was the concept of high-level decks separating peo-ple from traffic, an idea derived from Le Corbusier's *La Ville Radieuse*, and reinforced by the Buchanan Report for the Ministry of Transport, *Traffic in Towns*, 1963. The 1966 *City Centre Policy Report* would have extended this 'decks over racetracks' environment SW along the Centre. Thankfully that was never implemented. One surviving walkway leapfrogs across Lewins Mead, Rupert Street and Nelson Street, and there is the stub of another at the W end of Rupert Street, a stairway to nowhere. Small mercy that the planned council housing was never built: who would have willingly lived here?

67. Unitarian Meeting House, Lewins Mead, by W. Blackburn, 1787–91

elements have been woven through the old in a happy co-existence. In the first courtyard, there are piers of two C13 arcades, one embedded in a later wall, with cushion capitals of Norman character – perhaps reused C12 work. This was the hospital chapel, a double-aisled structure of four bays, with a s porch (now the gate through which we entered). The rest of the architecture is confused. Four Tudor doorways survive, and some C17 windows. One enters a further inner court through a Gothic school range, *c.* 1758–62. To the left, a range of 'model dwellings for the industrial classes', of 1856. Three storeys with balcony access. Outside again, and to the NE the walkway runs beneath and through **St Bartholomew's Court**, offices by *Alec French Partnership*, 1983, to emerge at **Lewins Mead**. Here is a brick exedra with a bronze **statue** of a gaunt cloaked horseman, by *David Backhouse*, 1984. Next the **Sugar House**, with a simple rendered front, small windows and a glass entrance canopy added in the conversion to a hotel, 1999. The last relic of the Bristol sugar industry. A sugar refinery was established here in 1728. A C19 engine-house chimney at the rear is now part of the hotel reception. On the right, an apparently C18 house with shell-hood door is a pastiche of 1922.

Immediately NE is the **Unitarian Meeting House**, 1787–91 [67], now offices. Once the home of Bristol's wealthiest Nonconformist congregation; in 1787 they commissioned a new meeting house from *William Blackburn*, the London prison architect. It appears that Alderman Richard Bright, a member of the meeting, made the choice, presumably having met the architect in connection with the prison Blackburn was then designing at Lawford's Gate, Bristol, for the county of Gloucestershire. Designed on a wide T-plan with the entrance at its foot and slightly recessed staircase wings filling the returns. The footprint is a rectangle 70 ft wide by 40 ft deep (21 by 12 metres). Ashlar façade with pedimented centre and a high rusticated basement. High centre window, a dignified tripartite arch with an order of acanthus and fern leaves. Elegant semicircular Ionic porch.

Inside is a suave rectangular hall, where one might believe in the Age of Reason. Five arched tripartite windows (identical with that on the front) line the sides and back. *Blackburn* used the same motif at the Watermen's Hall, London, 1778–80. Boldly coffered ceiling, suspended on chains from the roof trusses. Three galleries on thin cast-iron supports, the rear one now an organ loft. **Box pews** frame a semicircular lobby beneath the organ gallery. Graceful mahogany **pulpit** on an elegant stem. The pulpit stairs, box seats and a tiny railed communion table are all of a piece with the pulpit. Some C19 wall tablets remain. Converted to offices 1987–9 by *Feilden Clegg*, sensitively managed by glazing beneath the side galleries, although the central pews were necessarily sacrificed. Outside are carriage yards (formerly with stables), and schoolrooms perched on the cliff to the N.

NE of the Unitarian Meeting House, first the gigantic mass of **Greyfriars**, 1974, *Wakeford, Jerram & Harris*, two linked towers with first-floor entrances and external pedestrian decks. Pink aggregate wall surfaces, and shallow canted façades on the blank ends facing Lewins Mead. Built on the site of a Franciscan Friary (*c.* 1250). Immediately beyond is the even bulkier **Whitefriars**, 1976, by *D.A. Goldfinch Associates*, awkwardly massed above a high podium which was refaced in the late 1990s.

Lodge Street

Lodge Street is a steep cobbled hill between Trenchard Street and Park Row. On the NE side a late Georgian terrace of *c.* 1800–10, which by the 1970s was derelict and nearing collapse. It became a *cause célèbre* in Bristol's conservation battle and was substantially rebuilt *c.* 1980–2 by *Ferguson Mann* for the Bristol Churches Housing Association. With the new houses behind in **Lodge Place**, the scheme provided fifty-six homes. Six terraced two-bay houses with semicircular fanlights inside open pediments. At the top of the row, a double-fronted villa, with simple door surround; an elegant fanlight flanked by tapering fluted pilasters supporting a moulded cornice. On the sw side was formerly the Countess of Huntingdon's Chapel, a good Tudor Gothic structure of *c.* 1831, demolished *c.* 1967 for **Trenchard Street Car Park**, a multistorey monster.

Lower Maudlin Street

See Upper Maudlin Street.

Lower Park Row

A steep medieval lane from Colston Street up to Park Row.

Starting from the top at the junction of Lodge Street, first a terrace of six houses, *c.* 1790. No. 1 has a very fine iron porch on the Lodge Street side, over a Pennant stone plinth; leaded tent canopy, batwing spandrels and chinoiserie details. Further down at No. 10 an exceptional survival, a house of *c.* 1600–60 discovered beneath its Georgian refacing in 1978. The NE face has a cross-window and, on the upper floors, small round-headed windows at the NE corner, lighting deep cupboard-like recesses. Stringcourses at the first and second storeys, continuous around the building. The main front faces sw, now tight against the Ship Inn, with a narrow alleyway restricting the view. A five-window range under two gables, with two early C19 arched doorcases. The ovolo-moulded cross-windows contain much work from a comprehensive restoration *c.* 1980.

Marlborough Street

See Upper Maudlin Street.

Narrow Lewins Mead

See Lewins Mead.

Nelson Street

Bridewell Police and Fire Station of 1928 by *Ivor Jones* and *Sir Percy Thomas*, a neglected building of considerable quality, covers the block between Bridewell Street, Rupert Street and Silver Street, and incorporating the higher fire station to the N. The dramatic police-station entrance has massive blocked piers and exaggerated voussoirs beneath an open pediment, recessed inside an arch, perhaps after George Dance the Younger's Newgate Gaol. The disastrous w end of Nelson Street lacks vitality and humanity. Immediately w of Bridewell Street, the **Police Headquarters Extension** by *A.H. Clarke*, City Architect, 1967, a thoroughly dull eight storey tower. Further on, **Nelson House** (1967, by *Angus McDonald & Partners*), disjointed slabs and a web of first-floor decks.

An early C18 mercantile enclave laid out on the orchard ground of The Gaunt's Hospital to the NE of College Green. **Unity Street** was opened up in 1742, perhaps in conjunction with the anticipated construction of Park Street (*see* Walk 4, p. 189). On the NW side from the top, Nos. 2–4, built as a single composition with a central emphasis. No. 3, the central house, is of five bays with three-bay pedimented centre and Gibbsian blocked Ionic pilasters to the doorcase. Nos. 2 and 3 now mutilated by C20 shopfronts. *James Paty the Elder* has been suggested as author. Bath stone ashlar with deep V-groove rustication to the ground floors. The rest of the row is similar if less grand. At No. 8, the hallway has the usual

68. No. 28 Orchard Street, staircase, *c.* 1720

arch on fluted pilasters, with Gibbsian blocks, an unusual detail in an interior. The SE side of Unity Street is wholly taken up by the former **Merchant Venturers' Technical College**, an unfortunate Gothic concoction of red brick by *E.C. Robins*, 1880, rebuilt on the same footprint and to a similar design after a fire in 1906 by *Alfred Cross*. Now semiderelict.

Orchard Street, the NE continuation of Unity Street, was laid out in 1718 and completed 1722. Before Unity Street was constructed it was accessed from Denmark Street to the SE. As at Queen Square the Corporation leases specified uniform-height sash windows and brick fronts. Parapets replace modillion cornices, imitating the improved fire precautions of London building regulations. The whole street has unfortunately been painted white. No. 28 is unusually rich, having grotesque mask keystones over every window, and a fine cantilevered mahogany staircase [68]. At its NE end the street widens out into what is nearly a square; Nos. 15–18 have uniform open-pedimented doorcases on provincial stone brackets. No. 15 has excellent Rococo plasterwork of *c.* 1740–50 in the staircase hall, possibly by *Joseph Thomas* who worked at Clifton Hill House. In Orchard Lane and Hobbs Lane, SE, former service and mews buildings to the Orchard Street development.

Pipe Lane

Pipe Lane is a narrow lane connecting the bottom of Colston Street with Frogmore Street. Houses largely C17–C18, but demolition and major redevelopment on the S side in the 1980s for the St Augustine's Parade scheme (*see* below) has stripped away most of the historic fabric here. N side, *see* Colston Street.

The Pithay

See All Saints Street.

Rupert Street

Rupert Street was created by culverting over the River Frome in 1857 and 1879. Drastically remodelled in the 1960s (*see* topic box, p. 140). Between Lewins Mead and Rupert Street is **Froomsgate House** of 1971 by *Alec French & Partners*. The most offensive of the area's gargantuan monoliths, seventeen storeys of repetitive windows in drab concrete and orange brick. Directly NE of Froomsgate House, **Rupert Street Multi-storey Car Park**, 1960, by *R. Jelinek-Karl* with structural engineers *Munder & Partners* and *E.N. Underwood*. Oval in plan with a continuous spiral ramp. The first multi-storey in Bristol, following examples at Exeter, of 1957, and Coventry, of 1959.

St Augustine's Parade

St Augustine's Parade forms the W side of The Centre, from Mark Lane to Pipe Lane. An irregular row, largely of C18 and C19 houses, with later additions. They do not have the civic presence for such a situation,

ELEVATION TO ST AUGUSTINES PARADE

hence the (fruitless) plans to sweep all away after the Second World War. This row epitomizes Bristol's haphazard character.

From Mark Lane, Nos. 1–2 (formerly Halifax Building Society), by *Alec French*, 1937. Five storeys and block-like, in Portland stone with bronzed doors and a balcony with restrained Jazz Age motifs. French's Bristol & West complex of 1973–80 stands across The Centre, showing the youth and maturity of an architectural career (*see* p. 119).

Further N, the building line steps back for the **Hippodrome** [69], a theatre and music hall of 1911–12, the last major design of *Frank Matcham*: for Sir Oswald Stoll, for whom Matcham had designed the London Coliseum (1904). The auditorium sits well to the w on a broad plot created by demolitions N of Denmark Street. A narrow access to the site from St Augustine's Parade limited the opportunity for an appropriately grand façade, so Matcham chose to build upward. The narrow frontage had an attic storey and tall roof, topped by an illuminated revolving globe, all removed 1964. To the left is an extension of 1964, which continues the grooved channelling of Matcham's building. The domed **auditorium** is largely true to its original appearance. Two galleries and the mandatory array of gilded plaster terms and swags. The large stage enables the Hippodrome to take West End productions and international opera. It was built with a tank beneath the stage for water spectacles. The top of the dome slides back for ventilation.

The next three houses have been amalgamated as the **Horn & Trumpet** pub. The two on the left are C18, then one perhaps of *c.* 1700, with moulded wooden cornices at each floor level, showing the transition from medieval jetties to classical stringcourses. Then No. 18, a tall four-storey pedimented façade, unchanged since the 1820s except for late C19 window surrounds. Nos. 23–25, **Dominions House** was built as offices for Star Life, 1898, by *Arthur Blomfield Jackson*, with writhing Art Nouveau ornament over the windows, wide doorways with stretched swan-necked pediments, and gabled bays. A further two storeys and a steep chateau roof with domed turrets was planned; completion was still being mooted in 1905. Through the left-hand entrance is **St Augustine's Court**, a group of C18 houses and C19 rubble-stone ware-houses, converted to offices by *Moxley Jenner & Partners* and *Stride Treglown*, 1988–90. Nos. 26–30 St Augustine's Parade and the adjoining **St Augustine's Place** curving NW into Pipe Lane, were remodelled with St Augustine's Court, according to their appearance *c.* 1860. Vestigial timber frames were demolished for new offices etc. behind. No. 26, three-and-a-half storeys with gables and jetties, of C17 origin. No. 1 St Augustine's Place, *c.* 1890, of four storeys and a high shaped gable, large windows with continuous glazing behind a central cast-iron column.

St James's Parade

A pedestrian way running E–W beside St James (*see* City Churches, p. 97). To its S is the former churchyard, a park since 1882. On the N side, **St James Court**, by *Holder Mathias Alcock*, completed 1996. Four-storey offices of Bath stone, with recessed centre, nicely detailed windows and brises-soleil. It incorporates to the E the tower and triple-arched entrance to a former **Presbyterian church**, designed 1858, by *J.C. Neale*. Its slim spire was removed in 1956.

St Nicholas Street

St Nicholas Street is the SW segment of the circle of streets that ran just within the Saxon ringworks, later the line of the medieval walls. From the W end, the curving course of the walls is clear. On the N **side** is the **Stock Exchange**, by *Henry Williams* (1903), now a restaurant. The design is unapologetically backward-looking, and no doubt to the taste of Sir George White, who paid for it. A single-storey pavilion with heavy arcaded windows behind a small temple front of glossy black marble columns and a richly ornamented entablature. The unrelated doorcase derives from the porch at St Mary the Virgin, Oxford, of 1637. Inside, the U-shaped toplit basement staircase is an Art Nouveau extravaganza of tulips in ivory and green ceramic tiles. In the basement are palatial san-itary facilities with marble-lined walls and mahogany and brass fittings.

On the S **side**, the **Fish Market** of 1873 by *Pope & Son*, now a bar. A single-storey hall with an iron-framed roof, rusticated piers and broad segmental arches, the stonework badly weathered. Opposite, **The Elephant** pub by *Henry Masters*, 1867, with a carved elephant's head on the first floor. Then No. 18, **Gresham Chambers**, a three-storey shop of

1868 by *Ponton & Gough*, one of several High Victorian Gothic designs by them (*see* Avon Insurance building, Broad Street). On the ground floor, good sculpted heads in roundels. On the s wall of the Exchange Market a cast-iron **drinking fountain** of 1859, by *Coalbrookdale Foundry*, from a design by *W. & T. Wills* of London. Then **St Nicholas Chambers** by *Archibald Ponton*, c. 1866, a handsome stone-fronted range of shops of four storeys. Round-arched windows, and carved dragons in the spandrels. On the ground floor, cast-iron shafted columns; in place of capitals, moulded blocks which appear to be (but are not) the ends of transverse beams running back into the building – a picturesque if essentially dishonest device. The shopfronts are set back and thus visually distinct from the structural supports. Opposite is St Nicholas (*see* City Churches, p. 104).

St Stephen's Street

Working SE from Colston Avenue, Nos. 9–11 is a big overblown Victorian office, signed on the right side by *J.H. Hirst*, 1873–5. Beneath a hubbub of decoration is a double-height arcade, each divided with a subsidiary segmental arch beneath a projecting sill. The keystones are inadequately tied to the entablature. High and busy attics with Lombardic arches, etc. Next door a quieter four-storey office of 1878, with moulded brick frames to segmental and round-headed windows, and glazed yellow and blue brick walls. Terracotta heads of poets inset. s again is the former **Bristol Times and Mirror** offices, 1902–4 by *Foster, Wood & Awdry* (now a backpackers' hostel). Domestic Arts and Crafts applied with some success to offices of a reasonable size, which Gomme, Jenner and Little suggest is influenced by Lethaby's Eagle Insurance, Birmingham, of 1900, especially in the ground floor. The design borrows from late C17 Bristol merchants' houses. On the SW side, hidden from the street, St Stephen (*see* City Churches, p. 108).

Small Street

Part of the late Saxon street plan, and a favoured address for medieval merchants. Almost the whole SW side is now taken up by the Victorian former **Post Office**, now used as the Crown Courts. The earliest building (everything left of the central arch) is by *James Williams* of the Office of Works, 1867–8. *E.G. Rivers* extended to the right of the arch in 1887–9, being obliged to mirror the earlier work. Doric columns screen the recessed entrances. Extended to the s in 1908–9 by *John Rutherford* in a heavy and unimaginative Edwardian classicism. Facaded in 1994 for new **Crown Courts** by *Stride Treglown*, invisible from Small Street, but with good polychrome striped masonry towards The Centre.

On the NE side the **Assize Courts**, by *Popes & Bindon*, 1867–70. An asymmetric front, collegiate Perp at the right, with a tall central tower and a tight Gothic left flank. The parts are poorly balanced, and the details ugly. The building interconnects with the Guildhall in Broad Street, and was an attempt to mitigate the lack of space in the Guildhall

70. Bristol Royal Infirmary extension, by Adams & Holden, 1911–2. Postcard *c.* 1912

courts. Controversially, the first design competition was aborted, then, in the second, all three prizes were taken by *E. W. Godwin*. But *R.S. Pope* – still holding the firm's reins at seventy-six – persuaded or bullied the Corporation to show favour, and Godwin's much admired design was abandoned for one of precious little merit. Inside, the Law Library incorporated part of an arcade from a C12 hall house. After wartime bombing gutted parts of the interiors, this precious Norman arcade was demolished in 1961, on the pretext that its removal was essential for a modern court. It was not even considered worth saving the stonework, although the C19 replica hammerbeam roof over the hall was carefully stored.

Directly to its left, **Foster's Chambers**, once the house of the C15 merchant John Foster, although the visible remains are a patchwork of later pieces. Four-bay gabled C17 front, refenestrated in the C18. Interiors much altered.

Tailor's Court

See Broad Street.

Telephone Avenue for Armada House

See Baldwin Street.

Unity Street

See Orchard Street.

Upper Maudlin Street, Lower Maudlin Street, Marlborough Street

These streets are now so dominated by Bristol's main hospital that they are treated together. **Bristol Royal Infirmary** (BRI) was opened in 1737, funded by subscription, as part of a national trend for founding charitable hospitals in the early and mid C18. Its royal title was granted in 1850.

71. Bristol Royal Hospital for Children, Upper Maudlin Street, by Whicheloe Macfarlane, with sculpture by Andrew Smith, both 2001

On **Marlborough Street**, the first infirmary building, probably by *George Tully*, had its entrance facing SE to Earl Street. It was replaced by the present **Old Building**, designed in 1784 by *Thomas Paty*, in conjunction with *Daniel Hague* (probably as builder rather than architect). The unequal H-plan was constructed in stages, the E wing 1784–6, the centre block 1788–92, and the W wing, delayed by the Napoleonic War, 1806–9. It consists of a three-storey central block of eleven bays arranged 3:5:3, with recessed bays beyond linking the wings with the centre; the dignified design now spoiled by alterations of *c.* 1866, perhaps by *Henry Crisp* who designed the two-storey ward wing at the SW in that year. On the SE side, a lancet Gothic chapel with museum beneath, by *S.C. Fripp*, 1858.

Opposite on the N side of Marlborough Street is the Portland stone **King Edward VII Memorial Building** of 1911–12 [70]. By *H. Percy Adams & Charles Holden*, also responsible for the Central Library (*see* Major Buildings, p. 75), it is an important step in the movement towards a plainer, more abstracted architecture. Unconstrained by an adjoining historic building as at the Central Library, the building speaks through its massing and smooth surfaces. Hints are discernible of the geometries of Holden's London Transport Headquarters and University of

London Senate House. *Adams & Holden*'s design, housing 181 patients, was selected late in 1909, and built 1911–12. The cost of *c.* £70,000 was raised through a public appeal headed by Sir George White, founder of Bristol Aircraft Company. It is effectively White's chief memorial in the city. Now only the SE front is easily visible, the least interesting part. Ranged across the steeply sloping site are two tall blocks with towers at the ends, and between them a deep courtyard open at the SW. Two-storey columned loggias facing SW. The plan was intended to provide maximum air and daylight to the wards, objectives that had long been central to hospital design. A low wing with Lutyensesque dome fronts the street, with a recessed entrance court at the NE end. The competition specified that the design be easily extendible. But the 1960s building (below) hid the important SW elevations and destroyed the broad framing flight of steps, diminishing the design immeasurably. The long **Maudlin Street extension** (properly called Queen's Building) is by *Watkins Gray Group I*, designed *c.* 1965–6, opened 1973. Insistent repetition of grey concrete horizontals and slab-like mullions emphasizes the scale of the street front. The projecting beam-ends seemingly take after Northwick Park Hospital, Middlesex, by Llewelyn Davies & Weeks, where they were designed to enable later extension. Here they could never have that function; perhaps they are an attempt to relieve the visual tedium. The building masks two big blocks on the hill behind.

To the SW again, the yellow brick towers of **Bristol Royal Hospital for Children** by *Whicheloe Macfarlane*, completed 2001 [71], dominate **Upper Maudlin Street**. It replaced a predecessor on St Michael's Hill (*see* Walk 9, p. 247). The street front is varied with shallow projections, oriel bays, and over the entrance a glazed quadrant with sun visors at each storey. Window frames are painted jade-green and there are small areas of brilliant pink, yellow and green beneath the canopies and oriel bays. At the entrance, and highly visible from the street is a light sculpture, **Lollipop Bebop**, by *Andrew Smith*, 2001, of coloured and illuminated hoops on curving stainless-steel stems.

Returning E towards the King Edward VII block, a turn s into **Lower Maudlin Street** reveals an interesting group of subsidiary hospital buildings. On the SW side, a large brick house with a rainwater head dated 1753, a late date for segment-headed windows and stringcourses, and with a fine doorcase in the style of *c.* 1720. The next house (also of 1753?) is more in keeping with the style of *c.* 1770, but continues the stringcourses and parapet cornice of its neighbour. The attics were added in 1886. Then the big red brick **Eye Hospital** by *Kendall Kingscott Partnership*, opened 1986. Part of the planning brief was for elevational enrichment, a requirement more than fulfilled by *Walter Ritchie*'s The Creation [72], believed to be the world's largest hand-carved **brick sculpture**, nicely contrasting organic textures with crisply chamfered brickwork. The five panels also gain from being set against darkened glass and black-painted Micatex panels. Opposite and in complete contrast is the late C17 vernacular **White Hart** inn, updated with a Victorian pub front.

72. Bristol Eye Hospital, detail from The Creation, by Walter Ritchie, 1986

Wine Street

The E arm of the four late Saxon streets that converged at the site of the High Cross. Until 1940 it presented an intricate weave of small shops and lavish Edwardian department stores competing for business. Now perhaps the saddest post-Blitz transformation. From High Street, on the s side is the E wing of the former Bank of England premises (*see* High Street), and its weak extension of 1976, by *Easton, Robertson & Partners*, weakly set back over a parking access ramp. (Various schemes have been proposed since *c.* 1990 to redevelop the Bank of England site, with no decision at the time of writing.) Just three buildings occupy the entire N side of Wine Street as far as Union Street. **Prudential Building** (1957), dull stripped classicism of brown brick over an ashlar basement with token engaged portico. Then **Vintry House** (1958) and **Southey House** (*Ivor Hodges*, 1963) both singularly unimaginative.

The Inner City

Walk 1. Around Queen Square 154

Walk 2. Castle Park and Broadmead 169

Walk 3. Temple and Redcliffe 178

Walk 4. Park Street and Brandon Hill 189

Walk 5. Canon's Marsh 199

Around Queen Square

This walk covers the rectangular tongue of land s of the medieval city, then called Town Marsh, bounded by Baldwin Street on the N (*see* p. 116), the River Avon to the E and s, and the diverted Frome (St Augustine's Reach) on the w. The Marsh wall ran N of present King Street, with gates at both ends. Medieval quays extended s to the gates on the E and w. The undefended s end of the Marsh was an archery training ground for the city militia. By the C16 there was a bowling green and at least one tavern.

Planned development started in 1650 with King Street. Queen Square and Prince Street were laid out to the s in 1699 by the Corporation,

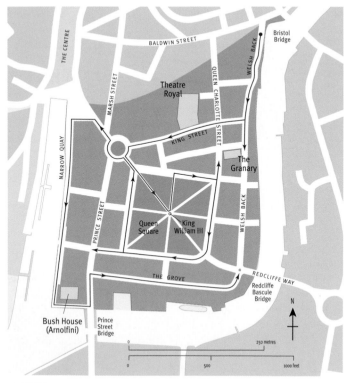

73. Walk 1

which still owns most of the freeholds. Queen Square remained the most fashionable Bristol address until the late C18 rise of Clifton, but became commercialized in the C19.

From Bristol Bridge (*see* p. 118), **Welsh Back** leads s along the waterside. After 1240 this was the city's secondary quay, serving the coastal trade with Ireland and Wales. No. 3, **West India House** by *Oatley & Lawrence*, 1903–4, has a narrow centrepiece with pilasters framing a double-height window, similar to the same architects' Scottish Provident Institution also of 1903 (*see* p. 126). Directly s, an office block of 1974 was remodelled as the **Brigstow Hotel**, by *Helical Bar Development*, 2001. The white-rendered front has clean grid lines and a strong vertical entrance bay, set off centre, with deep coving at the parapet. The ground-floor stonework is carefully done and the whole reads well at a distance. On the quayside, the **Merchant Seamen's monument** (2001), a granite bollard on a stepped plinth. Sinuous curving steel seats define the space. s of this is a sloped landing stage created from a Second World War bomb crater.

Passing the end of King Street, to the s, **The Granary**, 1869 by *Ponton & Gough* [74] brings the exoticism of Venetian, Moorish and Byzantine architecture to the Bristol quayside (*see* Introduction, p. 31). Gomme rightly calls it 'the most striking and piquant monument of the High Victorian age in Bristol.' Powerful massing, soaring angles, and intricate arcades of razor-sharp Cattybrook brick with black and buff polychromy. Comparison with Ponton's other buildings and the lack of structural clarity in Gough's work suggest *Ponton* was the principal designer. The ground-floor arcade perhaps derives from Street's nave arcades at All Saints, Clifton (*see* Walk 8, p. 236). Seven grain floors, with densely patterned ventilation openings. Each storey has a different arch form. Machicolated battlements, swallow-tail merlons and steep roofs. Ground-floor roundels were exit points for grain chutes. Flues within the walls delivered warm air from basement furnaces to dry the grain. Brick vaults insulated the structure above the ground floor, but the upper construction was not fireproof. Inside, massive brick piers carry ingenious wooden Y-beams transferring thrust onto the E and w walls, differently arranged at the E to avoid two furnace flues. These necessitated two brick piers in the E façade's uppermost arcade instead of stone columns. The floor joists are forcibly curved by cross-pieces to counteract the tendency of the floors to bow under the weight of grain. Converted to apartments, 2002 by *Barton Willmore Architecture*. Further s, the best late C20 building is the **Scottish Life** building of 1975, by *Burnet Tait Powell & Partners*, perhaps the earliest in Bristol to emulate the Victorian warehouse style with segmental window heads and a subtle play of crisp plum-coloured brick against recessed concrete lintels.

Return to **King Street**, perhaps the most rewarding street in Bristol both for its gently curving composition and harmonious juxtaposition of 350 years of buildings. Here are Bristol's best surviving Restoration merchants' houses. In 1650 the Corporation leased a plot s of the Marsh Wall to *Thomas Wickham*, carpenter, for six houses to be completed within ten years, providing that no 'noysome trades' were allowed. They backed on to the Marsh Wall. The s side remained open until 1663 when leases were granted specifying houses of regular design. The street thus formed, named after the newly restored Charles II, established Town Marsh as a fashionable address.*

On the s side, first the famous **Llandoger Trow** inn, *c.* 1664 [75]. Three showy timber-framed houses (five houses until bombed in 1940), the best Bristol survivors of their period. Three storeys and gabled attics, articulated by five full-height canted bays. The ground floors are raised over warehouse basements with shutters. The jettied ground floors were probably used for trading from the first. Shallow jetties and a broad unified composition give the houses a Renaissance feel. Glazing appears once to have been continuous between the bays and must have been most impressive. Some C17 arched 'Ipswich' windows remain. Renaissance details, e.g. tapered pilasters with lozenges and coarse Ionic capitals. Now interconnected within, but some older elements survive: parts of the lateral stair, a C17 German overmantel with Nativity scene, and an C18 shell-hooded corner buffet (No. 4); a panelled parlour with early C18 bolection moulding (No. 3); and in the first-floor great chambers, two simple Tudor-arched chimneypieces, and moulded ceilings.

On the N side, w of Queen Charlotte Street are the backward-looking **St Nicholas's Almshouses** begun in 1652. Eight regular gables

*The detailed research of Dr Roger Leech has been invaluable in writing the entry for King Street.

75. Llandoger Trow pub, King Street, *c.* 1664

to King Street (the three facing Queen Charlotte Street are C19). Mullioned windows with hoodmoulds, and a larger gabled entrance bay. Fifteen-panelled door, mid-C17. Over the entrance hall was a tiny chapel, the floor of which was removed during rebuilding 1959–61 under *John K. Maggs*, for *Donald Insall*. The double-height hall thus created has a plaster barrel vault dated 1656, with late strapwork and Symbols of the Four Evangelists, a daring Commonwealth affirmation of old ways. In the courtyard behind, a **D**-shaped mid-C13 **bastion** is the most complete visible remnant of the town walls.

To the w is the astonishingly beautiful Georgian **Theatre Royal**, actually a complex of various dates surrounding Britain's oldest surviving theatre auditorium, in almost continuous use since 1766. Forty-nine merchants subscribed £50 each to fund the first theatre inside the city boundary. The site behind King Street avoided the need for an architecturally significant façade. It received its royal patent and its name in 1778. It closed in 1942, but was saved by public appeal. In 1946 the renowned Bristol Old Vic was established here, and in 1972 improved backstage facilities and a studio theatre were created, with a new entrance through the adjacent Coopers' Hall, by then redundant. After two centuries, and at some cost, at last the theatre had a public face and facilities appropriate to its standing.

First, what is visible from the street? The **Coopers' Hall** is by *William Halfpenny*, 1743–4 [76], after the old hall was demolished for the Exchange. Corinthian order close to that in Book I of Isaac Ware's 1743 edition of Palladio. However, the proportions are quite un-Palladian: squat basement, a steep pediment raised over an attic flanked by massive volutes, and very tall sash windows (a Halfpenny hallmark). To the w *Peter Moro*'s 1972 **extension** for a studio theatre and offices, on the site of a small entrance front of 1903. Carefully modulated recessions and projections enliven the brown brick façade, while four gables echo the neighbouring warehouse and the pediments of Coopers' Hall.

The guild hall was on the first floor. *Moro* removed the staircase, floors and internal walls, and replicated the modillion cornice and coving over the hall. The glazed entrance now leads to Moro's processional stair with gallery landing around the walls. The finish is rightly reticent; plain rendered walls, glass and chrome. Moro's planning integrates the c18 and c20 elements and changes of level, and is compact and practical. A proposal to remodel the foyers and studio theatres is currently under discussion.

s of the upper foyer is *Moro*'s irregular octagonal **studio theatre**, and to the N the **auditorium** (1764–6) [77]. In 1764 the proprietors paid £38 16s. 8d. for a plan of Drury Lane Theatre, London, from its carpenter, Mr Saunderson, and engaged Thomas Paty to supervise construction of a theatre conforming as far as possible with that plan. Kathleen Barker's suggestion that the plan was of Richmond Theatre, Surrey, seems to be contradicted by the minutes. In any case, Paty was probably responsible

for all design decisions beyond the most basic principles of layout. The auditorium is semicircular rather than elliptical as was usual. Dress circle and upper circle originally arranged as boxes, the fluted Doric columns marking the now-removed partitions. The ceiling was raised for an additional gallery tier in 1800. Above the much-altered proscenium arch, acanthus plasterwork probably of 1766. Paired Corinthian pilasters, similarly decorated, flank two tiers of boxes. The remaining decoration dates from successive alterations, substantially achieving its current form by 1881, when the starred ceiling was installed and other changes made, by *T.S. Pope* and *C.J. Phipps*. The present pea-green colouring is based on descriptions of the late c18 scheme. Much was sacrificed for *Moro*'s remodelling, including an c18 stage apron, rare proscenium doors, and c18 backstage with c19 machinery. The 'thunder run' (a wooden trough down which balls were rolled to simulate thunder) survives above the ceiling.

Continuing the N side, at No. 36 a crisp red brick warehouse, perhaps *c.* 1900, very similar to No. 13 Queen Square and probably by the same architect. No. 35 of *c.* 1870, a distinctive Bristol Byzantine façade in dark brick, built as a cork warehouse and refurbished as offices *c.* 1975. Five arched window recesses are capped by narrow attic arcades grouped 2:2:3:2:2 and carved heraldic beasts. *Henry Masters* or *W.B. Gingell* have been suggested as architect. Nos. 33 and 34 are the only survivors of *Wickham*'s 1650 building lease; a three-storey Commonwealth merchant's house completed by 1658, with attached warehouse. No. 33 has stone party walls (the rear wall probably part of the c13 Marsh Wall) with a timber-framed gabled front; late c18 fenestration. The plan has two full-width rooms one behind the other, with dogleg stair and connecting lobby between. First-floor great chamber with elaborate plasterwork frieze, and ceiling panels [10]. At No. 34, Bristol's earliest surviving **warehouse**, originally separate from No. 33, but now interconnected. A beam and hook remain above the blocked hoist door.

Now for the s side, working w from Queen Charlotte Street. No. 6 shows off an early c18 six-bay brick front with fine shell-hood, and windows similar to Dowry Square (*see* Walk 6, p. 210) and Orchard Street (*see* p. 144). But the rear stair-tower, off-centre door and double-hipped roof instead of the usual ridge are evidence that two houses of *c.* 1665 were amalgamated and refronted with cut-back gables *c.* 1720. Nos. 7 and 8 (*c.* 1665) were built as a pair with outer party walls of stone but a central timber partition. Ground floors raised over half-basements with shuttered doors, as at the Llandoger Trow. Jettied upper floors with bays, pent roofs and big gables. The jerry-built framing consisted partly of reused ships' timbers and barrel staves.

Nos. 11–13, Kings Court (1988, *Ian Penrose Associates*), a low-rise office in carefully executed brick, maintains the street's scale. Then Nos. 14–15, a pair of c19 warehouses in Pennant stone. Unusual chamfered and brick-banded window surrounds have affinities with works by *W.B. Gingell*. Nos. 16–18 were built by *Francis Bayley*, shipwright, in 1663–6. No. 16 was refronted and the gable cut back in the c18. (It reportedly contains c17 moulded cross-beamed ceilings, one supported by a Samson post.) No. 17 was refronted in brick with a truncated gable *c.* 1700; still with cross-windows rather than sashes, but with moulded platbands instead of jetties. No. 18, the least altered, has a two-storey canted oriel and late c18 fanlight. Its elevation is continuous with Nos. 19–20 (*c.* 1665, now interconnected), possibly also by *Bayley*. At No. 20 a shopfront of *c.* 1800 with reeding and roundels, incorporating the c17 door.

w of King William Avenue, a coarsely detailed three-storey office block of the 1970s with aggregate-faced concrete panels. An early example of the influence of the conservation movement, echoing the neighbouring jetties, bays and general scale. Opposite is the **Old Library**, now a restaurant. In 1613, Robert Redwood gave his lodge here to the Corporation for a public library. The present building, of 1738–40, cost £1,301 8*s.* 1*d.* *James Paty* provided the ornamental carving and possibly the design. A five-bay front breaking forward to a three-bay pedimented centrepiece with Composite doorcase. Elaborate crestings, including studying putti over the first-floor windows and the City arms in the pediment, were removed during brutal repairs *c.* 1970.* The projecting w wing was added in the 1780s. The e gateway has an ogee

*One reading putto may be that now on the n wall of St Michael on the Mount Primary School, Park Lane (*see* p. 249).

78. Burning of the Mansion House, Queen Square. Painting, W.J. Muller, c. 1831

The Bristol Riots occurred on 29–31 October 1831. Bristol's Recorder Sir Charles Wetherell had told Parliament that Bristol was indifferent to parliamentary reform, prompting demonstrations on his return by supporters of the Whig reform agenda and by others protesting against Bristol's corrupt self-serving Corporation. Civil and military security were ineffectual, and the middle class proved unwilling to volunteer for the militia. Violence and looting quickly escalated; Queen Square and the Bishop's Palace and three prisons were burned. Britain's worst unrest since the Gordon Riots of 1780 scandalized the nation. The destruction was measured in hundreds of thousands of pounds of property destroyed and an uncertain death toll – probably at least one hundred. It may also have accelerated Clifton's popularity as a residential suburb outside the city.

gable of a type briefly fashionable in Bristol c. 1720–50. Fine oak staircase with acanthus tread-ends. The principal first-floor room was removed to the new Central Library in 1906 (see Major Buildings, p. 77).

At the w end of King Street, n side, the **Merchant Venturers' Almshouses** of 1696–9, with their coat of arms on the s wall. It follows Colston's Almshouses, St Michael's Hill, although humbler in detailing and materials, with a cheerful vernacular air. Cross-windows, and scroll-bracketed door canopies which sag at improbable angles. The carpenter was clearly taxed by the corner canopies. The missing w range of the quadrangle was bombed in 1941.

Now turn s to enter the NW corner of **Queen Square**, among the largest C18 squares in Britain, and Bristol's first piece of urban planning, laid out by the Corporation in 1699 for merchants' houses, presumably

79. Queen Square, statue of King William III, by J.M. Rysbrack, cast in 1733

with recent London developments (e.g. St James's Square and Red Lion Square) in mind. The Corporation was clearly also aware of London's post-Great Fire building regulations and the new classical regularity, for the leases specified storey heights, brick façades and modillion cornices. But there was no imposed terrace design; various carpenters built single houses or small groups. Building started slowly, peaked *c.* 1710–15 and finished 1727. It was already overshadowed stylistically by Grosvenor Square, London, and by 1729, Queen Square, Bath was showing the way to the unified square of palace-front terraces. The square was bisected diagonally SE to NW by Redcliffe Way in 1936–7, one councillor in favour of the scheme stating 'Gentlemen, there is no "architecture" in the square and you know it'. Rarely is a section of major road entirely obliterated, but here it was, with a visionary restoration by the Council's *City Centre Projects and Urban Design Team*, 2000–1.

At the centre is *J.M. Rysbrack*'s exceptional brass equestrian **statue of William III** [78], acclaimed by George Vertue (1733) as 'the best statue ever made in England'. Proposed in 1731 after a similar scheme in London had failed: the subject demonstrated the loyalty of Bristol's Whig oligarchy to the 1689 Revolutionary settlement. Designs were invited from Rysbrack and Peter Scheemakers, and Rysbrack's model won the day. (Scheemakers's statue went to Hull.) Cast in London 1733 and erected in 1736. The asthmatic king is transformed into a lean and powerful Roman wearing an athlete's band, exuding nobility and purpose.

The N side and most of the W side were burnt in the riots of 1831 (*see* topic box, p. 161). The Corporation imposed some aesthetic control on the rebuilding, inspecting plans to ensure that 'nothing really objectionable would be erected'. We start at the centre of the N side, at the **Custom House**, rebuilt 1835–7 by *Sydney Smirke*, Surveyor to the Customs Office. A bland design of five tall arched windows over a banded ground floor. Paired pilasters about the door and deep bracketed cornice. Working clockwise, Nos. 1–9 by *Henry Rumley*, *c.* 1833, an ashlar terrace with giant pilasters and fanciful Grecian capitals. Square, fluted doorcase pilasters and fanlights of interlaced circles. Four have lost their veranda balconies.

From the NE corner a short detour into **Queen Charlotte Street**, the S end of which was laid out with Queen Square. No. 59 (1709–11) was refaced probably in the mid 1730s with an uninhibited and showy Baroque façade [80], perhaps unparalleled in England of its size and type.* Each storey has different flanking pilasters and window surrounds. On the ground floor, eared window surrounds after Borromini's gallery doorcases at the Palazzo Pamphili, Rome, and inside the frames, little scribed voussoirs. Second-floor window keystones grow into lugged tablets. Rosewell House, Bath (1735) – previously ascribed to John Strahan but tentatively reattributed to *Nathaniel Ireson* of Wincanton – is so similar it must be by the same architect. Neither resembles Strahan's other known works. Ireson picked up elements of the Roman Baroque style through his work as builder to Thomas Archer, who in turn was influenced by Bernini and Borromini. Ireson's Ven House, Somerset, has tablets and keystones reminiscent of the Bristol design and his White Horse Inn, Wincanton, mixes motifs in equally uninhibited fashion. To the S, No. 61, *c.* 1705, shows the inexperience of Bristol builders in the use of brick.

Returning to the E side of Queen Square, a red-brick warehouse of *c.* 1900 at No. 13, two storeys higher than its neighbours (*see* p. 159). Nos. 14–16 (1967, *Alec French & Partners*) are representative of Queen Square's numerous mock-Georgian offices. Then the rhythm is interrupted by the **Port Authority Offices** by *W.V. Gough*, 1885, reviled for its complete insensitivity to context – as one might expect for its date. Built when Bristol Docks Committee took over Avonmouth Dock in 1884, to a lavish Flemish Renaissance design in red brick and buff terracotta, originally symmetrical except the right-hand doorway. Four statues of the Continents on the first floor. To the S a two-bay extension also by *Gough*, 1902, in the same style.

---

*The house had been leased by Jacob Elton since 1716 or before. Ison's supposition that he refaced the house on renewing his lease in 1736, remains unproven.

80. No. 59 Queen
Charlotte Street, attrib-
uted to Nathaniel Ireson,
mid-1730s

More early C18 houses on the s **side**. No. 29 (1709–11) is the showiest
[81]: a five-bay brick façade with superimposed Doric, Ionic and
Composite columns. The window pediments balance naïvely on the
keystones, while the columns stop short of the eaves. The doorcase is late
C18. Mid-C18 railings, wrought-iron gates, and ornamented gatepiers, all
recently reinstated. Central corridor hall with elliptical arch giving on to
an open-well staircase. A front and rear room on each side, some with
bolection-moulded panelling, and rear closet towers at the outer angles.
A late C18 modernization included Siena marble chimneypieces and the
rearrangement of the upper staircase. Narrow rear service court with
mid-C18 Gibbs window surrounds; within are remains possibly of the
early C18 kitchen fireplace. Houses such as this one near the quays com-
monly had associated warehouses and counting houses behind.

No. 30 is the best Neo-C18 replacement, with a concave curved porch
and finely judged materials, by *Edmund Cullis* of Gloucester, 1919–21.
At Nos. 33–35 by *Alec French Partnership*, *c*. 1990, the Postmodern details
do not succeed in such close proximity to the real article. Clumsy porch
and glazing patterns. w of Grove Avenue, three five-bay houses all of
c. 1703. Nos. 36 and 38 have stringcourses, quoins and Doric-columned
mid-C18 doorcases with open pediments. Between them, No. 37,
updated in the late C18 with rusticated ground floor and a Doric
columned porch. The w end of this row, all of 1981–2, replaced tall C19
warehouses with pastiche of the weakest sort. All the details are unconvincing. At the sw angle behind No. 46 is the disused **Seamen's Mission**
by *Voisey & Wills*, *c*. 1880, an institute with chapel above. The w front

bombed in 1940 and appallingly refronted with the most utilitarian concrete structure, now derelict. It demands imaginative reuse.

The w **side** of Queen Square dates from the 1830s rebuilding, except for two C18 survivors. Rebuilding was completed in 1840. The random distribution of decorative features makes a somewhat unsatisfactory whole. *Henry Rumley*'s authorship is documented for No. 57, formerly St Stephen's Parsonage. The Greek Revival details are seen throughout the rest of the w side, and at Nos. 1–9, N, which must be his too. The first-floor bracketed window pediments with wreath decoration appear only on the w side.

Now for the details. From the s, Nos. 49–50, completed in 1833 at a cost of £978, by *R.S. Pope*, the only houses on this side definitely not by *Rumley*. Precise tuck-pointed red brick, but old-fashioned five-stepped voussoirs. **Phoenix House**, 1834, was *Rumley*'s own residence and thus puts on some display. Shallow projecting centre, a semicircular Greek Doric porch, and a large stone phoenix on the parapet. Nos. 52–53, a pair completed 1838, have deep party-wall recesses instead of pilasters, a favoured device of *R.S. Pope*, who perhaps contributed here. Nos. 54 and 55 (*c.* 1710) survived the riots. No. 54 was modernized with a first-floor wreathed window pediment. At No. 55, an C18 door-hood, the shell much smaller than the hood. Nos. 69–72 (*c.* 1835), are the truncated and altered remains of the w half of the N side, a unified design, but weaker than the E half.

We leave Queen Square where we came in, at the junction of King Street and Prince Street. Here, the bulky **Broad Quay House**, 1981, dominates. By *Alec French & Partners* for developers Standard Life, replacing the similarly scaled Co-operative Wholesale Society building of 1906. The design evolved from a futuristic concept of 1973 with gold reflective glass, via a glass-walled bell-shaped building of 1977, to the existing red-brick polygon wrapped around a small courtyard. On the E (Prince Street) façade, good ceramic panels of Bristol's history by *Philippa Threlfall*. Around the N end of the building towards Narrow Quay, its warehouse character is expressed in segmental arches, paired windows and careful surface modelling. Slate mansards with buttress-like ties sit over a recessed storey, giving the roofs rather the appearance of a bell-tent. A bronze **fountain** of Sabrina, goddess of the River Severn, by *Gerald Laing*, hides nearby in the centre courtyard of Broad Quay House.

A little way along Narrow Quay is **Jury's Hotel**, formerly the Unicorn, by *Wakeford, Jerram & Harris*, 1964–6. Its multi-storey car park is raised on V-columns beneath screens of double-lozenge patterned white concrete into which the floor beams lock. An unusual construction, closer to bridge trusses than post-and-beam structures. Here, such strident pattern-making is crushing. s of Farr's Lane are three warehouses: vernacular C19 in stone; next a tall Cattybrook brick structure *c.* 1900, now a Youth Hostel; then a narrow three-storey sail loft of the early C18, remodelled as the **Architecture Centre** by *Niall Phillips Architects*, 1996, an effortless use of roughcast render, steel and glass.

At the s end on the cobbled quayside a forceful bronze **statue** of John Cabot (*Stephen Joyce*, 1986), Bristol's adopted maritime explorer, gazes westward. Behind him, **Bush House**, now the **Arnolfini Arts Centre** [82], commands the central position on Bristol harbour, the junction of the rivers Avon and Frome. Its four-square bulk has an unexpected nobility and, since its landmark rejuvenation in 1975, has come to symbolize a new Bristol. Built 1830–1 by *R.S. Pope* as warehousing and offices for Acramans, iron founders. The design was a development of Pope's Wool Hall (*see* Walk 3, p. 180). At the time it was Bristol's largest and most architecturally ambitious warehouse, of rugged Pennant sandstone with Bath stone dressings. The symmetrical s façade combines round arches, classical proportions and a sense of impending Victorian solidity. It was extended northward in 1835–6 for the same company to provide tea warehousing, after the East India Company's monopoly was lifted in 1833. Asymmetrical because of the two-phase construction: the E front has, from the left, three bays of 1830–1, then six bays of 1835–6. Here, the arches are linked at impost level, as at Zion Chapel, Bedminster, tentatively attributed to Pope. Giant arches, rock-faced basements and Pennant walls were widely exploited in the 1850s Bristol warehouse style – but for twenty years it stood alone. Pevsner believed it to be of 1847 and called it 'remarkably early for the *Rundbogenstil*' which makes the date 1831 all the more remarkable. The building was remodelled in 1975 by *JT Group Ltd* for the Arnolfini Arts Centre, with exhibition space, cinema, restaurant and shop, and offices

82. Bush House, Narrow Quay, by R.S. Pope, 1830–1, extended 1835–6

above. Internally, wooden floors on cast-iron Doric columns were replaced by reinforced concrete. A new shallow hipped roof on a glazed mansard gave an additional floor of offices. Interiors completely rebuilt again by *Snell Associates*, 2003–5.

Turning N, **Prince Street** is a bleak stretch of mediocre post-war buildings. Laid out *c.* 1700 with Queen Square and named after Prince George of Denmark, Queen Anne's husband, it runs N–S, linking Marsh Street with the harbour. All that remains is Nos. 66–70, an impressive group immediately N of Bush House. Nos. 68 and 70 were built for the deal merchant John Hobbs. In the pediments, Baroque cartouches display his badge of three hobbies. Leases were signed in 1725; the architect was probably *John Strahan* who laid out Kingsmead Square, Bath, for Hobbs. At No. 68, the Shakespeare Inn, a panelled ground-floor parlour, and an open-well staircase sited laterally in the centre of the house, leading up to a full-width chamber at the front – the same plan form used at King Street in the 1650s. No. 66 is of three bays, the narrow single-bay centrepiece framed by fluted giant pilasters under a segmental pediment. Ison suggests *William Halfpenny*'s hand, but *John Strahan* seems as likely.

Now turn E into **The Grove** where the unpolished character of a working dockside lingers in the cobbled quay with its iron railings and C19 hand crane. On this corner is a simple five-storey seed warehouse

83. Nos. 66–70 Prince Street, late 1720s

(now a pub) completed as late as *c.* 1878, but appearing to be fifty years earlier. Segment-headed openings are punched through the rock-faced Pennant walls.

The N side of The Grove, formerly the rear service ranges of Queen Square, is now mainly offices. E of Grove Avenue the Postmodern rear of Nos. 33–35 Queen Square by *Alec French Partnership*, *c.* 1990, has an oriel bay and heavy metalwork beneath the balconies. The former **Sailors' Home** was converted in 1874 from the warehouse behind No. 29 Queen Square. E again is the **Hole in the Wall** pub, thoroughly modernized but probably of C17 or C18 origin. The small projection with slit windows facing The Grove was supposedly a look-out for customs men or press-gangs.

Opposite, **River Station** restaurant was converted from a former river-police station by *Inscape Architects*, 1998. Of the early C20 structure, only the boat slip is now recognizable. Entrance and staircase in an angled glass projection. Steel balconies, curved roofs and tented canopies evoke a maritime quality. It gains from attention to finish – blue glass insets in the balcony, copper guttering and subtly textured render panels. The whole has a poetic lightness of touch. E towards Redcliffe Bridge is Bristol's earliest **transit shed** *c.* 1865; iron-framed and originally open-sided to speed up the unloading of cargo prior to transport or warehousing; the sides were later timber-clad. Converted to another restaurant *c.* 1998.

Walk 2.

Castle Park and Broadmead

This walk covers two areas of differing character with linked histories: an extensive open park NE of Bristol Bridge, and to its N a 1950s shopping precinct with some important earlier buildings amid the concrete gloom. Castle Park, to the s, was successively the site of Bristol Castle (C11–C17), then an area of late C17 houses and industry, and, by the late C19, Bristol's primary shopping district. It was heavily bombed 1940–1. N of Newgate, Broadmead developed around a C13 Dominican friary outside the town walls. From the C17 the area was a centre of religious dissent. By the 1930s it was a down-at-heel mix of business premises, chapels and C16–C19 housing. Here the bombing was lighter than in the Castle district. The post-war redevelopment is a half-hearted piece of planning.

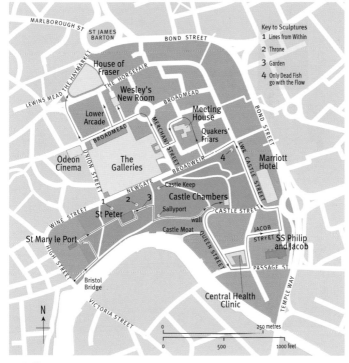

84. Walk 2

Bristol's docks and industries made it an obvious target for German bombing. There were six major raids between 24 November 1940 and 11 April 1941, and many minor ones. Over 1,400 people were killed. The first raid destroyed about a quarter of the medieval city (i.e. present-day Castle Park), four churches (St Peter, St Mary le Port, St Nicholas, Temple), and historic buildings including the Dutch House (1676) and St Peter's Hospital, a fine timber-framed house of 1612. A civilian recalled being 'ankle deep in broken glass, and the air so full of hot ash that I had to protect my face . . . I looked [towards] Castle Street and saw the most amazing spectacle . . . I was looking at a whole city burning.' Surprisingly, during the most perilous months of 1941 museum staff attempted to salvage important plasterwork and chimneypieces from the ruins of St Peter's Hospital. However, the action of intense heat and freezing weather caused them to disintegrate as they were brought out.

The impact on Bristol ran deeper than bricks and mortar. The Castle district, home to the glossiest pre-war cinemas, shops and cafés, had been packed with window-shopping promenaders on weekend evenings. Post-war Broadmead never resurrected that social function. Isolated by acres of bombed wasteland, the once-thriving Old Market district to the E descended to shabby dereliction. The linear continuity from Clifton in the W to Stapleton Road in the E was broken, a topographical dislocation still partly unresolved.

From Bristol Bridge, a path leads E along the N wall of the harbour into **Castle Park**. Created in 1978 as a watered-down version of a scheme by *Sir Hugh Casson*, and enriched in 1993 with new landscape features and art installations. The offices on High Street need redevelopment to bring some coherence to both streets and park. Behind them stands the ruined St Mary le Port (*see* City Churches, p. 102), one of two churches here gutted in the Bristol Blitz.

Between St Mary le Port and St Peter, a footbridge with sinuous steel balustrades designed by *Matthew Fedden*, 1993. The path here deliberately follows the line of a Saxon sunken road excavated 1962. The ruined church of St Peter (*see* City Churches, p. 106) has a herb garden to the s on the former churchyard, once framed by St Peter's Hospital, and rather bleak paving to the N and W. This is a good point to encompass the **public art** in the park, of 1992–3; *see* also the map. NW of the church, **Lines from Within**, a tall abstract bronze by *Ann Christopher*, evoking contemporary structures rising from medieval foundations beneath. Convex curved oak and steel seats by *Alan Tilbury*. E of St Peter a long hedged garden called **Beside the Still Waters**, by *Peter Randall Page* and *Bristol City Council Landscape Architects* [85]. To the N is *Rachel Fenner's*

85. Castle Park, Beside the Still Waters, by Peter Randall Page with Bristol City Council Landscape Architects, 1993

Throne, of French limestone, a reference to the castle's royal associations. SE towards the harbour wall a lively bronze **drinking fountain** by *Kate Malone*, with bas reliefs including the ship and castle from Bristol's coat of arms. At the park's NE corner, a sculpture installation, **Only Dead Fish Go with the Flow**, by *Victor Moreton*, of white-glazed *cerâmica do Douro*.

Now for the scattered surviving elements of **Bristol Castle** (*see* map for locations) which covered most of the park E of the shallow gully-like feature running N–S, marking the approximate course of the castle's W wall. To the N, the **keep** foundations (*c.* 1120), of which parts of the N and W walls, a well-shaft and a garderobe pit survive. Pennant rubble wall bases up to 16 ft (*c.* 5 metres) thick. The keep is thought to have been about 80 ft (24 metres) high, 80 ft square and faced with a pale limestone. On the s side of the park, above the harbour, the **sallyport**, a defensive stepped tunnel from within the castle down to moat level, allowing the castle defenders to prevent sappers undermining the walls. C20 walls above ground, with C12 or C13 door-jambs and tunnel visible behind an iron gate. Following the harbour wall E, shortly, a length of standing castle **wall** *c.* 6 ft 6 ins (2 metres) high, with two chamfered arrow loops, with fireplace openings from its incorporation in post-C17 structures. At the E end of the park, the **Castle Chambers**, with early C20 glazed arches and brickwork fronting two rooms of uncertain function, related to the King's Hall (rebuilt 1239–42, dem.) which stood nearby to the N. The s room, of *c.* 1225–50, was possibly a porch and has fine moulded ribs on five-part shafted columns, with some vigorous stiff-leaf capitals (recent replicas). It was perhaps part of the mid-C13 works at the castle overseen by the king's 'viewer', *William Mountsorrel*. The early C14 N room is simpler, with single-chamfered ribs, and may have been a separate entrance to chambers, later used as a chapel or antechapel.*

Here we leave Castle Park and move s down **Queen Street** across the **castle moat**; now a sluggish stream running from Broadweir beneath Lower Castle Street (known until the C19 as Castle Ditch). Only visible here where it empties into the harbour. This was the site of the castle orchard. By the C17 there were scattered houses, gardens and limekilns here.

s of the moat is **King's Orchard**, offices and housing by *Leach Rhodes Walker*, 1982. Hard orange brick, with broken rooflines and cardboard-thin 'towers'. At the s end, lower and more successful housing, with stucco walls and a courtyard over underground parking. Now s into **Passage Street**, where the former offices of **Wessex Water** stand opposite. By *BGP Group Architects*, 1978, a clean horizontal block raised on stilts over a recessed glass entrance foyer. Of red brick, with strip windows interrupted by widely spaced verticals expressing the frame. For the **Shot Tower** behind, see p. 180. On the N side of Passage Street is the **Central Health Clinic**, 1935, by *C.F.W. Dening*, the only pre-existing building incorporated in the 1940s plans for a Civic Centre. An integrated centre (a relatively new building type) with general, paediatric and dental clinics and a separate wing for tuberculosis cases. Brown brick and Portland stone. Deep U-shaped courtyard; stepped central tower, and gently canted ends to the rear wing.

Here, unexpectedly, SS Philip and Jacob (*see* City Churches, p. 107) sitting low in a spacious churchyard. It is overshadowed to the N by **Rogers' Brewery**, Jacob Street, by *W.B. Gingell c.* 1865, now offices (*see* Castle Gate, below). A tall Pennant rubble block with rock-faced rusticated basement, a much-altered fragment of the original powerful design.

A path E of the brewery leads N to Old Market roundabout and underpass (1968). Here, Temple Way bisects Old Market on its way towards Newfoundland Street, in fulfilment of the 1944 Reconstruction Plan. Swamped by post-war redevelopment. Behind to the sw, **Castle Gate**, speculative offices by *M.P. Kent Design Group*, 1980–2. Looking N, E of Temple Way the dark pink tower of **Mercury House** (*Elsom, Pack & Roberts*, 1971), and to its w, the **Marriott Hotel**, formerly Holiday Inn, completed 1972. Turning w then N into **Lower Castle Street**, the tall and

*Includes information from M.Litt. thesis by Michael Ponsford, 1979.

86. Quakers' Friars, roof of the Bakers' Hall, C14

intrusive office tower of Castlemead (*A.J. Hines & Co.*), begun 1973 but halted by the property crash and completed 1981. Unbroken concrete verticals with narrow glazing strips, terminating in a flared top.

Here begins **Broadmead**, Bristol's post-war shopping centre. For the long history of its planning, *see* Introduction, pp. 39–40, 42. The plan by the City Architect *J.N. Meredith*, provided for 145 shop units and was finalized in 1946–7. It was built piecemeal, with many changes, from 1950 to 1960. Here at the SE end of Broadmead, furthest from the flagship stores on The Horsefair, the architecture is dowdy and feeble. Here **Broadweir** runs W, where shortly is a narrow turning N into a rear service court, **Quakers' Friars**. Here is one of the most architecturally ambitious C18 Friends' meeting houses attached to fragments of a medieval Dominican friary. The simple, four-square **Meeting House** of 1747–9, by the Quaker *George Tully* and his son *William*, is now Bristol Register Office. Rendered walls with widely spaced segmental-arched sashes and pedimented E entrance door dated 1747. This and the other masonry details by *Thomas Paty*. Ramped corners to the parapet, an effective decorative device. Panelled interior now crudely partitioned for the Register Office, with central lantern and Doric columns supporting galleries on three sides. Pleasing caretaker's **cottage** attached at the left, perhaps by *George Dymond*, *c.* 1833–5, with wide eaves and sashes set in recessed arches.

To the W is a courtyard with fragments of the monastic ranges of the **Blackfriars**. Their church to the N was established here in 1227–8. At the Reformation, parts were adapted as a merchant's house and later fragmented for industrial use. N of the courtyard, **Cutlers' Hall** was possibly the friars' dormitory over the S cloister range, used by the Cutlers' Company from 1499 until *c.* 1770 and purchased by the Quakers in 1845 for use as a school. A long two-storey range of rubble stone, with big E window of three E.E. cusped lancets, moved here from the Bakers' Hall range (*see* below). Small single-light windows to the long N side, possibly lighting the friars' cells. The s wall was rebuilt in 1850 with two-light plate-traceried windows, by *William Armstrong*. But his pupil *E.W. Godwin* may have been responsible, for he wrote an account in *The Builder*. At the rear of the courtyard, **New Hall**, added in 1869 as a schoolroom over a covered play area, on the site of the C13 lesser cloister E range. It also links Cutlers' Hall with **Bakers' Hall**, in the s range, probably the friars' infirmary of *c.* 1230–60. A patchwork of masonry outside, with two arches of the lesser cloister in the N wall. Part of a Perp window from the friary nave was reset in the s wall in 1961. The upper hall has a crown-post roof [86] with arch-braced collar-beams and wind-braces, conjecturally C14: repaired 1971–4 under *Alan Rome*. All this sits in the unloveliest of settings, with the backs of shops, rubbish bins, car-parking and public toilets: surely Bristol's greatest planning failure of the 1950s. Plans by *Alec French Partnership* were approved in 2002 to remodel Quakers' Friars as part of the Broadmead extension, creating a new square from the surrounding service court, lined with shops and with flats to the s.

Then w on to Merchant Street, and the **Merchant Tailors' Almshouses**, dated 1701, symmetrical and U-shaped around a narrow courtyard. Central shell-hooded entrance and, above, the Merchant Tailors' arms with richly modelled Baroque mantling. Interiors completely removed for the shopping centre to which it is now attached: **The Galleries**, 1987–90, *Leslie Jones Architects*. It covers the entire sw quarter of Broadmead. Behind the almshouses there is much glass, with repetitive gables in the glazing pattern. Buff and orange brick with predictably thin Postmodern pediments and arches. Inside, the standard arrangement with shops facing three storeys of balconies around a full-height glazed atrium.

From Merchant Street N into the hub at the centre of Broadmead, designed by *J.N. Meredith*, with bland four-storey Bath stone quadrants. Then w into **Broadmead** (the street). On the N side, through a double-arched screen, a cobbled courtyard leads to **Wesley's New Room**, effectively the world cradle of Methodism and its first purpose-built place of worship. John Wesley arrived in Bristol in March 1739. Finding inadequate accommodation for the three groups of worshippers here, he organized the purchase of land for a 'new room' on 9 May. Building began three days later and by June the first meeting was held in the unfinished shell, proof of the Dissenters' dynamism. Major rebuilding and enlargement was needed by 1748; the present structure is probably almost entirely of that date.* In 1808 it became a Welsh Calvinist chapel, but was bought back in 1929 and restored by *George Oatley*, 1930.

In the long s courtyard, a bronze **statue** of John Wesley on horseback, by *A.G. Walker*, 1932. Here, external display was neither possible nor desired. A reticent roughcast façade with one round-arched

---

*Recent studies have made conflicting deductions as to which parts pre-date 1748.

87. Broadmead, Wesley's New Room, perhaps by George Tully, mainly 1748

window above a Gibbsian blocked porch (by Oatley, to the C18 plan but of conjectural design). The **interior** [87] exudes a magnetic calm; a plain, functional room with six Tuscan columns supporting the ceiling. Panelled E and W galleries lit by segment-headed windows. Stylistic similarities with the Friends' Meeting House (*see* p. 173) suggest *George Tully*'s hand here. The constricted site necessitated additional top-lighting, yet living space for visiting preachers had to be provided above too. These requirements were ingeniously reconciled by pushing an octagonal lantern through the upper room, with windows cut in the shaft to light the upper room. On the N wall, a two-tier **pulpit** (rein-stated in 1930) reached by stairs down from the gallery ends. To save space the pulpit sits over the N entrance lobby. Central block of box pews (1930, reconstructing C19 predecessors); but benches in and under the galleries. Light-green painted walls, originally pale grey limewash with stone-coloured painted woodwork. *Snetzler* **chamber organ**, 1761, installed in the gallery 1930. The upper **living room** (originally also the preachers' library) is reached from the E gallery or by an external N staircase. Study-bedrooms at the sides with functional window seats, and a writing slope in John Wesley's bedroom. In the **Garden Court** (of 1953–4) a bronze **statue** of Charles Wesley by *F. Brook Hitch*, 1938.

88. Lower Arcade, Broadmead, by James & Thomas Foster, 1824–5

Returning to Broadmead, directly w is **Lower Arcade** (by the brothers *James & Thomas Foster*, 1824–5) [88]. Its twin, Upper Arcade, was blitzed and the survivor narrowly escaped demolition for the new shopping development in 1948. Thirty-six two-storey shops arranged in nine bays marked by Ionic columns with a cast-iron frieze above, and narrow oriels inspired by the Burlington Arcade, London (1818). Glazed cast-iron roof with lion masks in the spandrel arches. The handsome Broadmead façade is a scaled-down version of *Smirke*'s Old Council House design (*see* p. 134). Smirke's frieze above the ground floor is here reduced to a moulding and the anthemion decoration promoted to the main entablature.

On the s side, the c18 façade of the **Greyhound Inn**, with two-storey canted bays flanking an arched carriageway. By the 1940s little survived within; everything behind the frontage was swept away for the Galleries shopping centre, c. 1987, the façade being 'preserved' as an entrance. To the w, what was once the most distinguished shopfront here, Nos. 77–79 Broadmead, by *Ellis E. Somake* for Dolcis shoes, 1952, remodelled as two shops c. 1970. Originally one double-height façade, of which the wider, left side was deeply recessed beneath the second-floor loggia, a sophisticated spatial arrangement. No. 78 Broadmead, **Marks & Spencer**, by *James Monro & Sons*, c. 1950, on classical lines suggesting columns and entablature, represents the run-of-the-mill Broadmead designs.

At the junction of Union Street and Broadmead the mildly Art Deco **Odeon** cinema, 1938, by *T. Cecil Howitt*. A full-height turret over a corner entrance, its coherence now destroyed by the extension of the vertical fins over the upper drum, and removal of the capping band. Flanks faced in cream faience, with green bands implying shutters to the horizontal upper windows on Union Street. Ground floor now shops, interiors gutted 1983–5 for studio cinemas. Across the road southward one of the few Victorian survivors here, now **Next**, by *Alfred Harford*, 1880.

At the lower N end of Union Street is **Broadmead Baptist Chapel**, by *Ronald Sims*, completed 1969. The Baptists were established here in 1671. Their C19 chapel was replaced by ground-floor shops and a new chapel above. Since removal of the laminated timber spire, the chapel is marked externally only by its canted and broken roofline. Ground-floor classrooms and ancillary accommodation, and, above, a chapel seating 720 and a meeting hall. Both spatially and in plan the chapel lacks coherence, the worship being focused on the long E side of the rectangle. A very long dais, with pulpit at one extremity and bench-like communion table at the other. In between, a wide space on which the seating is centred. Full-immersion baptistery built into the curved continuation of the pulpit wall. Raked w gallery backed by a glass wall, with C19 stained-glass panels from the old chapel. Timber-clad ceiling of varied and canted profiles with four full-width lights running E–W.

N along Union Street at the junction with The Horsefair, **St James's Place Gateway**, 1997 by *Fitzroy Robinson*, three curving steel masts supporting a glass canopy and advertising sails, announcing the entrance to Broadmead. Facing the junction, Broadmead's flagship store, **Lewis's** (now House of Fraser), by *Sir Percy Thomas & Son*, built 1955–7. Six storeys of Portland stone on a sloping triangular site. At the apex, a curved prow emphasized by a rectilinear grid with double-cell horizontal glazing strips divided by single-cell panels of stone. The upper storey is set back and topped by a roof terrace. Interiors refitted for Bentalls by *Stride Treglown* (1998). The perambulation ends here, appropriately in the heart of Bristol's shopping centre.

Walk 3.

Temple and Redcliffe

Temple and Redcliffe lie in the deep curve s of the River Avon, and SE of the city centre. Settlement here was established by the C12, prompted by the presence of Bristol Bridge and the roadways to Bath and Bedminster. In 1145 the E part was granted to the Knights Templar, who founded Temple Church and made the district their administrative centre in the w of England. The area was protected by a wall to the s from the C13, and the charter of 1373 brought it into the county of Bristol. Weaving became the major industry in Temple. The area is treated here in three walks starting at Bristol Bridge, St Mary Redcliffe and Redcliffe Bridge, which form a circle.

A note about spelling: Redcliffe usually has a final 'e', but sometimes not. This book follows modern maps for street names.

89. Walk 3

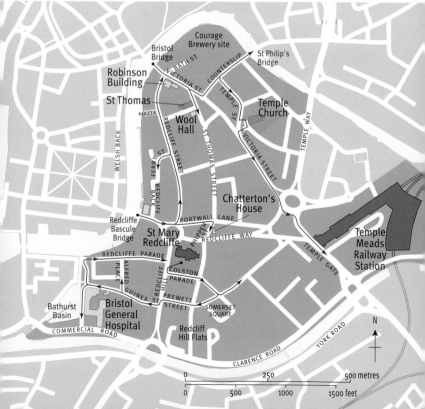

90. Nos. 2–16 Victoria Street, 1870s

Bristol Bridge to Temple Meads

Bristol Bridge is the natural starting point for a walk s of the river. The main route SE is now **Victoria Street**, proposed in 1845 to ease traffic from Temple Meads railway terminus to the city but completed *c.* 1872; the layout (but not the building design) was by *S.C. Fripp*. **Bath Street** is now a short cul-de-sac running E from Victoria Street. On the N side is the former **Courage Brewery** site (previously George's), which held the entire frontage between Bristol Bridge and St Philip's Bridge. The site had been a brewery since at least the 1820s, with Finzel's Sugar Refinery at the E end from 1857. Courage's closed in the 1990s. Remodelled as mixed offices and apartments, by *Atkins Walters Webster*, in 2001–2. The 1930s **Keg Store** in dark brick is on the left, and beyond, the **Tower**, *c.* 1925, tall and heavily classical. On the s side, a terrace of three-storey brick houses by *William Paty*, 1789, later brewery offices. (For the buildings opposite and s of Bristol Bridge *see* Redcliff Street, pp. 186–8.)

Back to Victoria Street, which was badly bombed and now makes a less than heartening gateway to the city. The NE side from Bath Street to Counterslip is a pleasing example of Victorian Gothic variety, the only part of the street to give some idea of its original appearance [90]. Most of this row was façaded for offices or apartments in the 1990s. On the corner of Bath Street, No. 2, the **Talbot Hotel** (*c.* 1873), in sub-Ruskinian commercial Gothic, with an arched entrance on the curve beneath a conical roof. Polychrome brick sets the tone for the street. Blitzed in 1940; everything above the first floor is almost undetectable reinstatement by *BGP Group Architects, c.* 1994. Nos. 4 and 6 await refurbishment. No. 8, reminiscent of No. 35 King Street (*see* Walk 1, p. 159), may be by

Henry Masters who did much work here. At No. 10, Platnauer Brothers' clockmakers' shop, Gothic was rejected for a pilastered grid of load-bearing masonry and plate glass. No. 16, 1871, by the London architect *J. Michelen Rogers*. Brick and patterned terracotta, with big arched first-floor window, and a florid dormer. (Ground floor, late 1990s.)

Opposite on the sw side, Nos. 25–31, four gabled houses of 1673–5.* Three storeys with gabled attics, jettied ground floors and bay windows. Running s here, **St Thomas Street**, an important medieval thoroughfare but now insignificant. On the right, St Thomas the Martyr (*see* City Churches, p. 110). s of Thomas Lane is the former **Wool Hall** (1828, *R.S. Pope*), now a pub and offices. Built for St Thomas parish as a market hall and warehouse, a spare classical design, but with robust Pennant masonry that feels very Victorian. Tall symmetrical façade with vermiculated plinth, a narrow pedimented centre, windows grouped vertically in arched recesses. A forerunner of Pope's Bush House (*see* Walk 1, p. 166). The centre of Redcliffe is quite barren: return to Victoria Street.

A short detour NE along **Counterslip** to the **Tramways Electricity Generating Station**, 1899, an early work by *W. Curtis Green* [91]. A hybrid of Neoclassical and Baroque elements, in red brick and Bath stone. Especially monumental SE façade. NE side rising almost sheer from the water, with five Venetian motifs. E of the river, but best viewed from St Philip's Bridge is the 141-ft (43-metre) high disused **Shot Tower** [20], of 1968–9. The engineers *E.N. Underwood & Partners* treated a functional concrete structure as an aesthetic object, to great effect. It replaced the demolished shot tower (1782) on Redcliff Hill, where the plumber William Watts invented the process of dropping molten lead from a height into water to form perfectly spherical lead shot. Distinctive angled top chamber over a **Y**-section shaft, the three arms carrying a staircase, a hoist for lead and the dropping shaft.

From Counterslip turn s into **Temple Street**, the main medieval way to Temple Gate and thence to Bath, superseded by Victoria Street. Where Temple Street re-joins Victoria Street is the C19 Gothic gateway to Temple Church (*see* City Churches, p. 111). Immediately s, No. 58, Victoria Street, by *W.V. Gough*, *c.* 1890s, for Temple vestry. Red brick with round-arched arcaded windows and a small Flemish pediment. Next door, the **King's Head**, a C17 core with late Georgian refronting and pub interior of *c.* 1865, a rarity in Bristol. It includes coloured mirror panels and a panelled snug at the back. To the SE is the **Shakespeare Inn**, with big oversailing gable, ground-floor jetty, and pent roofs at each floor. The date 1636, painted, unverified but quite plausible. The sw side of Victoria Street is dominated by mediocre post-war offices; the best is **Transport House**, 1959, by *Travis & White*, for the Transport and General Workers' Union. On the angled entrance is an intaglio sculpture of three heroic male figures bearing a torch.

*The painted date comes from a deed of 1456 referring to shops here.

91. Former Tramways
Generating Station,
Counterslip, by W.
Curtis Green, 1899

At the SE end of Victoria Street facing Temple Way roundabout
is No. 100 Temple Street, formerly the **London Life Building**, by *Wells
Thorpe*, 1982. Its staggered masses achieve a pleasing three-dimensional
quality. Five well-composed red brick storeys, screened by slim paired
supports of contrasting aggregate. Recessed upper floors reduce the
apparent bulk. s of the roundabout between Redcliffe Way and Temple
Gate two disused Victorian railway hotels: the **Grosvenor Hotel** (1875,
S.C. Fripp), high and four-square with coarse Flemish-looking attics;
and to the SE the **George Railway Hotel** (*c.* 1870) with a statue of Queen
Victoria presiding over the entrance. Under repair 2004. Opposite in
Temple Gate, Temple Meads Station (*see* Major Buildings, p. 88).

Around St Mary Redcliffe

Redcliffe sits upon a red sandstone bluff that gives the district its name.
Sited outside the medieval town *en route* to Bedminster is Bristol's most
famous church, St Mary Redcliffe (*q.v.* Major Buildings, p. 66). It
remains hugely impressive for its scale and magnificence, despite the
busy circuit road nearby. The route s and w of the church takes in much
good domestic architecture of the C18–C20, starting from the relative
quiet and shelter to the s of the church.

Colston Parade, s of the churchyard, is a pleasant row of C18 and C19
houses. From the w, No. 12 (*c.* 1772), with a w front of brick, and on the
N a symmetrical five-bay stucco front with central doorway. Fry's House
of Mercy, a small Gothic Revival almshouse of 1784, has Y-traceried windows symmetrical about the Tudor-arched entrance. Interiors rebuilt
after Second World War bombing. Nos. 1–5, *c.* 1760, possibly by *Thomas*

Paty, have banded rustication to the ground floors and Gibbsian blocked door surrounds, though without the usual stepped window voussoirs. At the E end, the **Ship Inn** has chunky window frames and carved detail of *c.* 1870, with an irregular C17 or C18 structure behind. Just to the E is **Redcliffe Methodist Church** by *Alec French & Partners*, 1962. A concrete box on a brick base, with a fully glazed (ritual) E wall framing St Mary Redcliffe. To the s, the area around **Somerset Square** and **Prewett Street** was redeveloped with the **Redcliff Hill flats** by the *City Architect's Department*, 1955–64. Designed under *J.N. Meredith*, the later phases under *A.H. Clarke*. Similar blocks were put up at Barton Hill in the E of the city. Reinforced concrete construction of *in situ* columns and partially pre-cast beams. The w section completed first, mainly of three- to five-storey blocks, but some blocks up to thirteen storeys. In the centre of Somerset Square is a strange confection, an C18 **conduit head** from the destroyed Georgian square of the same name.

To the E along Prewett Street, on the N the stump of a brick-built **glass cone**, now a hotel restaurant; the only surviving glass cone in the city (probably *c.* 1780), and a reminder that glass and pottery were major C18 and C19 industries in Temple and Redcliffe. Use for glass-making ceased by 1812 and the unstable upper parts were dismantled in 1936. Return w to **Redcliff Hill**, cleared for 1960s road plans, where the w side is dominated by *Whicheloe Macfarlane Partnership*'s **Phoenix Assurance** building of 1974. Four storeys of unremitting horizontals over a stilted base in pale concrete, with minimal articulation provided by a stepped elevation. The landscaped court facing Guinea Street is more successful. s of Guinea Street is **Waring House**, 1958–60 [92], the biggest of the Redcliff Hill flats (*see* above). A design of some distinction with, on the s side, scalloped roofline and barrel-vaulted canopy echoing the curved revetments of the river below.

From Redcliff Hill turn w into **Guinea Street**. On the s side, Nos. 10–12, built as one house in 1718 for Edmund Saunders, a slave trader, merchant and churchwarden at St Mary Redcliffe. No. 10 has the original entrance, with a mid-C18 Gothick door, and an ogee gable, perhaps added slightly after 1718. The house was divided into three before 1832, with the addition of cramped doorways. Wavy arrises in gauged and rubbed brick to the upper windows, and twelve grotesque window keystones, the best such group in the city. The original **plan** must have been a through-corridor from the door, then at right angles to it a hall running E–w to the staircase, with two rooms in front and two behind. At No. 12, a good original staircase, with expected early C18 features. Over it, a fine stucco ceiling, probably by a local craftsman. A frame of fruit in high relief contains a delightful bas-relief of hunting scenes in a rural landscape. In the cellar, a stone cistern on an odd teardrop plan, just possibly an early plunge bath. A few yards N in **Alfred Place**, two infill houses, both designed by architect-artist partnerships for themselves. No. 2, by *Jonathan Mosley* and *Sophie Warren*, completed 2002. A severe white-rendered box over black timber boarding,

92. Waring House, Redcliff Hill, by J.N. Meredith, built 1958–60

the rectilinearity countered by one subtle angle, a motif repeated inside. No. 4 by *Mike* and *Sandie Macrae*, completed 2001. Designed for energy efficiency, it has solarblock lower walls, lime-rendered upper parts with a jettied centre, and wave-like roofs of Evalon cladding.

Returning to Guinea Street, which slopes down to the w, Nos. 18–19 are possibly also part of Saunders's development here, *c.* 1718. At No. 18, an early C19 doorcase and fanlight.

On the slope to the w, the Pennant and Bath Stone **Bristol General Hospital** by *W.B. Gingell*, a competition win and one of his earliest Bristol works. Its core of 1852–7 is visible from the s and w, in an Italianate round-arched manner with a sw polygonal turret, originally with ogee dome. The hospital sits over basement warehousing of massive rock-faced masonry. *The Builder* criticized its 'ill chosen site' beside Bathurst Basin; Victorian fear of 'miasmas' – disease-causing vapours thought to prevail in damp atmospheres – obliged Gingell to install a powerful ventilation system. Fireproof construction, speaking tubes and steam-powered lifts were additional innovations. The L-shaped building was much extended, forming by the early C20 a courtyard plan entered from Guinea Street. The main additions were *Gingell's* Outpatients Department, designed 1871; N wing by *Crisp & Oatley*, *c.* 1895; a ward block next to the gates, 1905; a gate lodge, and SE wing with sun balconies, both 1912. All the work after 1900 was by *Oatley & Lawrence*. The building is spoiled by enclosed metal balconies, concrete-rendered additions over the s terracing, and by the loss of the dome and French-inspired dormered roofs.

From the point where Guinea Street meets Bathurst Basin, to the N is the **Ostrich Inn**. Truncated window pediments and margin glazing perhaps of *c.* 1830, but the asymmetric placing of the door and the ramped parapet suggest a mid-C18 structure beneath. Here the rock is peppered with tunnels, known as Redcliffe Caves, probably the result of excavating sand for glass-making, and certainly not the slave dungeons of Bristol myth (*see* topic box, p. 202). Steps bring us up on to **Redcliffe Parade**, two terraces with wide views N across the Floating Harbour and city. The W terrace and the first two houses E of Jubilee Place are of *c.* 1768–71; continued E with single-bay houses of *c.* 1800. At the W end, the return elevation of No. 13 has an early C19 tented porch and full-height canted bay with embattled parapet. Return E to Redcliff Hill and the end of this walk.

Redcliffe Bridge to Bristol Bridge

The third walk takes us from Redcliffe Bridge, NW of St Mary Redcliffe, back to Bristol Bridge. N of the church, Redcliffe Way was driven through to Queen Square in 1939, replacing tightly packed housing with a bleak and open corridor. Industrial remains are grouped at this end of Redcliff Street, with late C20 rebuilding further N.

Redcliffe Bascule Bridge, of 1939–42, took the inner circuit road towards Queen Square. Chunky concrete piers and D-shaped control cabins. It provides the best view of the mills and warehouses on Redcliff Backs rising sheer from the harbour. On the bridge's NE flank, **Custom House** apartments,* by *Architecture & Planning Group*, 2001, trumpet the reinvention of Bristol harbour as another London docklands. Seven storeys with a stack of near-circular balconies cantilevered from the corner. Visually fragmented by changes of colour and details; nevertheless it successfully terminates the long waterfront vista. The site was formerly occupied by the Western Counties Agricultural Association (WCA), whose **WCA Warehouse** [93], next door to the N, is by *W.H. Brown* of Leeds, 1909. A blend of gruff industrial and Edwardian classicism, and an early Bristol use of a reinforced concrete frame with brick cladding. On both the E and W fronts, three cantilevered two-storey oriels, originally housing hoists. Converted to housing in 1997 by *Architecton*, with an internal light well, and penthouses set back from the parapet.

Excavation here revealed that the river bank was moved some 165 ft (50 metres) westward between the C12 and C15, by dumping rubble to raise the ground level for building. A C13 slipway and two C14 docks were discovered. The present line of Redcliff Backs was under water until the C14. Towards St Mary Redcliffe from the Custom House apartments, on the N side is the WCA offices by *W.V. Gough*, in red and yellow brick, and quite old-fashioned for 1896–7.

From Redcliff Street, **Portwall Lane** runs E, formerly directly inside the C13 port wall. The wall and outer ditch ran E from the River Avon at Redcliffe Bridge, meeting the river again at the present Temple Quay

---

*A pointless and confusing name without historical precedent. The Custom House is in Queen Square.

93. WCA Warehouse, Redcliff Backs, by W.H. Brown, 1909

just N of Temple Meads. On Portwall Lane, N side, a good row of late C19 **warehouses** of orange Cattybrook brick. The best is No. 3, probably by *W.B. Gingell c.* 1880, with ground-floor segment-headed windows between firm square piers, brick cogging and an arched corbel-table. No. 4 (*Alec French Partnership, c.* 1990), the **Open University** office, is a well-mannered addition. Nearby on Phippen Street is **Chatterton's House** of 1749, the only remaining example of the small vernacular buildings that once crowded up to the church walls. Built by St Thomas parish for its schoolmaster, it was the birthplace in 1752 of the poet Thomas Chatterton. Facing Redcliffe Way is the pedimented façade of the **School House**, relocated here from nearby in 1939. Ashlar walls with two segment-headed windows, channelled pilaster strips and flanking doors, somewhat old-fashioned for the apparent date of 1779.

94. Canynges's House, c14 hall roof; early c20 photograph

William Canynges the Younger (1402–74) was the wealthiest and best-known of a great mercantile family, serving as an MP three times and mayor five times. He specialized by shipping other merchants' cloth to Europe in his ships. William Worcestre tells us Canynges employed a hundred men at one time. His ten ships, totalling nearly 3,000 tons, included the *Mary and John* of 900 tons. The family were major patrons of St Mary Redcliffe, but the tradition that William Canynges the Elder (grandfather of the younger) was solely or largely responsible for the Perp rebuilding is now questioned. Canynges's house was c14 or perhaps earlier, with a hall, chapel, and chambers extending w to Redcliff Backs. Here Canynges added a high tower, with bay windows 'highly decorated, like the rooms' (Worcestre). A richly patterned tile floor dated *c.* 1481–1515, is at the British Museum. The house was demolished for road-widening in 1937.

Return E to **Redcliff Street**, where on the E side is No. 60, **The Atrium**, by *J.H. Hirst* then *Henry Crisp*, 1882–3, a tobacco factory for Edwards, Ringer & Co. An eclectic jumble of motifs: round arcades, pink sandstone and Pennant stone polychromy, classical cornices and pediments. Inside, a central top-glazed iron atrium. Four lock-up shops fronted the street. Converted to apartments 2001. A few yards further on the w side is a medieval **wall** under a c20 roof, a fragment of the house of William Canynges the Younger (*see* topic box, above). Two blind arches without capitals, inserted in the c15 presumably

95. Robinson Building, Redcliff Street, by Group Architects DRG, 1960–3

to strengthen the C14 masonry. Within the right arch, a C15 ogee-arched stoup or wash-basin, and the masonry joins of a C14 arch. The wall formed the N side of a four-bay hall with an elaborate timber roof [94].*

*On Redcliff Backs and Guild Court is a C15 rubble wall, now with C20 flats grafted on. This wall has two blocked windows with relieving arches. It is on the same line as the Redcliff Street wall, and probably connected with it as part of the N boundary of Canynges's House.

N along Redcliff Street most of the w side has been redeveloped since the 1980s as speculative offices and apartments. The design concepts were negotiated 1970–7. The planners laudably insisted throughout that all new buildings continue the walkway along the harbour; only the s end remains to be completed. All the buildings here show their workaday faces to Redcliff Street, and are best viewed from Welsh Back across the harbour. At Ferry Street (cul-de-sac, w side), two brick towers of **Buchanan's Wharf**, 1884, a granary and flour mill, converted to apartments 1988. **Redcliff Quay** to the N is by *Alec French Partnership*. The planning brief was established in 1980 but the design only approved in 1989 after tortured negotiation, public inquiry and the intervention of the Secretary of State. Buff brick over a limestone plinth with brown marble banding, and red and chocolate detailing. On the long harbour façade, metal balconies and brises-soleil confuse the eye.

The narrow **piazza** to the N is dominated by a sculptural ceramic obelisk, **Exploration**, 1991, by *Philippa Threlfall* and *Kennedy Collings* with an armillary sphere by *James Blunt*. To its N, Discovery House is part of the Redcliff Quay development: then **Bull Wharf** and **Bristol Bridge House**, both by *Angus Meek/R. Diplock Associates*, 1985. The mid-1970s proposals for the former explicitly echoed the C19 warehouse aesthetic. That idea was replaced by standard 1980s arches, leaded mansards, etc. Bristol Bridge House is more satisfactory; carefully modelled buff brick alternates with sections of curtain walling. At the N end, **Number One Victoria Street**, by *Prudential Architects*, 1979–82, holds the prominent corner adjoining Bristol Bridge. In harsh orange brick with angular projections towards the water, giving the uncomfortable illusion that the lead mansards are dripping like molten wax down the wall faces. For Victoria Street, *see* p. 179.

On the opposite corner at No. 1 Redcliff Street, the **Robinson Building** [95], Bristol's first true tower block, of 1960–3, by *Group Architects DRG* (Dickinson Robinson Group owned the client, E.S. & A. Robinson). Sir Basil Spence approved it but had no part in the design. A custom-built post-war office block of such architectural quality is a rarity outside London, although, from the first, it has been criticized for its siting: it is certainly unsympathetic to its C17 neighbours in Thomas Street, and dominates views from some quarters. A square fifteen-storey tower of extreme elegance and simplicity, with stilted podium-like conference and training facilities adjoining to the s. Fully glazed foyer set behind external columns. Crisp structural mullions and pre-cast wall panels finished with white Carrara marble aggregate. Bronze-framed glazing set behind the openings, creating shadow and depth. The segment-headed windows are the first deliberate echo of the Victorian warehouse style in post-war Bristol, an alteration intended to appeal to the company board at final approval.*

*Information from Colin Beales and Elain Harwood.

Walk 4.

Park Street and Brandon Hill

From College Green, we take a circular route via the busy shops of Park Street, around Brandon Hill, then via the w side of the hill down to Deanery Road and back to our start point. Brandon Hill, topped by the landmark of Cabot Tower, is the highest point in central Bristol; an outcrop of Brandon Hill Grit, a pinkish sandstone much used locally. Park Street was laid out over Bullock's Park in the mid C18: a development of polite housing climbing towards Clifton. By the early C19 Brandon Hill was absorbed into the city.

Note: Park Street and parts of Brandon Hill are very steep.

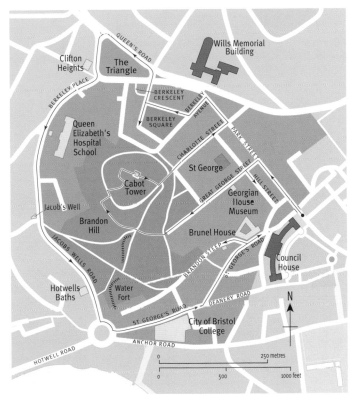

97. Park Street and the tower of the Wills Memorial Building

Park Street, first proposed in 1740, was laid out in 1758 by *George Tully*; building commenced in 1761. *Thomas Paty* and *James Paty* were among the first builders. At its bottom end Park Street crossed a narrow, steep-sided gully on the line of Frogmore Street. A cast-iron viaduct by *R.S. Pope* was opened in 1871, easing the ascent. On its NE side, Nos. 8–18, Italianate stuccoed shops by *W.H. Hawtin*, 1867 and 1872. Opposite, Nos. 7–11 by *Henry Masters*, 1871, four storeys and nine bays wide, with a repetitive froth of carving around the windows. The interiors (now occupied by bars and a club) are a different matter. In 1936 Ronald Avery purchased fittings from the Cunard liner RMS *Mauretania*, launched 1907, decommissioned 1934. The ship's interiors were designed *c.* 1906 by the architect *Harold Peto*. They were deftly reinstalled here by *W.H. Watkins*, who extended the premises of Avery's wine merchants here in 1936–8. The ground-floor lounge bar was the *Mauretania's* library, with mahogany panelling and an oval stained-glass dome; above Frogmore Street the first-class Grand Salon, more intimate, with luscious gilding after an C18 French boudoir. It all conjures up a slightly raffish Edwardian *belle époque*. Illuminated *Mauretania* logo (1938) on the SE façade, Bristol's first moving neon sign.

At the junction of St George's Road is the former **Bristol Philosophical and Literary Institution** (1821–3), an early work by *Charles Cockerell*. The Institution was founded in 1817 to provide library, lecture theatre and museum galleries. Cockerell's sculpture casts from Aegina were displayed here. The Institution became part of the new Bristol Museum and Library (*see* Walk 9, p. 241) in 1871, and the building was bought by the Freemasons, who still own it. Corner entrance beneath a circular Corinthian portico; the order comes from the Temple of Apollo at Bassae in Greece, which Cockerell excavated in 1811. The portico relates poorly to the weaker return elevations, where insistent horizontal mouldings accentuate the sloping site. Cockerell noted this fault during construction, perhaps when it was already too late to effect any improvement. Beneath the portico, a fine bas-relief panel by Bristol-born *E.H. Baily* depicting Bristol being introduced to the Arts, Sciences and Literature. The building was bombed in 1940 and restored 1957–8, though with much loss of character inside.

Park Street was perhaps Bristol's first hillside terrace of uniformly stepped houses [97]. Each pilaster is clasped by the cornices from each side, resolving the change of level. The ramped parapet employed on sloping terraces at Bath from the 1760s was never as widely used here. The houses are faced with Bath stone, three windows wide and quite plain. About one third were badly damaged by bombing in 1940, and all but one replicated after the war. Most now have unattractive c20 shopfronts. Either side of the junction at Great George Street, matching houses of *c.* 1762, of brick and with pedimented returns, attributed to *Thomas Paty*. On the s side, No. 47, Alfred Chillcott & Co., jewellers, added a shopfront *c.* 1865–70. Polished granite columns and round arches with dense carving, perhaps by *Foster & Wood* or *Pope & Son.*

Great George Street leads to Brandon Hill. First, in the service lane behind Chillcott's shop, No. 7 Hill Street, designed *c.* 1974 by *Whicheloe Macfarlane Partnership* for their own use. Elegant three-storey composition in concrete, with strong verticals and broad chamfered panels framing the windows. Back in Great George Street, on the SE side are several three- and five-bay detached houses by *William Paty* (Nos. 3, 7, 23, 25, 27), built 1788–91, with rusticated ground floors and his typical arched doorways with open pediments on pilasters. All are in Paty's spare and elegant Neoclassical manner; ashlar-fronted, with undecorated window openings. Plans and details varied according to the clients' wishes. No. 7, now the **Georgian House Museum**, was built for John Pinney who owned sugar plantations on Nevis in the Caribbean. His wide social circle, many of whom were entertained here, included Lord Nelson, Southey, Coleridge and Wordsworth. Remarkably complete **interiors**, with study [98] and powder room at the front, and rear reception rooms with restrained plasterwork and marble chimneypieces. Lateral stone staircase with geometric wrought-iron balustrade, basement quarters including, unusually, a stone-lined plunge bath. Given to the city in 1938 by Canon R.T. Cole.

Opposite is St George, Brandon Hill (*see* City Churches, p. 95), then **Royal Colonnade**, recently completed in 1828. Probably by *R.S. Pope*, judging by stylistic similarities, e.g. with his Royal Western Hotel (*see* below, p. 198). Projecting ends frame a recessed ground-floor colonnade, which is simply doubled up in the centre, making an ill-advised 1:2:2:1:1:2:2:1 rhythm. At the top of the hill, No. 31 Great George Street,

98. The Georgian House Museum, study, by William Paty, 1788–91

by *Alec French Partnership*, 1987–90 [21]. A finely judged mix of red brick and Bath stone, in overlapping terraced blocks that hug the hillside. Appropriate Regency references in the shallow roofs, projecting eaves and a bowed oriel with brises-soleil on the sw.

Now on to **Brandon Hill**, traditionally used to dry laundry, and now a public park with rights of access confirmed by the Corporation in 1533. The best visible remains of Bristol's **Civil War Defences** are here (*see* topic box, p. 246). First, on the lower s slopes, the overgrown earthworks of the **Water Fort**, on what was then an open promontory defending the harbour approaches. The trek down and back is recommended only for the keen. A linear **earthwork** runs almost due N up the hill, with a spur and outwork halfway up marked by a tree. At the summit, C17 stone walls with a bank and ditch define a long angular **bastion** to the NW of **Cabot Tower**, by *W. V. Gough*, 1896–8 [99]. It commemorates the four hundredth anniversary of John Cabot's voyage in 1497 from Bristol to Newfoundland. A tall pink sandstone tower with limestone dressings, carried off with considerable panache. Diagonal buttresses rise sheer without set-offs (giving rather the impression of a

99. Cabot Tower from Brandon Hill, by W.V. Gough, 1896–8

chamfered recessed panel to each wall); bulging balconies under free
Gothic gables, then a firm parapet balcony with corner pinnacles and
flying buttresses supporting a strange octagonal cap, with a winged figure of Commerce surmounting a globe. Despite Gothic enrichments, it
defies stylistic labels; the distant profile is distinctive and successful. On
the E side of the hill, picturesque gardens with waterfalls, *c.* 1910–36.

Leaving the park, first **Charlotte Street** [100], laid out by *Thomas and
William Paty* with parts of Park Street and Berkeley Square. Severe
façades, three bays and three storeys with attics behind the parapet; a
step down and a pilaster lesene between each house, sashes unrelieved
by architraves and rusticated ground floors. The late Paty style became
the standard in Clifton and elsewhere, even where other architects were
involved. Doric doorcases of a pattern-book design first used a few
years earlier (*see* Rodney Place, Walk 7, p. 224). Some good cast-iron tented
balconies of *c.* 1830 limit any tendency to tedium. Raised pavements,
also characteristic of Bristol. On the SE side, Nos. 19 and 20, two villas
of the 1820s. Projecting centres, and, over the ground-floor windows,
semicircular panels with Adamesque radial fluting, unusual for Bristol.

100. Charlotte Street, by Thomas and William Paty, *c.* 1780s; balconies, *c.* 1830

Charlotte Street joins the upper part of **Park Street**. At No. 81, a bold three-arched shopfront, *c.* 1865, but little else of note. Looking up Park Street, the view is dominated, as its architect intended, by the University's Wills Memorial Tower, 1915–25, (*see* Major Buildings, p. 83). At the crest of the hill on the left is Berkeley Avenue, leading to **Berkeley Square** (planned 1787, completed *c.* 1800), probably by *William Paty*, as Thomas, his father, died 1789. The main builder *James Lockier*, like others here, went bankrupt in the slump of 1793 (*see* topic box, p. 217). Like Dowry Square, Hotwells, Berkeley Square was planned with an open SE side facing the city, now filled by a soulless post-war University building in pastiche Georgian. Even without this, the square would be vexing. A trapezoid plan (no two sides equal or parallel) with the highest point at the w angle; each side is a sloping terrace, and any attempted symmetry hopeless. Nos. 9–10 has an Edwardian Baroque refacing by *John Bevan the Younger*, 1912. No. 15, Berkeley Square Hotel, largely rebuilt in replica after war-damage, makes a weak centrepiece to the NW side. Five bays (1:3:1), the centre broken forward under a starved pediment. Odd inconsistencies such as flanks of unequal width; a dentil cornice and Vitruvian scroll band on this house only; architrave mouldings to the pediment entablature but not the sides; and pilasters stilted on awkward plinths. In the central gardens, a fragment of *John Norton*'s near-replica **High Cross** (1851), first erected on College Green to replace the medieval original removed in 1764. It was dismantled in turn for the Council House landscaping in 1950 (*see* Major Buildings, p. 73) and the upper parts re-erected here in 1956.

Leaving the square at the N angle, on the left is **Berkeley Crescent**, built 1791–*c.* 1800 and planned with Berkeley Square. A tight curve of six houses on a high terrace pavement. Like the backs of Berkeley Square, it is of unfashionable brick. We emerge here on to **Queen's Road**. To the right, the Museum and Art Gallery, and, in front, the Venetian Gothic Brown's Restaurant (*see* Walk 9, pp. 239 and 241). To the left of Brown's, Queen's Road runs into the NE side of the **Triangle**, laid out in the early 1850s on former nurseries. It introduced grandiose metropolitan shops for a wealthy clientele, and gave coherence to an awkward no-man's-land at the approach to Clifton. On the right side, the Italianate **Royal Promenade** (1859, *Foster & Wood*), palatial in scale if repetitious, designed after *John Marmont*'s Royal Promenade, Clifton (*see* Walk 7, p. 227). Much altered, but the original façade survives, e.g. at No. 58.

Turning s into **Triangle West**, on the w side is **Clifton Heights**, Bristol's second tower block, 1962–5, by *Raymond Moxley*. Three-storey horizontal podium with colonnaded ground floor; cleanly articulated twelve-storey tower above. Controversial for its proximity to C18 Clifton, and the hilltop situation, magnifying its impact from a distance. A mixed scheme of shopping, restaurant, offices and flats, unusual for the early 1960s. Descending towards Jacob's Wells Road, a high revetment marks Upper Berkeley Place, with more *Paty* stepped terracing *c.* 1790, with pretty canted bays to six houses. Below in **Berkeley Place** is the **QEH Theatre** by *Moxley Jenner*, 1990, for the nearby school (*see* below). A restricted site beneath high walls: striped brick and a glazed drum foyer. Polygonal auditorium in the round, also reached by a bridge from the school grounds. Stretching along the steep hillside, **Queen Elizabeth's Hospital School** by *Thomas Foster & Son*, 1844–7 [101]. Founded in 1590 by the bequest of John Carr, a soap merchant. Picturesquely asymmetric gatehouse at street level, giving on to a vertiginous flight of steps up to the entrance tower, symmetrically composed, with double-height central oriel above. Three long, high

101. Queen Elizabeth's Hospital School, by Thomas Foster & Son, 1844–7

storeys of red rubble in a bare Tudor Gothic style. The structural members are cast-iron. Inside, an open-well staircase with enriched stone balustrade and heavy ogee-capped newel. Opposite the school, **Hill's Almshouse**, 1866–7, by *Charles Hansom*, founded by Thomas Hill of Clifton. A high E-plan façade to the road, Tudor Gothic, a picturesque composition with oriels, buttressing, gables and chimneys. Unusual rear elevation, with nine-bay cast-iron verandas on two storeys (now glazed in), with Gothic tracery. Low three-bay s chapel.

Here Berkeley Place becomes **Jacob's Wells Road**, running down a steep gully where the Woodwell stream ran s into the harbour. N of the junction of Constitution Hill is **Jacob's Well**, rediscovered in 1987. Inside an C18 or C19 stone structure, a warm spring flows from an opening in the wall. On a lintel above, a fragment of Hebrew script formerly interpreted as the word *zochalim* ('flowing'), believed to signify a C12 *mikveh* (Jewish ritual bath). In 2002, the script's interpretation was revised, and the bath is thought to be too deep for a *mikveh*. It may have been for the ritual washing of bodies prior to burial in a Jewish cemetery nearby on Brandon Hill. In any event, the lintel probably pre-dates 1142, when the spring became the property of St Augustine's Abbey. Further archaeology is needed.

Almost opposite, high on the side of Brandon Hill, a plain, domestic-looking **Police Station** of 1836; rubble walls and broad unmoulded window architraves. Lower down, replacing *Elijah Hoole*'s Artisan Dwellings of 1875, **Brandon House** (1959) by *A.H. Clarke*, the City Architect. Ten-storey slab-block local-authority housing, partly on a stilted basement, with living rooms running the full depth of the block and lit E and w to take advantage of limited light. The lacklustre aspect at the bottom of the hill is alleviated by the jolly red brick and yellow terracotta of the former Hotwells **baths** (designed 1881, opened

102. Brunel House, St George's Road, by R.S. Pope and I.K. Brunel, 1837–9

1887) by the City Surveyor *Josiah Thomas*, with Flemish, Loire and Queen Anne elements. Robust giant recessed arcades at the sides. It provided swimming and washing baths for a poor district. Now a dance studio. Here, Clifton is left behind and the city is heralded by the busy Hotwell Road junction. More local-authority flats on the right, **St Peter's House**, by *J.N. Meredith*, begun 1953; Bristol's first high block of council flats. Opposite, **Woodwell Crescent** (*Pope, Bindon & Clark*, 1853) on late Georgian lines, with paired round-arched windows beneath pediments. E into **St George's Road**, first, on the right, **Read's Dispensary** (*J.P. Sturge & Sons*, 1905), with Arts and Crafts half-timbering, red brick and green tile, marred by plastic windows. Next door, No. 126, of the same design as Woodwell Crescent. The rear was imaginatively remodelled,

2001. Full-height glass staircase bow above a toplit single-storey extension, with crisp **V**-shapes both in plan and elevation, and dark green edging tiles echoing its neighbour. Along St George's Road, on the s lies the **City of Bristol College**, 1998–2000 by *Unite*; long and symmetrical, with slightly canted flanks, and bowed recessed centre. Central triangular courtyard with glazed corner turrets, and an open spiral stair to the basement, with ceramics by *Linda Clark*. Artworks designed into the scheme: *Stephen Joyce* (lanterns, bronze globe, etched aluminium floor), and *Bill Guilding* (stair-drum mural).

Further E, St George's Road branches NE down into the aimless hollow behind the Council House: the site of the modestly mid-Georgian College Street, demolished early 1960s, now car parks. Down the slope (left side), small vernacular houses including No. 15, **Limekiln Cottage**, *c.* 1775. Behind, *c.* 100 yds (91 metres) up the short hill called **Brandon Steep**, **Brandon Cottage** of *c.* 1760–80, symmetrical and with ogee Gothick trim to the windows and door, perhaps by *Thomas Paty*.

Back on St George's Road is **Brunel House**, by *R.S. Pope*, perhaps with *Isambard Kingdom Brunel*, 1837–9 [102]. Built as the Royal Western Hotel, it was central to Brunel's visionary scheme for an integrated route from London to New York; via the Great Western Railway to Bristol, crossing the Atlantic on the S.S. *Great Western* after staying overnight here. The scheme never materialized and the hotel became a Turkish bath in 1855. It must have been very impressive in its day, following Jearrad's Queen's Hotel, Cheltenham, as one of England's earliest hotels to enjoy full architectural treatment. Four-storey Greek Revival front, façaded for offices by *Alec French Partnership*, 1984. Inset from the ends, single-bay projections with high round arches and two-storey upper parts with *antae* and attached columns. These projections embrace a giant Ionic colonnade of eleven bays. Above the colonnade, the upper parts are recessed, arranged 3:5:3, with attached giant columns in the centre. The Corinthian order comes from the Lysicratic Monument at Athens, also used by Pope at St Mary on the Quay (*see* City Churches, p. 103). Sketches by *Brunel* suggest that his was the idea of carriage entrances at the ends with high arches and radiating rustication. But it was surely Pope who synthesized these, and the elements characteristic of his own style, into a final design.

The right-hand arch was a carriage entrance, known as the Bazaar Ride; after closure it was used for horse-dealing. Through the arch, not open to the public, but visible from the road, a long narrow open space framed by gaunt ruined walls of a C19 building of uncertain provenance; an apsidal end with high round-arched windows abuts a quarry face at the rear. Was it finished then ruined, or left half-built? In the centre, a bronze resin **sculpture**, Horse and Man (*Stephen Joyce*, 1984). It makes a strangely surreal end to the walk.

Walk 5.

Canon's Marsh

Canon's Marsh, also called **Harbourside**, is an elongated D-shaped area N of the Floating Harbour and s of Brandon Hill. Originally it was water meadows owned by St Augustine's Abbey (the cathedral after 1542), but by the C18 shipyards and rope-walks had encroached. In the C19 it housed the gasworks, timber and stone yards and railway sidings. With the 1970s closure of the city docks, it became derelict. In the 1990s, the E end was reinvigorated with prominent offices for Lloyds Bank, and the At-Bristol Millennium project, which successfully interleaves buildings with high-quality and popular public spaces. Controversial proposals for the w end, indicative both of the potential and difficulties of harbourside regeneration, are now resolved.

The walk begins at the s end of The Centre, where the stepped cascade falls to the harbour (*see* City Centre, p. 125). w of St Augustine's Reach, a row of utilitarian transit sheds, mostly C20, converted to bars and restaurants. The first to be treated was the **Watershed Media Centre**, at the N end, iron-framed and originally with sliding doors to the quay-side, 1894, by *Edward Gabriel*; converted by *JT Group Ltd*, 1980–1, as part

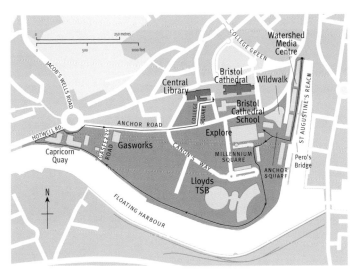

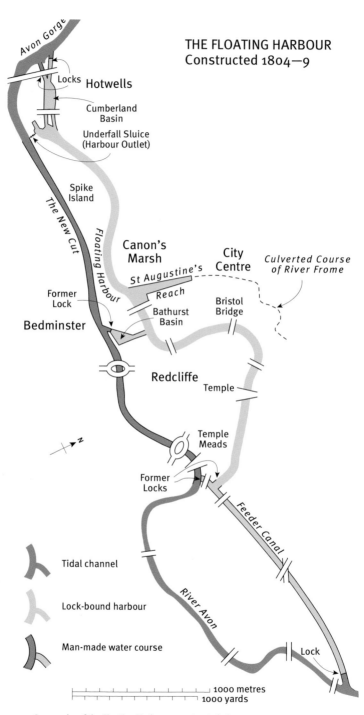

THE FLOATING HARBOUR
Constructed 1804–9

Avon Gorge

Locks Hotwells

Cumberland
Basin

Underfall Sluice
(Harbour Outlet)

Spike
Island

The New Cut

Floating Harbour

Canon's
Marsh

City
Centre

*Culverted Course
of River Frome*

St Augustine's

Reach

Bristol
Bridge

Former
Lock

Bathurst
Basin

Bedminster

Redcliffe

Temple

N

Temple
Meads

Former
Locks

Feeder Canal

Tidal channel

Lock-bound harbour

River Avon

Man-made water course

Lock

1000 metres
1000 yards

104. Geography of the Floating Harbour, constructed 1804–9

105. St Augustine's Reach, Pero's Bridge, by Eilis O'Connell, opened 1999

of the City Council's conservation programme. N gable end in red brick and Ham stone. Loire Renaissance pilasters, vigorous strapwork and figures in the gable, and a corner turret with octagonal ogee dome. Take the covered walkway s to **Pero's Bridge** [105], which crosses the s end of St Augustine's Reach. Designed 1993–4, opened 1999, by the artist *Eilis O'Connell* in collaboration with *Ove Arup & Partners*, and built by *David Abels*. Bristol's first example of the extrovert footbridges that have become a feature of harbour-regeneration projects. A hydraulic ram raises the centre of the bridge, with sculptural horns acting as counterweights. Despite some crudeness of finish, the staggered plan with refined opposing curves raises it above the run of footbridges. Named after Pero, one of few well-documented slaves, brought to Bristol in 1783 from the Nevis plantation of John Pinney (*see* Walk 4, p. 191). The naming was a symbolic acknowledgement of Bristol's role in the slave trade.

From Pero's Bridge turn W into **Harbourside**, of *c.* 1998–2000, carried out with Millennium Commission funding to a masterplan by *Concept Planning Group*. Immediately one enters **Anchor Square**, presided over by an alarming bronze rhinoceros beetle on a low plinth, by *Nicola Hicks*, 2000. On the N is **Rowe's Leadworks** (*c.* 1886), straightforward industrial, of Pennant and Bath stones. Tall brick chimney with wide projecting cap. Converted to a restaurant in association with the **At-Bristol** complex, opened in 2000, consisting of Wildwalk (formerly Wildscreen), a nature exploratory; Explore, a science exploratory and planetarium; and an IMAX cinema. Its two buildings flank Anchor Square. Adjoining the leadworks, **Wildwalk**, by *Michael Hopkins & Partners* with engineers *Buro Happold*. The wedge-shaped site is well exploited: at the apex, a blank brick drum of the IMAX, from which the structure radiates in descending layers. A sweeping tent-like canopy of ETFE on external steel masts covers the botanic garden. The relationship with the leadworks is unresolved, but Hopkins's interior spaces are excellent: a dark curving tunnel of sprayed concrete emerging into the high light-filled curve of the IMAX foyer [106].

The **Explore** building by *Wilkinson Eyre* with *Ove Arup & Partners* (structural engineers) was created from a goods shed designed in 1904 by *W. Armstrong*, engineer to the Great Western Railway, and *P.E. Culverhouse*. An early example of the French *Hennebique* system of reinforced concrete construction. Railway sidings ran through an arcaded ground floor with a single-storey warehouse above serviced by electric cranes. Surprisingly modern-looking concrete elliptical arches support the upper floor; best seen from the S and W. The new S screen

106. Wildwalk At-Bristol, IMAX foyer, by Michael Hopkins & Partners, 2000

wall is set behind a deep loggia, fronted by the mirror-finished metal globe of the **planetarium**. The glass N wall [23] is pleasingly ambiguous at the NE corner, becoming a free-standing external screen with an opening inviting passers-by to walk through. Inside, an elliptical beech-clad pod houses toilets and staircase. Outside the N front is **Small Worlds**, a cone sculpture in fibre and coloured cement blocks by *Simon Thomas*, inspired by Paul Dirac's Nobel-prize-winning work on anti-matter at the University of Bristol.

s of Explore is **Millennium Square**, by *Concept Planning Group*, framed E and W by striking piers with louvres and wide metal caps – the ventilation shafts for an underground car park by *Alec French Partnership*. At the E side *William Pye*'s **water sculpture** Aquarena: a broken arc of mirror-polished steel that shimmers with falling water forms the NE entrance to the square, then a series of fountains on stepped water terraces which can be drained to form a stage for events. At the S end two more steel water-walls form a narrow chasm. To the W, **statues** of Cary Grant by *Graham Ibbeson*, 2001; William Tyndale and Thomas Chatterton, both by *Lawrence Holofcener*, 2000. In the square's paving, **Zenith**, by *David Ward*, a figure-of-eight light sculpture.

Towards the harbour southward are offices for **Lloyds Bank** (now Lloyds TSB), by *Arup Associates*, 1988–90 [107]; a broad crescent faced in pale French stone, enclosing an amphitheatre towards the water (where stands a crane base of *c.* 1890). The design is similar to Arups' unexecuted scheme for Paternoster Square, London, of the late 1980s, which was also inspired by Beaux-Arts planning and civic gestures. In accordance with the planning brief, the Bristol design shuns the carefully cultured 1980s dockside aesthetic. Arups, a firm noted for its Modernist principles, chose instead Postmodern classical references such as rustication, and giant paired columns. Thin steel structures support the canopy above, but from a distance the disconcerting impression is of a free-standing screen of columns that supports nothing. The Postmodernist wit does not quite come off. Interior arranged around a curving toplit 'street', enabling a very deep plan. It sits uncomfortably with the later buildings behind, yet Lloyds moved here a decade before regeneration started in earnest, and there were no neighbours to consider. To the W is phase II, a rotunda completed 1994, linked by a low entrance pavilion. Circular staff restaurant with timber roof and a lantern.

Following the path w along the harbour wall, to the N is a roughly triangular area more or less derelict since the 1970s, the last big harbourside site to remain so. Construction work which will radically alter some of what follows began in 2004. It is chiefly occupied by derelict C19 gasworks, established here in 1823 by the Bristol and Clifton Oil Gas Company on the site of C18 limekilns and glass works. The site is bisected by the powerful Victorian streetscape of **Gasferry Road**, cobbled and narrow between unrelenting high walls, with distinctively Bristolian cast-iron kerbs. To its E and W are two derelict **retort houses**, probably of *c.* 1840, when the gasworks was expanded; and on the W, an **engine house** with brick chimney, of the same period. The retort houses are of rock-faced Pennant stone, with round arches, gabled ends and chunky voussoirs. If that date is correct they form the only surviving link between Pope's Bush House and the later *Rundbogenstil* warehouses by Gingell, (e.g. pp. 183, 267). But extensions were designed in this style as late as 1886, making certain dating problematic. The major elements will be incorporated in the planned redevelopment, probably as public spaces such as galleries and cafés (for a brief summary of this scheme, *see* Introduction, p. 47).

At the w apex of Canon's Marsh is **Capricorn Quay** apartments by *Alec French Partnership*, 1998–2002, making much of an awkward triangular sliver between the water and the busy Hotwell Road, yet opposite *ss Great Britain* and commanding the best position in the w harbour reaches. Two sweeping curved blocks, divided by a sunken garden on the footprint of Limekiln Dock (extant 1626–1903). Suggestions of playful seaside architecture in the repeated aquamarine balconies of perforated metal, timber masts supporting upswept canopy roofs, and glazed rotunda at the w end. From here return E along **Anchor Road**, where immediately the remodelled back of a C19 house draws the eye (*see* Walk 4, p. 197). Eastward, much new building *c.* 2001–3 on semi-derelict industrial sites s of Deanery Road.

Then **College Square**, a shabby cul-de-sac s of the Central Library and Bristol Cathedral (*see* Major Buildings, pp. 75, 50). It will be remodelled in the Canon's Marsh redevelopment to provide a better approach to both buildings. Directly s of the cathedral is **Bristol Cathedral School**, possibly of C12 origin and refounded in 1542 by Henry VIII. The buildings are a challenging puzzle of medieval monastic remains, altered and extended in every century since the Reformation. Facing w towards College Square, the former **Deanery** appears to be an early C17 house of seven bays and three storeys, altered in the C18. However the cellars are probably medieval, and the inaccessible s wall has four Norman windows and later medieval stonework: the present house is a rebuilding of something much earlier. C17 cross-gables at the back; those at the front were removed before 1734, and hipped dormers and sash windows were added. Ground-floor crenellated Tudor Gothic addition dated 1893, probably by *T.S. Pope* and *W.S. Paul*, with big mullioned-and-transomed windows, and a two-storey bay at the left. Inside, an open-well **staircase**, perhaps late C17, with newel posts continuous through three floors.

Adjoining the Deanery to the s, **Abbey House** has a late Norman door-way, c. 1150–60 [108] below ground level on the w front. Scalloped capitals and three orders of mouldings (two chevron bands, outer interlace pattern), perhaps by the mason of the nearby Abbey Gatehouse. It was a porter's lodge to the C12 abbey ranges eastward; the upper storeys were remodelled in the C17, damaged by fire in 1940 and rebuilt in the 1950s. Inside, a good chimneypiece with elaborate chamfer stops, c. 1590–1640, and a small room with plaster frieze of a similar date. Behind the Deanery and s of the cathedral cloister, the abbey **frater**, confused by C19 alterations, now forms the heart of the school buildings. Large C16 windows in the second floor and, at the w end, a fine if much-restored E.E. doorway of c. 1240, which has triple columns with stiff-leaf capitals, around a deeply moulded cusped and subcusped arch.*

Against the frater's s wall, a corridor is the only survival of the former **lesser cloister**. In the cellars beneath the frater, evidence of a medieval staircase between the main and lesser cloisters. The collegiate Tudor wings facing Anchor Road are by *Roland Paul, c.* 1920–35. Recent excavations suggest the monastic buildings extended s of the present Anchor Road. The walk ends with these reminders of the origins of Canon's Marsh as the property of a religious house.

*There is uncertain evidence that it may have been moved here from the NW angle of the cloister, the site now marked by a block arch.

Outer Areas

Walk 6. Hotwells and the Clifton Slopes 208

Walk 7. Central Clifton 221

Walk 8. North Clifton 232

Walk 9. The University and St Michael's Hill 239

Walk 10. Kingsdown to Stokes Croft 253

Walk 11. The Eastern Fringe 260

Walk 12. Spike Island 269

Walk 13. Bedminster 275

Walk 6.

Hotwells and the Clifton Slopes

Clifton, with its big stone-built Georgian and Victorian houses in a spacious and leafy setting, has been described as 'pre-eminent . . . among English suburbs', and who could deny it? It is bounded by Durdham Downs to the N, the Avon Gorge to the w, and a steep escarpment separating it from the city s and E. Below is Hotwells, nestling against the cliffs at the E end of the Avon Gorge. Together, Clifton and Hotwells cover just over one mile E–w, and nearly two miles N–s.

First a brief historical outline. Hotwells was part of the Manor of Clifton. A hot spring emerged here from the tidal mud in the mouth of the Avon Gorge, noted by William Worcestre in 1480. A spa was licensed by Charles I in 1630, perhaps influencing the Society of Merchant Venturers' purchase of the manor of Clifton in 1676. A new pump room (1696) prompted Early Georgian developments of lodging houses, e.g. at Dowry Square, and occasionally in Clifton too, nearby but steeply uphill. The Hotwells summer season dovetailed with the winter season at Bath, although always a poor relation. The social nuances of late C18 Hotwells are captured in Fanny Burney's novel *Evelina*. The spa declined in the C19; the Hotwell House was finally demolished in 1867.

The pattern of growth in Clifton went something like this. Before 1700 it was a scattered hamlet, centred on the parish church of St Andrew

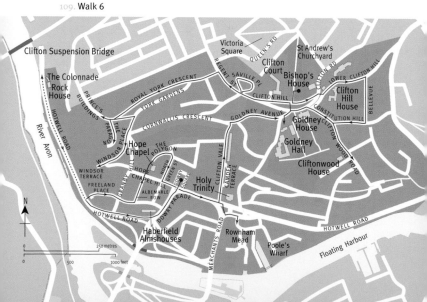

110. Hotwells, with Windsor Terrace (left) and The Paragon (right) above

(destroyed by bombing) on present-day Clifton Hill. Goldney and a few
similar large houses existed in the late C17, and building accelerated
somewhat after 1700. Pope mentions 'very pretty lodging houses' in 1739
and, in a relation to Bristol like that of Hampstead to London, some
wealthy merchants' houses near the church on the hill. The motivations
were exclusivity, a pastoral setting and pure air. From *c.* 1760, small-scale
speculative ventures began to feature, but nothing on a par with Bath.

Then in the 1780s a new borehole brought a hot spring to the top of
the Avon Gorge, which, with the attendant assembly rooms and hotel,
accelerated the building boom that produced Royal York Crescent,
Cornwallis Crescent, and much else. Architecturally they are unexceptional, even amateur. Their virtues are scenic ones, strung picturesquely
across the precipitous slopes above Hotwells. But the French War
brought everything to a catastrophic halt in 1793, bankrupting many
and leaving much unfinished. In 1807 a visitor could still write of the
'melancholy spectacle' of 'the silent and falling houses'. Building
resumed slowly at first, from *c.* 1810.

Efforts to make Clifton into a second Hotwells or indeed a second
Bath failed and it became happily suburban. It was incorporated into
Bristol only in 1835. The years *c.* 1815–*c.* 1850 saw the apotheosis of
Clifton architecture, with handsome and solidly built Grecian housing.
One cannot speak of town planning in the French or Beaux-Arts sense.
Clifton is planned for leisurely traffic, with not one straight main
thoroughfare pre-dating the mid C19. Irregularly planned squares are
interspersed with profuse planting and connected by obscure byways;
Clifton's abundant confusion is its great charm.

After the 1850s the terrace was supplanted by detached or paired villas for the best housing. But the Gothic Revival villa never caught on in Clifton, as it did in, say, Oxford. Instead, debased Italianate, Tudor or Jacobean villas sprawl across its N fringe, and E into Cotham and Redland. The plateau offers none of the scenic opportunities of the escarpment; the prodigious hulks of grey or lurid red stone soon pall. It makes a disappointing postscript.

Hotwells and Clifton present difficulties for both writer and reader. Many worthy buildings cannot be fitted sensibly into a walk; omission should not be taken as an indicator of lesser value. The most significant buildings are covered, along with representative examples of each period and type.

Hotwells

A circular walk starting in Dowry Square. Parts of the w slopes of Hotwells are very steep, especially Granby Hill, Freeland Place, Hopechapel Hill and Clifton Vale.

Dowry Square was the first significant C18 development associated with the spa. It was laid out from 1721, by *Thomas Oldfield* and *George Tully*, the Quaker carpenter-architect, who probably also designed many houses here. Building continued slowly until *c.* 1750. A three-sided square open at the s end, each side with a five-bay centre flanked by smaller (mostly three-bay) houses. Central gardens with spear-headed railings on a copper-slag block coping. On the w side, N of Hopechapel Hill, No. 1 of *c.* 1730, is a fairly unchanged example of the smaller houses. No. 3 (rebuilt 1822), is ashlar-fronted with giant pilasters to the upper floors; No. 4, the central house of this side, is possibly by *Thomas Paty*, *c.* 1747–8, of brick and Bath stone. Long and short quoining to a pedimented centre, five-stepped voussoirs, early C19 porch. No. 5 is of the same build. On the N side, Nos. 6–9 are of *c.* 1721–5, probably by *Tully*. At the NW corner, No. 6 has two narrow frontages. Here in 1799–1801 Dr Thomas Beddoes investigated the treatment of disease with inhaled gases at his Pneumatic Institute, assisted by Humphry Davy. No. 9 is double-fronted with broken-pedimented doorcase on Ionic pilasters. At the rear are symmetrical full-height closet towers. Nos. 10–11 (1746, probably also by *Tully*), similar to No. 9, are backward-looking, with segmental-headed windows and heavy stringcourses. On the E side is the small but distinguished **Clifton Dispensary** (1823). A well-proportioned doorcase with big fanlight under a Tuscan porch. Fully developed tripartite windows, the earliest known to survive in Bristol; they became a staple of Clifton buildings by the 1830s.

Across Hotwell Road, **Dowry Parade** continues the E side of Dowry Square to the s. Leases were granted in 1762 by the Society of Merchant Venturers for a speculative venture of lodging houses (*see* topic box, p. 25), and the houses built in 1763–4 by *Robert Comfort*, *Benjamin Probert* and others. The elevations imitate *Thomas Paty*'s Albemarle Row of 1762–3 (*see* below); but Paty avoided errors such as the thin cornice without parapet and the cramped proportions. The five-bay houses were subdivided, probably *c.* 1790–1800, resulting in crowded pairs of doors and blocked central windows. Single-bay houses of *c.* 1820 continue s. Opposite, **Chapel Row** (now Nos. 262–266 Hotwell Road) is the s continuation of the w side of Dowry Square, laid out *c.* 1725. Three houses with continuous stringcourses and cornices. No. 262 is particularly pleasing, double-fronted, doorcase with segmental pediment, flush sash-boxes and grotesque window keystones. Chapel Row terminates bleakly in 1960s flats on the site of St Andrew-the-Less (built 1873, demolished 1964). s of Dowry Parade the Cumberland Basin road system (*see* Walk 12, p. 273) required the demolition of much C18 housing. Continue w on **Hotwell Road** past **Haberfield Almshouses** (*Pope & Paul*, 1889), a restrained design in orange brick and terracotta with two-storey porches. Nos. 288–290 Hotwell Road, a late C18 pair (one double-fronted and a single), sport three full-height bows reminiscent of Cheltenham or Brighton. Past Granby Hill, the road curves N, revealing more of the Avon Gorge.

From the narrow junction of Freeland Place, an optional half mile round trip to the site of the Hotwell. Just N of Freeland Place, Hotwell Road affords fine views of the rubble-stone substructure of Windsor Terrace (*see* p. 217) soaring some 70 ft (21 metres). Further w, **St Vincent's Parade**, a terrace of lodging houses begun 1789, some with early C19 iron balconies. Then a Victorian terrace, and beyond it **Rock House**, of three storeys and five bays, depicted in an engraving of *c.* 1741. Deep Doric colonnade added *c.* 1800 or soon after, and a tented balcony above. Then **The Colonnade**, 1786, built by Samuel Powell, lessee of the Hotwell, as shops for spa visitors. Gently curving brick front of thirteen bays with shopfronts beneath a deep Tuscan colonnade. A few yards N where the road now runs was the Hotwell Pump Room. Some 240 ft (73 metres) above, *I.K. Brunel*'s Suspension Bridge (*see* Major Buildings, p. 85) vaults the gorge with breathtaking nonchalance.

Return E to **Freeland Place**, a steep backwater which even in the weakest sunshine, somehow evokes Tuscany. On the right, Nos. 22–23, a two-bay villa perhaps *c.* 1830 later extended left to make three bays, with central balconied porch. On the left, single-bay houses of *c.* 1820–5 step down to the Avon, pleasingly varied in details and most with small Gothic tented balconies. Where Granby Hill crosses, continue E into Cumberland Place, then N into **Albemarle Row** [111]. No. 1, first left, is a cheap addition (1812) to a brick terrace of 1762–3, built probably by *Thomas Paty* as lodging houses. No. 5, the pedimented centre house, bears the date 1763 and the cypher of its owner John Webb. The house widths are irregular (from bottom to top, 5:5:5:5:3:3:5), and the steps up uneven, negating the attempted unity of a palace front. Characteristic five-stepped voussoirs, even quoins at each party wall and some Gibbsian doorcases. The double-fronted houses have a central hall with

rear stair, and suites each side arranged as parlour and bedroom with closets at the rear.

In **Hopechapel Hill**, opposite the top of Albemarle Row is the Georgian Gothic **Hope Chapel**, possibly by *Daniel Hague*, 1788, now a community centre. Founded by Lady Hope and Lady Glenorchy as a proprietary chapel serving Clifton and Hotwells. Rendered rubble stone with hipped roof behind a parapet with gabled centre, tall Y-traceried windows (apparently from an enlargement of 1838) and twinned central doors. Panelled corner pilasters like those at *Hague*'s St Paul, Portland Square (*see* Walk 11, p. 262). A narrow alley on the uphill side leads to the **Polygon** (1826–9), a twelve-house crescent (angled as the name suggests) with the fronts on the convex side, probably designed by *Richard Jones* for the developer Henry Brooke. Simple houses of three bays and three storeys with Regency Gothic balconies, facing uphill on to banked gardens, which lend them a verdant rusticity.

Following the lower path past the crescent, from its E end return via North Green Street, then left on Hopechapel Hill and back into Dowry Square. Continue E on Hotwell Road: on the right, C18 and C19 houses. Where Merchants Road turns S, a small cast-iron **fountain** by *Tom Dove* of Birmingham, 1902, commemorating Simon Short, a missionary to seamen and pioneer of the Temperance Movement. SE of the junction with Merchants Road, **Rownham Mead**, private housing by

Hubbard Ford Partnership, completed 1980 on the site of Merchants' Dock (1765). The first big residential scheme of the harbourside regeneration, in the vernacular style at the insistence of the planners: red-brown Sussex brick, pantile roofs and stained timber-cladding. It harmonizes surprisingly well.

Back on **Hotwell Road**, opposite the Rownham Mead housing **Holy Trinity** church by *Charles Cockerell*, 1829–30. Paid for by subscription, it is the last example in Bristol of a Church of England building in the classical style, at least partly as a result of Cockerell's personal preference. Central s entrance with dominant arched recess without mouldings and with half-domed coffered head, a deliberate reference to S. Andrea, Mantua. The open pediment has a sculpture of the Holy Spirit as a dove. A small belfry with narrow arched openings, barely related to the composition below. The interiors were destroyed by bombing. Cockerell nave was at right angles to the entrance axis, with columns defining a cross-plan around a shallow saucer-dome, after some of Hawksmoor's London churches. *Tom Burrough*'s plain refurbishment, 1955–8, made no attempt at restoration, but echoed the old design with a big elliptical dome.

Clifton Vale, the steep hill N of Holy Trinity provides a link to the next walk. At the lower end, **Camden Terrace**, *c.* 1855–60, in the style of *Pope, Bindon & Clark*; then fifteen regular stepped houses of *c.* 1836–41 by *Foster & Okely*. Severe but pleasing, with gently battered door-frames and late Grecian balconies under the shallowest of pediments. At the top turn right through the Z-bend into Goldney Avenue and up to Clifton Hill.

Outliers: **Rutland House**, junction of Hopechapel Hill and Granby Hill; a large mid-C18 house; canted bays and doorcase with icicle-work blocks to attached columns.

Poole's Wharf facing the harbour s of Hotwell Road. By *BBA Architects* for Crest Homes, completed 1999. Pastiche Regency houses and flats, around a courtyard garden. The small scale and planning are successful. Harbour inlet with footbridge of high arching struts, by *HLD Ltd*.

Clifton Slopes

Starting from St Andrew's churchyard, this walk covers the most important C18 developments on the s slopes of Clifton Hill. Goldney House is referred to briefly en route, with a fuller account of the inaccessible interiors and gardens at the end of the walk.

On the N side of **Clifton Hill** is **St Andrew's Churchyard**. The Regency Gothic church, by *James Foster*, 1819–22, was bombed, and its tower pulled down in 1954; the foundations remain. Good Gothic wrought-iron gates (*c.* 1822) and overthrow with lamp bracket. The railed footpath through the churchyard, popularly known as Birdcage Walk, has had its tunnel of lime trees since at least the 1860s. From the gates, turn E along Clifton Hill. Directly next to the churchyard is **Bishop's House**, a fine design in Bath stone ashlar, dated 1711 above the door. Single-bay projecting centre with horizontal banded rustication, segmental pedimented doorcase on fluted Ionic pilasters, and a triangular pediment to the window above. The windows in the two-bay flanks have segmental heads and continuous architraves. The wings are later. *John Strahan* has been suggested as architect, although there is no certainty of his being in Bristol before *c.* 1725. *George Townesend* is another possibility. It is an exceptionally early Bristol example of fully realized classicism.

On the corner with Clifton Road, E, is **Richmond House** (*c.* 1701–3), probably the earliest survival of Clifton's mercantile settlement, built for Whitchurch Phippen, a mercer and linen draper. Three storeys and five bays arranged 2:1:2. Later in the C18, the front attic was raised half a storey and the original cross-windows replaced with sashes. Double-pile plan with central staircase. Relatively small service quarters, which may indicate a true villa conceived for private retreat from the city.

Below, set at an angle is **Clifton Hill House**, 1746–50 [112], a refined Palladian villa by *Isaac Ware*. Now a University hall of residence, not open to the public. It was built for the Bristol linen draper and

112. Clifton Hill House, garden front, by Isaac Ware, 1746–50

shipowner Paul Fisher, who had an earlier house here. In the mid C19 it was the home of the writer John Addington Symonds. An astylar Palladian entrance front facing w, of five bays and three storeys, with a porch added c. 1853, heavy but sympathetic to the C18 work. Fisher's cypher and the date 1747 are in the pediment. The carving is by *Thomas Paty*. He probably learned here the Palladianism that influenced his later work. The E-facing garden front (just visible from the gates of Manor Hall) is a tall astylar five-bay block, set on a podium with low wings: a composition similar to the Villa Ragona at Le Ghizzole by Palladio, whose *Quattro Libri* Ware had published in English in 1738. A remarkably reticent design of smooth ashlar, with unadorned window openings. Decoration is limited to a Gibbsian door surround, heavily rusticated podium, V-jointed rustication on the ground floor, and ornamented pediment. The **interiors** are equally reserved, except the drawing room and dining room, which have fine chimneypieces, and ceilings by *Joseph Thomas* with fanciful Rococo plasterwork in strongly defined compartments. Stone staircase, with iron S-scrolled balustrade, and a Rococo ceiling. Study embellished with a flamboyant Regency Gothic plaster vault and ogee door surrounds. A grand double staircase after Chiswick House leads to the garden. Wings raised one storey (the left in 1853, by or for 'EHSS', the right c. 1888), destroying the intended relationship of parts – but otherwise harmoniously done. The **gardens** are now a sloping lawn with trees, but there was a larger formal garden, before 1746, including two **gazebos** at the lower corners (the N one now collapsed), probably c. 1690–1700.

Now a brief diversion for lovers of hill-walking; to the N of Clifton Hill House, **Lower Clifton Hill** winds down past the bulky Neo-Georgian **Manor Hall** (*George Oatley*, 1932), a University hall of residence, to **Bellevue**, a speculative terrace begun by Harry Elderton, developer, c. 1792. His architect was probably *William Paty*. After the crash of 1793 (*see* topic box, p. 217) they were left incomplete until c. 1810–15. Two-bay stucco backs facing uphill on to a raised pavement, three-bay ashlar garden fronts with communal pleasure gardens. And so s along Bellevue and on to **Constitution Hill** which winds very steeply up to the w. At **Clifton Wood Road** we turn s into **Cliftonwood**, a little backwater distinct from Clifton but related to it, perched on a shelving narrow plateau, full of cranky corners and wide harbour vistas. In the C18 a few merchants settled here; humbler cottages clung to the slope above Jacob's Wells Road. Mid-C19 terraces fringe the escarpment. w of Clifton Wood Road, a large C18 stable block announces something earlier and grander: **Clifton Wood House**, of c. 1721, perhaps by *George Tully*. Eight bays and three storeys. Flanking the original and handsome timber doorcase, two deeply curved bows were added in c. 1800. At the back, the original fenestration is largely intact. Return past big Victorian villas with fanciful timber porches, and No. 9 Clifton Wood Road, a tiny Gothick cottage, perhaps c. 1790–1800, with triple-arched windows and a shaped gable. So back up to Clifton Hill.

Immediately SW of the Clifton Hill junction is **Goldney House**, another University hall of residence not normally open to the public. The exceptional C18 house and gardens are detailed at the end of this walk, *see* p. 218. From the road the only notable feature is an ugly and prominent tower with French pavilion roof, from *Alfred Waterhouse*'s alterations, 1864–5. Off Goldney Avenue, on part of Goldney House gardens, **Goldney Hall**, University accommodation by *Architects' Co-Partnership* (*c*. 1966), originally in nine separate blocks. Successfully remodelled in 1992–4 by *Alec French Partnership*. The exteriors were rendered to harmonize with Clifton's Bath stone, and the blocks linked to create an irregular courtyard, with a new L-shaped N block, visible from Goldney Avenue. Rooflines were varied, and turret-like fire escapes introduced. Interiors replanned as 'family' units, each for eight students.

To the N up the slope are the churchyard gates where we started. Immediately W, a mid-Georgian pair, **Beresford House** and **Prospect House**, built by *Thomas Paty c*. 1765 as lodging houses. Prospect House on the left, close to its original state, is overpowered by Paty's usual excess of Gibbsian blocks. The last of the big merchants' houses here is **Clifton Court** (now the **Chesterfield Hospital**), built *c*. 1742–3 for Nehemiah Champion and his wife Martha, Thomas Goldney III's sister. The Champions were central to Bristol's C18 brass industry; in 1723 Nehemiah patented an important process for granulating copper to improve the brass yield. An enjoyable design probably by *William Halfpenny*, aspiring to (but not achieving) Palladian correctness. Bath stone ashlar front but side walls of black slag blocks, a by-product of brass making. Five-bay centre block, one-and-a-half-storey wings. The design has similarities with Coopers' Hall (*see* Walk 1, p. 158).

Clifton Hill continues NW towards **Saville Place**, a small crescent on the N side shielded by trees; Nos. 1–5 here were started *c*. 1790 but completed in the early C19. Nos. 6–11 added 1838 by *Charles Dyer*, disjointed because a full half-storey lower and with canted-bay termination. Later cast-iron balconies obscure Dyer's signature over the door of No. 6. Here **Regent Street** begins, developed from the 1860s–70s as Clifton's main shopping street. Nos. 10–14, NE side, are shops by *Foster & Wood*, *c*. 1883, in Bath stone with carved festoons over triplet windows, and Mannerist inverted brackets to the attics. Soon on the SW is **Royal York Crescent**, *c*. 1791–1820, perhaps by *William Paty*. This most ambitious Clifton speculation describes a shallow sweeping curve of forty-six houses just below the crest of the down. Its developer *James Lockier* was bankrupted in 1793 (*see* topic box, facing), with ten houses substantially finished and fifteen incomplete. After an abortive plan to convert the whole to barracks, completion was achieved slowly from 1809 to 1820. Little need be said of the architecture: the stucco houses are quite plain, and with small irregularities of finish (some later additions). There are no centre or end pavilions, only a trivial projection of the central pair that is lost in the monumental scale. Its great strength lies in its contribution to distant views, contrasting an ordered sweeping composition with steep tree-clad curves and rocky outcrops of the gorge. There are richly varied iron balconies – some Gothic, some Neoclassical, and a few Victorian cast-iron. Finally, it stands on an impressive vaulted terrace pavement finishing at the w end some 20 ft (6 metres) above the road.

Here **Prince's Buildings** runs N to Sion Hill. By *William Paty*, an innovative design of 1789 with quasi-semi-detached pairs of three storeys with entrances in low linking wings. The rhythm, now largely destroyed by filling in above the links, is still visible at Nos. 2–3. At the s end of Prince's Buildings is the **Paragon**, a short crescent off to the sw. By *John Drew*, 1809–14, but the w end completed by *Stephen Hunter* to a modified design. Positioned spectacularly high on the escarpment, unusually the concave front faces uphill, and the convex rear faces the view. The backs have tented wrought-iron balconies; the fronts distinctive porches, elliptical in plan and standing almost free of the façades.

Lastly, down to the SE and the Victorian intrusion of **York Gardens** (*Henry Williams*, 1887), semi-detached with big mansards. Just below is **Cornwallis Crescent**, parallel to Royal York Crescent and almost as long. There is no need to follow it E again. Begun *c.* 1791, but completed *c.* 1835. They were originally known as Upper and Lower Crescent, perhaps deliberately echoing the relationship of Lansdown Crescent and Royal Crescent in Bath. At Cornwallis Crescent the plain stucco backs have the entrances, while the Bath stone s front, screened by trees and virtually invisible from all points, has a broad terrace walk raised on arches. Unusually the crescent is in two sections because of a pre-existing right of way.

At the w end of Cornwallis Crescent, Windsor Place leads inauspiciously off Granby Hill w to **Windsor Terrace**, built 1790–*c.* 1810 to designs possibly by *John Eveleigh* of Bath [113]. Its rampant disorder is, in its way, as instructive as all the perfection of Bath, and an object lesson

The Economic Collapse of 1793

The raised roadway at Windsor Terrace is the best place to appreciate (if that is the word) the effects of the collapse. War with France in 1793 created financial uncertainty and withdrawal of credit; Bristol was particularly badly hit, being on the crest of a building boom, with many builders and developers heavily over-committed. Over sixty went bankrupt in Bristol during the period of the Napoleonic Wars. Many half-finished properties were resumed from the late 1790s, but the recovery gathered pace only slowly. Key developments affected included Royal York Crescent, Cornwallis Crescent, Windsor Terrace and Portland Square. Sometimes reduced designs were substituted, to enable builders to complete them. At Cornwallis Crescent a builder appealed to the Merchant Venturers in 1828 to allow smaller houses, explaining optimistically that many authorities had advised him there would be no adverse effect on the design.

in how not to build a terrace. The speculator was William Watts, plumber, who invented a new production process for lead shot. Here, the site required a costly 70-ft (21-metre) high revetment. The two centre houses, completed by c. 1792, show the original conception, following Bath in its elaborate design. Building was interrupted by the collapse of 1793, which bankrupted all concerned. Work resumed in 1808 under *John Drew*, who evidently reused the pilasters already cut, despite having reduced the height of the new houses; hence the uncomfortable differences of scale. But he also failed to make the pilasters meet the cornice, with visually disastrous results. Illiterate details, e.g. the cutting of the grooved rustication over the windows.

Windsor Terrace is the end of the walk. From here, one can head s down Granby Hill to Hotwells, or N via Prince's Buildings to Sion Hill and the start of the next walk.

Now we deal with **Goldney House**, not fully described in the Walk (*see* p. 216). It was built for the Goldney family, Quaker merchants whose interests included investments in Woodes Rogers's circumnavigation of the globe (1708–11), and *Abraham Darby*'s ironworks, established 1707 in SE Bristol before transferring to Coalbrookdale, Shropshire. They remained intimately concerned with Darby's pioneering part in the Industrial Revolution. *George Tully*, also a Quaker, rebuilt an older house here c. 1722–4, for Thomas Goldney II, possibly leaving parts of

the old house as a service wing. The 1722 w front facing the garden, is of 3:1:3 bays, with a narrow central projection. In 1864–5 Lewis Fry insti-gated a dull remodelling by *Alfred Waterhouse*, who refaced the brick house in Bath stone, with an intrusive belvedere, plate-glass sashes, a big N porch and heavy staircase. The **Mahogany Parlour** survived almost intact; heavily panelled in Cuban mahogany imported by Thomas Goldney II, with fluted pilasters and inlaid Doric frieze. Baroque curved chimneypiece of brown Hotwell marble, and luscious fruit-and-game overmantel in lime and pearwood in the style of Grinling Gibbons [114].

The **gardens** were created largely by *Thomas Goldney III* (1696–1768). They are not large, but ambitious enough to be called by an C18 visitor 'a minor Stow'. The first improvement was the **grotto** (1737–64), one of the best in England, probably inspired by his father's account of a Utrecht silk merchant's grotto he had seen in 1725. Steps lead down to an arcaded chamber [115] with a pool fed by a cascade presided over by a river god. All is densely set with shells and minerals, including Bristol diamonds and tufa, probably executed by Goldney himself. At one side, a 'lions' den' – a low cave with stone lions. *Thomas Paty* laid the floor of marbled tiles from Coalbrookdale in 1762–4, and perhaps also designed the pretty Gothick façade added *c.* 1757. E of the house, an **orangery**, probably *c.* 1750, red brick with nine big segment-headed sashes, divided into groups of three by the two doors. On its axis is a **canal**

115. Goldney House, grotto, probably decorated by Thomas Goldney III, 1737–64

pond, 1758–9, very late for such a feature. The juxtaposition is similar to that at Frampton Court, Gloucestershire, of the late 1740s. Goldney later extended the garden s, with a **terrace** (1753–4) running E–W atop the Cliftonwood slopes. At its w end, a bastion with a Gothick **rotunda** (1757), formerly surrounded by a roofed colonnade. Red brick with ogee windows and battlements, perhaps reworking a structure mentioned in 1738. On the terrace a red sandstone **water tower** (1764), embattled and pinnacled, with Y-traceried lancets and porthole windows. It housed a *Newcomen* steam engine that fed the cascade in the grotto. Tower and rotunda may be by *Thomas Paty*. Nearby a lead **statue** of Hercules wielding his club, on a Baroque stone plinth, in place before 1768. On circumstantial evidence it may be one from Kingsweston by *John Nost the Elder*, 1715.

Central Clifton

For Clifton's historical development, *see* Walk 6, p. 208. This walk begins near the Avon Gorge Hotel on Sion Hill. Broadly, it covers Clifton from *c.* 1790 to the late Greek Revival of the 1820s–50s. Finally, with the grandeur of Worcester Terrace, Vyvyan Terrace and Victoria Square, Bristol's Belgravia arrives with a flourish.

Halfway up **Sion Hill**, a viewing platform affords excellent views of Clifton Suspension Bridge (*see* Major Buildings, p. 85) and the gorge. The buildings opposite were formerly the St Vincent's Rocks Hotel and Pump Room, where in the mid 1780s Thomas Morgan drilled a borehole from the Hotwell directly below, known as Sion Spring. Morgan also piped the water to several hundred houses on the hill. The project contributed to the acceleration of Clifton's building boom *c.* 1788–93. At the s end **Sion Spring House**, a five-bay house (perhaps 1810–30) with tented balcony, attached at the N to the four-storey building (of the 1780s) associated with the spring, with a seven-window range with canted bays. Much altered in the later C19. Converted to flats *c.* 2001, with first-floor curved glass front, remodelled from an awkward 1960s addition.

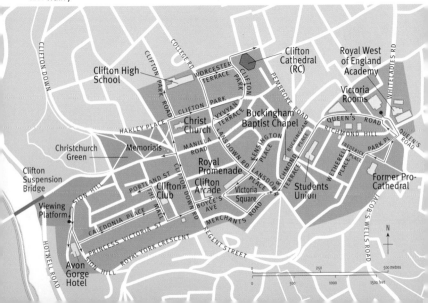

The view of the gorge and the proximity of Sion Spring were clearly the *raison d'être* for Thomas Morgan's haphazard development N on Sion Hill *c.* 1780–90 of four- and five-storey houses, the most desirable lodgings on the hilltop. Juxtaposed canted bays and curved bows recalling Brighton. Tented balconies added *c.* 1830. Every house has something worth seeing, and they achieve a delightful diversity (e.g. the porch, No. 8) within an overall harmony.

Back at our starting point is the long-derelict **Grand Spa Pump Room**, *Philip Munro*, 1890–4, a grandiose Neo-Renaissance building with caryatids and big windows on the entrance façade in Princes' Lane below. Built by the publisher and MP Sir George Newnes to revive Clifton's fortunes as a spa, in conjunction with the Clifton Rocks Railway, a hydraulic-powered funicular in an inclined tunnel from the Pump Room to the bottom of the gorge. Munro also designed the big Italianate **Avon Gorge Hotel** (1898) next door, which swallowed the top end of Prince's Buildings (*see* Walk 6, p. 217). Opposite the hotel is **St Vincent's Priory**, an intriguing Regency Gothic house built *c.* 1828–31. It is tall and narrow and dominated by a full-height bow, with narrow lancet windows. At the first floor this is vaulted out from little colonnettes and supported, visually at least, by twisting figures, said to be copied from St Mary Redcliffe. The Regency Gothic rarely achieves such vivacity in its surface decoration.

To the N of St Vincent's Priory, **Caledonia Place** runs E towards The Mall. Shortly it broadens out into a long narrow square, with the matching terrace of **West Mall** on the N facing a central garden. Both were built to a single design by *Foster & Okely*, 1833–40, as an extension to an C18 development which we shall reach shortly. Building began at the E end and worked W. Plain three-bay fronts are enlivened by fine cast-iron Grecian balconies with pedimented lattice panels, anthemion-topped verticals, cobweb spandrels and arrow braces. At No. 32 is the change to the C18 work, begun in *c.* 1788, probably to the design of *John Eveleigh* of Bath, with a thirteen-house terrace on each side. The ends and centre are pedimented and broken forward; inadequate devices to hold together a long composition. C19 attics and balcony additions (N side) do not help. Nevertheless they are (for Bristol at this date) an unusually formal conception. The E end house (s side) remodelled in Neoclassical style for National Provincial Bank, 1922.

At the E end is **The Mall**, a short street running N–S, and the closest thing to a centre in Clifton. A broad stone-fronted building faces W to close the square. It was originally the **Clifton Hotel and Assembly Rooms**, now the **Clifton Club**, 1806–11 by *Francis Greenway*, who had trained with Nash. Greenway and his two brothers ran a firm which undertook architectural design, building, statuary and landscaping, taking advantage of the vacuum that followed the collapse of 1793. They produced here one of the first big buildings in Bristol for over a decade. A nineteen-bay façade with bowed ends, recessed links, and a big projecting centre with Ionic giant order. Full attic interposed between entablature and pediment (cf. Coopers' Hall, p. 158). The desire for variety, and perhaps Greenway's inexperience, resulted in this somewhat incoherent design. *Joseph Kay* completed the interiors after Greenway's bankruptcy in 1809. Greenway was later transported for forgery, to become known as the father of Australian architecture. In the right flank, the high rusticated basement was replaced with canted projecting shopfronts by *J.H. Hirst*, 1856. Two tight oriels were recklessly squeezed into the central portico by *E. Henry Edwards*, 1894.

Now a brief optional detour N up The Mall and w into the narrow cul-de-sac of Portland Street. Here is **Carter's Buildings**, a complex of warehouse and workers' housing arranged in courts. Apparently of the 1790s, but altered probably *c.* 1850. The style suggests *Foster & Wood*. Virtually unique in Bristol for the courtyard housing, reminiscent of that in northern industrial cities: a reminder that about half the residents of Clifton were working people serving the needs of the other half.

At the s end of The Mall is **Princess Victoria Street**: despite its name, its origins were quite humble, many of the service premises now converted to shops at the E end, housing at the w. Immediately opposite the junction with The Mall, Nos. 29–31, two related Edwardian Baroque buildings probably by *James Hart*, 1906, for Cowlin & Son, builders. A recessed centre at No. 29, and both laden down with swags, window aprons, etc. To the E on the same side of the street, the modest Italianate Clifton branch **library**, built as Christ Church Schools, 1852, by *Charles Underwood*, but apparently altered by *Charles Hansom*, 1877.

Now into **Clifton Down Road**: on the NE side, is **Boyce's Buildings** probably by *Thomas Paty*, 1763. Originally three stylish lodging-houses for visitors to the Hotwell, a speculation by a wig-maker, Thomas Boyce. This must have been a lonely development, on a breezy plateau with views w to the gorge. Each house was of five bays, the central one

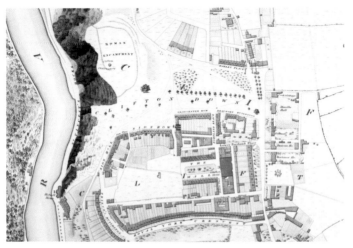

117 The N outskirts of Clifton, detail from Plumley and Ashmead's map, 1828

with pediment and Boyce's cypher; a well-mannered if repetitive design, but perhaps Bristol's first palace-front composition. All the windows have blocked Gibbs surrounds and stepped voussoirs. The right house was demolished for Merchants Road and the left house is crudely divided; shops now cover the gardens in front. Directly N is a side street, Boyce's Avenue, running E to a well-hidden oddity – **Clifton Arcade**, a delightfully indulgent mishmash of styles and references. Built as the Royal Bazaar and Winter Gardens by *J.W. King*, 1878, the venture soon failed and it became a furniture warehouse until 1992 when it finally opened for shopping. Red brick shops facing King Road, the window surrounds with vaguely Moorish decoration. The diminutive arcade has an upper gallery and simple wooden-framed roof on little cast-iron brackets with flying dragons. At the N end a tight but fully expressed imperial staircase. Behind is a blind Gothic wheel window that would be the envy of many a chapel.

Returning to Clifton Down Road, on the opposite side is **Rodney Place**, *c.* 1782–5, one of Clifton's earliest big planned terraces, in the late Paty style. Doric doorcases with single triglyph frieze and an arched fanlight beneath open pediment, probably the first Bristol example of a design that was soon widely used here, although very uncommon in C18 Bath. Paty may have taken it from a pattern-book design by *William Pain*, and there are similar examples in London from the mid C18. On the E side of the road three large late C18 houses. **Mortimer House**, probably of *c.* 1760–70, is in the manner of Clifton Hill House (Walk 6, p. 214). Single-storey wings mask higher rear wings. Then **Duncan House**, with a porch and mansard added by *Charles Hansom*, 1884, and, next door, **Freemantle House**, both somewhat later than Mortimer House. Freemantle House has an ornately carved ground-floor addition, also by *Charles Hansom*, 1884, under which one barely notices the Georgian carcase.

Shortly N we emerge on to the SE corner of **Christchurch Green**, a spur of the Downs which resisted development and now forms something akin to a wide house-lined village green. w of the road junction here, the former **Clifton Down Congregational Church**, 1868, by *Charles Hansom*, spiky Dec with a high transeptal apse at the (ritual) NW corner. Triple-arched porch, beautifully vaulted within and with mythical beasts on the hood stops. Converted to housing *c.* 1987–8, by *Bob Trapnell* and *Domus Design and Build*. On the green nearby are two **memorials**. A **sarcophagus** of 1766, an early War Memorial to the dead of the 79th Regiment in the capture of Manila (1763), erected by their commander General Sir William Draper of Manilla Hall. An **obelisk** commemorates William Pitt whom General Draper admired. Both resited when Manilla Hall, which faced the green s of Christ Church, was demolished in the 1880s.

Christ Church, at the NE corner of Christchurch Green, gives the distant impression of a large and prosperous suburban church in a unified E.E. design [118]. Very tall imposing spire. It has a disjointed building history. Designed by *Charles Dyer*, 1841, and consecrated 1844; further

118. Christ Church, Clifton, by Charles Dyer and others, from 1841

work was done by *Ewan Christian* in 1857, the steeple added 1859 by *John Norton*. N and S aisles by *W. Bassett Smith*, 1884–5.* Despite the sometimes coarse detailing, *Dyer*'s thoughtful handling of the E.E. is an early Bristol manifestation of movement towards archaeologically correct Gothic. Norton's steeple subtly suggests a transition to C13 Geometric Decorated. Pinnacles mask the broaches to the spire. Disappointingly mundane interiors, where the various building phases are more obvious. W gallery on timber-clad cast-iron columns, and odd triple chancel arches screening a broad polygonal apse. This chilly Anglicanism was crystallized in John Betjeman's scathing poem 'Bristol and Clifton': 'Our only ritual here is with the plate'.

Opposite the church to the N, a terrace of four three-bay houses probably of *c.* 1770, no doubt also once lodging houses given their size and fashionable details. To the E is **Clifton Park**, a leafy enclave developed in the 1830s and later with fine Greek and Gothic villas. But first, a short detour N along Clifton Park Road to the gates of **Clifton High School**, built as a house by *Stuart Colman* (1875), and sympathetically extended to the W by *George Oatley*, 1927. Colman's taste was experimental and

*A C19 history of Bristol incorrectly names the *Rev. Edward Young* as the principal architect. He lived nearby at No. 6 Clifton Park from 1838, and was the author of *Pre-Raffaelitism* (1857). Did he supply the impetus for Dyer's new archaeological approach?

often perverse: here, a rare and early Bristol example of Queen Anne. Confident red brick asymmetry, with quirky details such as the oriel on a miniature vault sprung from a column. Steep roofs, sunflowers on the chimneys and small rectangular dormers; at the rear, a gabled dormer bisected by a broad brick chimney. Returning to Clifton Park, on the N side, Nos. 1–4, two villa pairs in similar style, probably by *Charles Dyer*. A free and playful classicism is at work. Parapet with pilasters linked by little gables at Nos. 1–2, of 1836 (cf. Richmond House, Queen's Road, p. 231). Nos. 3–4, of 1845, are richer, with square tripartite bays and balustrading identical with Litfield House, Litfield Place (*see* Walk 8, p. 233). No. 5, now much mutilated, by *Charles Underwood*, 1849, was the home of the developer Edward Clark, who with Charles Savery employed Underwood on many developments.* The central bow and rosette frieze echo nearby Worcester Terrace. To the N in **College Road**, on the E side the return elevation of *Charles Underwood*'s **Worcester Terrace**, *c.* 1848–53 [119]. Constructed piecemeal, the ends and centre by 1849, and the gaps infilled by *c.* 1853. The returns are treated as separate villas, attached to the terrace only by their porches, a clever device but seemingly never repeated. The terrace front is refined and meticulously detailed, arranged 6:6:12:6:6 with every bay pilastered, except in the end pavilions. It is perhaps insufficiently varied. Curvaceous full-length balconies of cast iron.

To the E, the concrete Roman Catholic Cathedral (*see* Major Buildings, p. 63) makes a happy surprise in this suburban context. Turn s between the cathedral and Worcester Terrace, then w into Clifton Park again. The villas here, presumably also by *Underwood*, continue the Worcester Terrace style. But Nos. 8–9, of 1846, strike out on their own in unapologetic Perpendicular Gothic. Similar in many details to *R.S. Pope*'s Guildhall, Broad Street (q.v. City Centre): these may be his as well. Nos. 6–7 (1835), less convinced Regency Gothic, have haunched gables like their neighbour; perhaps by *Pope* or *Charles Dyer*.

To the s is **Vyvyan Terrace**, Clifton's most ambitious terrace. Designed *c.* 1833, almost certainly by *R.S. Pope* and named after Sir Richard Vyvyan, Tory MP for Bristol in 1832. Planned as a nineteen-house terrace, it was constructed piecemeal: Nos. 15–17 in 1833–4 (probably to entice developers and occupiers), the rest as late as 1841–7. Fifty-seven bays arranged [3:3:3]:12:[3:9:3]:12:[3:3:3]. Palatial centrepiece with eight giant Ionic columns *in antis*, reminiscent of Nash's Regents Park terraces. The end pavilions have attached columns and odd bowed balconies squeezed in. The twelve-bay recesses have Pope's characteristic first-floor loggias with panelled stone piers instead of iron balconies (cf. Buckingham Place, p. 231).

From the w end of Vyvyan Terrace, Lansdown Road runs s past **Manilla Road**. The outrageously ugly s side is by *Henry Williams*, 1888, raised on half-basements with mansards, porches and bays swamped

*Savery lived at a villa called Deepholme in Clifton Park from 1849.

119. Worcester Terrace, Clifton by Charles Underwood, c. 1848–53

with un-Bristolian buff terracotta. Further s, on the left is **Kensington Place**, worth a detour of a few yards to see Nos. 1–4, an elegant and controlled terrace by *Charles Underwood*, 1842, for the developers Savery and Clark, with tripartite windows in segmental recesses on the first floor.

Back again, and immediately into the NE corner of **Victoria Square**. On the left, **Lansdown Place**, now the NE side of the square, built for Samuel Hemming in 1842–5. Raised centre and ends, with slightly recessed links. Traditionally attributed to the firm of *Foster*, but Hemming's developers, Savery and Clark, frequently employed *Charles Underwood*. The restrained classicism is like his Worcester Terrace (*see* above), and at the SE end is a characteristic Underwood bow. Wide flagged pavement, and robust cast-iron area balustrades.

The development of the rest of Victoria Square is complex. The Society of Merchant Venturers owned the land, and in 1845–6 they produced plans for a small square here, with the back of one side facing Hemming's terrace. He objected to the consequent devaluation of his houses, and eventually paid £1,350 to secure the scheme's withdrawal. In 1847 the Society's surveyor *John Marmont* planned a new square incorporating Lansdown Place: he proposed two terraces: the NW was built 1847–c. 1851, and the SW only started in the 1860s. At about the same time villas were built on the SE side, not to Marmont's design.

Royal Promenade (NW) was complete by c. 1851, although some leases remained unsold until 1855. The builder was *William Bateman Reed*. An Italian palazzo design of some magnificence, with round-arched windows on the ground and second floors in the centre and ends. Continuous stone balconies with scrolled balustrades, and attic arcades combined with deep cornice brackets, producing a double staccato punctuation. Royal coat of arms in the attic. At the square's w angle is the related **Albert Lodge**, a handsome villa, and **Pharmacy Arch** leading to Boyce's Avenue, decorated with cameos of Victoria. Both are related to Royal Promenade and must also be by *Marmont* (a sketch for the arch is in the Merchant Venturers' archive).

The SE **side** of Victoria Square was developed *c.* 1865–72 with large detached villas. No. 30, the **Victoria Square Hotel**, 1865, by *Archibald Ponton*, was the vicarage to St James (*Pope & Bindon*, 1859–62, demolished). Firm angular window openings and judicious use of ornament. The rest are of 1869–70, probably by *J.A. Clark*. Some bland 1960s flats on the site of the church, and then villa pairs by *Pope & Bindon* in Merchants Road. The SW **side** was designed in 1863, also by *John Marmont*. Six houses at the N end were built by John Yalland, 1863–7, the rest completed 1874. The terrace is overburdened with powerful arcades of round and Lombardic arches: each bay is repeatedly subdivided vertically. Marmont rejected Yalland's proposal for columned porches, that might have relieved the horizontal repetition. This terrace pinpoints precisely that moment when Late Georgian order finally lapses into indiscriminate mid-Victorian eclecticism: it is perhaps a good point to finish the walk.

The East Side

We begin at the broad triangular junction where Whiteladies Road meets Queen's Road, on the main route from the city to Clifton. It is dominated by the **Victoria Rooms**, by *Charles Dyer*, 1838–42 [120], assembly rooms designed 'as well for business as festivity'. The designs were exhibited at the Royal Academy in 1838 and 1839. It exemplifies a European trend at this time, away from Neoclassicism and towards Roman Corinthian grandeur. A fine eight-columned portico, magisterially scaled. Pediment sculpture attributed to *Musgrave Watson*, 1841, depicting Wisdom in her chariot ushering in Morning and followed by the Three Graces; well-balanced and vivacious. Blind flanks with paired corner pilasters, not entirely successfully related to the centre. The Beaux-Arts emphasis on high blocked parapets is especially marked on the return elevations. Lateral main hall, disappointingly remodelled (1935) by *G.D. Gordon Hake* and *Eustace Button* for the University of Bristol after a fire. In the forecourt is the **Edward VII Memorial** designed by *E.A. Rickards* (1910–11, erected 1913) and executed by *Henry Poole* (much favoured by Rickards, e.g. at Cardiff City Hall). An equestrian statue was specified; Rickards, arguing for a less military approach, designed a rather weak seated figure, but finally a standing figure on a high plinth was settled upon. He presides over a curved **fountain** pool with writhing Art Nouveau bronze sculpture on aquatic themes. Roaring lions flanking the steps behind, also by *Poole*.

120. Victoria Rooms, Queen's Road, by Charles Dyer, 1838–42

Next door to the right, the former **Royal Colonial Institute**, designed in 1913 by the local architects *Bridgman & Bridgman*, achieves some presence by a narrow s front with a two-storey semicircle of giant Ionic columns. Unusual Mannerist treatment of the entablature: a continuous dentil cornice but separate blocks of frieze and architrave. The windows in between terminate in deep scrolls recessed beneath the cornice. In the attic storey, half-Atlas figures carry globes with the names of Britain's colonies. Angled right flank with a Venetian window at attic level. On the E side of Whiteladies Road, **Victoria Methodist Church** is by *Foster & Wood*, 1861–3. Geometric Dec in banded pink and cream stones, and extravagantly pretty.

On the E side of Queen's Road is the **Royal West of England Academy** [121], founded 1845 as an Academy of Fine Art with money from Ellen Sharples, mother of Bristol artist Rolinda Sharples. The present building (1854–7) is a conjunction of Victorian Renaissance façades by *J.H. Hirst* with plan and interiors by *Charles Underwood*. The glazed first floor was originally an arcaded entrance loggia reached by an external double staircase, but this was demolished for the entrance extension designed by *S.S. Reay* (1911–13), modified from a design by *H.D. Bryan* with advice from *George Oatley* (1908). It dampens the dynamism of the Victorian façade. Above, sculpture by *John Thomas*, c. 1857; in the left niche John Flaxman, and in the right Sir Joshua Reynolds, both of cast cement on slate armatures. Inside, Reay's marble-lined staircase hall leads up to a rectangular domed vestibule with painted lunettes (oil on canvas, not fresco) depicting Painting,

Sculpture, Craftsmanship and Architecture, by *Walter Crane*, 1913–14.

Across Queen's Road to the sw is **Park Place**. The terrace on the left is by *James Foster* (1822–*c.* 1835), for the Society of Merchant Venturers. Incongruous round-headed porches added later; they appear Edwardian. At the top of the rise is the Roman Catholic **Pro-Cathedral**, the saddest of Bristol's failed architectural visions. Begun 1834 by Peter Baines, Vicar Apostolic of the Western District, as a cathedral-in-waiting against the day when Catholic bishoprics were instituted. His architect, *Henry Goodridge* of Bath, envisaged a big Corinthian basilica. The steep quarried hillside subsided; by 1845 the project foundered with the walls and portico unfinished. In 1846–8, *Charles Hansom* completed it as a functioning if aesthetically displeasing church. A light timber roof caps columns left without capitals, supported within by round wooden arches and complex bracing. w narthex, hall and N porch added by Hansom from 1876, in Lombardic Romanesque with banded walls. It never became a cathedral. Unused since the R.C. Cathedral in Pembroke Road was opened in 1973 (*see* Major Buildings, p. 63), it is now crumbling away. Around the upper corner (w), Frederick Place leads to **Wetherell Place**, where in 1860 *J.A. Hansom* (designer of the Hansom cab and brother of Charles) designed for himself a pleasing Gothic house. In red brick with black diaper work, it is unexpectedly rectilinear, regular but not symmetrical. Two small picturesquely Gothic dormers.

Return N to the Victoria Rooms, passing on the central island the Gloucestershire Regiment's **South African War Memorial**, by *Onslow Whiting*, 1904–5. A bronze statue of a soldier loading his rifle. Take the w branch of Queen's Road to the left. Soon we come to a block of red brick flats on the right, by *Alec French*, 1935–7, in a faintly Moderne style with shops to the street, penthouses, and what was probably Bristol's first underground parking. Pevsner's fear that Clifton might be over-whelmed with such alien metropolitanism has thankfully proved groundless. Opposite are three large villa pairs, *c.* 1831–3, the model for Clifton Park and much else. From the Victoria Rooms, first **Edgecumbe House** and **Thornton House** by *Charles Dyer*. Edgecumbe has finely judged Grecian decoration and a deep verandah. Square bays with tripartite windows and arched motifs towards the road. The free blend of Grecian and Italianate typifies Dyer's work. Then the smaller **Bedford** and **Richmond**, with richly varied façades and symmetrical fronts to Richmond Hill, s. A further pair (Nos. 21 and 20) sit at the junction of Richmond Hill, where the end house has a rectangular bayed flank with recessed quadrant curves at the corners, quite a Baroque conception.

Beyond the junction with Pembroke Road, NW, Queen's Road rises gently SW to Victoria Square; dominated by the **University Students' Union**, by *Alec French & Partners*, completed 1965. Perhaps Clifton's most bruising post-war intrusion. A large textured concrete slab at the W end, central recessed entrance and the E end raised over a basement swimming pool. Inside, a free-flowing curved staircase in the foyer. Opposite is **Buckingham Place**, 1843–5, attributed to *R.S. Pope* on sty-listic grounds. First-floor loggias on paired stone piers (cf. Vyvyan Terrace, p. 226). Recessed strips between each house are another Pope trademark. The irregular stepped elevation disguises an otherwise sym-metrical composition.* Then **Buckingham Baptist Chapel**, 1842–7, by *R.S. Pope*, who donated his fees towards the decorative elements. The rich and aggressive French-influenced Gothic is rare for a Nonconformist church of this date, perhaps following *Butterfield*'s more English Gothic at Highbury Congregational Chapel (*see* Walk 10, p. 253). An over-steep gable with a splendid but sham rose window that does not light the interior. Arcades of blind niches flanking the entrance, and five-bay return elevations, poorly related to the front. Inside, a galleried hall with a false ceiling, flat and essentially classical but with moulded beams and oversized bosses. The roof structure above is supported on triangular trusses fronted by curved ribs spring-ing from large corbels with animated figures. Behind the dais-pulpit, a blind Gothic arch on classical pilasters. Scholarly Gothic and structural truth had yet to impinge here.

Richmond Terrace, further up on the opposite side of Queen's Road, is *c.* 1790 and later, probably by *William Paty*. A big speculative devel-opment of standard late Georgian design. The terrace pavement is high enough to fit in later shops beneath. More unusually, the terrace continues SE around two corners, effectively forming three sides of an outward-facing square. The walk ends at the wide junction between Victoria Square (*see* p. 227) and St Andrew's Walk which leads SW to Clifton Hill (*see* Walk 6).

*A similar composition, probably by *Pope*, is at Apsley Terrace, Apsley Road, Clifton, *c.* 1845.

Walk 8.

North Clifton

For Clifton's historical development, *see* Walk 6, p. 208. What follows is an account of some scattered buildings, not presented as a continuous walk. They are ordered from Christ Church, working w, along Harley Place, N via Clifton Down to the zoo; Clifton College and Pembroke Road; then Whiteladies Road, working s to N.

Starting from Christ Church (*see* Walk 7, p. 224), Nos. 1–9 **Harley Place** climb the slope to the w. A terrace begun *c.* 1788, but halted by the 1793 collapse (*see* topic box, p. 217), and not fully occupied until *c.* 1819. Stucco is abandoned here in favour of Bath stone ashlar, the favoured material for almost everything to come. No. 9 has segmental arches in

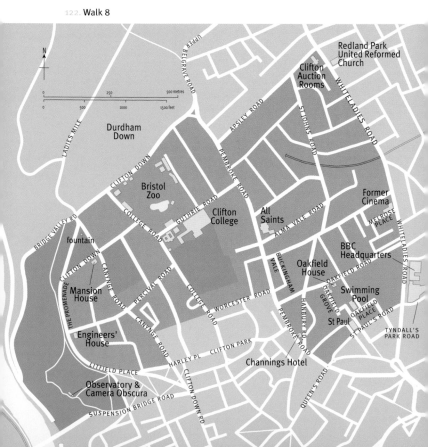

the ground floor, on the first floor a big tripartite arch-headed window with flanking niches beneath a Grecian tented balcony, and blind roundels above it. Shallow recessions and projections in the attic, and a blocked parapet. The composition is very similar to the centrepiece of the Bazaar, Quiet Street, Bath (1824–5, attributed to *Henry Goodridge*) and may thus be a refronting by him.

NE of the Suspension Bridge is **Observatory Hill**, an Iron Age earthwork of double banks and ditches above the Avon Gorge. At the highest point is the **Observatory**, a rubble-stone tower of an C18 windmill, recast in 1828–35 by *William West* as an observatory, in medievalizing dress. Camera obscura, open to the public, with fine views across the Avon Gorge.

Litfield Place curves NW from Camp Road to Percival Road. It was developed *c.* 1827–35 on land owned by the Society of Merchant Venturers, who controlled the designs carefully. At **Litfield House** (1829–30) the society rejected the intending occupier's plan, nominated *Charles Dyer* as architect and paid half his twenty-guinea fee. A blunt four-square façade, three bays with paired pilasters, Doric porch with colonnettes in the balustrades. Weak Roman consoled windows above ground-floor tripartite windows. Then Nos. 2–3 (1827), spare Late Georgian with good wrought-iron veranda. Nos. 4–5 (St Angela's Convent), 1827–8, are possibly by *Richard Jones*, with Victorian additions. At Nos. 6–7, 1830, *Dyer* amended another's design 'to render it consistent with architectural principles', which perhaps accounts for its blandness. **Dorset House**, 1833–4, must be by *R.S. Pope* (cf. Royal Colonnade and Brunel House, Walk 4, pp. 191 and 198); and if so, his too the indignity of seeing the Merchant Venturers submit the design to Dyer's chief clerk for approval. Recessed colonnaded centre perversely arranged 1:2:3:2:1, 'a disorderly use indeed of what is not without reason called the orders' (Pevsner). Lastly the ambitious **Engineers' House** (formerly Camp House), by *Charles Dyer*, 1830–1 [123], for the mayor Charles Pinney, with an American-looking two-tier portico and pedimented tripartite windows in the flanks, broad and squat and quite imposing.

The Promenade continues Litfield Place N, together forming a perfect continuum of domestic architecture of 1830–70, on the most substantial scale possible while maintaining an essentially suburban character. At **Promenade House**, 1836–8, giant Corinthian pilasters define a deep bow with heavy attics, remarkably similar to that at the demolished Priory, Cheltenham (*c.* 1825), attributed to *George Allen Underwood*. Promenade House may be his too, or a borrowing by his brother *Charles*. Then **Maxwell Taylor House** (originally Avonside), *c.* 1839 by *R.S. Pope*; windows framed by attached columns, and the same narrow wings as Dorset House. **Trafalgar House** (*c.* 1836) has a two-tier portico as at Engineers' House, and is probably also by *Dyer*. The lower tier has rusticated piers, with non-structural arched members between them – a solecism showing how architects were freeing themselves from the constraints of classical order.

From here on are several very large pairs, superficially classical, Jacobean or Italianate. At the N junction with Canynge Road, the **Mansion House**, formerly Elmdale, by *George & Henry Godwin*, 1867, was built for Alderman Thomas Proctor. He planned from the first to donate it to the city, accounting for its scale and massive rooms. Purple sandstone dug on site, with Bath stone dressings. Three big polygonal bays, and odd corbel-like eaves mouldings. Within, self-conscious modernity was expressed through varnished pickled-pine woodwork, plain-painted walls, bathroom with hot-water boiler, and a ventilation system fed from vents on the windward SW wall.

On **Clifton Down** towards Bridge Valley Road are more substantial villas, in various styles. Flemish Renaissance at **Sutton** and **Auburn House**; Italianate at **Avonbank** (now the Blue House) and **Llanfoist**, by *Henry Goodridge* (1857); Victorian palazzo at **Eaton** and **Glenavon**, *c.* 1853, with a row of four segmental pediments crammed between narrow belvederes; and Jacobean at **Tellisford** and **Trinmore**. In front, a triangular Gothic **drinking fountain** (*George & Henry Godwin*, 1872), big and canopied with much presence. Given by Alderman Proctor, commemorating the Society of Merchant Venturers' gift of free public access to Durdham Downs in 1860. Resited 1988.

Bristol Zoo, Clifton Down. Founded in 1835. The original landscape gardens by *Richard Forrest* of Acton largely survive. Of about the same date are two pretty Neo-Greek entrance **lodges**, with a C20 frieze of animal silhouettes. A glass entrance link by *LMP Architects* was added 1996. On the W side of the gardens, a **tea pavilion** and ballroom, 1929–30 by *W.H. Watkins*, extended with a tented canopy by *Peter Ware*, 1992. The **giraffe house**, *c.* 1860, is a Tudor Gothic villa all complete, with only the two-storey doorway hinting that the inhabitants are not human. *Charles Hansom* has been suggested as architect.

Clifton College, Guthrie Road, was one of the many new mid-C19 public schools. The first buildings, by *Charles Hansom*, opened in 1862. His later partner, *F.B. Bond*, continued after Hansom's death in 1888. The style is generally Perp, with a Dec chapel. The best views are from College Road [124]. From the left, the pink rubble-stone **Big School** projects S, a very high hall with large S window and strongly buttressed sides. Then in the centre **Percival Buildings** (1869 and 1875) with cloister and oriel, and some fluid ogee tracery. To the right a four-storey **gatehouse** tower, 1889. **Chapel** and belfry 1866–7, with N aisle added 1881. *Nicholson & Corlette* ingeniously recast this chapel in 1909–10. The central parts of the side walls were removed, and two chapels set diagonally on each side, breaking into the roofline. Rib-vaulting supports a green copper-clad lantern inspired by the Ely Octagon. Near the chapel, a South African **War Memorial**, a bronze statue of St George, armoured, virtuous and serene, by *Alfred Drury*, 1904. Of post-Edwardian work there is *A. Munby*'s **Science School** of 1927, plain and

123. Engineers' House, Litfield Place, by Charles Dyer, 1830–1

124. Clifton College, by Charles Hansom with F.B. Bond, 1862 and later

business-like, extended by *Eustace Button*, 1960s. *Charles Holden*'s **gateway** to College Road (1921) commemorates the school's war dead. Simplified Gothic, and crushingly mundane after the glory of his Central Library (*see* p. 75).

All Saints, Pembroke Road, 1962–7 by *Robert Potter* [125]. A strong High Anglican tradition has prevailed here since the C19. The church is designed on Liturgical Movement principles, emphasizing congregational participation. It replaced *G.E. Street*'s church (designed 1863, consecrated 1868) blitzed in 1940. *W.H. Randoll Blacking*'s restoration plan of 1947 foundered in years of tortuous delay. After Blacking's death, his partner Robert Potter (of Potter & Hare) decided the ruined walls were beyond repair, although his new design (1962–3) incorporates three surviving elements – the tower, sacristy and narthex. The stump of *Street*'s tower is topped by a slim laminated timber spire clad in aluminium. Nave to the N with canted E and W ends and vertical glazing strips, under folded and angled roofs. To the S are rubble-stone walls with slit windows for the ancillary buildings. Main entrance via the tower into a light cloister around a glazed atrium. The **sacristy**, SE, is by *F.C. Eden*, 1922–3, with fine panelling and elliptical barrel vault. The church lies N of the atrium; a calm space, not dark, but subdued due to the richly coloured windows. Coffered concrete roofs based on a massive X-beam. S gallery against a fully glazed wall, predominantly bright blue. Angled sanctuary, marked by two full-height red-glazed slit windows. *Blacking*'s incongruous Byzantine **ciborium** (1952) covers a Portland stone altar slab. – Engraved slate **piscina** by *John Skelton*, and silver **tabernacle** set with lapis lazuli (1923), designer *F.C. Eden*, makers *Barkentin & Krall*. – In the W angle, a **baptistery** with drum-shaped **font**. – W **windows** by *John Piper*, not abstract but powerful and primitive, representing the **River of Life** and **Tree of Life**, made of translucent fibreglass panels built up slowly *in situ*. – **Organ** by *Walker & Sons* in the NE corner, well integrated with the architectural setting. – N **chapel**, designed by *G.F. Bodley* as a narthex, 1907, recast as the Chapel of St Richard of Chichester. Three N windows (1909) and a weak E window by *Christopher Webb* (1967), with donor portrait of Fr Luetchford holding Potter's church.

At No. 1 Alma Vale Road, directly s of All Saints, **Edwards' Van Garage**, 1899, by *Drake & Pizey*. Quite lavish for a small and explicitly urban building type. *Fin-de-siècle* Baroque with Art Nouveau influences. A little way s, and E of Pembroke Road is **Buckingham Vale**, built up *c.* 1847–50 probably by *R.S. Pope* for the developer George Ashmead, founder of Buckingham Baptist Chapel and superlative Bristol mapmaker, who bought No. 13. At Nos. 12–13 [14], two houses are reconciled in an Ionic temple front *in antis*, with a blank central section: a common device in London villas of this date, but very unusual here. The broad proportions are uncharacteristic of Pope's work.

At the junction of Pembroke Road with Hanbury Road, **Channings Hotel**, originally called Pembroke Hall, by *Thomas Nicholson*, 1879–82. A gloriously brash and pompous Clifton villa. Two competing façades, all angles and bays, overwhelmed with incidental carving.

St Paul, St Paul's Road. Tower and broach spire by *Manners & Gill* of Bath, 1853, the rest rebuilt after a fire by *Charles Hansom*, 1868; porch by *H.C.M. Hirst*, 1905. Unexciting Pennant stone exterior. Five-bay nave with low pink sandstone arcade and sexfoil clerestory, wide aisles and tall narrow chancel under tie-beam roofs. Exceptionally complete **stained glass** sequence by *Hardman & Co.*, the E window probably of 1868, the rest 1871–87. Impressive timber **reredos** by *Powell & Sons* of Whitefriars, 1903, commemorating the marriage of Sir George White's daughter, with Perp niches framing *opus sectile* panels depicting the Ascension, Nativity and Crucifixion. In the aisles, ten more **panels** framed in pink marble, all made by *Powell's* between 1905 and 1927. They include a war memorial of 1919, an Angel of Victory with broken sword and shell case.

To the NE in Oakfield Place, the disused **Clifton Swimming Baths** (1849–50), an unusually early survival. Symmetrical façade with Grecian battered door-frame. Interiors and poolside buildings reportedly much altered. Threatened with redevelopment, 2004. N again, in Oakfield Road, **Oakfield House**, 1831, by *Charles Dyer*, signed on the porch. A substantial villa that appears from the rate books not to have been occupied until 1839. *Charles Underwood* perhaps added the rear bow window with rosette frieze.

Whiteladies Road forms the E boundary of Clifton. Now almost entirely commercial in character. There are many good Italianate villas of *c.* 1855–65, particularly at the s end, by *R.S. Pope* and *Henry Rumley* among others. Between Belgrave Road and Tyndalls Park Road, **Broadcasting House**, by *BBC Architects*, 1987. Now BBC regional headquarters, originally studios. Its massing and style maintains the street's

125. All Saints, Pembroke Road, by Robert Potter, 1962–7

character well. Two blocks with a columned recessed link containing the entrance, and round-arched windows in groups of twos and threes. Undeniably pastiche, but better than much else that carries that label. Further N, on the w side, the former **ABC Cinema**, Whiteladies Road, by *La Trobe & Weston*, 1921. An excellent example of the transition from Edwardian to Art Deco, but now closed and its future in doubt. It was the first purpose-built cinema to intrude upon Clifton, and included a dancehall and restaurant. Superior and flashy Hollywood motifs in the tall domed turret with pierced panels and carved stone, spread-eagle wings down the flank, etc.

Near the N end of Whiteladies Road a disparate group. On the w **side**, No. 106, **NatWest Bank** by *Drake & Pizey*, 1903–6, very high and bulky, in a free Baroque reminiscent of John Belcher. Immediately N, the church of **St John**, by *S.J. Hicks*, 1841, now **Clifton Auction Rooms**. Perp with open traceried w turrets after Rickman & Hutchinson's Holy Trinity, St Philip's, sitting awkwardly on short towers. On the E **side**, Nos. 155–157, three houses by *W.B. Gingell*, 1856, in a quirky *Rundbogenstil*. Ground floors much altered for shops. Three-and-a-half storeys, with two belvedere towers, central arcade, bays, and more variety than any building can sensibly bear. Then to the s, **Redland Park Congregational Church** (now United Reformed), 1954–7, in a simple and robust pared-down Gothic. By *Ralph Brentnall*, showing his continued allegiance to his late partner Oatley's style.

The University and
St Michael's Hill

This circular walk from Bristol University on Queen's Road, takes in C19 and C20 University buildings; the Royal Fort, site of Civil War fortifications and a dazzling Rococo villa; St Michael's Hill, a C17 and C18 urban landscape; and the sumptuous Elizabethan Red Lodge.

Note: the s end of St Michael's Hill is steep.

We begin at the Wills Memorial Building, Queen's Road, of 1912 onwards (*see* Major Buildings, p. 83), the centrepiece of a sequence of public buildings with some sense of civic grandeur, a rare thing in Bristol. Typical of Bristol's haphazard approach to such things, it faces the back of Berkeley Square and the untidy shops built on its gardens. Directly left of the University building is the **Museum and Art Gallery**, by *Frank Wills* with *Houston & Houston* of London, 1900–5. It follows the national

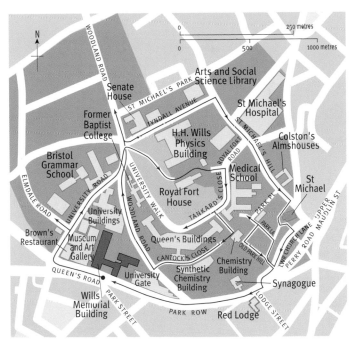

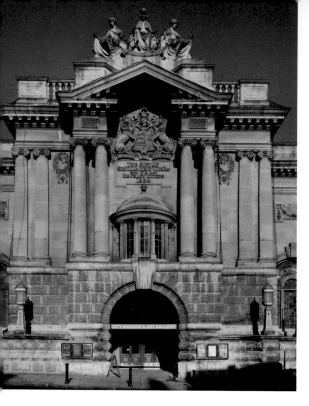

127. Museum and Art Gallery, Queen's Road, by F. Wills with Houston & Houston, 1900–5

trend for civic art galleries (cf. Preston, 1877; Sheffield, 1887; Bradford, 1900–4, to a very similar design). Originally the Art Gallery only; since 1940 it has housed the Museum too. Sir W.H. Wills of the tobacco firm donated the £40,000 cost and engaged his architect cousin, see p. 38. The result has been aptly described as 'fat Roman', less kindly as 'lunatic Baroque'. An overscaled thrusting centre over a porte-cochère; which was glazed to create a new entrance, 2004. Above, an applied Ionic portico beneath open pediment, with an inscription and the city coat of arms. The portico frames a bowed oriel. Heavy parapets with sculpture by *W.J. Smith* representing Architecture, Painting and Sculpture. The wings are set back, each with a big round-arched window: painted glass by *Joseph Bell & Son*, 1908.

Inside, two full-height halls with glazed barrel vaults. On the top floor, a sequence of toplit painting galleries around the front hall. Heavily articulated **front hall**, with balustraded gallery and the names of Old Master painters in swagged plaques above. Opposite the entrance, an imperial staircase descends through the thickness of the wall. Coppered brass electroliers by *Thursfield & Co.*, Birmingham. **Rear hall** added 1925–30 by *J.B. Wills*, Frank Wills's son. It has open two-tier arcades, lightening the effect. Walnut settees in the halls and galleries by the Bristol art furnisher *P.E. Gane*. In the rear café, a spectacular mid-c17 stone **chimneypiece** from Lewins Mead, some 12 ft (3.7 metres) high, with naïve Mannerist figures after Michelangelo's Medici tomb, but still with Jacobean strapwork. A fine example of the dissemination of the classical language through local masons.

Left again on Queen's Road, to **Brown's Restaurant**, the former **Museum and Library**, 'the West Country's greatest compliment to John Ruskin' (Pevsner). By *John Foster* and *Archibald Ponton*, 1867–72, the only known example of their collaboration; Foster designed the elevations and Ponton the plan. The façade is a Venetian Gothic rendition of *Foster & Wood*'s Colston Hall (*see* City Centre: Colston Street, p. 131), with two tiers of arcading and lancet niches between the upper arches. Venetian balustrades flank the broad steps leading to a full-length entrance loggia, now part-glazed. Rich foliate capitals with wild beasts on the ground-floor arcade. A row of shields above, added 1894–5. A design of great ambition, but much was never executed, including polychromatic masonry, sulphur inlay, balconies and carving. Much else was lost to bombing: a high pierced parapet with sculpture and corner canopies, ornamented cornices, etc. After the bombing, the museum collections were transferred to the Art Gallery (*see* above). The interior was not reinstated in *Ralph Brentnall*'s utilitarian rebuilding for the University refectory, 1949.

Left of Brown's Restaurant is **University Road**, a short hill running NE. Attached at the rear of Brown's is the former museum **lecture theatre** of 1874, by *Stuart Colman*. The angled façade expresses a domed polygonal plan. Mannered lancets of excruciating thinness, and an ogee-traceried window after the Ca' d'Oro, Venice. Parts of the interiors survive. Opposite, the **Eastern Orthodox Church**, 1888, by *Henry Rising*, built for the Irvingites in barn-like E.E. style. N of the church, turn left into **Elmdale Road**; Nos. 2–11 are thoroughgoing Gothic villas of 1883, reminiscent of Charles Hansom's Clifton College style. Nos. 8–11 have panels of lively carving depicting incidents from Aesop's fables.

Back on University Road, to the N is **Bristol Grammar School**, endowed by bequest of the merchant Robert Thorne in 1532, for boys 'to be instructed in good manners and literature'. The school moved here from premises in Unity Street, with the building of the Great Hall, by *Foster & Wood*, 1877–9 (visible from the N). Its Perp detail and composition look back to Clifton College and beyond to 1840s Tudor Gothic, yet the impression is bold, even quite handsome. Rubble walls of plum-coloured sandstone, with steep roofs, crowstepped gables, a narrow N tower and openwork bell-turret. It contains nine classrooms below a hall measuring 140 ft by 50 ft (42.7 by 15.2 metres), and 50 ft high. This was planned as a single schoolroom, still with its built-in cupboards and canopied masters' chairs. Two ranges towards University Road: to the N by *Frank Wills*, 1908, to the s by *W.V. & A.R. Gough*, 1912–14.

On the SE side of University Road is the first purpose-built home of **University College**, later the **University of Bristol** (for background, *see* Major Buildings: Wills Memorial Building, p. 83). This area is as close as the University gets to a campus or precinct: it occupies most of the quarter of a mile or so to the N, which yet retains the character of a prosperous Victorian suburb. All the University buildings before 1920 were sited in the triangle between Queen's Road, S, University Road, W, and Woodland Road, E. After a competition in 1879 failed to produce a winning design for new premises, one of the competitors, *Charles Hansom*, was appointed architect. He designed a quadrangular plan, asymmetrical and composed for a sloping site with no axial approach. It was over-ambitious, given the college's hopelessly inadequate funding; building was initially sporadic, and to reduced designs.

First, about two-thirds of the way up University Road, a bald grey stone range N of an open courtyard, built 1879–80. Intended as the first part of the quadrangle, to be hidden later by a W entrance range facing University Road. Instead, tacked onto its W end is *F.B. Bond*'s pink sandstone Albert Fry Memorial Tower of 1904, really just a large turret. The rear range E of the courtyard was built in 1883. Funding improved from 1889, enabling extensions to the S for Engineering and the Medical School (now Geography), in 1893–1904. By *Edward Hansom & F.B. Bond*, in their Clifton College style: sandstone rubble walls, cusped mullioned-and-transomed lights, varied by incidental turrets and oriel windows canted off little rib-vaulted bases. Facing **Woodland Road** is the Biology building by *Oatley & Lawrence*, 1910, originally Chemistry and Physiology. Perp tower, turrets, oriels and bays. To its W, at the apex of University and Woodland roads, the Zoology and Botany wing (1936–41), also by *Oatley & Lawrence*. Collegiate Tudor pared down to the minimum, lean and square with big mullioned and transomed windows.

To the E, above Woodland Road, is the former **Bristol Baptist College** [128], built in 1913–19 by *Oatley & Lawrence* for the world's oldest such establishment, founded 1679. Now also a University building. The style is Jacobean. Composed along a narrow, sloping site, with a N entrance tower. Good Doric doorcase. It is saved from severity by the homely red brick, and varied projections on the W front. Oatley's Arts and Crafts attention to quality and detail is evident in plain but solid interiors and fittings. Neo-Jacobean staircase of oak with pierced finials. Staircase window, by *Arnold Robinson*, with much purple and

128. Former Baptist College, Woodland Road. Architect's elevation, *c.* 1913

brown, commemorating Tyndale's English translation of the Bible. The former library and museum in the N wing has some C15 and C16 glass.

Now a circular tour of **Royal Fort**, to the N of Woodland Road. The historical background is complex. There were scattered buildings on the SE slopes below by the C15. On the open summit there was a windmill. Here, a five-sided fort was built *c.* 1644 by Royalist occupiers, hence its name (*see* topic box, p. 246). This was mostly demolished in 1655, and several big houses were built on the site. It became an exclusive and genteel place to live. Royal Fort House, a Palladian villa with sumptuous Rococo interiors, was built in 1758–61. Later, *Humphry Repton* landscaped the gardens. It became University property in 1917, and is now surrounded with University buildings of varying quality.

The entrance is at the junction of Woodland Road and Tyndall Avenue. Inside the gates, left of the drive beyond the shrubbery is the best of the University's additions, *Oatley & Lawrence*'s **H.H. Wills Physics Laboratory**, 1921–7 [129]. Closely modelled on Kirby Hall, Northants, of *c.* 1570: very big mullioned and transomed windows between fluted Ionic piers with scrolled brackets on top. Such emulation was old-fashioned by this date, but wholly in the spirit of the Willses' patronage.* The broad, high tower has window tracery and spiralled shafts at the battlements, suggesting C17 motifs. On the S front is

*Sir Ernest Newton's similar design for Uppingham School is exactly contemporary, but suggestions of cribbing are unsupported.

a big columned doorcase, with symbols representing discoveries in physics. Following H.H. Wills's wish to crown the Royal Fort with a ring of towers, the Physics Laboratory was just the NE corner of a great towered quadrangle which would have surrounded Royal Fort House, and for which *Oatley* drew up plans in 1918. The rest was never executed.

Opposite is **Royal Fort House**, Bristol's finest Georgian villa. In 1737 the Tyndall family leased a large house here, rebuilt by Thomas Tyndall in 1758–61. *James Bridges*, who made the wooden model still in the house, was claimed in 1763 to be its architect. A doggerel rhyme of 1767 suggests that Tyndall also consulted Thomas Paty and John Wallis; but this was written probably by Wallis himself, six years after the event. Wallis was Bridges' bitter rival for the design of Bristol Bridge, and his purpose in writing was perhaps to cast doubt on Bridges's authorship at Royal Fort House.

The house is almost square in profile and plan, of three storeys, in Bath stone. The Vanbrughian N entrance front has a tense narrow centre with arched first-floor windows. W front conventionally Palladian, of 1:3:1 bays. The pedimented centre breaks forward, and the ground floor has arched windows and V-grooved rustication. The S front has a full-height canted bay, small first-floor Venetian windows in the flanks, and two garden doors with pretty Rococo carving in the pediments. The relationship of the three façades is not entirely successful, yet the whole is undeniably pleasing.

Inside are incomparably the best C18 interiors in Bristol, at once playful and supremely elegant. The stuccoist was *Thomas Stocking*, and *Thomas Paty* was responsible for the masonry carving and fittings. The **plan** is simple: from the N front, a central entrance hall, with a triple-arched screen at the S, beyond which a lateral corridor leads left to a staircase in the SE corner. Drawing room, parlour, dining-room and study arranged around the hall. The **entrance hall** and corridor have a Doric plaster entablature, with elaborate trophies in the metopes. On the hall walls, four sculptural Rococo brackets. But the great surprise is the **staircase hall**, where **plasterwork** covers the walls with an all-over pattern reminiscent of C18 wallpaper [130]. The motif is sinuous vines, alive with birds and squirrels, with pastoral vignettes around the lower stems. Fine wrought-iron staircase balustrade of foliated S-scrolls. The **dining room** has a Rococo ceiling, a pine mantel carved with lively rocaille work, and delicately undercut drops of hunting trophies. The doorcase has wreathed Corinthian columns and an extravagant Chinoiserie overdoor. Attached to the E side, a big three-storey service wing, contemporary with the house, has a Delft-tiled niche in the corridor.

Attached to the E again, is **Stuart House**, simple but handsome, late C18 probably around a C17 core. The **garden** was sold for development in 1791 but, after quarrying had ruined it, the scheme foundered in the

130. Royal Fort House, 1758–61, staircase. Stucco work by Thomas Stocking

Bristol played a chequered role in the English Civil War: occupied by Parliamentarian forces in December 1642, it was taken by the Royalists in July 1643. Prince Rupert, Charles I's nephew, surrendered to Cromwell and Fairfax after brief fighting in September 1645. The city was vulnerable, having spread beyond its medieval walls, and in 1642 the Common Council ordered a defensive line to be built along the N escarpments and to the E of the city. This, and the refurbishment of the ruinous medieval castle, were executed by Cromwell's commander *Nathaniel Fiennes* in 1643. From a fort on Brandon Hill to defend the harbour approaches, the earthworks ran NE. At intervals there were palisaded redoubts, and larger wooden forts were built on the highest points, at Brandon Hill, Kingsdown (Prior's Hill Fort, now Fremantle Square) and St Michael's Hill. This last was rebuilt in 1643–4 by the Royalists, and was called the Great (or Royal) Fort. They also strengthened parts of the N line, but the Parliamentarians breached it quite easily in the E section in 1645. Bristol's defences, including the castle, were dismantled in 1655 on Cromwell's order. According to Jacob Millerd's 1673 map, Royal Fort 'being now demolished, is converted into houses and pleasant gardens'. There are significant remains on Brandon Hill (*see* Walk 4, p. 192), and the defensive line is discernible in boundary lines on later maps.

collapse of 1793. The Tyndalls resumed possession and *Humphry Repton* remodelled the gardens to hide both the scars and the new houses around Park Street. Small parts of Repton's scheme survive, as well as a small section of the C17 fort wall, s side.

Leave Royal Fort by the brick-vaulted **gatehouse** to the E, on the site of the Civil War gate, but so rebuilt that very little C17 fabric can remain. The outer arch is C18. Immediately on the right **Tankard's Close** takes one back s and then w round the hillside. On the left is the **Medical School**, by *Ralph Brentnall*, started 1959. Dull brown brick, swamping St Michael's Hill when seen from the city. In protest at its ugliness, students staged the Funeral of British Architecture, lowering a coffin into the foundations. Brentnall, with huge aplomb, attended *incognito* as an undertaker, saying that, as the murderer, he felt obliged to see her decently buried. Further w, the angular **Queen's Building**, or **Engineering School**, devised by *Oatley & Brentnall* in 1947. Executed in reduced form by *Brentnall*, 1951–8, in brick with green slate panels instead of the stone Oatley had wanted. Stylized classical references around the N entrance. It was incorporated in *Sir Percy Thomas & Partners'* masterplan of *c.* 1952, which proposed a grandiose symmetrical composition of buildings on terraces descending to Park Row, around an axial ceremonial stairway. Later buildings followed that plan only in general disposition, and the lower tiers went unbuilt.

The remains of the grand stairway lead s to the **Chemistry Building**, by *Courtauld Technical Services*, 1961–6. Two slab blocks with between them a podium overlooking the city. Predictably, on the s front, below a concrete panel of interlocking geometric shapes, is an angled cantilevered lecture theatre. Below the podium, a cloister-like sunken entrance court with pebble paving. From here **Cantock's Close** runs sw. On a high terrace is **Tower View**, a much-altered summer house of *c.* 1750–80 (extended with C20 brick). There were once many such structures on this hillside; this one was built as an adjunct to Lunsford House, Park Row (*see* p. 252). It had probably two rooms above a single-arched loggia. Dwarfing it to the s, the **Synthetic Chemistry Building**, by the *Percy Thomas Partnership*, opened 1999, injects some life. The plinth is Brandon Hill stone, with pale brick above. Curving triangular plan with a turret at the w apex. Full-height vertical projections, swept roofs and four lead-clad chimneys.

Woodland Road runs NW, back up to the Royal Fort entrance. N of this junction, the **Arts Faculty** is housed in big Victorian villas, by *George Gay*, *c.* 1862–72, E side. Linked by simple and unobtrusive rear extensions, by *MacCormac & Jamieson*, 1979–84, planned around garden courts, visible from St Michael's Park. Back s to **Tyndall Avenue**; at the junction is the **Senate House**, by *Ralph Brentnall*, opened 1965. A dispirited design of five storeys, ashlar faced, with bands of windows divided by narrow stone mullions. On a U-plan, but with no focal point. Immediately E the **Centre for Sport, Exercise and Health**, by *Nugent Vallis Brierley*, completed 2002. The long copper-clad upper parts bulge disconcertingly above a conventional brick ground floor. On the right side, *Brentnall's* **Physics Extension**, opened 1968, is notable only for its bulk and its desperate plainness, the result of a University cash crisis. Lastly the **Arts and Social Sciences Library**, by *Twist & Whitley*, opened 1975, repeating their design for Belfast University. Windows were reduced to a minimum to conserve heat, making the exterior fortress-like and austere. Indented corners and a second floor that reads like a big cornice, with long rows of small angled windows in box-like projections. Inside it is functional and well planned, although the staircase is too steep.

Turning s into **St Michael's Hill** we leave the University precinct. This was a main route from medieval Bristol towards Wales; the interest is in the happy mix of C17–C19 houses, framing the view of the city. On the E side, Nos. 78–100, a varied but harmonious row of late C18 houses, and a conservation success. After years of dereliction, they were repaired *c.* 1977–9 as flats. On the w side, the Tudor Gothic former **Children's Hospital**, by *Robert Curwen*, 1882–5. The main benefactor was Mark Whitwill, a Liberal politician and Congregationalist. Symmetrical front with cross-gabled ends, and the usual paraphernalia of bays, oriels and turret doorway. Opposite is **St Michael's Hospital** (opened 1975), a big concrete slab that unforgivably disrupts the street's scale and line. Take the picturesque raised and stepped **pavement** down the w side, from which the houses opposite are easily visible. w **side**, Nos. 65–67, probably by *George Tully c.* 1727. No. 67 has a shell-hood. On the e, Nos. 50–52, perhaps *c.* 1700–20, four storeys and a distinctive shared half-hipped gable. Then No. 46, of 1711, a four-bay stone façade with cornice and panelled parapet, and open segmental pediment on Tuscan columns. Below this, Winstone Court by *Derek Bruce & Partners*, 1977, a fine example of infill architecture incorporating, right, a late c18 house. The new work has chamfered window architraves, broken profiles and steps and walls making an excellent transition from the street. The left section floats above a glazed ground floor. Back on the w side, a long c18 row steps down the hill. Most were repaired by *Ralph Brentnall c.* 1960, the exteriors meticulously reconstructed from photographs but the interiors largely rebuilt. Nos. 49–51 are of *c.* 1711, No. 51 gabled, both updated *c.* 1770 with bays, etc. Nos. 39–41 are of *c.* 1700 and have later Georgian features.

Colston's Almshouses, 1691–6 [131], on the e side, was founded by Edward Colston, and was probably Bristol's first classical public building. More polished than the Manor House (*see* below), but, given the coincidences of place, date and style, they may have some connection. A homely open courtyard of warm limestone with hipped roofs, arranged symmetrically around a steeply pedimented three-bay chapel with an inscription flanked by two oval windows. On the roof, a domed bellcote. Cross-windows, the lower ones with alternating pediments over pulvinated friezes. The doorways have gabled canopies on brackets, except the chapel, which has a flat canopy with a segmental pediment. Below are three tall gabled houses of 1695, built to provide income for the almshouses. Two are now pubs.

131. Colston's Almshouses, St Michael's Hill, 1691–6

132. Manor House, Park Lane, *c.* 1691

More of the C17 on the w side: Nos. 23 29, the upper pair *c.* 1637. Three storeys, gabled with jettied first floors and second-floor moulded stringcourse. Bay windows with C18 sashes. Immediately after, turn right to St Michael (*see* City Churches, p. 104). To its s, the former **rectory** in Old Church Lane has a pretty C18 Gothick façade, red rendered with ogee-arched windows with intersecting glazing bars, presumably by *Thomas Paty* and of the same date as the rebuilt church, i.e. 1775–7. But the core is C16 or earlier: late C16 panelling was removed in 1910 (*see* Red Lodge, below). **Lower Church Lane** leads w, where good minor houses of C15–C17 origin were cleared in the 1950s.

To the N in Old Park Hill, an alleyway leads to **St Michael on the Mount Primary School**, by *W.V. Gough, c.* 1895, a Board School in Gough's gruff version of Queen Anne. On the N gable an C18 sculpture of a putto (*see* Old Library, Walk 1, p. 160). Just up the hill in Park Lane, the **Manor House**, rebuilt after a fire in 1691 [132]. This is the city's earliest surviving classical house, in a provincial interpretation of the Restoration-Dutch mode. A handsome façade of six bays and two storeys, with tiled hipped roof and dormers. Single-storey wings, probably from an earlier house shown on Millerd's 1673 map. A shell-hood door placed off-centre. The cross-windows post-date a fire that destroyed much of the interiors in 1978.

Back s down **Old Park Hill**, to **Savory's Printing Works**, now a University building. By *Mowbray Green*, 1905, extended to a design of 1909. The high façade above Park Row shows some Arts and Crafts influence in the roughcast render and timber balconies. At the front, a ramp leads down sw to Park Row.

Red Lodge, *c.* 1577–85, now a museum, is on the s side of Park Row. A remarkable late Elizabethan lodge with exceptional interiors. The site belonged to a c13 Carmelite foundation. In 1568 John Young acquired it and built a mansion (demolished for Colston Hall, 1863). There in 1574 he entertained Queen Elizabeth, who knighted him. For his tomb, *see* Bristol Cathedral, p. 61. Red Lodge was Young's garden lodge, of Brandon Hill sandstone, originally rendered and painted deep red, two-and-a-half storeys with an arched loggia to the garden – an Italian Renaissance idea. It was an independent dwelling by 1595, extended in the c17 and comprehensively altered *c.* 1720–30, with hipped roofs and eaves and cornice replacing gables, and long sashes. The N side was remodelled around a new staircase, and the loggia was incorporated into the rooms behind.

Interiors. On the ground floor, the **reception room** has an c18 bolection-moulded chimneypiece. To the E, in the **parlour**, a c16 ribbed and moulded ceiling and chimneypiece with scrolled frieze. At the NW corner, the **New Oak Room** was refitted in 1965. The fireplace, of perhaps *c.* 1600, came from the demolished Ashley Manor, Ashley Down (now a N suburb), and the panelling from St Michael's rectory (*see* above). Only during installation was it realized that the elaborate cornice is virtually identical to that in the Great Oak Room, and presumably by the same maker.

133. Red Lodge, Park Row, *c.* 1577–85; Great Oak Room

The open-well **staircase** is C18, of oak and nobly proportioned. Three twisted balusters per tread and Ionic column newels. It leads to a fully panelled chamber, called the **Great Oak Room**, among the most elaborate English interiors of its date [133]. Not an inch escapes embellishment. Entry is via a timber inner porch, as at, e.g., Montacute House in Somerset; now believed to be contemporary with the room. Shell-headed doors are framed by paired Composite columns. The lower entablature has a frieze of winged beasts and foliage. Above is a second tier, even richer, with paired terms instead of columns, and the arms of Young and his wife, projecting so far they seem to float over the structure. The porch's upper cornice matches neither the lower one, nor that above the panelling around the room. The walls have an arcaded dado separated by fluted pilasters, and above this, a regular grid of panels each framing a classical arch. Another geometric ribbed ceiling, with five pendants, vase and foliage motifs, winged cherubs, pomegranates, etc., and dim Gothic remembrances in ogee trefoils. Dominating all is the only major Bristol school chimneypiece still *in situ*. It is very big and high, of richly carved limestone. Alabaster panels depicting Hope, Faith, Justice and Prudence surround Young's arms, set in a strapwork cartouche flanked by paired terms. The cartouche and terms derive from two mid-C16 suites of engravings by Jan Vredeman de Vries.

In Red Lodge gardens is a C20 annexe known as the **Wigwam**, a barn-like structure by *C.F.W. Dening c.* 1920 for the Savages, a society of painters. In the main room, two chimneypieces, one of 1682 from the demolished Goat in Armour Inn, Alderskey Lane (formerly off Prince Street), with broken segmental pediment and seated figures, but still a cambered fire-opening. The other, inscribed 16 RMS 74, came from the house of Richard Stubbs, a wine merchant of St Michael's. The overmantel has arabesques, vine trails and tapering pilasters.

The **Synagogue** (1869–71) is on the N side of Park Row, opposite Red Lodge. Bristol's C18 Jewish community settled largely in the Temple district s of Bristol Bridge: the first permanent synagogue (1786) was at Weavers' Hall, the second (1842) nearby in Temple Street. Development of Victoria Street (*see* Walk 3, p. 179) forced the move to a new site, purchased by Samuel Platnauer. Structural and exterior design by the Corporation surveyor *S.C. Fripp.* Unprepossessing rubble exterior with Serlian entrance arch and rectangular triple windows above, overshadowed by the Reader's House at the right. Interiors by *Hyman H. Collins* of London [134]; women's galleries with lattice-work panels around three sides. Ark with curved mahogany doors, E (probably *c.* 1786), brought from Weavers' Hall. Over it an arched canopy on columns, with gilded symbolic plants on the scrolled capitals and on the canopy. Central **bimah** (cantor's stage), with columnar brass lamps from Temple Street. Eight-branched brass **menorah** (candelabrum), of C17 Dutch origin on C18 base.

134. Synagogue, Park Row, interior by Hyman H. Collins, 1869–71

Directly w, behind high walls and just visible from across the street is **Lunsford House**, refronted *c.* 1738–9 around a C17 core, and with a C19 wing at the rear. Three storeys and an attic, in Flemish bond brickwork; a two-bay projecting centre, with a Venetian window above a single-arched loggia. Lower two-bay wings, the change of level resolved by a ramped parapet. Then the **Vandyck Press**, 1911, by *Mowbray Green*, now a University building. A high rough-hewn rubble plinth, battered and faintly fortress-like, and a plain symmetrical front, divested of historicism. Brick side walls with scalloped and angled parapets. Opposite, more Arts and Crafts: first, four gabled brick shops with broad mullioned and transomed bays, by *Edward Gabriel*, 1905, and w of these Nos. 20–24, by *James Hart*, 1902. Originally a decorator's showroom with houses either side. Eclectic references, e.g. Doric colonnades, and C17 domestic in the wings. Baroque and Adam plasterwork in the centre. The party walls and ends marked by unusual buttresses sloping streetward. At the junction with Woodland Road, **public conveniences** of some distinction, with a pilastered temple front and dated 1904. Nearing the end of our circular tour is **University Gate**, the University's Engineering faculty by *Atkins Walters Webster*, opened 1996. It incorporates part of the very long façade of the Coliseum, a skating rink then cinema, 1910; an old-fashioned and pretentious design of Italianate arches, etc. This sits uncomfortably with the new building, of which the Woodland Road front and the w end nearest the Wills Memorial Building are the best parts, with juxtaposed roofs of swept curves.

Kingsdown to Stokes Croft

This walk covers the residential NE fringe of the centre, from the boundary with Cotham at the top of St Michael's Hill, across C18 Kingsdown, perched magnificently on steep slopes, and down to Stokes Croft. John Betjeman described Kingsdown in the late 1950s as 'this airy suburb, this place of Georgian view-commanding terraces, trees, cobbled streets, garden walls and residential quiet'. That atmosphere is not lost. The lanes from Somerset Street down to Dove Street (Montague Hill, Spring Hill) are extremely steep.

Cotham Parish Church stands where St Michael's Hill meets Cotham Road. Begun by *William Butterfield*, 1842–3, as Highbury Congregational Chapel; Church of England since the 1970s. Butterfield's first work is remarkably faithful for its date to the model of a Perp country church, especially considering its Nonconformist origins. Butterfield was the nephew of the main benefactor, W.D. Wills of the tobacco family. The building cost £2,765. Pennant rubble with limestone dressings, nicely composed on a shallow rise, formerly the site of the city gallows. On the N wall a **memorial** to five Marian martyrs burned at the stake here in 1555–7. Five-bay aisled nave, with four-centred arcade on crisp octagonal piers. Shallow clerestory of quatrefoils grouped in threes (and out of step with the arcades below). w gallery. In 1863 *E.W. Godwin* added the apse and a s tower with, beneath it, a galleried bay beyond the aisle,

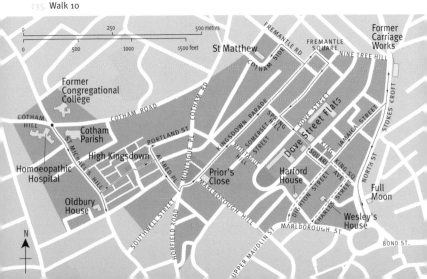

136. Former Western Congregational College, Cotham Road, by H.D. Bryan, 1905–6

giving the appearance of a double-depth aisle or a sort of transept. The apse was extended E by one bay, *c.* 1892–3. W window of 1950 commemorating the Rev. K.L. Parry, hymn-writer. On the corbel terminating the N nave arcade, a memorial **sculpture** to the Rev. H. Arnold Thomas d. 1924, by *Eric Gill*, depicting the Good Shepherd, with beautifully cut inscription.

N of the road junction is the Arts and Crafts **Western Congregational College**, by *H.D. Bryan*, 1905–6 [136]. Now a medical practice. Symmetrical in plan and elevation, and loosely Jacobean, although the first design was bigger and classical. **Y**-shaped plan, with a central entrance, behind which was an assembly hall. Angled wings containing, to the right, a library, and left, common room. The wings have big double-height bays, and decorative turrets flank the entrance. To the E, the Principal's House is suitably domestic, lower and half-timbered. A scalloped boundary wall with ball- and obelisk-finials at the gates exemplifies the Edwardian charm which Bryan could produce so well.

Opposite to the W, *Oatley & Lawrence*'s **Homoeopathic Hospital**, 1920–5, in a late Arts and Crafts Cotswold idiom. The £123,000 cost was paid by Melville and Gertrude Wills in memory of their son, killed in the First World War. A big Tuscan porch faces the road, with high gabled wings, simple mullioned windows and diagonally set chimneystacks in groups. Men's and women's wards were on different floors, all with E-, S- or W-facing arcaded sun balconies. There was an operating theatre on the top floor. The statement that the design was made as early as 1908 is unverified, but seems unlikely. Formal gardens of 1926–7 with rockeries of Pulhamite, an artificial stone.

St Michael's Hill runs S, here a shopping street, originally Regency and Victorian housing. Shortly, some earlier houses, particularly No. 121, **Oldbury House**, on the right. Now a University building, built as a gentry house *c.* 1679–89, and updated perhaps *c.* 1750. Six bays and three storeys, with three gables. Sash windows and a Gibbsian doorcase with pediment in the Paty style (cf. Quakers' Friars). For the s continuation of St Michael's Hill, *see* Walk 9, p. 239.

Opposite, alleys lead E into the very successful **High Kingsdown** housing complex, by *Whicheloe Macfarlane* and *JT Group Ltd*, 1971–5 [137]. The area was largely dilapidated Georgian housing; in *c.* 1965 the City Council proposed a destructive scheme of high- and medium-rise flats, rejected in 1968, after a local and national campaign. Unusually, the council transferred the project to the private sector, retaining ownership until completion so that no developers made a profit on the land. A new masterplan by *Whicheloe Macfarlane* proposed s- or w-facing low-rise houses of pale brick and tile, on a herringbone layout, with walled gardens. These features were inspired by Jørn Utzon's housing at Fredensborg, Denmark (1962–5), which the architect *Anthony Mackay* had seen. After approval, JT Group replanned it to increase the traffic-free areas, and built it in phases, 1971–5. A green space and Victorian pub were left in the centre. On the N boundary, a long slab of flats at right angles to St Michael's Hill, intended to shelter the houses from an unexecuted road scheme (cf. Ralph Erskine's Byker estate, Newcastle, planned 1970). Three- and four-bedroom houses are grouped mostly in zigzag ranges of three or four. All the main rooms face the gardens. Single-pitch roofs, strip windows, and weatherboarding between the storeys. In some, a fourth bedroom bridges the walkways. Alleys and courtyards create a sense of enclosure. For high-density housing of this

137. High Kingsdown housing, Whicheloe Macfarlane and JT Group Ltd, 1971–5

date, such privacy is remarkable. The only comparable English scheme is Bishopsfield, Harlow, by Neylan & Ungless, 1963–6.

Walking through the scheme by any route from w to E, one emerges soon at Alfred Place. A short distance E in **Portland Street**, is **Knightstone House**, by *Bruges Tozer*, *c.* 1974–9, on the site of Portland Methodist Chapel. Twenty-nine wardened flats over four storeys; tiled roofs and red brick with blue soldier courses. Planned at angles around a rear courtyard. It incorporates the chapel's Lutton Memorial Hall (*Foster & Wood*, 1883), round-arched and pedimented. Remarkably responsive to its site, especially given its date. Returning to **Alfred Place**, on the E side, an eight-house terrace of *c.* 1788, in two sections: hipped double-pile roofs to Nos. 16–24, and mansards at Nos. 26–30. Two- and three-storey canted bays with timber pilasters and cornice mouldings. To the s, six houses by *Moxley Jenner*, 1985. A contextual design in red brick. To the sw in Southwell Street, a white hospital **chimney**, 1965, which towers above the city and is unsympathetic to Kingsdown's character.

Now E across Cotham Road South, to the heart of Kingsdown; two long Georgian streets running NE, and overlooking the city: Kingsdown Parade and Somerset Street below, of different origins. Somerset Street (*see* p. 257) was laid out probably *c.* 1737–8 by *George Tully*, at the northern limit of the grid-like blocks N of King Square, but building had not begun by 1742. Above it, **Kingsdown Parade** was developed piecemeal: a few houses at its w end existed by 1742, but none is recognizable now. The E end was laid out with planned terraces in the later C18. At the corner with Marlborough Hill, s, **Prior's Close**, by *Inscape Architects*, 2000–4, a community-led development of houses, maisonettes and flats (*see* Introduction, p. 46). The tallest houses hold the C18 line and height, but the style and materials – buff brick, render and aluminium-clad penthouse roofs – thankfully avoid pastiche Georgian.

There follow selected points of interest, not a house-by-house coverage. Many good details (e.g. railings, bootscrapers, door knockers) are not remarked. Nos. 20–28 are typical of the piecemeal w end houses, unified by bays etc. **Devon House**, No. 34a, is unusually grand for Kingsdown. An ashlar front in the late style of *William Paty*, *c.* 1790: wide arched doorway with attached columns. At the NE end, both sides of the street were developed jointly *c.* 1791–1800, for a respectable middle class, by the developer Charles Melsom, probably to the designs of *William Paty*. On the s side, Nos. 48–86 form a near-uniform terrace, brick fronted under later stucco, with freestone dressings. The doorcases are a hybrid of two standard types: the imposts carrying both curved brackets to an open pediment and a moulded inner arch around the fanlight. The design first appeared in 1784 at Brunswick Square, also attributed to Paty. The deeds permitted canted bays to the rear parlours. On the N **side**, Nos. 65–101 are in pairs raised over high basements, and linked by single-storey entrance wings. The rhythm is now lost to infilling, except at e.g. Nos. 65–71. This seems to be a special variant of William Paty's style (*see* Introduction, p. 27). Nos. 81–85 are grouped in three to emphasize the centre. Long front gardens with brick walls and pedimented gates (surviving at, e.g., No. 71), and no rear gardens at all.

At the NE end of Kingsdown Parade we turn NW into Fremantle Road, then SW into **Cotham Side**. Here is **St Matthew**, 1833–5 by *Thomas Rickman*, who defined the accepted chronological terms for Gothic architecture. Pennant rubble and Bath stone exterior, mildly Perp, of six bays with four-stage W tower. Rickman was archaeologically minded enough to put a Bristol spirelet over the stair-turret. At the nave E end, chimneys disguised as turrets with big quatrefoiled caps. **Interior** divided at gallery level in 1989 to give a hall beneath and church above. Four-centred nave arcades on square sectioned piers with moulded angles. High clerestory with an ogee-headed niche on a big corbel between each bay. Flat panelled ceiling. – **Stained glass.** E window, 1927, by *Powell & Sons* of Whitefriars. – In the hall, four windows by *Arnold Robinson*, 1931–45. – **Organ** at the W end, with a strident Gothic case by *John Smith Sen.*, 1840. – In the N gallery a bronzed plaque with enamelling, to the Rev. John Clifford, d.1886, by *Singer & Sons* of Frome.

Return to Kingsdown Parade, where Nos. 1–4 **Apsley Villas** (s side) face the end of Fremantle Road. Nos. 1–2 are dated 1840: Nos. 3–4, *c.* 1850, have upper windows in big elliptical recesses. Both employ the narrow central recesses favoured by *R.S. Pope*. Directly NE is **Fremantle Square**, built on the site of a Civil War fort (*see* topic box, p. 246). On the NW side, big villa pairs, similar to Nos. 1–2 Apsley Villas (above). The other three sides are by *William Armstrong, c.* 1841–2; terraced, stuccoed two-bay houses with reticent late classical features such as first-floor windows recessed in blind arches. Good teardrop fanlights.

138. Somerset Street, detail of doorcase, late C18

From the sw corner, **Somerset Street** runs back to the sw, parallel and below Kingsdown Parade. A charming and relaxed backwater of smaller houses of *c.* 1750 and after. At the exit from Fremantle Square, No. 36 has an unusual bowed oriel with fan-shaped underside on slender cast-iron stanchions, perhaps *c.* 1810–20. Haphazard extension seems to have been the order of the day, perhaps suggesting a rise in the street's status at the end of the C18. Examples include No. 34, a mid-C18 cottage at the right, with a new door and three-storey extension at the left *c.* 1790. At Nos. 26–27, *c.* 1790, the left-hand house shows the original arrangement, while the right-hand was enlarged perhaps *c.* 1810 with a canted bay where the side courtyard once was. Further sw, Nos. 19, 18 and **Spring Hill House**, *c.* 1770–80. The builders may have been *Thomas* and *Isaac Manley*, who built the very similar No. 26 Cumberland Street, St Paul's (*see* Walk 11, p. 261). Homely and relaxed brick houses, mixing canted bays, Venetian and tripartite sashes on each house. The return elevation of Spring Hill House has a big Gibbsian arched doorway.

Descend by either of two steep setted lanes – Spring Hill, or Montague Hill further w. Both emerge on to Dove Street, dwarfed by **Dove Street Flats**, by the *City Architect's Department*, 1965–8. Three fourteen-storey slabs with lower linking blocks, and of little architectural merit. Despite protests, a swathe was cut through the shabby and part-derelict Georgian houses here, to provide 347 flats, just a handful more than the number of houses demolished: the conservation ethos had yet to gain acceptance, and building new was cheaper. Just below is **King Square**, laid out *c.* 1740 by *George Tully* and built up slowly *c.* 1740–75, perhaps with houses by both Tully and *Thomas Paty*. The SE and NE sides are dull post-war infill after bombing. On the sw side, Nos. 2–7 (*c.* 1762) are brick with pedimented doorcases and some Gibbsian blocks, all suggesting *Thomas Paty* (cf. his Albemarle Row, Walk 6, p. 211). They step up the slope unevenly, and No. 5 crams in an extra storey. At No. 3, a panel of icicle-work in the door pediment. On the N return of No. 7, a good Greek Doric porch, *c.* 1830 and a rare original coach house at the rear, *c.* 1760s, now derelict. The NW side is bisected by Spring Hill. To its left, unexciting 1980s work at Maple House: to the right, Nos. 12–15 of *c.* 1760–70, with early C19 timber porches. Ugly extensions spoil the E end.

Now an optional diversion: From the lower (s) side of King Square, turn sw into **Dighton Street**. Shortly on the right is No. 2, **Harford House**, a mid-sized Palladian villa modelled after Clifton Hill House (*see* Walk 6, p. 214). Probably by *Thomas Paty*, *c.* 1760. Three-storey pedimented centre of 1:3:1 bays, with lower wings set back. The right wing has been built up to three storeys, giving a lopsided appearance. A few yards E, turn E on to Marlborough Street, then first left into **Charles Street**, a bleak back street. Nos. 4–5 are a pair of modest brick houses of *c.* 1750. No. 4, occasionally open to the public, was from 1766 to 1771 the home of the Methodist leader Charles Wesley, and his son, the

composer Samuel Wesley. Simple and evocative mid-Georgian furnishings, and a re-created C18 rear garden. Continue NE along Charles Street and left via King Square Avenue to King Square.

From the SE corner of King Square, **Jamaica Street** runs NE. On the right, Nos. 2–6 have simple and refined Greek Doric doorcases of *c.* 1810–20. Nos. 37–39 were built *c.* 1905 by *J.L. Priest & Co.*, iron founders, as a carriage works; heightened by two storeys in 1909. Bristol's belated first experiment in exposed iron-framed construction; Glasgow had examples by the 1850s, Liverpool by the 1860s. Slim columns with perfunctory capitals frame a fully glazed façade on the lower floors. Half-glazed between brick piers in the upper addition. It faces the angled junction with **Stokes Croft**, currently shabby, deserving of better treatment and very slowly getting it. The street was built up by the late C17. No. 104 is a fine example of the Bristol warehouse style, built as **Perry's Carriage Works** by *E.W. Godwin*, 1862 [139]. Coursed Pennant rubble and limestone, ten bays by three storeys. On the ground floor, five broad segmental arches, originally open. Above, ten-light round-headed arcades to each floor, terminated by narrower pointed arches which lend the design a subtle tension. Disgracefully derelict, given the significance of both style and architect. To the s, Nos. 74–76, a pair of Gothic shops also by *Godwin, c.* 1865, now disfigured by later shopfronts. The deeply recessed windows, stepped party wall on the roof, tumbled and cogged brick and gabled half-dormers hint at their former quality. At the s end of the street, the former **Full Moon Inn**, *c.* 1695, has a three-storey gabled range at right angles to the street, with C18 sashes and early C19 porch. A good iron overthrow to the courtyard.

Walk 11.

The Eastern Fringe

Two walks cover the E outskirts of the city centre: St Paul's, N, and s
from Old Market through St Philip's.

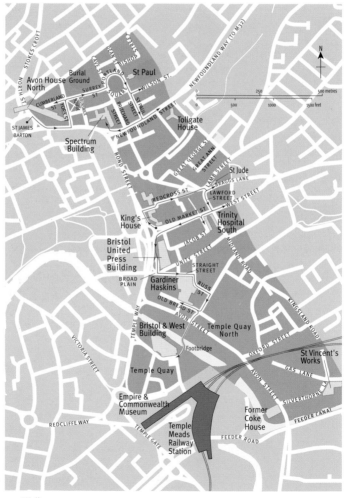

140. Walk 11

St Paul's

The district of St Paul's expanded in the late C18 to accommodate rapid population growth on the fashionable N fringe. Two good squares remain. It became industrialized from the mid C19, with boot- and furniture-making prominent. Post-war dereliction exacerbated racial tensions here, but the area has been turned around since riots in 1981. New commercial development vied with reuse of Georgian buildings in the late C20. Repairs started to the Georgian Gothic St Paul's church in 2002.

St James Barton roundabout N of Broadmead makes an unpromising start. On its N side, and to the E, are **Avon House North** (which bridges North Street), **Barton House** and **York House**, by *Whicheloe Macfarlane* and *R. Towning Hill, c.* 1969–74. Long concrete elevations, with slit windows and monolithic service towers, angled E into Bond Street. Avon House North was converted to flats *c.* 2001. Just E of the roundabout was St James's Square, laid out *c.* 1707, partly destroyed by wartime bombing, and the rest levelled *c.* 1965 for this complex. Turn N from Bond Street into York Street and the Georgian parts of St Paul's.

Immediately, one enters **Brunswick Square**, a rather haphazard Georgian scheme, laid out with Cumberland Street to its W in 1766, by *George Tully*, although he did not design the houses. Building proceeded only fitfully: the S side and Cumberland Street in 1766–*c.* 1771; the W side begun in the same years but never completed; and the E side not until 1784–6. The N side remained open until a chapel was built in the 1830s.

Now for the details: first, off to the W is **Cumberland Street**, a cul-de-sac truncated by Barton House (*see* above). The builders, *Thomas* and *Isaac Manley*, were probably left to provide their own designs, resulting in a compendium of parts put together without regard for the rules. Bays, Venetian and sash windows mixed willy-nilly in each façade, e.g. No. 26, S side. The N side has replica façades with offices behind, by *Hubbard Ford & Partners, c.* 1985–7, using oversized bricks. Better-preserved S side, with a good mid Victorian shopfront at No. 28. Back in **Brunswick Square**, the W **side** is an incomplete terrace of three, overladen with Gibbsian blocks at every window and door. These and the S **side** are attributed to *Thomas Paty*, the latter built *c.* 1766–71 by *Edmund Workman*. It is more orderly than the W side, and has a pedimented centre and stepped voussoirs. Seemingly five houses arranged 5:3:5:3:5 bays. In fact each end is two houses, the doors to the outer ones on the return walls; the divisions are visible at roof level. By the 1970s, the terrace was nearing collapse and demolition was authorized. Instead it was façaded for offices by *Towning Hill & Partners*, 1981–3, at least preserving the character of the square. The rear parts are sympathetic in scale and proportions, but the biscuit-coloured brick is alien to Bristol. The E **side** was funded by a Tontine subscription (*see* Introduction, p. 25). Probably by *William Paty, c.* 1784–6. The centre is de-emphasized in favour of the ends, which have higher pavilions, a Neoclassical characteristic.

Unusually for Bristol there are no lesenes between the houses, but it has the outdated stepped voussoirs beloved of the Patys.

William Armstrong's former **Congregational Chapel** (1834–5) dominates the N **side**, of boxy profile with heavily detailed attached Ionic portico and channelled rustication. Greek Revival merges into Italianate with arched upper windows and vase balustrades. To the right the low Greek **Surrey Lodge**, *c.* 1830, was the entrance to the Unitarian Burial Ground behind. Domestic-looking and conventionally Greek except in the recessed elliptical entrance arch flanked by Doric columns. Next door on Surrey Street, E, the site of Pevsner's wildly 'Moresco-Gothic' Surrey Villa is now occupied by nondescript 1980s offices in lurid orange brick.

Surrey Street forms the W approach to **Portland Square**, laid out by Act of Parliament (1787) on land owned by John Cave, William Pritchard and the Dean and Chapter of Bristol. It was named for the 3rd Duke of Portland, then High Steward of Bristol. The houses partly financed a new church for the growing population of St James's parish. Planning and elevations were by *Daniel Hague c.* 1787–8; his church was built 1789–94, but the houses were completed only *c.* 1823. It was planned together with surrounding streets to give vistas across the square; an ambitious piece of town planning for Bristol. The first design was in brick, soon modified by bigger end pavilions and the substitution of Bath stone. Although spartan by the standards of London or Bath, the architecture is controlled, even quite refined. The main developer was *James Lockier*, and *Thomas Pope*, father of R.S. Pope, was one of the builders. After a break caused by the collapse of 1793, building continued slowly and, unusually, the scheme was completed to the intended designs (*see* p. 217).

The terraces are continuous on the N and S sides; four-bay centre and ends with full attics and, in the centre only, pilasters with acanthus capitals. Deeply cut Ionic doorcases beneath open pediments, and plain window openings. The W side is bisected by Surrey Street and the E side by St Paul's church. Spacious roads frame a large oval garden. The **side streets** are simpler, and developed slowly, e.g. **Cave Street**, NW, its short E side built 1828 on the garden of No. 28 Portland Square (which once had an octagonal gazebo or conservatory on the roof, probably contemporary with the house). No. 27 retains much of its interior arrangement and fittings.

St Paul, by *Daniel Hague*, 1789–94, is a likeable oddity: externally Gothick of the Strawberry Hill variety, pretty and quite unconvincing, but hybrid-classical within (cf. St Michael, p. 104). Controversy surrounded its design: *Hague* and *James Allen* submitted designs, Allen's 'Grecian' plans being selected in 1787. Then the building committee rejected Allen in favour of Hague, apparently on grounds of cost. There were bitter and libellous public recriminations, and it was widely rumoured that Hague had allowed the vicar, the Rev. Joseph Small, to influence his design. Allen was eventually paid off with 100 guineas.

141. St Paul, Portland Square, by Daniel Hague, 1789–94

Hague acted as the mason, and *Joseph Shepherd* was the carpenter. Bath stone ashlar exterior of essentially classical proportions. Applied Gothic trim of ogee windows with intersecting and Y-tracery, pilaster strips with sunken round-ended panels, lozenges and quatrefoils, etc. The tall w steeple was inspired, according to Hague, by the tower of the second Royal Exchange, London (1667–71). A three-stage tower [141], then two further stages diminishing in wedding-cake fashion, and a stumpy pinnacle on top. The shallow decoration does not read from a distance. A w door beneath the tower leads to a four-bay nave with aisles. Three-light windows with solid quatrefoil bands reflecting the former galleries, removed 1901. Shallow chancel with correct Perp extension by *John Bevan*, 1893–4, clashing hopelessly with the style of the rest. Nave arcades of tall columns with fluted necks and acanthus-leaf capitals. Flat ceilings to the aisles, but over the nave deep coves at the sides, running into a flat centre. Gilded plaster arabesques on the ceiling, and left and right of the chancel arch. Originally the organ was on the w wall, framed by a mural of curtained windows. The altar cloths, etc., were of purple velvet; it must have been quite theatrical. Repaired 2002–4 after decades of redundancy; new uses are being sought.

In **Wilson Street**, SE, is the best survivor of C19 industry here: Pope & Co.'s boot and shoe factory behind No. 14 Portland Square, by *William Holbrow*, 1895. Red brick with stone banding over cambered windows and a decorative Neo-Baroque doorcase. Now Portland Lofts apartments. E on Wilson Street, a terrace of *c.* 1830, with round-headed doors framed by reeded mouldings, and pretty teardrop fanlights. From the w end of Wilson Street, s into **St Paul Street**, where 1980s office buildings at the s end have atrocious pseudo-Georgian façades, badly proportioned and crudely detailed. More of the same on Newfoundland Street, s, and Pritchard Street.

A short way E along **Newfoundland Street**, N side, is the former **Magnet Cinema** by *Holbrow & Oaten*, 1913–14. Edwardian classical, with heavy architraves, apron-panels, segmental arches and oculi. Top storey added later. Opposite, **Tollgate House** by *Stride Treglown & Wyeth*, completed 1975, a miserably crude sixteen-storey Y-plan office tower, to be demolished if the Broadmead extension (*see* below) goes ahead.

Returning w toward Bond Street, s of Newfoundland Street, the no-man's-land of **St Jude's** lies between the two walks, where setted streets run between levelled plots. Developed from *c.* 1700, as can be deduced from the names of Great Anne Street and Great George Street. This part was cleared gradually *c.* 1930–70. If current plans come to fruition, the E extension of Broadmead will rise here, with Bond Street rerouted E around it. We end at the **Spectrum Building** by *BGP Group Architects*, completed 1984, on a simple L-plan with screen walls of blue glass. Prominently sited and lit at night with blue neon, it brightens a junction which is hardly a sparkling introduction to the city.

South from Old Market

The walk explores the area around Old Market, an early medieval street, now an attractively varied arterial route into Bristol from the E. A swathe of bomb damage to the w cut it off from the city, causing near-terminal decline. Much has been repaired since the 1970s, and many C17–C19 buildings remain, mostly of artisan character. St Philip's, to the s, was established with C18 and C19 industry; fragmentary remains can be seen amidst the semi-dereliction. We finish with the concentration of 1990s development N of Temple Meads Station.

Starting at the big roundabout at the w end of Old Market, to the N (E side of Temple Way) is King's House (1981) an orange brick office block. Directly to its N, a pedestrian way leads right into **Redcross Street**, now a shabby backwater. No. 7, N side, a fine stone house of *c.* 1715–20, was the birthplace of Sir Thomas Lawrence, portraitist to George III and IV. Three storeys by five bays, with elliptical shell-hood doorcase, the windows connected vertically by aprons and horizontally by stringcourses. Once the centre of a three-house terrace, but now horribly enveloped by pink aggregate-faced offices (*Elsom Pack & Roberts*, 1974).

Now E to the junction with Lawford Street and Lamb Street. **St Jude**, by *S.B. Gabriel*, 1848–9, locked up and stranded in traffic, was among the first Bristol churches to conform to Ecclesiological requirements. Most of the cost of £2,979 was met by Bishop Monk of Bristol and Gloucester. Done well in Pennant rubble with low buttressed nave and w tower, showing careful observation of the forms of the C14 parish church. Dec windows, and snaking tracery on the tower parapet. Attached to the NE, school buildings with something of the angular simplicity of Pugin. N of the church in Braggs Lane is **Guild Heritage House**, by *Frank Wills & Sons*, 1912–13; an early building designed for the disabled.* Built for the 'Guild of The Brave Poor Things', a private charity founded by Ada Vachell; it soon discarded the crushingly emotive title. Blunt red brick exterior with chapel-like gabled centrepiece over sturdy Doric columns. It provided a hall, stage, classrooms, workshops, billiard room with wheelchair access, and a shop (the big window at the right). Now local authority offices.

s via Lawford Street to the crossroads with Old Market. At the NE corner is the **Palace Hotel**, Nos. 1–2 West Street: an absurdly high and pretentious gin palace, 1869–70, a speculation by Thomas Morgan to profit from a new railway station nearby. 'TM 1869' is repeated across the front. The distinctive draughtsmanship of the unsigned plans appears to be by *W.H. Hawtin*, who worked for Morgan elsewhere. Except the King's Head, Victoria Street (*see* Walk 3, p. 180), Bristol's richest Victorian pub interior. A partly surviving bar with bar-back on brass barley-sugar columns, patterned ceramic panels and voluptuous if repetitive plasterwork. To the E is **West Street**, an ancient thoroughfare, now mostly late C19 commercial. Some C18 houses remain (the best is No. 8) and further E, No. 20, a derelict C17 gabled house with Victorian half-timbering.

Return w to the crossroads at Lawford Street. **Old Market** runs w, getting broader at the site of the medieval Shambles. **Trinity Hospital South**, in the sw angle of the crossroads was founded in 1395 by John Barstaple and rebuilt in stages from 1857 to 1883 by *Foster & Wood*. The style is Tudor Gothic, the later parts with Burgundian details, cf. their Foster's Almshouses, Colston Street (*see* City Centre, p. 132), 1861 and later. Here, there are two Pennant stone facing ranges, running N–S. The NE section, of 1857–8, has many breaks and projections, aiming at variety but verging on confusion. w range with a Perp N chapel, 1867. SE addition of 1881–3, with a timber staircase-turret richer than that at Foster's Almshouses. Excellent w elevation hidden in Jacob Street; a shallow balconied courtyard with rich cusped and quatrefoiled timberwork. Little dogs on the gables, and a good iron lamp bracket, right. N of Old Market, the red brick **Trinity Hospital North**, 1913, by *Frank Wills & Sons*, Tudor Gothic again but resolutely dull.

*Deaf, dumb and blind facilities were reasonably common from the early C19; nationally there seem to be few if any other purpose-built facilities for wheelchair users of this date.

Most of the incident at the w end of Old Market is on the s side; the N can be appreciated without crossing over. No. 53, s, the **Mason's Arms**, perhaps *c.* 1630–50, is gabled with one jetty. No. 42, N, a well-proportioned early C18 house with three alternating pediments, and double-bowed shopfront, *c.* 1800. Second floor replaced *c.* 1980. To its w, No. 41 of *c.* 1630–80, probably with full-width jetties at first and second floor before partial C18 refronting. Then Nos. 36–38, built together in the mid C17, both bayed and jettied. This row was rebuilt except for the fronts *c.* 1980, destroying the C17 timber frames. Back on the s side, No. 59, **Kingsley Hall**, dated 1706, three storeys in Flemish bond brick chequered with paler headers. It oversails the pavement on five stout columns with trumpet capitals. Bolection-moulded windows with gauged brick heads. Then the big brick Gloster Regiment **Drill Hall**, by *Paul & James*, 1914 (disused), bombastic and hidebound. Nos. 70 and 71 are more gabled houses of the mid C17. No. 70, the **Long Bar**, has pent roofs to each floor, stop-moulded door-frame and two scrolled jetty brackets with pendants. At No. 71, one small jetty bracket with lozenges, pendant and floral motifs on the scroll. Finally the **Stag and Hounds** pub, once home of the medieval **Pie Poudre Court**, which heard market disputes. Rebuilt *c.* 1690–1710 with oversailing upper floors on columns, flat brick front with timber pilasters and string-courses, and some cross-windows. N side, w end: the former **Methodist Central Hall**, by *Kitchen & Gelder*, 1924, coarse Neo-Baroque with copper dome on a dumpy turret. Converted to flats *c.* 1990, when the big horseshoe-plan hall behind was demolished. No. 21 has a full-height Gothic-arched centre, *c.* 1885; cf. Frank Wills's tobacco-factory style.

Here at Temple Way we turn s, where immediately on the left is the **Post and Press**, properly the Bristol United Press Building, by *Group Architects DRG*, 1970–4. It has always been well regarded. Glass-walled foyer at the w, the rest faced in muted purple tile and glazed brick. The largely impenetrable façades were a response to early 1970s fears of terrorist bombings. Staggered and set-back upper tiers, grouped towers with rounded angles for vertical counterpoints. It provided a printing hall and seven storeys of offices, with forward-looking ventilation and heat recirculation systems. Directly to the s is **Broad Plain**, a triangular space with trees in the centre. On the s side of Broad Plain, C18 houses of various dates. No. 5, *c.* 1720, has an attractive shell-hooded door, straight quoins, and windows with serpentine brick arches, foliate keystones and brick architraves. The E end of the row has several one- to three-storey bay windows with Doric trim, grafted onto earlier houses *c.* 1780.

To the E of Broad Plain is the former **Thomas's Soap Works**, bounded by Unity Street, N, and Old Bread Street, s. Soap boiling, an important Bristol industry from the C12, began here *c.* 1783. Thomas's Soap Works was here from 1841, taken over by Lever Brothers, 1912–53. All the buildings now altered for Gardiner Haskins's store. N of Straight Street, a four-storey block facing Broad Plain dated 1884, remodelled possibly by *W.B. Gingell* from an 1850s building. A plaque on the w

142. Former Soap Works, pan building, perhaps by C. James 1881

front of an Assyrian bull (a Thomas's trade mark) is now weathered and unreadable. Adjoining on Straight Street a three-storey block of 1865, in Gingell's warehouse style with giant arcade and rock-faced ground-floor arches. s of Straight Street, a five-storey block with chequered curtain wall (*A.E. Powell*, 1957–8). Adjoining to the E, a red brick range of 1912 by Lever Brothers architect *J. Simpson*, plain but carefully detailed. s of these, visible from Russ Street, the distinctive pan building where the soap was boiled; five storeys of dark brick, a landmark of great charisma [142]. Recast in 1881, by *C. James*, from a lower 1840s building, adding machicolated chimneys like corner turrets, a corbel-table and crenellated parapet after the Palazzo Vecchio, Florence. Much altered after a fire in 1902, now stripped of much decorative brickwork and its chimney-crowns. Other remains of the soapworks on **Old Bread Street**, s: a two-storey Pennant stone block by *Foster & Wood* 1865–7, arcuated like Colston Hall (*see* City Centre, p. 131). Taller brick block to the w, 1881–2, by *C. James*. Both derelict, but proposed for conversion to apartments.

Temple Quay North, s of Avon Street, is here a wasteland of weeds; a mixed development around two angled towers by *Urbed* was approved for the site in 2002. A snaking **footbridge** supported on an angled mast, by *W.S. Atkins & Partners Overseas*, 2000, leads s to **Temple Quay**, formerly occupied by a railway goods depot and historically part of Temple. Included here as it is cut off by Temple Way, w. Redevelopment was planned c. 1990 by the controversial Urban Development Corporation (*see* Introduction, p. 46), and largely completed c. 1997–2002. Dominating the waterfront is the **Bristol and West Building**, by *Chapman Taylor* and *Stride Treglown*, 1997–2000. Well planned, with a s entrance between angled wings, but unimaginative elevations with repetitive boxy

143. St Vincent's Works, entrance hall, by R.M. Drake, 1891–3

windows. Stone-faced basements below contrasting yellow and red bricks, which attempt to break up its bulk. **Temple Quay House** (*Stride Treglown*, completed 2001) is in a faintly 1930s idiom with horizontal windows either side of a glazed recessed entrance. The glazed and angled N side is crisply done.

Outliers

In the hinterland E of the Floating Harbour, some enjoyable industrial remains. From Temple Quay North via **Avon Street** one passes beneath *Brunel's* **viaduct** of *c.* 1840 that carried the Great Western Railway into Temple Meads. Further along, on the w side, the former **coke house** of Bristol Gas Light Company works, *c.* 1850s, possibly by *W.B. Gingell.* Big and round-arched, in rock-faced Pennant rubble with nine-bay s front under later brick gables. **Silverthorne Lane** runs E, intimidatingly narrow beneath the towering rubble walls of the 1820s gasworks. At the junction with Gas Lane, **St Vincent's Works**, formerly Lysaght's galvanized ironworks. Facing the crossroads, its offices by *R.M. Drake,* 1891–3, with battered gateway and turreted corner entrance. Neo-Romanesque style, perhaps inspired by the adjoining *Rundbogenstil* factory of *c.* 1860, possibly by *Thomas Lysaght* who briefly partnered W.B. Gingell and whose brother owned the ironworks. The office has an octagonal two-storey entrance hall [143] beneath a glazed dome, with a painted frieze of shipping. The walls are wildly encrusted with *Doulton* tiles with Renaissance-inspired grotesquerie, extremely fine. Dog-leg staircase to one side, also with ceramic decoration.

Spike Island

Spike Island is the narrow strip of land s of the harbour from Bathurst Basin in the E to Cumberland Basin in the w. It became nominally an island in 1809 with the digging of the New Cut to the s (*see* Introduction, p. 24). The name may relate to the siting of a prison here (cf. Spike Islands at Cork Harbour, Ireland, and Sholing, Southampton, both with prisons). Building at Queen Square to the N from 1699 prompted the removal of shipyards to the s side of the harbour. At the present-day Princes Wharf, William Patterson built Brunel's ss *Great Western* (1837), and his ss *Great Britain* further w from 1839. By the late C19 timber wharves dominated the w of Spike Island, replaced with expensive housing and leisure facilities in the recent harbour regeneration.

Starting at **Prince Street Bridge**, to the SE is **Merchants Landing**, the second big harbourside development, by *Ronald Toone Partnership*, 1980–4, with meticulous refurbishment elements by *Roger Wilson*. Bland and bulky office buildings s on Wapping Road, and to the E red brick and rendered houses of two to four storeys, with first-floor oriels: details are nicely varied within an overall homogeneity. Walk E, with St Mary Redcliffe's spire (*see* Major Buildings, p. 66) visible over the wharf ahead. At the lock, s into **Bathurst Basin**. On the w the **warehouse** and **offices** of Robinson's Oil Seed manufactory by *W.B. Gingell*, 1874, façaded for squash courts and flats as part of Merchants Landing [16]. A lively example of the Bristol Byzantine style (*see* Introduction, p. 31). Two buildings of gaudy yellow and red brick, similar but not identical, unified by continuous cornice and stringcourses. Venetian ogee window heads in the left (warehouse) building set in Moorish arches

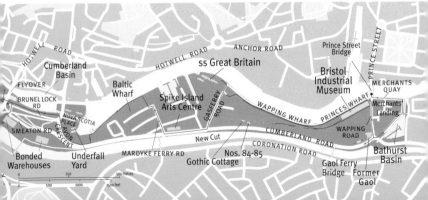

145. Princes Wharf, with Bristol Industrial Museum, by N.A. Matheson, 1948–51

of pointed horseshoe form. Plenty of cogging courses and panels of diagonal brickwork.

Bathurst Basin was formed where the Malago stream flowed N from Bedminster into the River Avon; the site of a medieval watermill, Trin or Treen Mill. During construction of the Floating Harbour in 1804–9, the mill pond was enlarged to form a small shipping basin, named after Charles Bathurst, then a Bristol MP. Small Regency houses on the N side, probably of *c.* 1820, were refurbished as part of the Merchants Landing scheme. To the SW, the lock to the New Cut is now closed. On its N side, the **Louisiana Inn**, formerly the Bathurst Hotel of *c.* 1820, has elegantly fragile tented balconies on cast-iron columns following the curved corner. W of Wapping Road, ruined fragments of the **New Gaol** by *Henry Hake Seward*, 1816–20. A high curving curtain wall leads W to a ruinous gatehouse. The gaol was burned in the Bristol Riots of 1831 (*see* topic box, p. 163) and rebuilt by *R.S. Pope*, probably in the same form. It was closed in 1883. Here we cut N up Wapping Road to the harbour, returning to Cumberland Road further W. The sporadic incidents at the E end of Cumberland Road are dealt with as outliers.

At the N end of Wapping Road, to the w is **Princes Wharf**, a general cargo wharf [145] with most of its equipment intact, now a national rarity. Bristol Harbour Railway was laid here in 1872–6. On the left, **Bristol Industrial Museum** by the Docks Engineer *N.A. Matheson*, 1948–51, converted 1978. It was the last transit shed built in Bristol. Utilitarian mottled brick on a steel frame, with sliding doors towards the harbour. On the quayside, four electric **cranes** by *Stothert & Pitt*, 1951, saved by a pressure group, City Docks Ventures, in 1975; now being restored to use by the Museum. These gaunt structures establish the industrial character of this part of the harbour. Beyond the Museum on a semicircular bastion sits the elephantine **Fairbairn steam crane** (1875–8), with a curved box-girder jib. Behind (s), sandwiched meaninglessly between blocks of flats, a fragment of *Henry Woodyer*'s St Raphael's church, 1858–9, demolished 1953. A stump of wall, buttressed by unusual transverse three-quarter arches. Further w on Wapping Wharf, **The Point** [146], by *Feilden Clegg Bradley,* 1999–2001, several large rectilinear apartment blocks on a triangular site. Big contrasting render panels of red and electric blue, and gunmetal-grey trim. The central block terminates in an astonishingly sharp point of five stacked balconies. In the w block, red walls predominate uncomfortably. A contentious design, either loved or loathed.

The restored **ss Great Britain** by *Isambard Brunel*, built 1839–43, sits s of the elbow in the harbour, salvaged from decay in the Falkland Islands and returned here in 1970. Surrounding structures include the Pennant stone **dry dock** with single-leaf iron caisson gate, where the ship was constructed. A white-rendered dockside **office** has a first-floor oriel with exceptionally wide N-facing sash window to light the draughtsmen's desks. Albion Dock to the w is not publicly accessible; instead take **Gasferry Road** s. On the right, the **McArthur Building**, *c.* 1896–7, a large red brick malthouse by the brewers' architect *William Bradford*. Demolition is proposed. Beyond it to the s, a villa perhaps of *c.* 1825, seemingly for the owner or manager of Hilhouse's shipyard (later Albion Dock). At the junction with Cumberland Road, No. 129, well detailed two-storey Italianate offices of *c.* 1860–70, for Charles Hill & Sons' shipbuilders. To the w, soon a grey brick building with a long box-framed concrete balcony announces the **Spike Island Arts Centre**, formerly Brooke Bond's tea-packing warehouse by *Beard Bennett Wilkins & Partners*, 1960. Function dictated the plan; tea was dropped down blending chutes into a long transverse packing hall, toplit by a glass-block barrel vault. Lower undulating roofs at the w end. Converted to exhibition and studio space 1998, by *Niall Phillips Architects*.

Immediately w, turn N along Mardyke Ferry Road.* Quickly one enters **Baltic Wharf**, by *Halliday Meecham Partnership*, complete by 1986, a private housing development of yellow brick with superficial

---

*The harbour walkway's w gates from Underfall Yard to Cumberland Road are locked at night. Then one must double back via Mardyke Ferry Road.

146. The Point, Wapping Wharf, by Feilden Clegg Bradley, 1999–2001

Postmodern arches-and-pediments, inexplicable cottagey half-hipped roofs and mock-timbering. At Cumberland Close bear slightly left and through an alley to the quayside, enlivened by three **sculptures**. First, *Vincent Woropay*'s bronze Hand of the River God, 1986; a disembodied hand holds aloft a plinth, the crowning Hercules lifting an obelisk (after Bernini) now missing. Then to the w, Atyeo by *Stephen Cox* 1986, of red-veined Verona marble, fluid and abstract. w again, *Keir Smith*'s less successful Topsail, 1987 – a sail before leaden clouds, of Portland stone. Here there are fine open views of the w harbour reaches. Opposite, more housing (*see* Walk 6, pp. 212–213): Poole's Wharf, Neo-Regency; to the w the tawny brick Rownham Mead highlights Baltic Wharf's shortcomings.

Continue w into **Underfall Yard**, a working shipyard housing the crucial harbour outlet sluices, and the Cattybrook brick **pump house** (1888) with sharp, elegant octagonal chimney. It provides hydraulic power to all harbour locks and bridges. Pedestrian gates E of the Harbourmaster's Office lead back to Cumberland Road.

Continue w; the road soon curves N, past Avon Crescent, a terrace of c. 1831–4. At its N end is the **Nova Scotia Hotel**, a three-storey pub with tripartite windows to the angled corner above an arched carriageway. A gatepier reputedly once bore the date 1811, but it appears on maps between 1821 and 1828. Opposite the hotel on the island, two low terraces built by the Bristol Docks Company (1831) for its dock workers, with gabled porches, wide eaves and half-dormers. Now a short stroll w along the quayside at **Cumberland Basin** (1804–9), with locks to the w, which allows ships to await high tide before emerging into the Avon [147]. On the s, a conspicuous feature of Bristol's w approaches, three red brick **bonded tobacco warehouses**, designed 1903 by *W.W. Squire*, the Docks Engineer, and built by *William Cowlin & Son*. Forbidding and bare, yet nobly proportioned. Carefully composed in three colours of brick, with clasping corners and projecting centres, nine storeys high and eighteen bays wide (grouped 7:4:7). Two bonds are on Spike Island: 'A' Bond (built 1903–6) at the E, with steel- and iron-framing with unreinforced concrete jack-arching, and 'B' Bond (1906–8) to the w, identical externally but not structurally. It is the first major English use of the *Coignet* system of reinforced concrete. 'C' Bond (1919) is in Ashton, s of the New Cut and invisible from here. 'B' Bond is occupied by Bristol Record Office and Create, an environmental-awareness centre. On its E flank, **Ecohome** by *Bruges Tozer Partnership*, 1996, built as a demonstration of environmental best practice. Of brick and timber cladding, on a square plan set diagonally, with single-pitch roof canted s for maximum solar gain.

Cumberland Basin flyover complex, 1962–5, is the w hub of Bristol's road system carrying traffic over Cumberland Basin from Bedminster in the s, Avonmouth in the w, and from the city centre. By the City Engineer's Department under *J.B. Bennett*; consulting engineers

147 Cumberland Basin (1804–9) with tobacco bonds beyond

Freeman, Fox & Partners. Elegant gullwing double-arched swing bridge on a central pivot. Beneath and just w of this, *I.K. Brunel*'s two **lock bridges** (1844–8) with decks suspended beneath tubular structural members of wrought-iron plates. Brunel employed this principle again at Saltash Bridge, Devon.

One may retrace one's steps E on Spike Island, or cross the harbour to Hotwells (q.v., Walk 6). Ferries run from Poole's Wharf, Hotwells, into the city centre.

Outliers

All on Cumberland Road, E to W.

Gaol Ferry Footbridge, 1935. A small and pretty iron suspension bridge with openwork piers, crossing the New Cut just w of the gaol gatehouse.

Nos. 84–85 Cumberland Road. A three-storey pair in Greek Revival style, *c.* 1835–40, sharing a shallow full-width pediment. Prominent central niche, pedimented and with overscaled acroteria and guttae, perhaps by *Henry Rumley* (cf. Queen Square).

Gothic Cottage, No. 91 Cumberland Road, 1840 [148]. Three-storey symmetrical Tudor Gothic, with central porch, and mullioned bay windows, square on the ground floor, canted oriels above. Pierced bargeboards to double gables. Converted to apartments 2002–3, when ludicrous half-timbered side-wings were stuck on.

Walk 13.

Bedminster

The manor and village of Bedminster existed before Bristol was founded. Its church, St John, was the mother church to St Mary Redcliffe. Early C19 industrialization was based on coal seams. As well as mining, iron-founding, brewing, glue-boiling, tanning and paper-making were big employers. But from *c.* 1880 to 1980 it was synonymous with W.D. & H.O. Wills's tobacco factories. Bedminster spawned aggressively Non-conformist sects of every variety, some of whose chapels survive; and it is rich in good C19 Board Schools. Yet in 1958 Pevsner considered Bedminster unworthy of separate mention. Losses include *John Norton*'s St John of 1855 (bombed), the best Victorian chapel (Ebenezer Methodist; remodelled) and, inconceivably, *Sir Edwin Lutyens*'s marble Great War memorial at the Wills factory (sold for salvage in 1986). But there is still plenty left to reward the inquisitive.

In 1804–9 the New Cut was dug, separating Bedminster from Redcliffe. **Bedminster Bridge**, built 1883, is the second bridge on this site. Good w side, with cast-iron parapets of interlaced rope-and-chain panels. sw on Coronation Road is the robust **Zion Congregational Chapel**, 1828–30 [150]. Paid for by the oilcloth manufacturer John Hare in fulfilment of a youthful promise; also known as the Church of the Vow. Pennant rubble with Bath stone dressings. Pedimented front with Doric columned

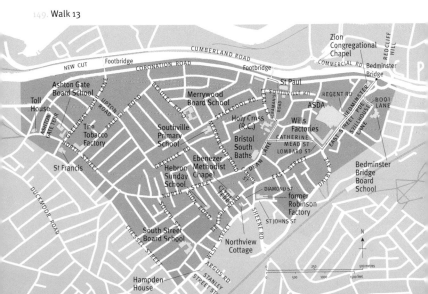

150. Former Zion chapel, Coronation Road, possibly by R.S. Pope, 1828–30

151. Former Wills's factory, Lombard Street block, by Frank Wills, 1906–8

entrance and round arches connected by impost mouldings. Similarities with Bush House (the Arnolfini, *see* Walk 1, p. 166) suggest *R.S. Pope* as architect. Excellent interior (subdivided as offices, but reversible) with cast-iron balcony on Ionic columns.

Bedminster Parade runs s from the chapel. Now a short detour: E along Boot Lane, to **Stillhouse Lane**. At the N end, the RNIB's **Vision Care Centre**, by *Alec French Partnership*, 1993. Buff brick, long and low with hipped roofs and tall angle-windows. Excellent use of materials, light and colour to create a functional and enjoyable environment. Next door is **Bedminster Bridge Board School**, by *W.V. Gough*, *c*. 1895. Shaped gables, and massive brick chimneystacks contrasting with Pennant stone walls. Big central window in the recess between two wings, round-arched and with Flemish-looking tracery. Returning to **Bedminster Parade**, on the w side is the derelict **police and fire station**, opened 1882, from the office of *Henry Crisp* but largely the design of his pupil *George Oatley*, then just eighteen. Ebullient castellar style, squat central tower with machicolations. Nearby, s, the red brick **library** by *Frank Wills*, 1913, with turgid Baroque embellishments on a steel and concrete frame. The s flank has a boldly projecting tower. Conversion of the police station and library to flats, café, etc., is proposed (2003).

The sw continuation of Bedminster Parade is **East Street**. To the w, the sprawling Postmodern ASDA store, *c*. 1987, on part of the **Wills Factories** site. To understand the Wills family's enormous significance to Bristol (*see* topic box, p. 38) one must first come here to see the ciga-rette factories that made their fortune. Cigarette smoking became a national habit from *c*. 1880; W.D. & H.O. Wills (Imperial Tobacco from 1901) caught the moment with brands like 'Three Castles' and 'Wild

Woodbine'. By 1914 the firm employed *c.* 3,800. Production moved to Hartcliffe on the fringe of s Bristol in the 1970s. The last Bedminster factory closed *c.* 1980, and the Hartcliffe site in the 1990s. At East Street, the red brick factories form an impressively ordered three-storey rank running s. All were designed by the Willses cousin, *Frank Wills*. At the N end, No. 1 Factory, 1883–6, has a central entrance tower with steep pavilion roof over a big recessed Gothic arch. Symmetrical wings, each with three giant Gothic arches and plate-traceried windows. Corbel-table integrated with groups of narrow attic lights. Converted to shops and offices in the 1980s, when a walkway was made behind the façade. The factory was extended s *c.* 1888, in the same style but with taller arcading, and the windows integrated more logically with their framing arches. Further s is the terracotta-faced Lombard Street block (1906–8) [151], in which Gothic is discarded for classicism, handled less surely. Subsidiary Tuscan columns frame the windows. Rounded corner with bulging Venetian oriel and copper-domed turret. Converted to offices *c.* 1985 with an extra storey over the attics. Some office and boardroom interiors remain, with plain oak panelling and Neo-Jacobean chimneypieces.

Opposite the Lombard Street corner, No. 29 East Street has a striking Art Nouveau shopfront, probably by *F. Sage & Co.*, London, *c.* 1905. Curving upper-window panels in the French manner. Turn NW into Lombard Street then w via Catherine Mead Street to **Dean Lane**. The open space here was formerly Dean Lane Colliery. To the left of the junction, **Bristol South Baths**, by *C.F.W. Dening*, 1931 in the faintly Moderne brown brick style that he applied to his public buildings. Just to the right is **Holy Cross Church** (**R.C.**), 1921–6, a Byzantine-Romanesque concoction in hard orange brick, by *John Bevan Jun.* Clustered around **Acraman's Road** to the N are small and pretty middle-class villas of *c.* 1830–40, with elliptical arches, Gothic arches and Grecian porches freely mixed. The stimulus for their construction was **St Paul's church**, Coronation Road, by *Charles Dyer*, 1829–31. Commissioner's Gothic style with narrow tower, spindly mouldings and pinnacles. It cost £10,196 including the site and accommodated *c.* 1,550 people. Nave and chancel were rebuilt after wartime bombing in an anaemic apology for Tudor Gothic by *Eustace Button*, reopened 1958. To the s, the former **St Paul's Vicarage**, Southville Road, plain and solid Gothic Revival by *S.B. Gabriel*, 1860. **Coronation Road**, running for a mile on the s side of the New Cut, was constructed *c.* 1820 as a carriage ride on the bank of spoil from the excavations. w of St Paul's, Nos. 69–78 probably begun *c.* 1835, but finished as late as 1852, by *Henry Rumley*.

Outliers

Bedminster and its neighbour Southville consist largely of C19 and C20 terraced housing; widely scattered points of interest do not make coherent walks. Outliers are grouped around West Street and Ashton Gate. A further group deals with Victorian and Edwardian Board Schools.

Around West Street

St John's Street (corner with East Street). Former Robinson's paper factory, by *Henry Crisp*, 1887. Red brick, originally single-storeyed; two storeys added *c.* 1899 probably by *George Oatley*. Segment-headed windows in groups of two and three, and gabled to East Street.

Off **British Road**, buried behind the w side of Diamond Street is **Northview Cottage**, a mid-C18 farmhouse seemingly connected with the Ashton Court estate. Coursed Lias stone with handsome bracketed door canopy, and iron lamp bracket. Fairly humble interiors, but in the parlour a surprising Rococo ceiling with medallion heads. To the N in British Road, **Ebenezer Methodist Chapel**, by *Herbert Jones*, 1885–6. Once Bedminster's most grandiloquent chapel, with Lombardic side windows. A grandly Corinthian pedimented front was amputated in 1974–5, for a deplorable façade of aggressively ribbed brick. A little to its W, **Hebron Sunday School**, Sion Road, 1885. Big and extravagantly Jacobean-Queen Anne, almost certainly by *Foster & Wood*.

Hampden House, No. 119 West Street, a symmetrical five-bay house, *c.* 1720–30. Brick with limestone quoins, heavy architraves, keystones and segmental porch on small curved brackets, all typical of Bristol *c.* 1720. Mullioned basement lights show lingering C17 influence. Panelled parlour with elaborate pedimented doorcase and mahogany chimneypiece.

North Street and Ashton Gate

At the corner of North Street and Raleigh Road, the **Tobacco Factory**, by *R. Earle* for Imperial Tobacco, 1912. Converted to an arts space, theatre, restaurant, etc., by *Ferguson Mann c.* 2000. It was originally the factory of Franklyn Davey, part of Imperial Tobacco Group, in which Wills was the major partner from 1901; Earle superseded Frank Wills as their architect in 1912 but continued his factory style. Red Cattybrook brick, a very C20 grid treatment of the exterior, with unmoulded three-storey piers, and no remnant of masonry framing between windows and piers. Sloped sills with weatherings.

On North Street and Greenway Bush Lane, the Pennant stone **Ashton Gate Board Schools** by *Charles Hansom*. Built in phases, 1876–89, the later parts with *Frederick Bligh Bond*. Stridently Gothic, with polychrome roofs and a steep-roofed tower with dormers (cf. Assize Courts, Small Street); chapel with twelve-light circular window. Opposite, **St Francis' church** (1950–3) by *Robert Potter*, replacing one blitzed in 1941. The style is simplified traditional: shallow roofs, yellow brickwork and big rectangular windows. N door framed by a rounded concave aedicule. E window by *Christopher Webb*. Immediately W is the high malthouse of **Ashton Brewery** (*George Adlam*, 1905). Brick and Ham stone with blind lunettes beneath shaped gables. NW at the junction of North Street and Ashton Road the **Ashton Gate tollhouse**, the only survivor of those built for the Bristol Turnpike Trust; *c.* 1820–30. Bow front with veranda on thin cast-iron columns. Mullioned windows with square hoodmoulds.

Victorian Schools

Following the Education Act of 1870, Bristol operated a School Board from 1871 to 1903. By 1891 it had built twelve schools and enlarged four more, mainly in the industrial suburbs. Many architects were employed, and the Board favoured no one style, although many were baldly Gothic. The Bristol Board took up Queen Anne cautiously and late, in the 1890s. Bedminster has five Victorian and Edwardian schools, the

152. Former Merrywood Elementary school, gables, by H.D. Bryan, 1907

richest concentration in Bristol. Two have been dealt with (Bedminster Bridge, p. 276; and Ashton Gate Board Schools, p. 279).*

Merrywood Board School, on a big sloping site at Beauley Road and Stackpool Road, Southville, by *Edward Gabriel*, 1894. Now partly demolished, the remainder used as a Community Centre and housing. Low spreading red brick blocks with gable ends, linked at their angles. Central square lantern topped by a bell-stage.

Merrywood Elementary Council School, Merrywood Road, Southville, now Southville Primary School [152]. By *H.D. Bryan*, 1907, in his most charming Queen Anne idiom. Red brick with white-painted arched windows, gables, etc. Single-storey classroom wings surround a higher central hall with cupola. Decorative carved brick panels; good wrought-iron gates.

South Street School, by *W.V. Gough*, 1893–4, two storeys and imposing, with shaped Flemish or Jacobean gables, tall half-dormers, and soaring chimneys. Bigger and less varied than his Bedminster Bridge Board School.

*A British School of 1846, in British Road, was burnt down and subsequently demolished in 1999.

Excursions

Arno's Vale 282

Ashton Court 285

Blaise Castle and Blaise Hamlet 288

Kingsweston House 291

Tyntesfield House 293

Arno's Vale

On the A4 (Bath Road) ¾ m. (1.2 km.) SE of Temple Meads railway station. Buses to Brislington and Bath, alight at Arno's Vale Cemetery.

Named from Peter Arno who kept an inn here in the C18. There are two attractions: a huge Victorian cemetery with many fine monuments; and nearby, the Gothick retreat of an C18 industrialist with stables in the form of a miniature Romantic castle.

Arno's Vale Cemetery

Established by Act of Parliament in 1837 and opened in 1839, this private cemetery was an alternative to the overcrowded city churchyards, and fast became Bristol's most fashionable burial place. An example of the

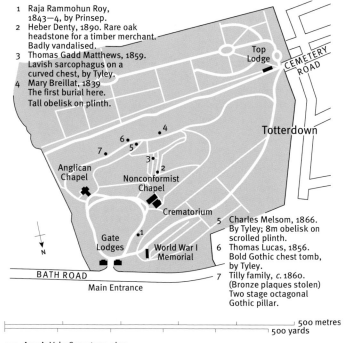

1 Raja Rammohun Roy,
1843–4, by Prinsep.
2 Heber Denty, 1890. Rare oak
headstone for a timber merchant.
Badly vandalised.
3 Thomas Gadd Matthews, 1859.
Lavish sarcophagus on a
curved chest, by Tyley.
4 Mary Breillat, 1839.
The first burial here.
Tall obelisk on plinth.

Top
Lodge

CEMETERY
ROAD

Totterdown

Anglican
Chapel

Nonconformist
Chapel

Crematorium

Gate
Lodges

World War I
Memorial

BATH ROAD

Main Entrance

5 Charles Melsom, 1866.
By Tyley; 8m obelisk on
scrolled plinth.
6 Thomas Lucas, 1856.
Bold Gothic chest tomb,
by Tyley.
7 Tilly family, c. 1860.
(Bronze plaques stolen)
Two stage octagonal
Gothic pillar.

500 metres
500 yards

153. Arno's Vale Cemetery, plan

154. Arno's Vale Cemetery, tomb of Raja Rammohun Roy, by W. Prinsep, 1843–4

Rammohun Roy was a Bengali Hindu, a pioneering cultural, religious and political reformer regarded as the father of the Indian Renaissance. He formed strong associations in Bristol, died here in 1833 and was buried at the house where he had stayed. In 1843 he was reinterred at Arno's Vale. His elaborate tomb [154] was designed in 1842 by *William Prinsep*, an artist to the East India Company, and built by the mason *John Brown*, 1843–4. A striking example of Indian-inspired Victorian architecture, its leafed dome, broad canopy and columns derive from authentic Hindu and Jain forms.

national trend for private cemetery companies, e.g. Kensal Green, London, 1833–7. Space ran out *c.* 1987 and closure was threatened. The crematorium closed in 1998, and the private owners faced minimal income but high costs occasioned by vandalism, theft and decay. Bristol City Council therefore gained ownership in 2003 and a charitable trust was established to maintain and repair it.

The sliding cast-iron gates are flanked by correct Greek Doric **lodges** by *Charles Underwood*, 1837–8. Arno's Vale is outstanding for its idyllic and painterly Arcadian landscape, with a circular drive backed by steep wooded slopes, against which are Underwood's two derelict mortuary **chapels**: Greek Ionic for the Nonconformists, Roman Italianate for the Anglicans. The latter has a projecting entrance, shallow Corinthian capitals and an arched and pedimented belfry.

Arno's Court

About ¼ m (0.4 km.) E on Bath Road. Arno's Court (now Arno's Manor Hotel) was bought by the brass-manufacturer William Reeve *c.* 1740 (*see* topic box, p. 202). That house became the service wing to a three-storey addition towards the road, of *c.* 1755–60. The new work was plain mid-Georgian, with two full-height bays, and is traditionally attributed to *James Bridges*, without solid evidence. But the steeply canted bays at Arno's Court remind one of several Bristol houses by unknown hands.* The 1750s wing was given a superficial Gothick trim *c.* 1764, when the estate buildings were Gothicized (*see* below). All the Gothick work is perhaps by *Thomas* and *James Paty*.

SE entrance front with full-height canted bays, Gothick ogee window heads and some sashes with intersecting tracery. Central porch with Gibbsian blocks, icicle work, and Rococo pediment. Within, two mildly Rococo ceilings attributed to *Thomas Stocking*. Cheerless 1850s additions to the N for a girls' reformatory, by *Foster & Wood*.

Across Bath Road to the N, a decorative **gateway** originally abutting the stables, and relocated *c.* 1992. Much Gothic panelling, termini and ogee battlements, and four statues, *c.* 1990, replicas of medieval originals – an example of Reeve's antiquarian interests. Ambitious **stables** in the form of a mock-medieval castle, among the finest of their date in the country, now the Black Castle pub [11] and, on the whole, well kept. Built of black slag blocks from Reeve's brass furnaces, with contrasting limestone dressings; in 1766 Horace Walpole claimed he had mistaken it for 'the Devil's Cathedral'. In the courtyard, some antiquarian fragments (e.g. a C16 tomb surround, head of Henry VIII, two C17 terms; much more now lost). The group effect is marred by the road between house and stables, and the removal of a Gothick bath house in 1957. Its façade is at Portmeirion, North Wales.

*Rownham House, dem.; Nos. 22–24 Clifton Wood Road; No. 106 Stokes Croft, dem.

Ashton Court

Off Kennel Lodge Road, Bower Ashton, *c.* ¾ m. (1.2 km.) sw of
Cumberland Basin.

NB: the house is oriented sw–ne, but all accounts refer to the sw
entrance as w; for simplicity this convention is maintained. The dates
of all building campaigns before the c19 are conjectural.

Set in beautiful parkland w of Bristol, **Ashton Court** is at once exciting, puzzling, neglected and intensely sad. A manor was recorded in the
Domesday book. The core of the present house is *c.* c14–c15. It was
owned by the mercantile Smyth family from 1545 to 1946. There were
major remodellings in the late c16, c17, c18 and c19. Deliberate historicism and imported fittings make interpretation a minefield. Purchased
by Bristol City Council in 1959; parts of the house are now used for
functions, but other parts are a shell and in dangerous condition,
despite the building's Grade I listing.

We begin at the w, entrance court. It has a c16 gabled e range, with shallow two-storey porch to the hall. Left of the hall is a c15 cross-wing, not
visible from here. The fanciful Gothic outer porch and Perp windows
all round the courtyard are *c.* 1803, inspired by one genuinely Perp hall
window. The porch is identical in detail to the s porch at St James (*see*
City Churches, p. 97), and so probably by *James Foster*. At the inner
angles are matching buttressed projections: at the right, c16, and at the
left, *c.* 1767, built for internal access to the nw wing of the same date.
This wing, with ogee Gothick trim, is perhaps by *Thomas Paty*. It has an
imitation Elizabethan stair-turret and gables with blind ovals and
Doric chimneys, either of the 1760s or 1803, but echoing the c17 work of
the s wing, which is masked by a two-storey corridor added to its n side
c. 1803.

Now to the s front. The sw wing is late c16. Its classical refronting of
1633–4 was spuriously attributed to Inigo Jones by the late c18. The
builder was Thomas Smyth (1609–42), an MP and a member of the
committee to raise money for Jones's refurbishment of St Paul's
Cathedral. Smyth married into the Poulett family, who did similar work
in the 1630s at Brympton D'Evercy and Hinton St George in Somerset.
This connection perhaps produced Smyth's mason-architect, who
was undoubtedly familiar with Jones's innovations. Thirteen windows
are arranged 5:3:5, their random spacing probably dictated by the

pre-existing structures. They have alternating pediments on the ground floor, straight cornices on rusticated brackets above. All probably had wooden cross-windows. There are paired shell-headed niches at ground level, and oval attic windows; all up-to-date C17 features, but crudely disposed. In the centre of the s front is a turreted **gatehouse** [155], possibly C16 and leading originally to the service court, with attached farm and stable buildings to the E. It gained its present form substantially in 1803 when the new Gothic SE stable wing was added, all probably by *James Foster* (*see* above). On the E is a **stable yard**, a three-part façade, altered later. The stable (now a tearoom) retains unusually fine cast-iron Gothic stalls. Service wing in the court behind the stables, including a possibly C15 kitchen, all demolished *c.* 1960.

The w porch leads into the **Great Hall**. The C18 chimneypiece incorporates an earlier carved alabaster panel. The N cross-wing has a C15 arch-braced **timber roof** of six bays, with three tiers of wind-braces, much renewed 1977–8. Now partly open, the space was perhaps originally a first-floor solar with service rooms beneath – a common Somerset layout. The NW **wing** was built *c.* 1767 to provide a new Dining Room. Now badly decayed, it is perhaps the most important surviving Gothick interior in Bristol. Lavish stucco decoration, maybe of *c.* 1803.

C18 panelled rooms at the E end of the sw wing, planned in enfilade with the now gutted **Long Gallery**. This contains a huge C17 Ionic black marble chimneypiece. At the sw corner of the Hall is a Restoration revival **staircase**, part of a big updating by *C.E. Davis*, the City Architect of Bath, 1885. Upstairs in the sw wing, a lavish chimneypiece of the 1630s, in rose marble with Jonesian details. The 'Great Chamber over ye Hall' is mentioned in a 1691 inventory. It has C16 stop-moulded chamfered door-frames. E of the Great Hall, the remains of *Davis*'s 1885 **Winter Gardens**; a wildly Gothic arcade and fan-vaulted hall inside the s gatehouse. At the same time the long stable to the E was converted to a 'Museum room'. It has an oak-panelled roof and two big chimneypieces, C15 French in character, with spiral mouldings.

The s front overlooks a lawn flanked by two long walls made up of shaped Jacobean gables; the w wall pre-dates 1760, with gables perhaps reused from an earlier house. The matching E wall was added before 1829. The **deer park** was created by successive purchases from the C16. Of *Humphry Repton's* scheme *c.* 1802, some planting was probably carried out. Sir J.H. Greville Smyth planted the Wellingtonias s of the house in the late C19; their removal is now proposed.

155. Ashton Court, s front, C17 (left) and early C19 (right)

Blaise Castle House and Blaise Hamlet

Henbury Road, Henbury. Approximately 4 m. (6 ½ km.) NW of Bristol city centre; buses to Cribbs Causeway stop at Blaise Castle House.

'What, is it really a castle, an old castle?'
'The oldest in the kingdom.' . . .
'Are there towers and long galleries?'
'By dozens.'

Jane Austen, *Northanger Abbey*, 1798–1803

On Bristol's NW outskirts is a small Georgian country house (now a museum of social history) with additions by *John Nash* and *Charles Cockerell*, and a sham medieval turret in a dramatic *Humphry Repton* landscape. But *Nash*'s Blaise Hamlet is perhaps the pre-eminent achievement of English Picturesque ideals.

In 1795–6 *William Paty* designed **Blaise Castle House** for the Quaker banker John Scandrett Harford. A restrained and graceful Neoclassical Bath stone box. NW front of five bays with a semicircular projecting Ionic porch, cleverly backed by its mirror-image carved, as it were, out of the building. Banded rustication to the ground floor. Five-bay SE façade, extended (right) in 1832–3 by *Charles Cockerell* with a six-column Ionic portico, into which the Picture Room projects, almost touching the four central columns. To the E is a detached Doric **conservatory** by *John Nash*, *c.* 1805–6, on a concave quadrant plan, with Venetian openings at the ends. In the hall, Neoclassical relief medallions by *Bertel Thorwaldsen*, *c.* 1833, and a plaster copy of part of the Parthenon frieze, *c.* 1820s. Cockerell's **Picture Room** has an oval domed lantern framed in an octagon. Bas-reliefs here also by Thorwaldsen. Scagliola Corinthian columns and a good marble chimneypiece. Well-proportioned library with free-standing Corinthian columns screening one end. Toplit staircase with interlaced wrought-iron balustrade.

The house sits in a contemporary landscape by *Humphry Repton*, whose Red Book of 1795–6 for the site was, unusually, implemented almost in full: a remarkably complete example of Picturesque ideals. (The balustraded terraces and big urns around the house are Cockerell's additions.) Repton's judicious tree-felling in the wooded parks exposed Picturesque vignettes. The long driveway included hairpin turns, caves, rocks and hanging woods, to give arriving visitors shudders of terror. A quarter of a mile SW on Blaise Hill is the **Castle** – the object of Catherine

Morland's naïve wonderment in *Northanger Abbey*. A triangular sham-Gothic tower with corner turrets, of the type made popular by Fort Belvedere, Windsor. It was designed by *Robert Mylne* in 1766 for the previous owner Thomas Farr, and made a popular excursion from Georgian Bath and Bristol. – Pretty thatched **dairy** by *George Repton*, *c.* 1804, perhaps under Nash's direction. – **Woodman's cottage**, *c.* 1797, designed to give views from the house of homely smoke drifting from a woodland clearing, now obscured by trees. – On Henbury Road is a Tudor turreted **lodge** by *Repton*, and shortly to the w, **Timber Lodge**, probably *c.* 1840–50, encased in knotty bark-covered logs reminiscent of C18 root-houses. – **Stratford Mill**, an C18 watermill from West Harptree, re-erected here in 1954 when its site was flooded for a reservoir.

Blaise Hamlet, ¼ m. (0.4 km.) N on Hallen Road, is owned by the National Trust (free entry to the grounds, but no access to the houses). In 1810–11 *John Nash*, assisted by Humphry's son *George Repton*, designed ten dwellings as a place of retirement for Harford's estate workers. Pevsner called it 'the *nec plus ultra* of picturesque layout and design' which charms rather than irritates because of 'its smallness, its seclusion ... and the nicely maintained degree of artificiality throughout.' Nine buildings are scattered around an undulating green with an emphatically off-centre pillar which is both pump and sundial [156]. Avoiding the regimented almshouse model, each cottage differs from the others, or rather combines the same forms and materials differently. Limestone rubble, thatch, boarded gables, stone-tiled roofs, and brick are arranged to create Picturesque variety. Wide thatched eaves, dormers, gables or half-hipped roofs cover the low compact cottages; each has at least one special feature, e.g. a dovecote gable or a sheltered seat. Oversized chimneystacks of decorative cogged brickwork, some round, some square, set diagonally or in groups to break the rooflines. **Circular Cottage**, with its dormer set symmetrically on a semicircular end, is perhaps first for Picturesque effect. Double Cottage combines two dwellings in one building. The hamlet is hidden behind a stone wall with a simple gate; Nash recommended modesty to maintain the pride of the recipients of Harford's generous charity. The villa-retreat of Park Village, Regents Park, London (built from 1824), was a development by Nash of the Blaise concept of the Picturesque village.

Kingsweston House

On Kings Weston Lane, *c.* 5 m (8 km.) NW of Bristol city centre; buses to Cribbs Causeway stop at Kings Weston Lane.

On a wooded escarpment overlooking the Severn estuary is one of *Sir John Vanbrugh*'s finest compact houses, built for Sir Edward Southwell, Queen Anne's Secretary of State for Ireland, *c.* 1710–22. Maximum drama is wrenched from just a few simple architectural elements judiciously disposed. The usually quoted start date of 1710 may be a year or two late: some high timbers are dated 1711. However, the walls went up quickly, and the house was completed probably in 1719, although work continued on subsidiary buildings into the 1720s. The master mason was *George Townesend*. It was much altered by *Robert Mylne*, 1763–8, for Edward Southwell III, and by Thomas Hopper 1846–7 (executant architect Henry Rumley). It is now a conference centre.

One arrives at the NE rear courtyard of a U-shaped plan, based on that of the preceding Tudor house. The ochre stone, quarried on site, weathers to a glowing orange-pink. Vanbrugh recessed the three-bay centre between angle turrets, but *Hopper* brought the centre forward, destroying the carefully recessed planes. His kitchen wing NE of the courtyard was demolished *c.* 1938. The severe NW façade commands wide views across industrial Avonmouth. A recessed centre between tower-like projections was replaced by Mylne's canted bay.

On the entrance front [157], SW, a projecting three-bay pedimented centre with two-bay flanks achieves monumentality through the plasticity of its elements. Round-arched windows in the centre, between big Corinthian pilasters, paired at the ends, with a lunette in the pediment. The flanking windows have brutally big flat surrounds. Parapet vases of *c.* 1717. One must stand well back to see Vanbrugh's memorable square arcade of chimneys, rising above the roofs to evoke the 'Castle air' he sought elsewhere, e.g. at the corner towers of Blenheim Palace. In 1713 Vanbrugh proposed 'to make some tryall with boards about height, etc, before they are carried up.' Chimneys rebuilt in 1968, unfortunately in Bath stone. The garden front, SE, has a narrow centre broken forward with, an applied Doric temple front of heavily rusticated pilasters and open pediment framing the garden entrance. Above is a square-hooded window tightly compressed by round-arched side windows. Over the central attic, a big blocking course with scrolled

157. Kingsweston House, SW front, by Sir John Vanbrugh, *c.* 1710–19

supports; an alternative design with pediment was presumably never executed.

Inside, a double-height **saloon**, remodelled by *Mylne* with three tiers of festooned picture frames, and a high dado with palmettes. Chimneypiece by *John Devall*, with a marble tablet of fighting putti, replacing Vanbrugh's central door to the three-storey **staircase hall**. Here, an original hanging staircase rises apparently unsupported. Surrounding balcony landings had open arcades, replaced with balustrades by Hopper, destroying Vanbrugh's complex spatial layering. The outer walls retain arched niches with *trompe-l'œil* painted statues and urns of *c.* 1719. Geometric parquetry on the underside of the quarter-landing.

The park was once heroic in scale; Kip's illustration of *c.* 1709 shows a vast avenue to the SW and formal parterres to the SE, all smoothed away in the mid C18. The best lodge, at Penpole Point, was demolished in 1950. – **The Echo**, a roofless summerhouse by *Vanbrugh*, terminates the SE axis. Arcaded façade with heavy rustication. – N of the house, the Corinthian **Banqueting Loggia** has a Venetian centrepiece, being adapted in 2003 as the entrance to a new house. Nearby, *Vanbrugh*'s domestic-looking **Brewhouse** *c.* 1718–20 has a theatrically overscaled keystone to the door, reaching the sill of the lunette above, and machicolations attempting a romantic medievalism a generation ahead of its time. (The Brewhouse and Loggia are private.) – NE on **Napier Miles Road**, *Mylne*'s **stables** of 1763, a simple and robust three-sided court with lunettes over each door, and end walls modelled as blind triumphal arches. Fine setting with matching lodges opposite, flanking a large lily pond, which originally supplied ice for the house.

Tyntesfield

8 m. (13 km.) w of Bristol city centre, ½ m. (0.8 km.) E of Wraxall on the B3130. Check with the National Trust for visiting arrangements. Initially visitors must take Park and Ride buses from Nailsea.

A High Victorian country house exceptional both for its architecture, and for the near-intact survival of most of its works of art, furnishing, estates, and ephemera of the lives of owners and servants. Built for William Gibbs (1790–1875), who made fortunes importing Peruvian guano for fertilizer. His family originated from Devon and ran their business in London: their Bristol connections were coincidental, and Tyntesfield was made possible by the railway age. Gibbs's modest Regency house, bought in 1843, was greatly enlarged by *John Norton* in 1863–5. His dramatic and strident Gothic mansion is without any hint of gloom, and beautifully sited on wooded slopes. William Gibbs's great-grandson, the reclusive 2nd Lord Wraxall, died in 2001. His complex will made the sale of Tyntesfield seem inevitable; perhaps the last such complete Victorian ensemble to be threatened with dispersal. After a national campaign it was bought instead by the National Trust in 2002.

The main approach is from the SE up a long slope, giving glimpses of high turrets and pinnacles. The s front has a tower-like centre with canted bay [158]. This central motif is virtually all that is recognisable of the Regency house, raised one storey by Norton. On the left is Norton's drawing room, with arcaded loggia probably by *Henry Woodyer*, added as part of a major remodelling for Gibbs's son Antony in 1887–90. E entrance courtyard with a low library wing s of the porch. A high tower over the porch was demolished in 1935. Fine naturalistic stone carving by a *Mr Beates*, e.g., the porch bosses. The entrance corridor leads to a spectacular **library** lined with golden oak, with an arch-braced collar-beam roof, fitted bookcases and *Minton*-tiled window seats. The **dining room** was extended E by *Woodyer* in 1887–90, with three bay windows screened by columns. Oak-panelled ceiling integrated with the chimney-surround. Toplit **hall**, with an impressive timbered roof, by Norton, the staircase and balcony-landings on arcades of coloured marble and granite added by *Woodyer*. **Drawing room** 51 ft (15.5 metres) long, with panelled ceiling. The Renaissance revival chimneypiece is an uncomfortable addition of 1910. **Billiard room** with timber clerestory roof: the central-heated billiard table was supplied by *James Plucknett, c.* 1889. Tyntesfield's high-quality furnishings include library sofas and carpet by *J.G. Crace*, and much by *Collier & Plucknett* of Warwick.

Gibbs was devoutly High Church: in 1873–5 he added to the N of the house a magnificent private **chapel**, by *Arthur Blomfield*. It is reached by a bridge from the first floor of the N wing. Inspired by the Sainte Chapelle in Paris and Sir George Gilbert Scott's Exeter College Chapel, Oxford. Perhaps Blomfield also had an eye to Butterfield's Keble College Chapel, also at Oxford, which Gibbs paid for. The chapel's crypt-like basement is let into the hillside. SW belfry turret with large crocketed pinnacle. Three-bay stone-vaulted nave, with W gallery, shallow transepts and apsidal sanctuary. **Stained Glass** all designed by *Henry Woolridge*, maker *Powell & Sons*; that in the nave is more muted. Arcaded **reredos** with mosaics designed by *Wooldridge* and made by *Salviati*. On the N wall, family memorial **crosses** set with gems, by *Barkentin & Krall*. Tessellated **floors** of faience, marbles, bluejohn and onyx by *Powell & Sons*. A private chaplain held daily services, with Gibbs's servants supplying the choir.

The National Trust has purchased about 500 acres (200 hectares), roughly one quarter of the original estate. S and W of the house are formal **terraces**, with specimen trees and rose gardens. **Stable Court** by *Woodyer*, 1889. Walled **kitchen garden** with bothy and badly dilapidated orangery, both *c.* 1894–7, probably by *Walter Cave*. The supporting paraphernalia is remarkably intact, notably the red brick **electricity-generating house** of 1889, probably by *Woodyer*. The farms, saw mill, water supply and gasworks must have ensured near self-sufficiency, typifying the practical thinking of a Victorian entrepreneur.

158. Tyntesfield, S front, by John Norton, 1863–5

Further Reading

Bristol's coverage of architectural and local history writing is perhaps as extensive as any major city outside London. The following list is necessarily partial, but the bibliographies listed below, with those in any of the recent books, will point the reader in the right direction. The many books on particular aspects of local history are not covered here for reasons of space.

Recent **bibliographies** for Bristol include N. Dixon's *An Historical and Archaeological Bibliography of Bristol*, 1987, updated by J. Brett for 1987–94. The computer database by the Regional History Centre at the University of the West of England brings things up to date. Of **archaeological** and **historical journals**, the *Transactions of Bristol and Gloucestershire Archaeological Society* (hereafter TBGAS), published from 1876 in 121 volumes, contain much of value; the proceedings of Clifton Antiquarian Club (late C19), *Bristol and Avon Archaeology*, (from 1982) and *Avon Past* are also useful. Local survey histories include John Latimer's excellent *Annals of Bristol*, four volumes covering the C16–C19, published 1887–1901; MacInnes and Whittard's *Bristol and its Adjoining Counties*, 1955; and Smith and Ralph's *A History of Bristol and Gloucestershire*, 1972. The best serial publication is the academic Bristol Record Society (BRS) volumes 1–55, (1930–2003), while the Bristol Branch of the Historical Association (BBHA) has a consistently excellent series of over seventy pamphlets. Publication of detailed archaeological reports in the 1980s was somewhat patchy: Jon Brett's forthcoming summary of Bristol's archaeology, for English Heritage, will help to plug that gap.

The definitive **architectural account** is *Bristol: An Architectural History*, by Gomme, Jenner and Little (1979), arranged chronologically. The list of Bristol architects and their main works at the back remains unique. T. Burrough's *Bristol* (City Building Series, 1970) is briefer but still useful. Burder, Hine and Godwin's *Architectural Antiquities of Bristol...*, 1851, provides a historical viewpoint. Works by period or topic are more numerous. For **medieval** Bristol, the unique and indispensable starting point is Frances Neale, *William Worcestre: The Topography of Medieval Bristol*, BRS, 2000, rigorous and academic. Virtually nothing systematically covers the architecture of *c.* 1530 to *c.* 1700, odd since so much survives: **Georgian** Bristol is better served. First, C.F.W. Dening's *The Eighteenth Century Architecture of Bristol*

(1923), beautifully illustrated, covers much that is now lost. Walter Ison's *The Georgian Buildings of Bristol* (1952) sensibly extends into the c19. Timothy Mowl contributed *To Build the Second City*, 1991, and with Brian Earnshaw, *An Insular Rococo*, 1999, covering the links between the Irish and English Rococo, with much on Bristol. Gordon Priest's *The Paty Family, Makers of Eighteenth Century Bristol*, 2003, includes a catalogue of previously unpublished drawings. J.R. Ward covers *Speculative Building at Bristol and Clifton 1783–93*, in Business History, XX, and John Neale's *Bristol: A Georgian Group Report*, 1998, comments on recent treatment of Georgian buildings.

There is less on **c19 Bristol**; Clare Crick's *Victorian Buildings in Bristol*, 1975 remains the best survey and uses excellent contemporary illustrations. Timothy Mowl's *Bristol: Last Age of the Merchant Princes*, 1991 covers more industrial and commercial work too. For the last hundred years, there is *c20: Bristol's Twentieth Century Buildings*, by Tony Aldous, 2000, especially good on post-war work; John Punter's invaluable *Design Control in Bristol 1940–1990* (1990), covering the role of the Planning Department in commercial development; and J. Hasegawa's *Replanning the Blitzed City Centre: a Comparative Study of Bristol, Coventry and Southampton, 1941–52*, (1992). Bristol Civic Society produced a brief survey, *Modern Buildings in Bristol* in 1975. Priest and Cobb's *The Fight for Bristol: Planning and the Growth of Public Protest*, 1980 is complemented by Tony Aldous's *Changing Bristol: New Architecture and Conservation, 1960–1980* (1979).

Religious Buildings are dealt with in J.H Bettey's *Historic Churches and Church Life in Bristol* (BRS, 2001); the medieval context is covered in the British Archaeological Association's Conference Transactions XIX, *Bristol in the Middle Ages; Almost the Richest City*, 1997 (ed. L. Keen). Dr. Roger Leech's *The Topography of Medieval and Early Modern Bristol* (BRS 48, 1997) deals with property holdings in and near the walled town. See also J. Harvey, *The Medieval Architect*, 1972; and D. Dawson, *Handlist of Medieval Places of Worship in …Bristol*, CBA Bulletin 34, 1986. On the Reformation, see J. Bettey's *Suppression of the Religious Houses in Bristol* (BBHA 1990) and M. Skeeters, *Community and Clergy; Bristol and the Reformation*, 1992. Ralph and Cobb's *New Anglican Churches in Nineteenth Century Bristol* (BBHA, 1991) is useful, and J. Harding's *The Diocese of Clifton 1850–2000*, 1999, covers the Roman Catholic churches. J. Samuel's *Jews in Bristol*, 1997, deals with the synagogues.

For Bristol Cathedral, see N. Pevsner, *Bristol, Troyes, Gloucester: the character of the fourteenth century in architecture*, Architectural Review, 113, 1958; J. Bony, *The English Decorated Style*, 1979; G. Cobb, *English Cathedrals, the forgotten centuries*, 1980; N. Pevsner and P. Metcalf, *The Cathedrals of England*, 1985; J. Bettey, *St Augustine's Abbey, Bristol*, (BBHA 1996), and *Bristol Cathedral, the rebuilding of the nave*, (BBHA 1993). *Almost the Richest City* (see above), includes the reassessment of the cathedral by R. Morris, C. Grossinger on the misericords, and much else. J. Rogan ed., *Bristol Cathedral, History and Architecture*, 2000 has a useful bibliography. Jon Cannon, 'The Absent Figure: on authorship and meaning in the Fourteenth-Century Eastern Arm of St Augusine's, Bristol', *Trans. Anc. Monuments Soc.* 48, 2004, debates the significance of the Berkeley family as patrons. Recent sources for St Mary Redcliffe include Warwick Rodwell, *Historical Report for the Conservation Plan for St Mary Redcliffe*, 2003; Linda Monckton, 'The Myth of William Canynges and the Late Medieval Rebuilding of St Mary Redcliffe', in *Almost the Richest City*, 1997; and M.Q. Smith, *St Mary Redcliffe, An Architectural History*, 1995.

Bryan Little's *Bristol: The Public View* (1982) deals with public buildings in detail; while K. Mallory's *The Bristol House* (1985) surveys domestic work. Robinson's *West Country Manors* (1930) and Robert Cooke's *West Country Houses*, 1957, remain invaluable for large houses nearby. *Rural Houses of North Avon and South Gloucestershire, 1400–1720* by Linda Hall, 1983, provides useful vernacular comparisons with Bristol architecture. The starting points for industrial archaeology are Buchanan and Cossons, *Industrial Archaeology of the Bristol Region*, 1969, and Bristol Industrial Archaeology Society (BIAS) Journals, 1970 onwards. There are several studies of specific industries, such as Joan Day's *Bristol Brass; the History of the Industry*, 1973.

For building **materials**, see E. Stonebridge, *Bristol Heritage in Stone* (1999), and R. Savage, 'Building Stones of Bristol' in *Nature in Avon: Proceedings of the Bristol Naturalists Society*, 1988. For the **topography** of specific districts, see e.g., Donald Jones, *A History of Clifton*, 1992, and Penny Mellor's excellent *A Kingsdown Community* (1985) and *A Kingsdown Collection* (1987). Dr Roger Leech's study *The St Michael's Hill Precinct of the University of Bristol* (BRS 52, 2000) examines early property leases in detail. **Building types** are less well represented; Bristol deserves a good architectural summary of its banks and commercial buildings. For inns, see C.F.W. Dening's *Inns of Old Bristol*, 1943. Earl and Sell's *Guide to British Theatres 1750–1950*, 2000, covers the Bristol examples well. James Russell deals best with *The Civil War Defences of Bristol*, 1995, while, for individual **buildings**, see M. Ponsford's M.Litt. thesis, *Bristol Castle: the Archaeology and History of a Royal Fortress*, (University of Bristol, 1979). John Wood's *A Description of the Exchange of Bristol...* (1745, reprinted 1969) is invaluable. For Temple Meads, the best detailed architectural account is John Binding *Brunel's Bristol Temple Meads*, 2001. Douglas Merritt's *Sculpture in Bristol*, 2002 is both accessible and authoritative.

Lastly, there are excellent **illustrative sources**. Selections from the Braikenridge Drawings can be found in Sheena Stoddard's *Bristol Before the Camera: the City in 1820–30*, 2001. Reece Winstone, followed by his son John, published some forty volumes of historic photographs grouped by date, mainly titled *Bristol As It Was*. They are under-used for detailed architectural analysis, as are Samuel Loxton's line drawings of Edwardian Bristol; see *Loxton's Bristol*, 1992.

Glossary

Acanthus: *see* [3D].

Acroteria: plinth and/or ornament on apex or ends of a pediment.

Aedicule: architectural surround, usually a pediment on two columns or pilasters.

Ambulatory: aisle around the sanctuary of a church.

Anthemion: *see* [3D].

Apron: raised panel below a window.

Apse: semicircular or polygonal end, especially in a church.

Arcade: series of arches supported by piers or columns (cf. colonnade).

Arched brace: *see* [2A].

Art Deco: a self-consciously up-to-date interwar style of bold simplified patterns, often derived from non-European art.

Ashlar: large rectangular masonry blocks wrought to even faces.

Atrium: a toplit covered court rising through several storeys.

Attic: small top storey within a roof. Also the storey above the main entablature of a classical façade.

Baldacchino: solid canopy, usually free-standing and over an altar.

Ballflower: C14 Gothic ornament, like a globe with three petals enclosing a ball.

Barrel vault: one with a simple arched profile.

Bartizan: corbelled turret.

Batter: intentional inward inclination of a wall face.

Beaux-Arts: a French-derived approach to classical design, at its peak in the later C19–early C20, marked by strong axial planning and the grandiose use of the orders.

Billet: *see* [1A].

Bolection moulding: convex moulding covering the join between two planes; common in the late C17–early C18.

Broach: half-pyramid attached to the lower corners of an octagonal spire.

Capital: head feature of a column or pilaster; for types *see* [1B, 3].

Cartouche: *see* [4].

Castellated: with battlements.

Chamfer: surface formed by cutting off a square edge or corner.

Chancel: the E part or end of a church, where the altar is placed.

Chapter house: place of assembly for the members of a monastery or cathedral.

Choir: the part of a great church where services are sung.

Ciborium: fixed canopy over an altar.

Clerestory: uppermost storey of an interior, pierced by windows.

Coffering: decorative arrangement of sunken panels.

Cogging: decorative course of bricks laid diagonally.

Colonnade: range of columns supporting a flat lintel or entablature (cf. arcade).

Corbel: projecting block supporting something above.

Composite: classical order with capitals combining Corinthian features (acanthus, *see* [3F]) with Ionic (volutes, *see* [3C]).

Corinthian; Cornice: *see* [3D; 3A].

Cove: a broad concave moulding.

Crenellated: with battlements.

Crocket: *see* [1B].

Crown-post: *see* [2B].

Cupola: a small dome used as a crowning feature.

Dado: finishing of the lower part of an internal wall.

Decorated (**Dec**): English Gothic architecture, late C13 to late C14.

Diocletian window: *see* [1].

Doric: *see* [3A, 3B].

Double-fronted (of a house): with rooms on both sides of the entrance.

Drum: circular or polygonal stage supporting a dome.

Dutch or **Flemish gable**: *see* [5].

Early English (E.E.): English Gothic architecture, late C12 to late C13.

Embattled: with battlements.

Entablature: *see* [3A].

Faience: moulded terracotta that is glazed white or coloured.

Flying buttress: one transmitting thrust diagonally, usually by means of an arch or half-arch.

Frieze: middle member of a classical entablature, *see* [3A, 3C]. Also a horizontal band of ornament.

Garderobe: a medieval privy, usually built into the thickness of a wall.

Geometrical: of tracery, *see* [1C].

Giant order: a classical order that is two or more storeys high.

Gibbs surround: *see* [4].

Gothic: the style of the later Middle Ages, characterized by the pointed arch and rib-vault (*see* [4]).

Groin vault: one composed of intersecting barrel vaults.

Guilloche: *see* [3D].

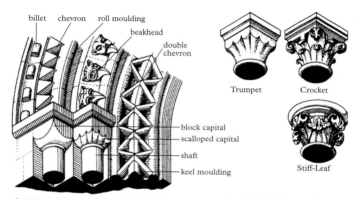

A) NORMAN AND EARLY DETAIL

B) ORNAMENTED CAPITALS

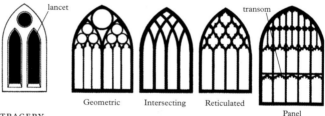

C) TRACERY

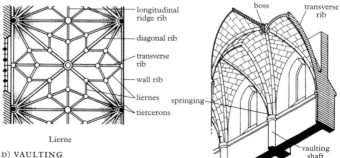

D) VAULTING

1. Medieval

Guttae: *see* [3B].

Half-hipped roof: with the upper part of the gable hipped (compare [5]).

Half-timbering: non-structural decorative timberwork.

Hammerbeam: *see* [2A].

Herm: head or bust on a pedestal.

Hipped roof: *see* [5].

Hoodmould: projecting moulding above an arch or lintel to throw off water.

In antis (Latin) : of columns, set in an opening (properly between simplified pilasters called antae).

Ionic: *see* [3C].

Italianate: a classical style derived from the palaces of Renaissance Italy.

Jack arches: shallow segmental vaults springing from iron or steel beams.

Jamb: one of the vertical sides of an opening.

Jettied: with a projecting upper storey, usually timber-framed.

Lancet: *see* [1C].

Lantern: a windowed or traceried turret crowning a roof, tower or dome.

Lesene: a pilaster without base or capital.

Lierne vault: *see* [1D].

Light: compartment of a window.

Lintel: horizontal beam or stone bridging an opening.

Loggia: open gallery with arches or columns.

Louvre: opening in a roof or wall to allow air to escape.

Lunette: semicircular window or panel.

Machiolation: openings between corbels that support a projecting parapet.

Mannerist: of classical architecture, with motifs used in deliberate disregard of original conventions or contexts.

Mansard roof: *see* [5].

Metope: *see* [3B].

Mezzanine: low storey between two higher ones.

Modillion: *see* [3E].

Motte-and-bailey: early castle type with an earthen mound (motte) within a timber enclosure.

Moulding: shaped ornamental strip of continuous section.

A) HAMMERBEAM ROOF WITH BUTT PURLINS

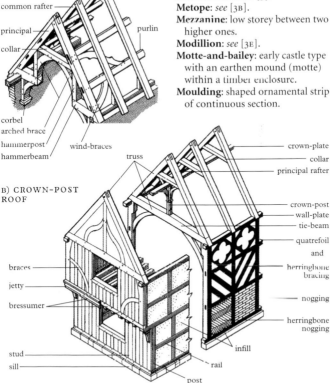

common rafter

principal

collar

purlin

corbel

arched brace

hammerpost

hammerbeam

wind-braces

truss

B) CROWN-POST ROOF

crown-plate

collar

principal rafter

crown-post

wall-plate

tie-beam

quatrefoil and

herringbone bracing

braces

jetty

bressumer

nogging

herringbone nogging

stud

sill

infill

rail

post

2. Timber framing

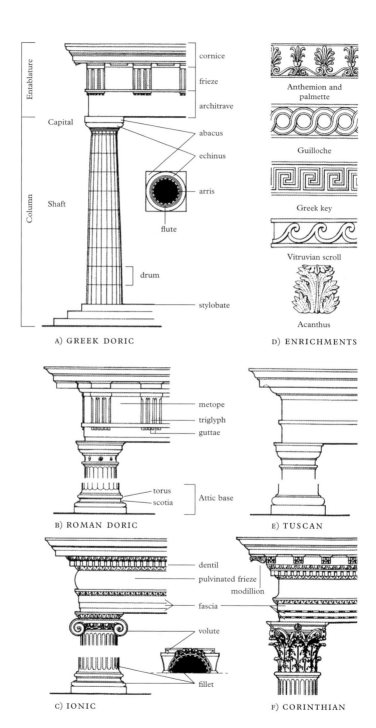

A) GREEK DORIC

- cornice
- frieze
- architrave
- abacus
- echinus
- arris
- flute

Entablature

Column

Capital

Shaft

drum

stylobate

D) ENRICHMENTS

Anthemion and palmette

Guilloche

Greek key

Vitruvian scroll

Acanthus

B) ROMAN DORIC

- metope
- triglyph
- guttae
- torus
- scotia

Attic base

E) TUSCAN

C) IONIC

- dentil
- pulvinated frieze
- modillion
- fascia
- volute
- fillet

F) CORINTHIAN

3. Classical orders and enrichments

Mullion: vertical member between window lights.

Nailhead: Gothic ornament consisting of small pyramids regularly repeated.

Narthex: enclosed vestibule or porch at the main entrance to a church.

Newel: central or corner post of a staircase.

Norman: the C11–C12 English version of the Romanesque style.

Oculus: circular opening.

Ogee: of an arch, dome, etc., with double-curved pointed profile.

Opus sectile (Latin): decorative or pictorial mosaic-like facing.

Orders (classical): for types *see* [3].

Oriel: window projecting above ground level.

Ovolo: wide convex moulding.

Palladian: following the examples and classical principles of Andrea Palladio (1508–80).

Parapet: wall for protection of a sudden drop, e.g. on a bridge, or to conceal a roof.

Parclose screen: one enclosing a chapel inside a church.

Pavilion: ornamental building for occasional use; or a projecting subdivision of a larger building (hence pavilion roof).

Pediment: a formalized gable, derived from that of a classical temple; also used over doors, windows, etc. For types *see* [4].

Pendentive: part-hemispherical surface between arches that meet at an angle to support a drum, dome or vault.

Penthouse: a separately roofed structure on top of a multi-storey block of the C20 or later.

Perpendicular (**Perp**): English Gothic architecture from the late C14 to early C16.

Piano nobile (Italian): principal floor of a classical building, above a ground floor or building and with a lesser storey overhead.

Pier: a large masonry or brick support, often for an arch.

Pilaster: flat representation of a classical column in shallow relief.

Piscina: basin in a church or chapel for washing mass vessels, usually wall-set.

Porte cochère (French): porch large enough to admit wheeled vehicles.

Portico: porch with roof and (frequently) pediment supported by a row of columns.

Portland stone: a hard, durable white limestone from the Isle of Portland in Dorset.

Presbytery: a priest's residence.

Prostyle: of a portico, with free-standing columns.

Pulvinated: of bulging profile; *see* [3c].

Quadripartite vault: *see* [1D].

Quatrefoil: opening with four lobes or foils.

Queen Anne: the later Victorian revival of the mid-C17 domestic classical manner, usually in red brick or terracotta.

Quoins: dressed or otherwise emphasized stones at the angles of a building.

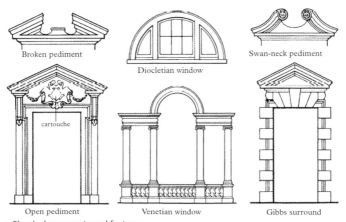

Broken pediment

Diocletian window

Swan-neck pediment

cartouche

Open pediment

Venetian window

Gibbs surround

4. Classical ornaments and features

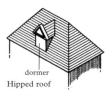

Hipped roof

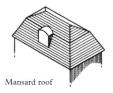

Mansard roof

Dutch or Flemish gable

5. Roofs and gables

Rainwater head: container at a parapet into which rainwater runs from the gutters.

Render: a uniform covering for walls for protection from the weather, usually of cement or stucco.

Reredos: painted and/or sculpted screen behind and above an altar.

Rib-vault: *see* [4].

Rock-faced: masonry cleft to produce a natural, rugged appearance.

Romanesque: round-arched style of the c11 and c12.

Rood: crucifix flanked by the Virgin and St John, carved or painted.

Rubble: of masonry, with stones wholly or partly rough and unsquared.

Rustication: exaggerated treatment of masonry to give the effect of strength.

Sacristry: room in a church used for sacred vessels and vestments.

Saddleback roof: a pitched roof used on a tower.

Sanctuary: in a church, the area around the main altar.

Scagliola (Italian): composition imitating polished marble.

Sedilia: seats for the priests in the chancel wall of a church or chapel.

Sexfoil: a six-lobed opening.

Single-fronted (of a house): with rooms all to one side of the entrance.

Slype: in a greater medieval church, a covered passage leading E from the cloisters between transept and chapter house.

Spandrel: space between an arch and its framing rectangle, or between adjacent arches.

Stanchion: upright structural member, of iron, steel or reinforced concrete.

Stellate: star-like.

Stiff-leaf: *see* [1B].

Stilted (of an arch): with vertical sections above the springing point.

Stoup: vessel for holy water.

Stucco: durable lime plaster, shaped into ornamental features or used externally as a protective coating.

Swan-neck pediment: *see* [4]

System building: system of manufactured units assembled on site.

Terracotta: moulded and fired clay ornament or cladding (cf. faience).

Tie-beam: main horizontal transverse timber in a roof structure.

Tracery: openwork pattern of masonry or timber in an opening. For types *see* [1C].

Transept: transverse portion of a church.

Transom: horizontal member between window lights.

Trefoil: with three lobes or foils.

Triforium: middle storey of a church interior treated as an arcaded wall passage or blind arcade.

Triglyph: *see* [3B].

Trumpet capital: *see* [1B].

Truss: braced framework, spanning between supports.

Tunnel vault: one with a simple elongated-arched profile.

Tuscan: *see* [3E].

Tympanum: the area enclosed by an arch or pediment.

Undercroft: room(s), usually vaulted, beneath the main space of a building.

Venetian window: *see* [4].

Vermiculated (of stonework): carved with patterns like worm-trails.

Vitruvian scroll: *see* [3D].

Volutes: spiral scrolls, especially on Ionic columns (see [3C]).

Voussoirs: wedge-shaped stones forming an arch.

Weathering: inclined, projecting surface to keep water away from the wall below.

Wind-brace: *see* [2A].

Index
of Artists, Architects and Other Persons Mentioned

Names of artists, architects etc. working in Bristol are in *italic*; page references including relevant illustrations are in *italic*.

Abels, David 201
Abercrombie, Sir Patrick 40
Adams, H. Percy 75
Adams (H. Percy) & Charles Holden 149–51
Adlam, George 279
Aldworth, John and Francis 102
Aldworth, Alderman Robert 14
Allen, James 110–11, 262
Allen, Ralph 4
Allies & Morrison 62
Archer, Thomas 163
Architecton 77, 184
Architects' Co-Partnership 216
Architecture & Planning Group 184
Armstrong, John 74
Armstrong, W. 202
Armstrong, William 107, 174, 257, 262
Arno, Peter 282
Arup Associates 45, 47, 204
Arup (Ove) & Partners 201, 202
Ashmead, George 223, 237
Asshe, Abbot 51
Atkins (W.S.) & Partners Overseas 267
Atkins Walters Webster 179, 252
Aumonier, William 75
Austen, Jane 288–9

Avery, Ronald 190

Backhouse, David 142
Bacon, John Sen. 61
Baghott, Sir Paul 101
Baily, E.H. 60–1, 98, 134, 191
Baines, Peter 230
Baldwin, Samuel 61
Barkentin & Krall 236, 294
Barry, Sir Charles 121
Barry, E.M. 80
Barstaple, John 265
Barton Willmore Architecture 156
Bathurst, Charles 270
Bayley, Francis 160
Baynton, Dame Mary 102
BBA Architects 213
BBC Architects 237
Beard Bennett Wilkins & Partners 271
Beates, Mr 293
Beckford, William 84, 101
Beddoes, Dr Thomas 210

Belcher, John 238
Bell, Joseph 71, 99
Bell (Joseph) & Son 58, 98, 108, 240
Bengough, Henry 102
Bennett, J.B. 273
Bennett, William 71
Bentley, J.S. 103
Berchet, Pierre 17
Berkeley family 50, 59–60
Berkeley, Lady Joan 55–6, 60
Berkeley, Maurice III, 7th Lord 60
Berkeley, Sir Maurice and Lady Ellen 101
Berkeley, Maurice, 9th Lord 60
Berkeley, Sir Richard 101–2
Berkeley, Robert Fitzharding, 1st Lord 50
Berkeley, Robert, 3rd Lord 72
Berkeley, Thomas, Lord 60
Bernard, W.L. 35
Bernini, Gian Lorenzo 163
Betjeman, John 225, 253
Bevan, John 116, 263
Bevan, John Jun. 195, 278
BGP Group Architects 172, 179, 264
Biddulph, Thomas 98
Biggs, William 78
Bindon, John 30
Birde, William 101
Birkett, Stanley 117
Blackburn, William 21, 141–2
Blacking, W.H. Randoll 236
Blackwell, Jonathan 126
Blanket, Edmund 109
Blisset, Troth 93
Blomfield, Sir Arthur William 66, 96, 294
Blunt, James 188
Board, Ernest 58
Bodley, G.F. 237
Boehm, Sir Joseph 128
Bond, Frederick Bligh 35, 36, 235–6, 242, 279
Borromini, Francesco 163
Bourne, J.C. 89
Boyce, Thomas 223–4
Bradford, William 271
Braikenridge, George Weare 19
Brentnall, Ralph 84, 238, 241, 246, 247, 248

Bridges, James 21, *104–5*, 118, 244, 284
Bridgman & Bridgman 229
Bright, Alderman Richard 142
*Bristol City Council Landscape
    Architects* 170
Britton, John 66
Brooke, Henry 212
Brooke, John 72
Brown, John 283
Brown, W.H. 36, *184–5*
Browne, Hugh 122
Bruce (Derek) & Partners 248
Bruges Tozer Partnership 46, 256, 273
Brunel, Isambard Kingdom 29,
    85–7, 88–90, 119, *197–8*, 211, 268, 271,
    274
Bryan, H.D. 35, 36, *229, 254, 280*
Bubb, John G. 137
Burke, Edmund 125
Burlington, Lord 80
Burnet Tait Powell & Partners 44, 156
Burney, Fanny 208
Buro Happold 202
Burrough & Hannam 77
Burrough, T.H.B. 40, 213
Burton, Abbot 54
Busby, Charles A. 26, *136–7*
Bush, Bishop *13*, 60, 61
Butler, Joseph 60
Butterfield, William 32, 231, 253, 294
Button, Eustace 228, 236, 278

Cabot, John 73, 166, 192
Campbell, John 60
Canynges family 12, 66, 72, 186
Canynges, William the Younger 11,
    72, 186
Carpenter, Mary 60
Carr, John 195
Casson, Conder & Partners 40
Casson, Sir Hugh 170
Cauchferta, Angello del 74
Cave, John 262
Cave, Walter 294
Cawthra, Hermon 137
Champion family 216
Chantrey, Sir Francis 60–1, 102
Chapman Taylor 267
Chatterton, Thomas 185, 204
Christian, Ewan 225
Christopher, Ann 170
City Architect's Department 42, 104,
    182, 258
*City Centre Projects and Urban
    Design Team* 162
Clark, Edward 226, 227
Clark, J.A. 33
Clark, Linda 198
Clarke (sculptor) 106

Clarke, A.H. 77, 143, 182, 196
Clayton & Bell 71, 109
Clifford, Rev. John 257
Coalbrookdale Foundry 148
Cockerell, Charles 24, 26, 28, 77,
    119–20, 190–1, 213, 288
Codrington, Robert 60–1
Coignet system 35–6, 273
Cole, Canon R.T. 191
Colley, Thomas 136
Collier & Plucknett 294
Collings, Kennedy 188
Collins, Hyman H. *251–2*
Colman, Stuart 225, 241
Colston, Edward 17, *93,* 125, 202, 248
Colston, Sarah 94
Colt, Maximilian 102
Comfort, Robert 210
Comper, Sir J. Ninian 72
Concept Planning Group 47, 125, 201,
    204
Cookin, John 102
Cookson, Elizabeth 61
Cossins, John 18
Court, Charles & William 95
Courtauld Technical Services 247
Cowlin (William) & Son 35–6, 73, 223,
    273
Cox, Stephen 272
Cox, Thomas 20
Crace, J.G. 294
Crane, Walter 230
Crawfurd, Emma 60
Crisp, Henry 126, 150, 186, 276, 278
Crisp, Nicholas 79
Crisp & Oatley 183
Cromwell, Oliver 246
Crosett, Mary Spencer 60–1
Cross, Alfred 145
Crosse, Benet 110
Cullinan (Edward) Architects 47
Cullis, Edmund 164
Culverhouse, P.E. 90, 202
Curwen, Robert 247

Dance, George the Elder 78
Dance, George the Younger 95, 143
Daniel, Eleanor 61
Darby, Abraham 17, 218
David, Abbot 52, 60
Davis, C.E. 287
Davy, Humphry 210
Dening, C.F.W. 38, 131, 172, 251, 278
Denny & Bryan 129
Devall, John 292
Dighton, Henry 98
Domus Design and Build 224
Doubleday, John 119
Doulton & Co. 35, 36, *122–4,* 268

Dove, Tom 212
Drake & Pizey 95, 237, 238
Drake, R.M. 35, 127, 268
Draper, Elizabeth 61
Draper, General Sir William 224
Drew, James 104
Drew, John 217, 218
Drury, Alfred 60–1, 235
Dyer, Charles 24, 26, 27, 32, 216,
    224–5, 226, 228–9, 231, 233, 237, 278
Dymond, George 134, 173

Earle, R. 279
Easton, Robertson & Partners 139, 152
Eden, F.C. 236
Edney brothers 92
Edney, Simon 18
Edney, William 18, 71, 101, 108
Edward I 105
Edward III 105
Edward VII 228
Edwards, E. Henry 127, 223
Edwards, J. Ralph 108, 132
Edwards, Mary 98
Edwards, Thomas 98
Elderton, Harry 215
Elizabeth I, Queen 71, 250
Elliott, Dean Gilbert 51, 61
Ellis & Clarke 38, 131
Elsom, Pack & Roberts 172, 264
Elton, Abraham and Mary 117n.
Elton, Jacob 163n.
Elwyn, Mary Brame 60
Elwyn, William Brame 60–1
Elyot, Abbot 57
Erskine, Ralph 255
Eveleigh, John 217–18, 222
Everard, Edward 122

Farr, Thomas 289
Fedden, Matthew 170
Feilden Clegg 142
Feilden Clegg Bradley 271–2
Fenner, Rachel 170
Ferguson, Malcolm 101
Ferguson Mann 96, 126, 143, 279
Fiennes, Nathaniel 246
Fisher, Paul 215
Fitzroy, Robert 105
Fitzroy Robinson 177
Flaxman, John 93, 229
Forrest, Richard 235
Forsyth (sculptor) 61
Foster family 30, 227
Foster, James the elder 26, 30, 97, 213,
    230, 285–7
Foster, James the younger 30
Foster, James & Thomas 176
Foster, John (c15) 132, 149

Foster, John (c19) 29, 30, 241
    see also Foster & Wood
Foster, Thomas 30
    see also Foster & Okely
Foster (Thomas) & Son 35, 195–6
Foster & Okely 213, 222
Foster & Wood 29, 31, 35, 96, 120, 126,
    130, 131, 132–3, 191, 195, 216, 223, 229,
    241, 265, 279, 284
Foster, Wood & Awdry 148
Fox, Francis 90
Fox, Sir Charles 90
Foy, John 108
Frampton, Sir George 60
Frampton, Walter 11, 100
Freeman, Fox & Partners 274
Freeman, James 122
Freke, Philip 60
French, Alec 38, 131, 139, 146, 230
French (Alec) & Partners 42, 117, 119,
    129, 138, 139, 145, 163, 166, 182, 231
French (Alec) Partnership 45, 118, 124,
    141, 164, 168, 174, 185, 188, 192, 198,
    204, 205, 216, 276
Fripp, Samuel C. 60, 90, 98, 150, 179,
    181, 251
Fry family 38
Fry, Lewis 219

Gabriel, Edward 35, 36, 117, 136, 199,
    252, 280
Gabriel, Samuel B. 32, 265, 278
Gane, P.E. 240
Gaunt, Maurice de 100, 102
Gay, George 33, 247
Geoffrey of Coutances, Bishop 7, 105
Gibbes, Henry 98
Gibbons, Grinling 77, 219
Gibbs family 293
Gibbs, James 93, 98
Gibbs, William 293–4
Gill, Eric 254
Gillinson, Barnett & Partners 139
Gingell, W.B. 30, 31, 32, 117, 126, 136,
    137–8, 159, 160, 172, 183, 185, 205,
    238, 266, 268, 269
Gingell (W.B.) & T.R. Lysaght 30, 134–5
Glascodine, Samuel 80–1, 139
Glenorchy, Lady 212
Gloucester, Robert Earl of 97, 98
Godwin & Crisp 107
Godwin, E.W. 29, 31, 32, 107, 149, 174,
    253, 259
Godwin, George 29, 66–7
Godwin, George & Henry 235
Goldfinch (D.A.) Associates 142
Goldney family 218–20
Goldney, Thomas II 218–19
Goldney, Thomas III 21, 216, 219–20

Goodridge, Henry 25, 230, 233, 235
Gore, Major W. 60–1
Gough, W.V. 35, 110, 117, 131, 155–6, 163, 180, 184, 192–3, 249, 276, 280
Gough, W.V. & A.R. 241
Gournay, Robert de 100, 102
Grant, Cary 204
Gray, Bishop 60
Green, A. Mowbray see Mowbray Green, A.
Green, W. Curtis 35, 180–1
Greenway family 222
Greenway, Benjamin and Daniel 78
Greenway, Francis 26, 222–3
Griffin, John 78
Group Architects DRG 42–3, 187–8, 266
Guilding, Bill 198

Hague, Daniel 21, 23, 150, 212, 262–3
Hahn, Jean 83–4
Haig, Henry 65
Hake, G.D. Gordon 228
Halfpenny, William 18, 19, 78, 122, 158, 167, 216
Halliday Meecham Partnership 271
Hansom, Charles 35, 108, 127–8, 196, 223, 224, 230, 235–6, 237, 241, 242, 279
Hansom (Edward) & F.B. Bond 242
Hansom, J.A. 230
Hardman/Hardman & Co. 58, 71, 109, 237
Hardman, Beryl 74
Hare, John 275
Harford, Alfred 177
Harford, John Scandrett 288–90
Harris, E. Vincent 37, 73–4
Harris, John 111
Harris, Renatus 95
Harris, Thomas 101
Harrison, Thomas 26
Hart, James 36, 223, 252
Hawkshaw & Barlow 87
Hawksmoor, Nicholas 96, 213
Hawtin, W.H. 33, 129, 190, 265
Heathman & Blacker 125
Heaton, Butler & Bayne 34, 72, 107
Helical Bar Development 155
Hemming, Samuel 227
Hems, Harry 108
Henderson, A.A. 61
Hennebique system 35, 202
Henwood, Luke 92
Hicks, Nicola 202
Hicks, S.J. 238
Hill, R. Towning see Towning Hill
Hill, Thomas 196
Hilliard, William 102
Hines (A.J.) & Co. 173
Hirst, H.C.M. 237

Hirst, John H. 148, 186, 223, 229–30
Hitch, F. Brook 175
HLD Ltd 213
Hobbs, John 20, 167
Hodges, Ivor 152
Hogarth, William 71, 105
Holbrow & Oaten 264
Holbrow, William 264
Holden, Charles 36, 37, 41, 75–7, 84, 149–51, 236
Holder Mathias Alcock 147
Holiday, H. 93
Holofcener, Lawrence 204
Hoole, Elijah 33, 196
Hope, Lady 212
Hopkins (Michael) & Partners 46, 202–3
Hopper, Thomas 291, 292
Hosking, William 66
Houston & Houston 239
Howitt, T. Cecil 38, 177
Hubbard Ford & Partners 261
Hubbard Ford Partnership 213
Hughes, Catherine 128–9
Hughes, Walter 129
Hunt, Abbot 51, 57
Hunt, G.J. 59
Hunter, Stephen 217
Hutton, James 117

Ibbeson, Graham 204
Innys, Andrew 100
Insall, Donald 157
Inscape Architects 45, 46, 168, 256
Ireson, Nathaniel 20, 163–4

Jackson, Arthur Blomfield 147
James, C. 267
James, Thomas 102
Jay, John 72
Jearrad, R.W. and Charles 198
Jelinek-Karl, R. 145
Jennett, F.S. 63
Jessop, William 24
Jones, Herbert 279
Jones, Inigo 14, 78, 285
Jones, Ivor 143
Jones (Leslie) Architects 174
Jones, Richard 212, 233
Jones, Terry 65
Jowett, Benjamin 83
Joy, William 54–5
Joyce, Stephen 166, 198
JT Group Ltd 46, 166, 199, 255
Juyn, John 72

Kamptz, F. von 111
Kay, Joseph 223
Kendall Kingscott Partnership 151
Kent (M.P.) Design Group 172
Killigrew, William 111
King, J.W. 224

Kip 292
Kitchen & Gelder 266
Kitchin, Robert 109
Knowle, Abbot 50–1

Laing, Gerald 166
Langley, Batty 21
La Trobe & Weston 129, 238
Lavington, John 72
Lawrence, G.C. 73
Lawrence, Sir Thomas 264
Leach Rhodes Walker 172
Lean, Vincent Stuckey 38, 75
Lethaby, William R. 148
Livermore Brothers 117
Llewelyn Davies & Weeks 151
LMP Architects 235
Lockier, James 194, 216, 262
Luetchford, Fr 237
Lutyens, Sir Edwin 73, 125, 275
Lysaght family 268
Lysaght, Thomas 117, 268

MacAdam, John 29
MacCormac & Jamieson 247
McDonald (Angus) & Partners 143
McFall, David 73–4
Mackay, Anthony 255
Mackintosh, Charles Rennie 36, 75–6
Macrae, Mike and Sandie 183
Maggs, John K. 157
Malone, Kate 171
Mander & Partners 145
Manley, Isaac 258, 261
Manley, Thomas 258, 261
Manners & Gill 237
Marmont, John 195, 227–8
Mason, Mary 60–1
Masters, Henry 147, 159, 180, 190
Matcham, Frank 33, 146
Matheson, N.A. 271
Matthew, Dr Tobias 75
Mede, Thomas and Philip 72
Meek (Angus)/R. Diplock Associates 188
Melsom, Charles 256
Meredith, J.N. 39, 132, 173, 174, 182–3, 197
Merrett, Henry 108
Mew, Frederick 127
Middleton, Harriet 60
Millerd, Jacob 14, 246, 249
Minton 293
Mitchell, William 65
Monk, Bishop 265
Monnington, W.T. 74
Moore, J.F. 60
Moreton, Victor 171
Morgan, Thomas (c18) 221–2
Morgan, Thomas (c19) 265

Moro, Peter 158–9
Morris, William 122
Mosley, Jonathan 182
Mountsorrel, William 172
Mowbray Green, A. 249, 252
Moxley, Raymond 42, 130, 195
Moxley Jenner 44, 195, 256
Moxley Jenner & Partners 42, 130, 140, 147
Munby, A. 235
Monro (James) & Sons 177
Munro, Philip 222
Mylne, Robert 22, 289, 291–2

Nash, John 136, 137, 226, 288–90
Neale, J.C. 147
Neatby, W.J. 36, 122–4
New, Keith 59
Newbery, Abbot 60
Newcomen 220
Newland, Abbot 12, 51, 60, 62
Newnes, Sir George 222
Newton family 60–1
Newton, Sir Ernest 243n.
Newton, Sir Henry 60
Newton, Sir John 60
Neylan & Ungless 256
Nicholson, Thomas 237
Nicholson of Malvern 109
Nicholson & Corlette 235
Norris, Canon J.P. 51, 60, 62, 96
Northcliffe, Lord (Alfred) 131
Norton, John 33, 74, 195, 225, 275, 293–5
Nost, John the Elder 19, 220
Nugent Vallis Brierley 247

Oatley, Sir George 36, 37, 67–8, 82–4, 92, 174–5, 215, 225, 229, 238, 244, 276, 278
Oatley & Brentnall 246
Oatley & Lawrence 37, 116, 126, 132, 136, 155, 183, 242–3, 254
O'Connell, Eilis 201
Okely, William 30
Oldfield, Thomas 210

Page, Peter Randall 170–1
Pain, William 224
Paine, J. 60–1
Palladio, Andrea 79–80, 158, 215
Palmer, F.C. 138
Palmer-Palmer, Jordan 61
Parry, Rev. K.L. 254
Parsons, Robert 78
Pascoe, Edward 108, 132
Patrick, Brother 65
Patterson, William 269
Paty family 23, 30, 93, 95, 193, 195, 255
Paty, James (brother of Thomas) 21, 284

Paty, James the Elder 30, 72, 95, 144, 160, 190
Paty, James Jun. 108
Paty, Thomas 18, 21, 23, 30, 71, 78, 80, 92, 102, *104–5*, 118, 126, 150, *158–9*, 173, 181–2, 190, 198, 210–11, 215, 216, 219–20, 223, 244, 249, 258, 261, 284, 285
Paty, Thomas and William *193–4*
Paty, William 23, 27, 30, *94–5*, 101, 104, 137, 179, *191–4*, 215, 216, 217, 231, 256, 261, 288
Paul, Roland 206
Paul, W.S. 205
Paul, William 92
Paul & James 266
Pearson, F.L. 57
Pearson, J.L. *50–1*, 57, 62, 100
Pedlar, Richard 132
Penn, Admiral William 72
Penrose (Ian) Associates 160
Pepys, Samuel 12
Percival, Rev. John 83
Percivall, Joseph 104
Pero 201, 202
Peto, Harold 190
Pevsner, Sir Nikolaus 8–9, 32, 36, 51, 54, 56, 66, 68, 70, 75, 83, 84, 85, 94, 105, 120, 121, 166, 231, 233, 241, 262, 275, 289
Phillips (Niall) Architects 166, 271
Phippen, Whitchurch 214
Phipps, C.J. 35, 159
Pibworth, Charles 62, 76
Pigou, Dean 61
Pinney, Charles 233
Pinney, John 191, 201, 202
Piper, John 41, 236
Pitt, William 224
Platnauer, Samuel 251
Plucknett, James 294
Pollen, Patrick 132
Ponton, Archibald 29, 30, 120–1, 148, *155–6*, 228, 241
Ponton & Gough 31, 120–1, 148, *155–6*
Poole, Henry 228
Pope, Alexander 124, 209
Pope, Richard Shackleton 25, 27, 28, 29, 31, 81, 88, *103*, *121–2*, 134, 136, 149, 165, *166–7*, 180, 190, 191, *197–8*, 205, 226, 231, 233, 237, 257, 270, 276
Pope, Thomas 30, 262
Pope, Thomas Shackleton 30, 51, 118, 159, 205
Pope & Bindon 228
Pope, Bindon & Clark *197*, 213
Pope & Paul 108
Pope & Son 147, 191
Popes & Bindon 29, 98, 134, 148
Poremba, A. 63

Portland, 3rd Duke of 262
Potter, Robert 41, *236–8*, 279
Poulett family 285
Powell, A.E. 267
Powell, Samuel 211
Powell, William 60, 61
Powell & Sons 237, 257, 294
Poyntz, Sir Robert 11, 101
Pradhan, Niranjan 129
Priest (J.L.) & Co. 259
Priestley, J.B. 37
Pring, Martin 109
Prinsep, William 283
Pritchard, William 262
Probert, Benjamin 210
Proctor, Alderman Thomas 235
Prudential Architects 188
Pugh, William 109
Pugin, A.W.N. 88, 265
Pye, William 204

Randall, John 19, 126
Reay, S.S. 229
Redfern, James 51
Redwood, Robert 75, 160
Redwood (R.S.) & Associates 116
Reed, William Bateman 227
Reeve, William 21, 284
Repton, George 289
Repton, Humphry 243, 246, 287, 288–9
Reynolds, Sir Joshua 229
Ricci, Sebastiano 105
Richardson, Jonathan 94
Richman, Martin 126
Rickards, E.A. 228
Ricketts, Charles 129
Rickman, Thomas 24, 257
Rickman (Thomas) & R.C. Hussey 26
Rieger 65
Rising, Henry 241
Ritchie, Walter 44, 136, *151–2*
Rivers, E.G. 148
Robins, E.C. 145
Robinson, Arnold 58–9, 93, 242, 257
Rodway & Dening 37
Rogers, J. Michelen 180
Rogers, Woodes 218
Rome, Alan 174
Roques, A.W. 137
Rowley, Thomas 100
Roy, Raja Rammohun 129, 283
Rumley, Henry 163, 165, 237, 274, 278, 291
Ruskin, John 29, 241
Russell, Sir James 98
Rutherford, John 148
Rysbrack, J.M. 18, 19, *93–4*, 98, 100, 162–3

Sage (F.) & Co. 278
Salley, Bishop Miles 11, 100, 101
Salviati 294
Sampson & Son 108
Sandford, Richard 72
Sansovino, Jacopo 30, 134
Saunders, Edmund 182–3
Savery, Charles 226, 227
Scheemakers, Peter 163
Scipio Africanus 202
Scott, Sir George Gilbert 51, 294
Scott, Gerald 108
Scott, Sir Giles Gilbert 37–9, 84, 131, 137
Searchfield, William and Anne 101
Seale, Gilbert 136
Seward, Henry Hake 270
Sharples, Ellen 229
Shaw, Norman 127, 131
Shepherd, Joseph 263
Shipward, John 108
Short, Simon 212
Sidnell, Michael 93, 98
Simpson, J. 267
Sims, Ronald 177
Singer/Singer & Sons 61, 257
Skelton, John 236
Smirke, Sir Robert 24, 26, 95–6, 119, 134, 176
Smirke, Sydney 163
Smith, Andrew 150–1
Smith, John Sen. 257
Smith, Keir 272
Smith, W. Bassett 225
Smith, W.J. 240
Smyth family 285
Smyth, Sir J.H. Greville 287
Smyth, Thomas 285
Snell Associates 167
Snetzler 175
Snow, Abbot 51
Snygge, Sir George 109
Soane, Sir John 137
Somake, Ellis E. 177
Southey, Robert 60
Southwell, Sir Edward 291
Southwell, Edward III 291
Spence, Sir Basil 188
Squire, W.W. 273
Stammers, Harry J. 72
Stanhope, Elizabeth 60–1
Stevenson, J.J. 131
Stocking, Thomas 22–3, 244–5, 284
Stoll, Sir Oswald 146
Stothert & Pitt 271
Strahan, John 18, 20, 163, 167, 214
Street, G.E. 32, 41, 51, 57, 58, 96, 103, 156, 236
Stretton, Mary 104

Stride Treglown 44, 147, 148, 177, 267–8
Stride Treglown & Wyeth 264
Stuart, James 60–1
Stubbs, Richard 251
Sturge (J.P.) & Sons 197
Sumsion, Thomas 92
Symonds, John Addington 215

Taylor, Sir Robert 95
Telford, Thomas 86–7
Theed, William 125n.
Thomas, Rev. H. Arnold 254
Thomas, J. Havard 60, 125
Thomas, John 121, 135, 229
Thomas, Joseph 22, 145, 215
Thomas, Josiah 35, 118, 197
Thomas, P. Hartland 37
Thomas, Sir Percy 143
Thomas (Sir Percy) & Partners 246
Thomas (Percy) Partnership 41, 63, 247
Thomas (Sir Percy) & Son 177
Thomas, Simon 203
Thorwaldsen, Bertel 288
Threlfall, Philippa 166, 188
Throkmorton, Lady Margaret and Sir Baynham 102
Thursfield & Co. 240
Tijou, Jean 18
Tilbury, Alan 170
Toone (Ronald) Partnership 269
Townesend, George 19, 92, 214, 291
Towning Hill, R. 261
Towning Hill & Partners 261
Townsend, C. Harrison 124
Trapnell, Bob 224
Travis & White 180
Trelawny, Bishop 60, 61
Trent, N.A. 61
Tristram, E.W. 54
Tully, George 21, 78, 129, 150, 173, 175, 190, 210, 215, 218, 248, 256, 258, 261
Tully, William 173
Twist & Whitley 44, 247
Tyddesley, Sir Walter 109
Tyley/Tyley & Sons 60–1, 93, 95
Tyndale, William 204, 243
Tyndall family 244–6

Underwood, Charles 26, 27, 223, 226–7, 229–30, 233, 237, 284
Underwood, E.N. 145
Underwood (E.N.) & Partners 43, 180
Underwood, George Allen 233
Unite 139, 198
Upton, George 102
Urbed 267

Vachell, Ada 265
Vanbrugh, Sir John 20, 291–2
Vaughan, Sir Charles 61
Verity, Simon 65
Vernon & Evans 90
Verrio, Antonio 17
Vertue, George 162
Vick, William 85
Victoria, Queen 128, 181
Villam le Someter 60
Viollet-le-Duc, E.E. 90
Vitruvius 80
Voisey & Wills 164
Vries, Jan Vredeman de 251
Vyvyan, Sir Richard 226

Wakefield, Benjamin 127
Wakeford, Jerram & Harris 116, 128, 139, 142, 166
Walker, A.G. 174
Walker & Sons 237
Wallis, John 244
Walpole, Horace 20, 104, 284
Walsh, J. 104
Walter, Henry 102
Ward, David 204
Ware, Isaac 22, 158, 214–15
Ware, Peter 132, 235
Warren, Sophie 182
Waterhouse, Alfred 35, 126–8, 216, 219
Watkins, W.H. 38, 136, 190, 235
Watkins Gray Group I 151
Watson, Musgrave 228
Watts, William 180, 218
Webb, Christopher 237, 279
Webb, John 211
Weeks, R. 63
Weeks, Ronald 65
Weir, James 136
Wells Thorpe 181
Wesley, Charles and Samuel 258–9
Wesley, John 21, 174–5
West, Benjamin 101
West, William 232
Westmacott, Sir Richard 60–1
Wetherell, Sir Charles 161
Wheeler, Charles 73
Whicheloe Macfarlane 150–1, 255, 261
Whicheloe Macfarlane Partnership 182, 191

Whinney, T.B. 136
Whinney, Son & Austen Hall 131, 136
White, Sir George 38, 126, 147, 151, 237
White, George (c17) 79
White, Thomas 58
White, Thomas and Chrystina 100
Whiting, Onslow 230
Whitson, John 106
Whitwell, Mark 247
Wickham, Thomas 156, 159
Wilkinson Eyre 46–7, 202
William III, King 19, 162–3
Williams, Henry 95, 122, 147, 217, 226
Williams, James 148
Wills family 36, 38, 83, 243, 275–7
Wills, Sir Frank 35, 119, 239–40, 241, 266, 276–7, 279
Wills (Frank) & Sons 265
Wills, Sir George Arthur 83
Wills, Henry Herbert 83, 244
Wills, Henry Overton 83
Wills, J.B. 240
Wills, Melville and Gertrude 254
Wills, W.D. 253
Wills, Sir W.H. 240
Wills, W. & T. 148
Wilson, Roger 269
Wilstar, John Jacob de 78
Witney, Thomas 53
Wood firm 95
Wood, John the Elder 20, 78–81, 92, 134
Wood, Joseph 30
    see also Foster & Wood
Woodyer, Henry 32, 271, 293–4
Wooldridge, Henry 294
Worcestre, William 104, 110, 186, 208
Workman, Edmund 261
Woropay, Vincent 272
Worrall, Georgiana 60
Wraxall, 2nd Lord 293
Wren, Sir Christopher 92
Wyatt, Matthew Digby 88–90

Yalland, John 228
Young, Rev. Edward 225n.
Young, Joan 61
Young, Sir John 61, 250–1

Index

of Localities, Streets and Buildings

Principal references are in **bold** type; page references including relevant illustrations are in *italic*. 'dem.' = 'demolished'

Abbey House **206**
ABC Cinema (former) **238**
Acramans' Ironworks *see* Bush House
Acraman's Road **278**
Albemarle Row 23, *211–12*, 258
Albert Lodge **228**
Albion Chambers 119
Albion Dock **271**
Alderskey Lane 251
Alfred Place 46, *182–3*, **256**
All Saints:
    Clifton 32, 40–41, 156, *236–238*
    Corn Street 7, 9, 17, 40, *92–4*
All Saints' House **116**
All Saints Lane and Court **80**, 116
All Saints Street 42, **116**
Ambrose Road *47*
Anchor Road **204–6**
Anchor Square **201–3**
Apsley Terrace 231n.
Apsley Villas **257**
Architecture Centre **166**
Armada House (former Bristol Water Works offices) **117n.**
Arnolfini Arts Centre *see* Bush House
Arno's Court (Manor Hotel) 21, 23, 202, **284**
Arno's Vale and Cemetery *17–18*, *282–284*
Art Gallery *see* Museum and Art Gallery
Artisan Dwellings (dem.) 33, 196
ASDA **276**
Ashley Down 27, 250
Ashley Manor (dem.) 250
Ashley Place *27*
Ashton 273
Ashton Brewery **279**
Ashton Court 14, 15, 21n., 278, **285–6**
Ashton Gate 29, **279**
Ashton Gate Board Schools **279**
Assembly Rooms *see* Clifton Club
Assize Courts 12n., 29, **148–9**, 278
Asylum and School of Industry for the Blind (dem.) 26
At-Bristol 46–7, *48*, **202–3**
Atrium, The **186**
Auburn House **235**

Avery's wine merchants (former) 190
Avon Crescent **273**
Avon Gorge Hotel **222**
Avon House North **261**
Avon Insurance **120–1**
Avon Street **268**
Avonbank (now Blue House) **235**
Avonside *see* Maxwell Taylor House

Back, The *see* Welsh Back
Back Hall (dem.) 117
Bakers' Hall *173–4*
Baldwin Street 36, **116–17**
Baltic Wharf **271–2**
Bank of England:
    Broad Street *see* Branch Bank of England
    High Street **139**, 152
Barber-Surgeons' Hall (dem.) 81
Barton Hill 41–2, 182
Barton House **261**
bastion *see* walls
Bath Street **179**
Bathurst Basin *32*, 183, **269–70**
Bathurst Hotel **270**
BBC *see* Broadcasting House
Bedford House **231**
Bedminster 12, 24, 25, 35, 39, **275–80**
Bedminster Bridge **275**
Bedminster Bridge Board School **276**, 280
Bedminster Parade **276**
Bell Lane 6
Bellevue **215**
Bentalls (former) **177**
Beresford House **216**
Berkeley Crescent **195**
Berkeley Place **195–6**
Berkeley Square 23, 193, **194–5**, *239*
Bigwood's (former) 117
Birdcage Walk **213**
Bishop's College (dem.) 26
Bishop's House **214**
Bishop's Palace (dem.) 161
Bishopsworth 20
Black Castle *17–18*, **284**
Blackfriars (Dominican priory and church) 7, *173–4*

Blaise Castle and Blaise Hamlet 21–2, **288–90**
Blue House *see* Avonbank
Bond Street 42, **264**
Boyce's Avenue 224
Boyce's Buildings **223–4**
Braggs Lane **265**
Branch Bank of England (former) 28, *119–20*
Brandon Cottage **198**
Brandon Hill 4, *45*, 46, 95, 189, **192–3**, 196, 246
Brandon House *196–7*
Brandon Steep 21, **198**
Bridewell Police and Fire Station 118, **143**
Bridewell Prison (dem.) 118
Bridewell Street 45, *118*
Bridge House **117**
Brigstow Hotel **155**
Brislington 6, 16, *17–18*, **282**
Bristol Baptist College (former) 36, **242–3**
Bristol Bridge 6, 7, 8, *9*, 21, 104, 117, **118**, 124, 178–9, 244
Bristol Bridge House **188**
Bristol Castle *see* Castle
Bristol Cathedral *see* Cathedral
Bristol Cathedral School 7, **205**
Bristol Docks Company housing **273**
Bristol Eye Hospital 44, *151–2*
Bristol Gas Company *see* Colston House
Bristol Gas Light Co. works (former) **268**
Bristol General Hospital 31, **183**
Bristol Grammar School 35, 71, 140, **241**
Bristol Harbour Railway 271
Bristol Industrial Museum **270–1**
Bristol Municipal Charities Offices *see* Quay Head House
Bristol Museum and Library *see* Museum and Library (former)
Bristol Philosophical and Literary Institution 26, **190–1**
Bristol Record Office **273**
Bristol Register Office **173**
Bristol Royal Hospital for Sick Children **150–1**
Bristol Royal Infirmary 36, 37, 38, **149–51**
Bristol South Baths **278**
Bristol Times and Mirror (former) **148**
Bristol United Press Building *see* Post and Press
Bristol Water Works offices 15, **117n.**
Bristol & West Buildings:
　Broad Quay 45, **119**, 146

Temple Quay **267–8**
　see also St Stephen's House
Bristol Zoo **235**
British Road **278–9**, 280n.
Broad Plain 20, **266**
Broad Quay **119**, **125–6**
Broad Quay House 45, **165–6**
Broad Street 15, *31*, 36, **119–24**, 134
Broadcasting House **237–8**
Broadmead (district and street) 12, 21, 39–40, 42, 43, 47, 169, 170, **173–7**, 264
Broadmead Baptist Chapel **177**
Broadweir **173**
Brooke Bond warehouse (former) **271**
Brown's Restaurant *see* Museum and Library
Brunel House (former Royal Western Hotel) 29, 191, **197–8**
Brunswick Square 44, 256, **261–2**
Buchanan's Wharf **188**
Buckingham Baptist Chapel 32, **231**, 236
Buckingham Place 226, **231**
Buckingham Vale 27n., *28*, **236**
Bull Wharf **188**
Bullock's Park 189
Burton's Almhouses (dem.) 110
Bush House (Arnolfini Arts Centre; formerly Acramans' Ironworks) 31, 44, 46, *166–7*, 204, 276

Cabot Café (former) **129–30**
Cabot Tower *192–3*
Caledonia Place 27n., **222**
Camden Terrace **213**
Camp House *see* Engineers' House
Canon's Marsh (Harbourside) 45–6, 47, *199–206*
Cantock's Close **247**
Canynges's House (dem.) 12, *186–7*
Capital & Counties Bank (former) **127**
Capricorn Quay 45, **205**
Carlton Chambers **117**
Carmelites *see* Whitefriars
carriage works (former):
　Jamaica Street 36, **259**
　Perry's, Stokes Croft 31, *259*
Carter's Buildings **223**
Castle 6, 7, 12, 16, 106, **171–2**, 246
Castle Chambers **172**
Castle Gate **172**
Castle Park 39, 41, 44, 106, 125, *169–72*
Castle Street 38, 39
Castlemead **173**
Cathedral (St Augustine's Abbey) *vii*, 2, 7, *8*, 9, 12, 32, *50–62*
　furnishings 6, 11, **57–8**, 93, 111n.
　monuments *13*, **59–61**
　precinct and related buildings 7, 12, **62**, 128, 199, **205–6**

Cathedral (R.C.) *see* Clifton Cathedral
Cathedral School *see* Bristol Cathedral
    School
Cave Street **262**
Cenotaph **125**
Central Health Clinic 38, **172**
Central Library 36, 37, 38, 41, **75–7**, 84
Centre, The (Tramways Centre) 40,
    44, 116, 119, **124–6**, 130
Centre Gate **140–1**
Champion's Dock *see* Merchants' Dock
Channings Hotel (Pembroke Hall) **237**
Chapel Row 20, **211**
Chapel of the Three Kings of Cologne
    132
Charles Street **258**
Charlotte Street 23, *193–4*
Chatterton's House **185**
Chesterfield Hospital *see* Clifton Court
Children's Hospital (former) 151, **247**
Chillcott (Alfred) & Co. (former) **191**
Christ Church:
    Broad Street 21, *94–5*
    Clifton 32, *224–5*
Christ Church Schools (former) **223**
Christchurch Green **224**
Christmas Steps *126* 7
City of Bristol College **198**
city gates 8, 154
    Lawford's Gate 105
    Newgate 105
    Redcliff Street 8
    St John 8, **98**, 119
    St Leonard's 126, 138
    south gate (St Nicholas Street) 104
    Temple Street 8
    see also walls
Civic Centre project 39, 41, 172
Civil War defences 12, **192**, 243, 246
Clare Street *126–8*
Clevedon Court 21n.
Clifton 3, 4, 17, 23, 25, 26–7, 37, **208–10**,
    213–38
Clifton Arcade **224**
Clifton Auction Rooms **238**
Clifton Cathedral (R.C.) 41, *63–5*
Clifton Club (former Clifton Hotel
    and Assembly Rooms) 26, *222–3*
Clifton College 29, 35, **235–6**, 241, 242
Clifton Court (Chesterfield Hospital)
    20–1, **216**
Clifton Dispensary **210**
Clifton Down 33, **233–5**
Clifton Down Congregational
    Church (former) **224**
Clifton Down Road *223–4*
Clifton Heights 42, 130, **195**
Clifton High School **225–6**
Clifton Hill *213–16*

Clifton Hill House 21, 22, 145, ***214–15***,
    224, 258
Clifton Hotel *see* Clifton Club
Clifton Park 27, **225–6**
Clifton Rocks Railway 222
Clifton Suspension Bridge 29, 44, *85–7*
Clifton Swimming Baths **237**
Clifton Vale 27n., *213*
Clifton Wood House **215**
Clifton Wood Road 20n., **215**, 284n.
Cliftonwood **215**
coke house, Avon Street **268**
Coliseum (former) **252**
College Green 4, 73–4, ***128–30***
College Road **226**, 235–6
College Square *205–6*
College Street (dem.) 198
Colonnade, The **211**
Colston Avenue 35, 38, 124, **130–1**
Colston Centre 42, 119, **130–1**
Colston Hall 7, 29, 32, 38, **131–2**, 241, 250
Colston House (former Bristol Gas
    Company showrooms) **131**
Colston Parade **181**
Colston Street *130*, **131–3**
Colston's Almshouses 15, 19, 161, 202, ***248***
Colston's House 12
Commercial Rooms 26, *136–7*
Congregational Chapel (former),
    Brunswick Square **262**
Constitution Hill **215**
Coopers' Hall (former) 19, 20n., 122,
    157–8, 216, 223
Corn Market (dem.) 14
Corn Street 4, 6, 30, **80**, 131, *134–8*
Cornwallis Crescent 209, **217**
Coronation Road **278**
Corsham Court 21n.
Cote House (dem.) 21n.
Cotham 26, 253
Cotham Parish Church (former
    Highbury Congregational Chapel)
    32, 231, *253–4*
Cotham Side **257**
Council House (present and previous)
    37, *73–4*, 134
Counterslip 35, *180*
Countess of Huntingdon's Chapel
    (dem.) 143
County Fire Office (former) **127**
Courage Brewery (former; previously
    George's) 46, *179*
Court House **122**
Create **273**
Crown Courts (present and previous)
    44, *148*
Culver Street 139
Cumberland Basin 24, 36, 46, *273–4*
    road system 210, *273–4*

Cumberland Road 270, **273–4**
Cumberland Street 258, **261**
Custom House **163**
Custom House apartments **184**
Cutlers' Hall **173–4**

Dean Lane **278**
Deanery (former) 7, **205**
Deanery Road 129
Denmark Street **138**
Devon House **256**
Dighton Street **258**
docks and quays 7, 8, 29–30, 37, 43,
    44, 45, 47, 48, *124*, 154, 184, *199–201*,
    270–1
    see also Floating Harbour
Dominican Priory *see* Blackfriars
Dominions House **147**
Dorset House 27n., **233**
Dove Street Flats **258**
Dowry Square and Dowry Parade 20,
    21, 160, 194, 208, **210–11**
Drill Hall **266**
drinking fountains:
    Castle Park **171**
    Centre **125**
    Clifton Down **235**
    Exchange Market / St Nicholas
        Street **148**
Duncan House **224**
Dunlop & Mackie (former) **116–17**
Dutch House (dem.) 14, 139, 170

earthworks, Observatory Hill **233**
East Street **276–8**
Eastern Orthodox Church **241**
Easton 36
Easton Way 40
Eaton **235**
Ebenezer Methodist Chapel **279**
Ecohome 46, **273**
Edgcumbe House **231**
Edinburgh Chambers 36, **117**
Edwards, Ringer & Co. (former) **186**
Edwards' Van Garage **237**
Electricity House 38, **131**
Elephant, The (pub) **147**
Elmdale *see* Mansion House (Clifton)
Elmdale Road **241**
Engineers' House (formerly Camp
    House) **233–4**
Ernst & Young *see* One Bridewell
    Street
Everard's Printing Works 36, *122–4*
Exchange and markets 3, 20, 40,
    78–81, 148
Explore (former GWR goods shed)
    35, 46–7, *48*, **202–3**
Eye Hospital *see* Bristol Eye Hospital

Fairfax Street **116**
Feeder Canal 24
Fish Market **117**, **147**
Fishponds 39
Floating Harbour 24, 33, *200*, 270
    see also docks and quays
Foster's Almhouses 29, 126, *132–3*,
    264
Foster's Chambers **149**
fountains (public):
    Clifton **228**
    Hotwell Road **212**
Franciscan Friary 7, 142
Franklyn Davey factory (former) *see*
    Imperial Tobacco
Fraser, House of *see* Lewis's
Freeland Place **211**
Freemantle House **224**
Fremantle Road **257**
Fremantle Square 246, **257**
Friary House **132**
Friends' Meeting House 21, **173**
Friends Provident Building (former)
    37–8, 131, **137**
Frogmore Street **139**, 190
Froomsgate House **145**
Fry (Albert) Memorial Tower *see*
    University of Bristol
Fry's chocolate factories (dem.) 116
Fry's House of Mercy **181**
Full Moon Inn (former) **259**

Galleries shopping centre **174**, 176–7
Gaol Ferry Footbridge **274**
Gasferry Road **205, 271**
gasworks, Canon's Marsh **205**
gates *see* city gates
Gaunt's Hospital, The (dem.) 100,
    138, 144
Gaunt's House, The 42, **138**
George Railway Hotel **181**
Georgian House Museum *191–2*
glass cone, Redcliffe 23, **182**
Glenavon **235**
Goat in Armour Inn (dem.) 251
Goldney Hall 44, **216**
Goldney House 17, 19, 21, 209, 213,
    216, *218–20*
Gothic Cottage **274**
Granary, The 31–2, 46, 121, **155–6**
Grand Hotel (now Thistle Hotel) *31*,
    120
Grand Spa Pump Room **222**
Great Anne Street **264**
Great Britain, ss 45, 271
Great Fort *see* Royal Fort
Great George Street:
    Brandon Hill *45*, **191–2**
    St Jude's **264**

Great Western Railway goods shed
  see Explore
Gresham Chambers 147–8
Greyfriars 7, **142**
Greyhound Inn **176**
Grosvenor Hotel **181**
Grove, The 45, **167–8**
Guardhouse Arch 12
Guild Court 187n.
Guild Heritage House **265**
Guild of the Holy Cross *see* St John
  the Baptist, Broad Street
Guildhall (present and previous) 11,
  15, 28–9, **121–2**, 134, 148, 226
Guinea Street 17, 20, 23, **182–3**
GWR *see* Great Western Railway

Haberfield Almshouses **211**
Halifax Building Society (former) 38,
  146
Hampden House **279**
harbour *see* docks and quays
Harbourside 199, **201–3**
Harford House **258**
Harley Place **232–3**
Hartcliffe 277
Hatchet, The (pub) **139**
Hebron Sunday School **279**
Henbury 202, **288–90**
High Cross 11, 139, **195**
High Kingsdown 42, **255–6**
High Street 6, 14, 30–1, **81**, 139
Highbury Congregational Chapel *see*
  Cotham Parish Church
Hill (Charles) & Sons (former) **271**
Hill Street **191**
Hill's Almshouse **196**
Hippodrome 33, 138, *146*
Hobbs Lane **145**
Holbeck House **119**
Hole in the Wall pub **168**
Holiday Inn (former) **172**
Holy Cross Church (R.C.) **278**
Holy Trinity:
  Hotwells 24, 40, **213**
  St Philip's 24, 238
Homoeopathic Hospital 38, **254**
Hope Chapel **212**
Hopechapel Hill **212**
Horn & Trumpet (pub) **146** 7
Hort's pub **121**
Hotwell House (dem.) **208**
Hotwell Pump Room (dem.) **211**
Hotwell Road 205, **211**, **212–13**
Hotwells (district) 3, 12, 20, 23, 24, 45,
  46–7, **208–13**, 274
Hotwells baths (former) 35, **196–7**
House of Fraser *see* Lewis's
HSBC Bank, Corn Street **136**

Imperial Tobacco buildings (former)
  276, **279**
Inland Revenue (former) **117**

Jacob Street **265**
Jacob's Well **196**
Jacob's Wells Road 33, **196**
Jamaica Street 36, **259**
Jewish buildings **196**, **251–2**
Jubilee Place **184**
Jury's Hotel **166**

Kensington Place **227**
King Square 21, **258–9**
King Street 8, 12, 14–15, *16*, 20n., 44,
  156–61, 167, 179
Kings Court **160**
King's Hall (dem.) **172**
King's Head 31, **180**
King's House **264**
King's Orchard **172**
Kingsdown 3, 19, 23, 26, 44, 46, 246,
  253, **255–8**
Kingsdown Parade 25, 27, **255–6**
Kingsley Hall **266**
Kingsweston House 19, 20, 220, ***291–2***
Knightstone House **256**
Knowle West 39

Langton's Mansion (dem.) 15
Lansdown Place 27n., **227**
Lawford's Gate 105
Leigh Woods 36
Leonard Lane 6, 138
Lewins Mead 7, 8, 17, 21, 33, 40, 42,
  116, 131, ***140–2***, 202, 240
Lewis's (House of Fraser) 42, **177**
libraries:
  Bedminster **276**
  Clifton branch **223**
  King Street (former) *see* Old
    Library
  see also Central Library
Limekiln Cottage **198**
Limekiln Dock (dem.) **205**
Litfield House 226, **233**
Litfield Place 27, 226, ***233–4***
Little Brothers of Nazareth (R.C.) *see*
  St James (Whitson Street)
Little Peter Street 38
Liverpool, London and Globe
  Insurance *see* NatWest (Corn Street)
Llandoger Trow inn 15, *156–7*, 160
Llanfoist **235**
Lloyds TSB Bank:
  Canon's Marsh (HQ) 45, 47, ***204***
  Corn Street (originally West of
    England and South Wales
    District Bank) 30, *134–6*

lock bridges **274**
Lodge Street and Lodge Place **142–3**
Lombard Street *277–8*
London & Lancashire Assurance **136**
London Life Building (former) 45, **181**
London and South Western Bank (former) **136**
Long Bar **266**
Lord Mayor's Chapel *see* St Mark
Louisiana Inn **270**
Lower Arcade 43, *176*
Lower Castle Street *172–3*
Lower Church Lane **249**
Lower Maudlin Street *see* Upper Maudlin Street
Lower Park Row **143**
Lunsford House 20n., 247, **252**
Lutton Memorial Hall **256**
Lysaght's ironworks *see* St Vincent's Works

McArthur Building **271**
Magnet Cinema (former) **264**
Mall, The 26, **222–3**
Manilla Hall (dem.) 224
Manilla Road **226–7**
Manor Hall **215**
Manor Hotel *see* Arno's Court
Manor House 15, **249**
Mansion House:
　　Clifton (originally Elmdale) 29, 33, **235**
　　Queen Square (dem.) *161*
Maple House **258**
Mardyke Ferry Road 271
Mark Lane 145, 146
Market Chambers **81**
Market Gate **81**
Market Hall **81**, 117
Market Tavern **80**
markets *see* Exchange and markets; Fish Market; St Nicholas Market
Marks & Spencer **177**
Marlborough Street **149–50**, 258
Marriott Hotel (former Holiday Inn) **172**
Marsh Wall *see* walls
Mason's Arms **266**
Maxwell Taylor House **233**
Mayor's Chapel *see* St Mark
Meeting House *see* Friends' Meeting House
Merchant Street 32, **174**
Merchant Tailors' Almshouses 19, **174**
Merchant Tailors' Hall (former) 19, **122**
Merchant Venturers' Almshouses **161**
Merchant Venturers' Hall (dem.) 18–19, **126**
Merchant Venturers' Technical College **145**

Merchants' Dock (Champion's Dock; dem.) 23, 213
Merchants' Hall *see* Merchant Venturers' Hall
Merchants Landing 45, **269–70**
Merchants Road 224, **228**
Mercury House **172**
Merrywood Board School (former) **280**
Merrywood Elementary Council School (Southville Primary School) **280**
Methodist Central Hall (former) **266**
Miles and Harford's Bank (former buildings) 136, 137
Millennium Beacons **126**
Millennium Square 44, **204**
Montpelier 26–7
monuments and sculpture (public):
　　Aquarena **204**
　　Atyeo **272**
　　Beside the Still Waters *170–1*
　　I.K. Brunel **119**
　　Edmund Burke **125**
　　John Cabot **166**
　　Cenotaph **125**
　　Thomas Chatterton **204**
　　Edward Colston **125**
　　Creation, The 151, *152*
　　Edward VII Memorial **228**
　　Exploration **188**
　　Cary Grant **204**
　　Hand of the River God **272**
　　Horse and Man **198**
　　Lines from Within **170**
　　Merchant Seamen's monument **155**
　　Neptune 19, **126**
　　Only Dead Fish Go with the Flow **171**
　　Pitt memorial **224**
　　Raja Rammohun Roy **129**
　　Small Worlds **203**
　　South African War Memorial **230**
　　Throne **170–1**
　　Topsail **272**
　　William Tyndale **204**
　　Queen Victoria **128**
　　War Memorial, Clifton Down **224**
　　William III 19, *162–3*
Mortimer House **224**
Museum and Art Gallery 15n., 35, 38, 41, *239–40*
Museum and Library (former; now Brown's Restaurant) 29, 190, *239–40*

Narrow Lewins Mead **140–1**
　　see also Lewins Mead
Narrow Quay 20n., 23, 31, *166–7*
National Provincial Bank, Clifton **222**

National Westminster Court **124**
NatWest Bank:
    Corn Street (originally Liverpool,
      London and Globe Insurance
      and Stuckey's Bank) 30, **136**
    Whiteladies Road **238**
Nelson House **143**
Nelson Street 8, 42, 140, **143**
Neptune statue 19, **126**
New Bristol Centre **139**
New Cut 24, 269, 270, 274
New Gaol **270**
New Minster House **117**
Newfoundland Street **264**
Newgate 105
News Theatre (dem.) 38
Next **177**
North British & Mercantile
    Insurance (former) **119**
North Street **279**
Northcliffe House 38, **131**
Northview Cottage 23, **278–9**
Norwich Union Building (former) **139**
Nova Scotia Hotel **273**

Oakfield House **237**
Observatory and Observatory Hill **233**
Odeon Cinema 38, **177**
Old Bread Street **267**
Old Bristol Bridge *see* Bristol Bridge
Old Council House 26, 119, **134**, 176
Old Library (former) 20n., **77, 160–1**
Old Market (district) 12, 14, 31, 44,
    170, 172, **264–5**
Old Park Hill **249**
Oldbury House **254–5**
One Bridewell Street 45, *118*
Open University office **185**
Orchard Street and Orchard Lane 17,
    20, 23, *144–5*
Ostrich Inn **183–4**

Palace Hotel 31, **265**
Paragon, The *209*, **217**
Park Lane **249**
Park Place **230**
Park Row 14, 20n., 33–5, 36, 246, *249–52*
Park Street 21, 37, 39, 43, 144, **189–95**,
    246
Passage Street 45, **172**
Pembroke Hall **237**
Pembroke Road **236–8**
People's Palace 33, **117**
Pero's Bridge *201*
Perry's *see* carriage works
Pharmacy Arch **228**
Philosophical and Literary
    Institution *see* Bristol Philosophical
    and Literary Institution

Phoenix Assurance **182**
Phoenix House **165**
Pinney house *see* Georgian House
    Museum
Pipe Lane **145**
Pithay House 42, **116**
Pithay, The 42, **116**
Pizza Express, Corn Street **137**
Platnauer Brothers **180**
Point, The *271–2*
Pointing's Chemist (dem.) 30–1
Police Courts **118**
Police and Fire Stations:
    Bedminster (former) **276**
      Nelson Street *see* Bridewell Police
      and Fire Station
Police Headquarters Extension **143**
Police Station, Brandon Hill **196**
Polygon, The **212**
Poole's Wharf **213**, 272
Pope & Co. (former) **264**
port *see* docks and quays
Port Authority:
    Offices 35, **163**
    transit sheds *see* Watershed Media
      Centre
Portland Lofts **264**
Portland Methodist Chapel (dem.) 256
Portland Square 23, 217, **262–3**
Portland Street:
    Clifton **223**
    Kingsdown **256**
Portwall Lane 8, **184–5**
Post Office, Small Street (now Crown
    Courts) 29, **148**
Post and Press (Bristol United Press
    Building) 42–3, **266**
Presbyterian church (former), St
    James's Parade **147**
Prewett Street **182**
Prince Street 19, 20, 21, 122, 166,
    167–8, 251
Prince Street Bridge **269**
Prince's Buildings 23, 27, **217**, 222
Prince's Theatre (dem.) 29, 33–5
Princes Wharf 45, 269, *270–1*
Princess Victoria Street **223**
Prior's Close 46, **256**
Prior's Hill Fort (dem.) 246, **257**
Pritchard Street **264**
Pro-Cathedral (R.C.) 25, 63, 64, **230**
Promenade, The 33, **233**
Promenade House **233**
Prospect House **216**
Prudential Building:
    Clare Street (former) 35, *126–8*
    Wine Street **152**
public conveniences, Park Row **252**
pump house, Underfall Yard **273**

QEH Theatre *see* Queen Elizabeth's Hospital School
Quakers' Friars 7, 47, *173–4*, 255
Quay Head House (former Bristol Municipal Charities Offices) 35, **131**
quays *see* docks and quays
Queen Charlotte Street 20, 157, *163–4*
Queen Elizabeth's Hospital School 35, 140, **195–6**
    QEH Theatre 44, **195**
Queen Square 15, 17, 19–20, 44, 145, 154–5, 159, *161–5*, **168**, 269
Queen Street **172**
Queen's Road 26, 27, **195**, **228–31**, *239–41*

Read's Dispensary **197**
Red Lodge 14, 15, *250–1*
Redcliff Backs 12, *184–6*, 187n.
Redcliff Hill 23, 180, *182–3*
Redcliff Quay **188**
Redcliff Street 8, 15, *184–8*
Redcliffe (district) 4, 7, 16, 23, 39, 42, 178, 180, **181–4**
Redcliffe Bascule Bridge **184**
Redcliffe Caves 184
Redcliffe Methodist Church **182**
Redcliffe Parade **184**
Redcliffe Way 40, 162, **184**
Redcross Street **264**
Redland (district) 32
Redland Chapel 18, 20, 111
Redland Park Congregational (now U.R.) Church **238**
Refuge Assurance (former) **117**
Regent Cinema (dem.) 38
Regent Street **216**
Richmond House:
    Clifton Hill **214**
    Queen's Road 226, **231**
Richmond Terrace **231**
River Station 45, **168**
Robinson Building 42, *187–8*
Robinson's Oil Seed manufactory *see* Bathurst Basin
Robinson's paper factory (former) **278**
Rock House **211**
Rodney Place **224**
Rogers' Brewery 31, **172**
Roman sites 6
Rowe's Leadworks **202**
Rownham House (dem.) 284n.
Rownham Mead 45, **212–13**, 272
Royal Bazaar and Winter Gardens *see* Clifton Arcade
Royal Colonial Institute (former) **229**
Royal Colonnade **191**
Royal Fort (or Great Fort) **243–6**
Royal Fort House 21, *22–3*, 38, *243–5*
Royal Hotel 29, **129**

Royal Promenade:
    Triangle **195**
    Victoria Square 27n., 194, **227–8**
Royal West of England Academy 38, **229–30**
Royal Western Hotel *see* Brunel House
Royal York Crescent 23, 209, **216–17**
Rummer Inn **80**
Rummer pub **139**
Rupert Street 140, **145**
    Multi-storey Car Park **145**
Rutland House **213**

Sailors' Home (former) **168**
St Andrew, Clifton (dem.) 208–9, **213**
St Andrew-the-Less, Clifton (dem.) 210
St Angela's Convent **233**
St Anne's 46
St Augustine the Less (dem.) 40, 129
St Augustine's Abbey 7, 12, 128, 199
    see also Cathedral
St Augustine's Court **147**
St Augustine's Parade 44, *145–7*
St Augustine's Place **147**
St Augustine's Reach 7, 124, *199–201*
St Bartholomew's Court **141**
St Bartholomew's Hospital 7, 12, 33, **140–1**, 241
St Ewen (dem.) 95
St Francis **279**
St George, Brandon Hill 24, *95–6*, 103
St George's Road *197–8*
St James:
    Clifton (dem.) 228
    Whitson Street (now Little Brothers of Nazareth) 7, 13, *97–8*, 111n., 285
St James Barton 42, 261
St James Court **147**
St James's Parade **147**
St James's Place Gateway **177**
St James's Priory *see* St James, Whitson Street
St James's Square (dem.) 20, 261
St John:
    Bedminster (parish church, dem.) 33, 275
    Whiteladies Road (now Clifton Auction Rooms) **238**
St John the Baptist, Broad Street 7, 8, 9, 11, 13, *98–100*, 105–6, 122
    Churchyard **122**
St John's Conduit **98**
St John's Street **278**
St Jude 32, **265**
St Jude's (district) 39, **264**
St Leonard (dem.) 126, 138

St Mark (Lord Mayor's Chapel) 7, 11, 13, 18, **100–2**, 112n.
St Mark's Hospital (dem.) 7, 12
St Mary le Port 6, 9, 40, **102**, 111n., 139, 170
St Mary on the Quay (R.C.) 25, *103*
St Mary Redcliffe 7, 9, *10*, 11, 18, 29, *34*, 56, *66–72*, 105, 186, 222
St Matthew **257**
St Michael on the Mount Primary School 160n., **249**
St Michael on the Mount Without 9, 21, **104**
 former rectory 21, **249**, 250
St Michael's Hill 4, 12, 14–15, 19, 44, 239, 246, **247–9**, **254–5**
St Michael's Hospital **247**
St Nicholas 7, 11, 21, 22–3, 100, *104–6*, 108, 111n., 170
St Nicholas Chambers **148**
St Nicholas House **139**
St Nicholas Market **80–1**
St Nicholas Street 6, 30, 81, **147–8**
St Nicholas's Almshouses **156–7**
St Paul:
 Bedminster 24, **278**
 Portland Square 21, 212, *262–3*
 St Paul's Road **237**
St Paul Street **264**
St Paul's (district) 23, 39, **260–4**
St Paul's Vicarage (former) **278**
St Peter, Castle Park 6, 9, 40, *106*, 111n., 170
St Peter's Hospital (dem.) 14, 170
St Peter's House **197**
SS Philip and Jacob 7, 13, **107–8**
St Philip's (district) 23, 24, 35, 39, 42–3, 238, **264–8**
St Philip's Marsh 46
St Raphael (dem.) 32, 271
St Stephen 9–11, 13, 18, 40, *108–10*, 111n.
St Stephen's House (Bristol & West Building Society) 38, **131**
St Stephen's Street **148**
St Thomas the Martyr 7, 11n., 18, 21, 99, **110–11**, 180, 185
St Thomas Street 14, **180**, 188
St Vincent's Parade **211**
St Vincent's Priory **222**
St Vincent's Rocks Hotel and Pump Room (former) 221
St Vincent's Works (formerly Lysaght's ironworks) 35, *268*
St Werburgh 6, 9
Saville Place **216**
Savory's Printing Works **249**
Saxon sites 6, 8, 106, 119, 147, 170
School House **185**
Scottish Life 44–5, **156**

Scottish Provident Institution **126**
sculpture *see* monuments and sculpture
Sea Mills 39
Seamen's Mission (former) **164–5**
Shakespeare Inn **167**, **180**
Shambles (dem.) 265
Ship Inn **182**
Shirehampton 23, 36, 39
Shot Tower (present and previous) 23, *42–3*, **180**
Silverthorne Lane **268**
Sion Hill **221–2**
Sion Spring House **221**
Small Street 6, 119, **148–9**
 aisled hall house (dem.) 7, 12n.
 No. 7 (dem.) 117n.
Sneyd Park 36
Somerset Square **182**
Somerset Street *257–8*
South Street School **280**
Southey House **152**
Southville *278–80*
Southville Primary School **280**
Southwell Street **256**
Spectrum Building **264**
Spicer's Door *11–12*
Spike Island 45, *269–74*
 Arts Centre **271**
Spring Hill House **258**
Stag and Hounds **266**
Star Life (former) *see* Dominions House
statues *see* monuments and sculpture (public)
Stillhouse Lane **276**
Stock Exchange (former) 38, **147**
Stoke Park 21n.
Stokes Croft 31, 253, *259*, 284n.
Stuart House **244–6**
Sugar House 17, **142**, 202
Sun Alliance House **128**
Surrey Lodge **262**
Surrey Street **262**
Surrey Villa (dem.) 262
Suspension Bridge *see* Clifton Suspension Bridge
Sutton House **235**
Synagogues *251–2*

Tailor's Court **122**
Talbot Hotel **179**
Tankard's Close **246**
Telephone Avenue **117n.**
Tellisford **235**
Temple (district) 7, 16, 39, **178–81**, 251, 267
Temple (or Holy Cross) Church 7, 9, 17–18, 40, 58, 71, 72, 101, *111–12*, 170, 178
Temple Gate **180–1**
Temple Meads Station 29, 48, **88–90**, 268

Temple Quay 46, **267**
Temple Quay House **268**
Temple Quay North 46, **267**
Temple Street 8, 14, **180–1**, 251
Temple Way 40, 43, 172, 181, 264, **266**, 267
Theatre Royal *157–9*
Thistle Hotel *see* Grand Hotel
Thomas's Soap Works (former) *266–7*
Thornton House **231**
Three Sugar Loaves (pub) **126**
tobacco warehouses 36, **273**
Tollgate House **264**
tollhouse, Ashton Gate 29, **279**
Tolzey (dem.) 14, 134
Totterdown 29, 40, 46
Tower House **116**
Tower Lane 6
Tower View **247**
Town Marsh 8, 12, 154, 156
town walls *see* walls
Trafalgar House **233**
Tramways Centre *see* Centre, The
Tramways Generating Station (former) 35, *180–1*
transit sheds:
    The Grove **168**
    St Augustine's Reach *see* Watershed Media Centre
Transport House **180**
Trenchard Street Car Park **143**
Triangle and Triangle West 39, 42, **195**
Trin (Treen) Mill (dem.) 270
Trinity Hospitals North and South 29, **265**
Trinmore **235**
Tyndall Avenue **247**
Tyntesfield *293–5*

Underfall Yard **273**
Union Street 177
Unitarian Meeting House 21, *141–2*
Unity Street 21, **144–5**
University of Bristol 35, 37, 38, 41, 44, 83, 119, 195, 228, **241–7**, **249**, **252**
    Arts and Social Sciences Library 44, **247**
    Albert Fry Memorial Tower 38, **242**
    halls of residence 44, **214–20**
    H.H. Wills Physics Laboratory 38, **243–4**
    Students' Union **231**
    Wills Memorial Building 2, 36, 37, 38, **82–4**, 190, 194, 239
University College *see* University of Bristol
University Road **241–2**
Upper Arcade (dem.) 176
Upper Maudlin Street 6, *149–52*

Vandyck Press (former) **252**
viaduct, Avon Street **268**
Victoria Methodist Church **229**
Victoria Rooms 26, 38, **228–9**
Victoria Square 27, **227–8**
Victoria Square Hotel **228**
Victoria Street 46, *179–81*, 251
    Number One **188**
Vintry House **152**
Vision Care Centre **276**
Vow, Church of the *see* Zion Congregational Chapel
Vyvyan Terrace 27, **226**, 231

walls 8, 147, 246
    bastion (King Street) 8, **157**
    inner (Leonard Lane) 6, 138
    Marsh Wall 8, 12, 154, 156, 160
    north (Nelson Street) 8
    port wall (Portwall Lane) 8, 184
    St John's 8, 98
    see also city gates
Wapping Road **269**, 270
Wapping Wharf *271–2*
Waring House 42, *182–3*
Water Fort **192**
Watershed Media Centre 35, 44, 46, **199–201**
WCA Warehouse and offices *184–5*
Weavers' Hall 251
Welsh Back (The Back) *11–12*, 15, 46, 121, 122, **124**, *155*
Wesley's New Room 21, *174–5*
Wessex Water offices (former) 45, *172*
West of England and South Wales District Bank *see* Lloyds TSB Bank
West India House **155**
West Mall 27n., **222**
West Street:
    BS2 **265**
    BS3 *278–9*
Western Congregational College (former) 36, *254*
Wetherell Place **230**
White (George) offices (former) **126**
White Hart **151**
White Lion (dem.) 15
Whitefriars **142**
Whitefriars or Carmelite foundation 7
Whiteladies Road 228, **229**, **237–8**
Wigwam 15n., **251**
Wildwalk 46, **202–3**
Wills Factories (former) 35, *276–8*
    war memorial (dem.) 275
Wills Memorial Building *see* University of Bristol
Wilson Street **264**
Windmill Hill 46

Windsor Terrace *209*, 210, **217–18**
Wine Street 14, 125, **152**
Winstone Court **248**
Woodland Road 44, **242–3**, 247, 252
Woodwell Crescent **197**
Wool Hall (former) 166, **180**
Worcester Terrace 27, **226–7**

YMCA (former) **132**
York Gardens **217**
York House **261**

Zion Congregational Chapel (former;
    Church of the Vow), Bedminster
    25, 166, **275–6**

Illustration Acknowledgements

Every effort has been made to contact or trace all copyright holders. The publishers will be glad to make good any errors or omissions brought to our attention in future editions. We are grateful to the following for permission to reproduce illustrative material:

English Heritage (James O. Davies): 1, 3, 4, 5, 7, 8, 9, 10, 11, 12, 14, 15, 16, 17, 18, 19, 20, 21, 22, 23, 24, 26, 27, 28, 29, 31, 33, 34, 35, 36, 37, 38, 39, 42, 43, 44, 45, 46, 47, 49, 50, 52, 54, 55, 56, 57, 59, 60, 61, 62, 63, 64, 65, 66, 67, 68, 71, 72, 74, 75, 76, 77, 79, 80, 81, 82, 83, 85, 86, 87, 88, 90, 91, 92, 93, 95, 97, 98, 99, 100, 101, 102, 105, 106, 107, 108, 110, 111, 112, 113, 114, 115, 118, 119, 120, 121, 123, 124, 125, 127, 129, 130, 131, 132, 133, 134, 136, 137, 138, 141, 142, 143, 145, 146, 147, 148, 150, 151, 152, 154, 155, 156, 157, 158
Alan Fagan: 25, 30, 32, 41, 104, 153
Alison Farrar: 48
Bristol City Council: 2, 53, 73, 84, 89, 96, 103, 109, 116, 122, 126, 135, 140, 144, 149
Bristol Museums & Art Gallery: 13, 40, 58, 70, 78, 117
Bristol Record Office: 69
Bristol Reference Library (Braikenridge Collection): 6
Reece Winstone Archive: 94, 139
The Master and Fellows of Corpus Christi College, Cambridge: 51
University of Bristol Special Collections: 128